The Cambridge Guide to
Learning English as a Second Language

THE CAMBRIDGE GUIDES SERIES

Authoritative, comprehensive and accessible guides, addressing both the theoretical and the practical aspects of key topics in second language teaching and learning.

For more information on these titles, please visit: www.cambridge.org/elt

Other titles in this series:

The Cambridge Guide to Blended Learning for Language Teaching
Edited by Michael McCarthy

The Cambridge Guide to Research in Language Teaching and Learning
Edited by James Dean Brown and Christine Coombe

The Cambridge Guide to Second Language Assessment
Edited by Christine Coombe, Peter Davidson, Barry O'Sullivan and Stephen Stoynoff

The Cambridge Guide to Pedagogy and Practice in Second Language Teaching
Edited by Anne Burns and Jack C. Richards

The Cambridge Guide to Second Language Teacher Education
Edited by Anne Burns and Jack C. Richards

The Cambridge Guide to Teaching English to Speakers of Other Languages
Edited by Ronald Carter and David Nunan

The Cambridge Guide to

Learning English as a Second Language

Edited by

Anne Burns
Jack C. Richards

CAMBRIDGE
UNIVERSITY PRESS

CAMBRIDGE
UNIVERSITY PRESS

University Printing House, Cambridge CB2 8BS, United Kingdom

One Liberty Plaza, 20th Floor, New York, NY 10006, USA

477 Williamstown Road, Port Melbourne, VIC 3207, Australia

4843/24, 2nd Floor, Ansari Road, Daryaganj, Delhi – 110002, India

79 Anson Road, #06–04/06, Singapore 079906

Cambridge University Press is part of the University of Cambridge.

It furthers the University's mission by disseminating knowledge in the pursuit of education, learning and research at the highest international levels of excellence.

www.cambridge.org
Information on this title: www.cambridge.org/9781108408417

First published 2018
First published in 2018

20 19 18 17 16 15 14 13 12 11 10 9 8 7 6 5 4 3 2 1

A catalogue record for this publication is available from the British Library

ISBN 978-1-108-40841-7 Paperback
ISBN 978-1-108-40842-4 Apple iBook
ISBN 978-1-108-40843-1 Google ebook
ISBN 978-1-108-40844-8 Kindle ebook
ISBN 978-1-108-40845-5 eBooks.com ebook

CONTENTS

ACKNOWLEDGEMENTS

THE CO-EDITORS

A substantial number of people have supported us in the development of this volume and we are grateful for their contributions. First, we would like to thank all the authors for their willingness to write the various chapters and for their patience over the time it took to bring the volume to fruition. The anonymous reviewers helped to shape the volume further through their useful and thought-provoking feedback. Karen Momber, Jo Timerick, Joanna Garbutt and Sarah Almy offered us their excellent editorial, content, and copy-editing expertise and their guidance has been much appreciated. Finally, the many students we have taught over the years and the curiosity they have shown about the learning of English as a second language inspired us to edit this book in the first place.

Anne Burns
Jack C. Richards

THE CO-EDITORS AND THE PUBLISHERS

The authors and publishers acknowledge the following sources of copyright material and are grateful for the permissions granted. While every effort has been made, it has not always been possible to identify the sources of all the material used, or to trace all copyright holders. If any omissions are brought to our notice, we will be happy to include the appropriate acknowledgements on reprinting and in the next update to the digital edition, as applicable.

John Benjamins Publishing Company for the diagrams on p. 44 from *Third Language Acquisition in Adulthood* edited by Jennifer Cabrelli Amaro, Suzanne Flynn, and Jason Rothman. Copyright © 2012 John Benjamins Publishing Company. Reproduced with kind permission; Oxford University Press for the text on p. 60 from *The New Oxford English Dictionary* edited by Judy Pearsall and Patrick Hanks. Copyright © 1998 Oxford University Press. Reproduced with kind permission; Dagmar Abendroth-Timmer and Eva-Maria Hennig for the text on pp. 95–96, adapted from *Plurilingualism and Multiliteracies: International Research on Identity Construction in Language Education* by Dagmar Abendroth-Timmer and Eva-Maria Hennig, published by Peter Lang AG. Copyright © 2014 Dagmar Abendroth-Timmer and Eva-Maria Hennig. Reproduced with kind permission; Stephen D. Krashen for the figure on p. 186, adapted from *Second Language Acquisition and Second Language Learning* by Stephen D. Krashen, published by Pergamon Press Inc. Copyright © 1981 Stephen D. Krashen. Reproduced with kind permission; Cambridge University Press for the figure on p. 205 from *Teaching Speaking: A Holistic Approach* by Christine Chuen Meng Goh and Anne Burns. Copyright © 2012 Cambridge University Press. Reproduced with kind permission.

INTRODUCTION

Learning English as a Second Language

Anne Burns and Jack C. Richards

RATIONALE FOR THE BOOK

In modern society, the majority of the world's citizens speak one or more second languages and learning a second or third language in childhood is a normal part of the lives of many people. In many countries, such as Singapore, Indonesia, Finland, India and Nigeria, it is often an aspect of socialization typical of a multilingual and multicultural environment. The bilingual or multilingual communicative repertoire that many people make use of in such settings is an important part of their identities. For many others, learning a second language may commence later in life, either at primary or secondary school, and may be essential for education, employment or social survival, as well as many other purposes. Fluency in a second language, particularly an international language such as English, is now mandated by educational policies in many countries, and the teaching of second languages requires a considerable investment of resources at many different levels, including investment in policy and curriculum development, teaching and teacher training, textbook development, technology, and assessment.

While it is now important to be cognizant of the plurilingual nature of language learning and use, and the increasing relevance of translanguaging in multicultural education (e.g., García and Wei, 2014), a key focus is on the learning of English as a second or additional language. The learning of English has been the subject of a considerable amount of research and theorizing in applied linguistics for over half a century, particularly since the research domain of second language acquisition (SLA) emerged in the 1970s. A great deal has been researched and written since then within SLA studies, from cognitive, interactionist, and sociocultural perspectives. Much of this research has focused on the acquisition of the grammatical system of English as a second or additional language and on the role of input and output in promoting grammatical development, as well as the contribution of individual factors such as age, motivation, aptitude, affect, and personality. The benchmark for acquisition has typically been the monolingual native speaker of the target language. Missing from the SLA perspective, however, has been a broader view of the nature of second language knowledge and use – one, for example, that considers the second language in its own terms as a component of the speaker's bilingual or multilingual competence, rather than being a defective form of the native-speaker's language. In addition, the SLA paradigm has typically excluded a focus on other dimensions of language knowledge and use apart from grammar, such as the skills of reading, writing, listening and speaking, pronunciation and vocabulary, as well as the acquisition of pragmatic and intercultural second features of language use. This gap in the literature prompted the present book.

THE PURPOSE OF THIS BOOK

The chapters in this collection seek to move the study of learning English as a second language beyond its typical narrow focus and to provide a more comprehensive overview of learning. To do this, we invited a number of scholars and applied linguists to contribute chapters on language learning processes as they occur across a wide range of domains of language use. The intention was to provide a variety of different perspectives, since no single learning theory can account for all aspects of the development of English as a second language.

The book is aimed at an audience of pre-service and in-service teachers and teacher educators who are seeking a comprehensive coverage of the field, as well as graduate and postgraduate students wishing to gain an authoritative and up-to-date starting point for their studies or research. To that end, the book offers tasks for further reflection and suggestions for essential reading, as well as coverage of the various topics included.

The contributors were asked to address three main areas:

1. The nature of the domain/construct/skill: a brief overview of the topic of the chapter and its key dimensions.

2. The key learning issues for this domain: the issues covered would depend on the topic, but could include:
    *   factors that influence the development of proficiency in the domain;
    *   how development is characterized;
    *   differences between novices and experts;
    *   links to proficiency frameworks.

3. The implications for teaching and assessment.

Contributors were invited to use the areas above as a framework for their chapter, or to adapt this structure according to the domain they wrote about. While, as we have mentioned, the focus of the book is primarily on the learning of English, several authors also included the learning of other languages in relation to English. This book may also be relevant, therefore, to readers whose interests lie in languages other than English.

The guide contains nine sections, which aim to organize and reflect different dimensions of the diverse and complex scope of learning English as a second or additional language.

IMPLICATIONS FOR AN UNDERSTANDING OF LEARNING ENGLISH AS A SECOND LANGUAGE

The chapters contained in the various sections of the book present a wide and diverse range of perspectives on the learning of English. Nevertheless, there are themes and implications that permeate the chapters as a whole, and we outline four of the major themes below.

LEARNING AND LEARNERS

One major motif that runs throughout the guide is the focus on who language learners are, as the authors reflect on:

LEARNERS AS EMERGENT BILINGUALS OR MULTILINGUALS

Discussion of L2 learners' language development and use has traditionally foregrounded the monolingual native speaker as the reference point. The target of learning has been narrowly defined and referenced to L1 norms, failing to acknowledge the distinct role that the L2 and other languages may play in shaping learners' multilingual and multi-cultural identities. Many of the contributors argue that a second or additional language forms part of the learner's multilingual competence (or translanguage competence). Second language learners can more appropriately be described as emergent bilinguals or multilinguals who integrate their use of an additional language with other languages they know.

THE ROLE OF AGENCY AND IDENTITY

Agency has been defined as "the socioculturally mediated capacity to act" (Ahearn, 2001: 112). Kalaja, Alanen, Palviainen, and Dufva (2011: 47) comment: "L2 learners are no longer viewed as individuals working on their own to construct the target language, but very much as social agents collaborating with other people and using the tools and resources available to them in their surrounding environment". In many of the examples in this collection, the learners are engaged actively and purposefully in their language-using experiences. The learners set goals for themselves and make use of the situation and resources available to them to achieve their goals.

Identity refers to how learners position themselves in relation to speakers of other languages, and how this positioning is shaped by their experience of self in their other language or languages. L2 learners, particularly adults, are often positioned as novices, despite the fact that they may be proficient in several other languages. In the case of learning in academic contexts, L2 learning involves entry into a community of practice and the development of a disciplinary identity as learners acquire disciplinary knowledge.

LEARNING AND LANGUAGE

Language is viewed by contributors to this book as a complex and dynamic phenomenon. Language learning thus involves taking account of:

THE SITUATED NATURE OF SECOND LANGUAGE LEARNING

Second language learning takes place in a diversity of both formal and informal contexts, each of which reflects a different configuration of elements that shape the nature of interactions learners are engaged in. Contexts include the home, classrooms, workplaces, social situations, heritage learner environments and technology-enhanced learning contexts, each of which involve different roles, participants and power structures, as well as different purposes and means for using a second language.

A DYNAMIC RATHER THAN A STATIC UNDERSTANDING OF LANGUAGE

As summarized by Pennington (2015: 149), this view of language involves a shift in perspective "from monocompetence, defined as knowledge of an autonomous, unvarying, and uniform system acquired in a homogeneous speech community, to multicompetence, defined here as use of an interactive, variable, and non-uniform system acquired in a heterogeneous world of intersecting groups and individuals".

SECOND LANGUAGE LEARNING AS MORE THAN THE ACQUISITION OF GRAMMAR

Contributors demonstrate the need to broaden the focus of research well beyond the acquisition of the grammatical system of language. In contrast to the traditional SLA approach to learning, which focuses on the acquisition of grammatical rules that develop in a linear fashion, language learning is no longer viewed simply as a cognitive issue involving mastery of the linguistic system. Instead, it is seen to involve a multidimensional change in both the resources learners use to fulfill socio-communicative goals and the affordances beyond the traditional classroom space they make use of in acquiring them (Jenks, 2010).

MULTIMODAL INTERACTIONS IN DIVERSE SITUATIONS THAT MERGE TRADITIONAL VIEWS OF LANGUAGE AS SEPARATE SKILLS

The spoken and written texts learners encounter and use are increasingly integrated and multimodal. Pedagogical approaches for developing literacy and communication skills described by many of the contributors are based on a view of language as social practice, i.e. one in which the different skills are often 'merged' through learners' participation in real-world activities that involve multimodal forms of communication.

LEARNING AND LANGUAGE DEVELOPMENT

As many of the contributions reflect, there is a need to broaden current concepts of language learning to expand understanding of:

THE NATURE OF 'DEVELOPMENT' IN SECOND LANGUAGE LEARNING

No single theory of development or acquisition can account for how learners progress in their language learning trajectories. Perspectives in this guide view development in a number of ways: as incremental improvement in proficiency as determined by greater fluency, accuracy and pragmatic effectiveness, as well as growing confidence and risk-taking; as a movement from novice to expert language user; as a transition from outsider to insider within a community of practice; as acquiring an expanding range of learning resources and affordances; as developing membership of different kinds of communities through social media; as developing a metalanguage for talking about language and texts; making a transition from collaborative and independent practice; as reconstructing one's understanding and view of the world and one's place in it; and as the ability to transfer learning from one context (e.g., the classroom) to the workplace.

MULTIDIMENSIONAL UNDERSTANDING OF SECOND LANGUAGE LEARNING

Contributors emphasize the need to recognize the multifaceted nature of language learning and of language use. Atkinson (2011) emphasizes that second language acquisition is a very complex phenomenon with many different dimensions. It requires multiple theories of second language acquisition to provide a complete understanding of it. Contributors to this book refer to different views of learning to explain dimensions of L2 language learning: incidental learning; scaffolded learning; learning as socialization; learning through participation and apprenticeship within social groups; learning through observation and participation in social practices; autonomous and self-directed learning; learning through modeling and guidance from experts; and language learning as the negotiation and development of identities.

LEARNING AND LEARNING CONTEXTS

The role of context is highly significant in language learning. New perspectives offered in these chapters highlight the need to consider language learning contexts in terms of:

THE NEGOTIATION OF CROSS-CULTURAL ENCOUNTERS

A second or additional language is a resource for participation in cross-cultural encounters and experiences and for the development of intercultural communicative competence. This involves the ability to mediate and translate between languages and cultures in diverse settings involving speakers with multiple linguistic and cultural backgrounds.

CHANGING LEARNING AFFORDANCES

The new opportunities or 'affordances' for language learning that are available through technology, the internet and the media, and the resulting shift from classroom-based learning to out-of-class learning as a primary source of both input and output for many second language users, has prompted the need to reconceptualize the nature of second language learning. New learning affordances provide opportunities for different kinds of interaction and language use, as well as access to different learning processes that are available in classroom-based teaching.

RECONFIGURATIONS OF THE NATURE OF SECOND LANGUAGE TEACHING

While from a cognitive perspective it was often suggested that a language was not teachable but could be 'acquired' through experientially based learning, drawing on implicit rather than explicit instruction, contributors to this guide offer different perspectives on instructional contexts. Contributors describe a variety of roles for explicit classroom-based instruction, including strategy training, modeling expert language use, comparing pragmatic features of languages, and translation activities, as well as activities that involve implicit learning. Explicit and implicit teaching are seen to tap into different learning processes.

CONCLUSION

This introductory chapter foregrounds our aim in editing this book – to expand the range of current perspectives on what it means to learn English as a second or additional language. Our intention in the following pages is to provide readers with a broad and composite set of accounts of language learning, written by authors well-versed in the topics that are covered, that can be used as a starting point for further reflection, reading and investigation. In compiling this collection, we stressed to the contributors that they did not need to take any particular theoretical stance on language learning, but to offer their own theoretical frameworks and perspectives. In this respect, we hope that the book opens up many avenues for further discussion, exploration and research in an area that is of the utmost importance for the field of English language teaching.

References

Ahearn, L. M. (2001). Language and agency. *Annual Review of Anthropology*, 30, 109–137.

Atkinson, D. (Ed.) (2011). *Alternative Approaches to Second Language Acquisition*. London: Routledge.

García, O., & Wei, L. (2014). *Translanguaging: Language, Bilingualism and Education*. Basingstoke, UK: Palgrave Macmillan.

Jenks, C. (2010). Adaptation in online voice-based chat rooms: Implications for language learning in applied linguistics. In P. Seedhouse, S. Walsh, & C. Jenks (Eds.), *Conceptualising 'Learning' in Applied Linguistics* (pp. 147–162). London: Palgrave Macmillan.

Kalaja, P., Alanen, R., Palviainen, Å., & Dufva, H. (2011). From milk cartons to English roommates: Context and agency in L2 learning beyond the classroom. In P. Benson & H. Reinders (Eds.), *Beyond the Language Classroom* (pp. 47–58). Basingstoke: Palgrave Macmillan.

Pennington, M. P. (2015). Research, theory and practice in L2 phonology: A review and directions for the future. In J. A. Mompean & J. Fouz-González (Eds.), *Investigating English Pronunciation: Current Trends and Directions* (pp. 149–173). New York: Palgrave Macmillan.

SECTION I

LEARNERS AND LEARNING ENGLISH

The first section focuses on who second language (L2) learners are, which, in the case of English, is becoming increasingly diversified across the world, as learners begin their learning at a variety of different ages and with a multiplicity of learning and language(s) backgrounds and repertoires.

In the first chapter on the language learner, **Yuko Goto Butler** examines features of L2 learning in children, comparing first language (L1) and L2 learning, as well as differences between young and older learners. She highlights the different contexts in which young learners acquire additional languages, and discusses how context impacts the goals and processes of a learner of English as an L2. She also describes how age factors relate to the learning of phonology, vocabulary, morphosyntax and literacy, and reviews the role of implicit learning, explicit learning, and learning strategies.

In the next chapter, **Tracey Costley** explores the different contexts in which adolescents learn L2s, and the particular attributes and dispositions that influence both their understanding or 'idea' of English and their approaches to learning. She highlights the role of social contexts and maturational factors on L2 learning, discusses how age, gender and language-learning background influence language learning in adolescents, and points out the implications of these factors for the teaching of adolescent learners.

In their chapter on language learning among adults, **Carol Griffiths** and **Adem Soruç** review research findings on adult learners and outline the characteristics and dispositions of this group of learners. They discuss neurological, psycho-affective, sociocultural and other factors that affect the English language learning outcomes of adult learners, and suggest that research findings prompt a rethinking of the common assumption that adults are often unsuccessful in their attempts to learn additional languages.

In the next chapter, **Judit Kormos** examines the impact of specific learning difficulties on L2 development, particularly those difficulties that are neurological in origin and often inherited, rather than those that reflect socio-environmental dimensions. She discusses factors that may influence many components of English language proficiency, including grammar, vocabulary and reading, writing and listening skills.

John Witney and **Jean-Marc Dewaele** examine how learners acquiring a third language can draw both on metalinguistic awareness and on familiarity with learning strategies developed from learning previous languages. They suggest that learners acquiring a third or further language have greater metalinguistic awareness, make use of a great number of learning strategies and use them more frequently.

The chapters in this section draw our attention to the very extensive range of learner factors that need to be considered in L2 learning. They highlight the importance of being cognizant of, and sensitive to, these factors in determining the goals and needs of learners at different points in their life trajectories, and also the kinds of linguistic and learning resources they bring with them, whether their learning takes place in actual or virtual settings.

CHAPTER 1

Learning as a Child

Yuko Goto Butler

INTRODUCTION

For children, learning a second language (L2) differs in important ways from learning a first language (L1), as well as from learning an L2 as an adult. After all, children are still in the process of their cognitive, social-affective, and linguistic (L1) development, which in turn influences their L2 learning in various ways. Educators must consider such differences when teaching and assessing children who are learning an L2. Although the research on children's L2 learning still remains relatively limited, this chapter summarizes researchers' current understanding of children's L2 learning, so that educators can make use of this emerging knowledge. To that end, I begin by describing who young L2 learners are and their varying L2-learning contexts and needs. I then discuss key characteristics of child L2 learning. I conclude by suggesting ways that educators can put these findings to work for teaching and assessing young L2 learners.

OVERVIEW

WHO ARE YOUNG L2 LEARNERS?

Young L2 learners are often defined as children of preschool and primary school age who are learning a second language. Although the exact age range for preschool and primary school differs depending on educational systems, it is generally between 4 and 12 years old. I should note, however, that young L2 learners can be defined in alternative ways. Researchers who subscribe to some notion of a critical period in L2 acquisition – a hypothesis that one can no longer acquire 'native-like' proficiency in the target language once they reach a certain age – may argue that young L2 learners should be defined as children who are exposed to their L2 sometime after birth but before the critical period ends. However, the existence of a critical period is debated among researchers, and even among supporters the exact range of such a period in L2 is controversial. Some researchers also distinguish young L2 learners from children who have regular contact with two languages from very early in their lives; such children, sometimes referred to as simultaneous bilingual children, are considered to have two L1s. Here again, however, the cut-off point – the age children need to be exposed to two languages to qualify as speaking two L1s – is not clear: it ranges from two months to three years of age (Unsworth and Blom, 2010). So, while acknowledging that the age range of four to twelve years old for young L2 learners has some critics, this is the range frequently used within the pedagogic and policy community, and it is the range I use here.

VARYING LEARNING CONTEXTS AND GOALS OF YOUNG L2 LEARNERS

Young learners are by no means homogenous, and the contexts of their L2 learning differ greatly. Young L2 learners include language minority children who have a minority language (or languages; see Chapter 5) at home and learn a majority language in the community and school as their L2. Depending on circumstances (e.g., their home language became a less dominant language), children's home language can be considered an L2, in the form of a heritage language to be maintained or relearned. Young L2 learners also include children who have a majority language as their home language but are enrolled in an immersion program and receive academic instruction (at least partially) through their non-home language (L2). Lastly, children learning a foreign language (FL) are also considered to be young L2 learners, and this type of young L2 learner is growing rapidly in number worldwide. In principle, FL-learning children are assumed to have limited exposure to the target language outside of the classroom, but the amount and quality of children's exposure to the target language vary substantially by region and by socio-economic status.

Reflecting such variability in learning contexts, the goals of L2 learning differ substantially – not only across the above-mentioned L2 groups but also within any given group. While sometimes the goal of young L2 learning is to develop age-appropriate basic linguistic knowledge and skills that allow children to converse daily with target-language speakers, at other times the goal is to develop high L2 proficiency in academic contexts (i.e., academic language) so that learners can acquire content subject knowledge (e.g., mathematics and science) through the target language. Academic language is generally considered to be "the vocabulary, sentence structures, and discourse associated with language used to teach academic content as well as the language used to navigate the school setting more generally" (Bailey and Huang, 2011: 343); however, it is important to note that researchers disagree about what constitutes academic language abilities and, further, that the relationship between academic language abilities and content subject learning is not yet well-understood.

KEY LEARNING ISSUES

Considering such diversity of learning contexts and goals of L2 learning for young learners, we can expect that learning outcomes vary as well. Various social contextual factors, as well as individual factors (e.g., motivation, aptitude, etc.; see Chapters 6 and 7), influence their L2 development. As mentioned already, it remains controversial if the ultimate attainment of L2 is affected by the onset of first exposure to L2; researchers debate if a critical period exists, and if it does, when it is and what domains are affected by it. In FL contexts, learning L2 from a very young age may not be most effective. In this section, I sketch major aspects of young L2 learning that we know so far, first in the domain of language development and then in the domains of learning styles and strategies (see Chapter 9).

PHONOLOGY DEVELOPMENT

Among the general public, there is a widespread belief that children can acquire 'native-like' sounds in their L2/FL with ease. Researchers have found, however, that the influence of a child's L1 is persistent and observable. Although research directly examining phonological development among young L2 learners remains very limited, retrospective research has shown that non-native accents can be perceived, at least in some properties, even among learners who started being exposed to their L2 before the age of three. Researchers have proposed models for phonology development that may explain the reason for the persistence of non-native accents even among those who started learning L2 at a very young age (see Chapter 17). One such model is Flege's Speech Learning Model. According to this model, both L1 and L2 share a common phonetic space, and L2 learners perceive new L2 sounds based on their existing L1 phonetic categories, either through assimilating or disassimilating the L1 categories, depending on similarities and dissimilarities between novel L2 sounds and L1 sounds (Flege, 1999).

A number of studies have examined the relationship between the age of onset of L2 and the ultimate L2 phonology acquisition, as measured by perceived accent ratings, as well as by physical phonetic and phonemic properties (e.g., voice onset time). Such studies have generally found correlations between the age of onset and phonology acquisition. However, researchers disagree on whether there is any cut-off point in the course of phonology development (i.e., a critical period) and, if so, when exactly the critical period is.

In addition to the age young learners are first exposed to the target language, a few other factors have been suggested as influencing their L2 phonology acquisition. Most notably, the amount and type of L2 input (which is usually negatively correlated with the amount of use of L1) has been found to be an important predictor of L2 phonology attainment. Also influential are the learner's desire to acquire 'native' sounds in L2, and how the learner identifies himself or herself in relation to his or her L1 and L2. Moreover, phonological differences between L1 and L2 cannot be ignored. For example, Flege and Fletcher (1992) found that among children who had been immersed in English since they were five to eight years old, Chinese L1 speakers had more perceivable non-native accents in L2 (English) than their Spanish L1 counterparts.

Unlike in L2 contexts, in FL contexts where learners usually have limited target language input, 'the earlier, the better' is not warranted. In fact, most existing studies have found no advantage for young starters in perceiving and producing FL sounds. In FL contexts, the amount and quality of instruction appear to be more influential over one's phonology acquisition than the age of onset of FL instruction (Muñoz, 2014).

LEXICAL DEVELOPMENT

In L2-learning contexts, young L2 learners' lexical processing (i.e., the process of recognizing, accessing, and producing words that are stored in one's mental lexicon) improves gradually throughout their primary school years, consistent with the general development pattern observed among L1 monolingual children. However, it is often reported that lexical processing among child L2 learners is less efficient or slower, compared with their monolingual peers. Researchers have also found that L2 learners' vocabulary size (both receptive and productive vocabulary) in both their L1 and L2 is smaller than the vocabulary size of their monolingual counterparts (Bialystok, 2009).

A caution is necessary, however, when we compare young L2 learners – namely, children with various degrees of bilingual/multilingual abilities – with monolingual children. Researchers such as Grosjean (2010) argue that bilingual children's language knowledge and processing are *qualitatively* different from those of monolingual children. Under this view, it does not make sense to evaluate L2 learners' linguistic abilities against monolingual norms. In addition, we need to keep in mind that there are substantial individual differences in vocabulary development among young L2 learners, as well as among monolingual children learning their L1 (Murphy, 2014).

Among young L2 learners, older learners tend to acquire lexical knowledge faster than young learners, due to their greater cognitive maturity and richer experiences. From a multilingual developmental perspective, it is also important to note that children who have an opportunity to develop basic literacy skills in their L1 tend to keep developing their L1 vocabulary better than children who do not have a chance to develop basic literacy skills. Retrospective research often shows that children who immigrate to an L2 environment when they are around eight to ten years old, as well as L2-learning children who receive instruction in both their L1 and their L2, have a better chance of developing grade-equivalent (or higher) L2 vocabulary while retaining a high level of L1 vocabulary.

MORPHOSYNTAX DEVELOPMENT

Morphosyntax acquisition patterns of young L2 learners are often similar to those of monolingual L1-learning children. For instance, morphologies acquired late by L1-learning children also tend to be acquired late by young L2 learners, and common errors observed among young L2 learners have also been found among L1-learning children. However, young L2 learners also exhibit different patterns from L1 learners. For example, the overgeneralization of the copula (e.g., "I am play baseball") and the omission of a subject (e.g., "play baseball") are frequently observed among young L2 learners, irrespective of their L1 (Paradis, 2005). These phenomena may be largely attributable to children's cognitive maturity rather than other factors, such as L1 influence. It is important to note, however, that most current research on this topic was conducted among children whose L1 and L2 are European languages; more research looking at different language combinations is necessary. Indeed, while earlier studies claimed that children's L1 plays little role in their L2 morphosyntax acquisition (e.g., Dulay and Burt, 1974), more recent studies suggest that children's L1 may play a larger role than we used to believe. Similarly, the extent to which young L2 learners' morphosyntax acquisition is different from that of adult L2 learners remains unclear.

As with phonology development, there is no consensus on whether the age of initial exposure to L2 affects the ultimate attainment of morphosyntax; it remains unclear if there is a critical period in morphosyntax acquisition and, if so, when it is. However, when it comes to efficiency of acquisition, young L2 learners can pick up morphosyntax knowledge faster than L1-learning younger children, due to the older L2 learners' greater degree of cognitive maturity. Similarly, research conducted in FL contexts has shown that later starters of FL learning develop morphosyntax more efficiently than earlier starters (e.g., García Mayo and García Lecumberri, 2003).

LITERACY DEVELOPMENT

For young minority-language-speaking children who receive education in their L2 context, acquiring sufficient literacy skills (see Chapter 26) in L2 is a pressing issue. Existing studies, primarily conducted in North America and the United Kingdom, repeatedly report that many young L2 learners lag behind in their reading comprehension and academic studies. Interestingly, however, as far as the research from North America is concerned, young L2 learners on average perform equally well with their monolingual L1-speaking peers in word-decoding skills. Such word-decoding skills, which include phonological awareness, lexical access, and working memory, have long been known as critical elements for successful reading comprehension. But young L2 learners tend to have a weaker vocabulary, academic vocabulary in particular, which influences their reading comprehension. Oral language proficiency also seems to be associated with young L2 learners' reading comprehension, although the precise relationship remains unclear. Nonlinguistic factors, including socio-economic background, individual characteristics (e.g., motivation, personality, learning strategies, etc.), and type of instruction they receive, all contribute to young L2 learners' literacy development in complicated ways. For example, research has shown that teacher-centered instructional approaches tend to work better for quiet and analytical learners, while more activity-based instructional approaches appear to work better for active and outgoing children (Murphy, 2014).

When considering these findings, it is important to remember that many studies measure children's reading comprehension using standardized tests, while usually setting monolingual L1 children's performance as the norm, and what counts as literacy skills is usually defined narrowly. Studies also tend to pay almost exclusive attention to learners' L2 literacy skills, and ignore their literacy in L1 or any other language(s) that they may know. Increasingly, scholars are questioning such narrow, monolingual-based conceptualizations of literacy, and are advocating instead for multimodal and multilingual approaches to literacy (e.g., the translanguaging approach advocated by García and Wei, 2014).

LEARNING STYLES AND STRATEGIES

It is often assumed that children learn L2 more implicitly (i.e., learning through an unconscious and unintended process), whereas adults tend to learn L2 more explicitly (i.e., learning through a conscious and intended process) (e.g., DeKeyser, 2003; Ellis, 2005). However, empirical studies on implicit and explicit learning among young L2 learners are so scarce that it is unclear to what extent such assumptions are based on evidence. Lichtman (2013) suggested that our perceptional bias toward implicit L2 learning for children and explicit L2 learning for adults might, at least in part, be due to the fact that children tend to receive implicit instruction while adults tend to receive explicit instruction. Research conducted in FL learning contexts reports that older children (upper grade primary school students) appear to benefit from receiving both explicit and implicit instruction. When it comes to academic language, however it is defined, it needs to be explicitly instructed.

Young L2 learners may exhibit age-specific language learning strategies, such as incorporating body movements to interact with word meanings, and repeating and playing around with sounds. They appear to use some of these strategies (e.g., repeating sounds) unconsciously. As children become more cognitively mature and gain more experiences, they start incorporating many of the same language-learning strategies that are observed among adult L2 learners. The use of L1 as a strategy (e.g., memorizing L2 spelling using L1 phonetic knowledge) has also been observed (Mihaljević Djigunović, 2009).

It is also important to point out that many children today grow up immersed in technology. Prensky (2001: 52) argued that cognitive styles of children who are used to technology are different from previous generations in a number of ways, in that:

- they can process information much faster than the conventional speed;
- they are good at parallel processing rather than linear processing;
- they access information randomly as opposed to in a step-by-step fashion;
- they rely on graphics first rather than texts;
- they are accustomed to being connected with others as opposed to being unconnected;
- they prefer active learning to passive learning;

- they see *play as work* as opposed to *play vs. work*;
- they make constant decisions between payoff and patience;
- fantasy, rather than reality, pervades their lives;
- they view technology as their friend, not their enemy.

Although we still need more empirical evidence to affirm Prensky's observations, it is important for educators to pay close attention to children's learning characteristics when designing material and instruction for them.

IMPLICATIONS FOR TEACHING AND ASSESSMENT

In the following sections, I translate the preceding research findings into a few practical suggestions for teaching and assessing young L2 learners.

IMPLICATIONS FOR L2 TEACHING

USE MEANING-FOCUSED, HOLISTIC APPROACHES TO L2 LEARNING, SUCH AS TASK-BASED LANGUAGE TEACHING

Children have a strong drive both to make meaning while interacting with other people and to acquire new knowledge and skills playfully (Bland, 2015). Task-based language teaching (TBLT) can be used as an effective pedagogical approach, particularly if the learning goal is mainly to acquire age-appropriate communicative competence in L2. In TBLT, real-life communicative tasks are employed as instructional materials or syllabus designs, while primarily focusing on meaning rather than linguistic accuracy. Thus, it is particularly suitable for young learners.

When designing or choosing tasks for young learners, it is important to carefully consider young learners' unique characteristics, such as their cognitive maturity and experiences, as well as their language proficiency. Children's affective elements, such as their motivation, must be considered as well. And given children's affinity for stories and fantasies, narrative and fantasy features can be incorporated into task designs in order to motivate and engage children. Educators can control cognitive demands for completing tasks in a number of ways. For example, *tell a story based on pictures*, a common task introduced to young L2 learners, can be made less cognitively demanding by using fewer pictures, providing the pictures in sequential order, using a simpler plot line, and offering sufficient planning time prior to the task. Cognitive demands can also be reduced by providing children with scaffolding, such as incorporating whole-class brainstorming of major plot lines and ideas, or allowing children to work together in groups or pairs (Pinter, 2015).

AVOID 'ONE-SIZE-FITS-ALL' APPROACHES TO L2 INSTRUCTION

If the learning goal is mainly to acquire academic language, young L2 learners need to receive explicit instruction in vocabulary, syntax, and discourse associated with academic learning. A number of instructional strategies have been suggested in order to assist learners in comprehending content subjects (e.g., mathematics and science) through their L2. Learners' L1 can be used effectively as well. Multilingual- and multimodal-based literacy exercises may need to be promoted, depending on the children's background and purpose of the study. For example, educators can encourage children to construct texts involving multiple languages or incorporate various audio and visual materials into their learning. Importantly, there are substantial individual differences among children, both in their L1 and L2 development and in their needs. To meet such diversity, teachers must be flexible in their approach to L2 instruction. After all, there is no 'one size fits all' teaching method or strategy for young L2 learners.

IMPLICATIONS FOR ASSESSMENT

ADOPT AN ASSESSMENT APPROACH THAT SUPPORTS ONGOING LEARNING

In assessing young learners, measuring their abilities makes sense only if the results directly assist their learning. In other words, learning should be the core purpose of the assessment. Therefore, assessment for learning, a concept that has received substantial attention in recent assessment research, is particularly relevant to young learners. In assessment for learning, as opposed to assessment of learning, the primary goal of assessment is not to measure learners' learning outcomes accurately and consistently, but to obtain information about the process of learning in order to inform and assist their ongoing learning (Black and Wiliam, 1998). Thus, some researchers (e.g., Davison and Leung, 2009) argue that traditional psychometric notions of validity and reliability may need to be reconceptualized in assessment for learning.

In the assessment for learning paradigm, critical concerns include how best to provide the learners with diagnostic information and how best to assist them to be in charge of their own learning. Grounded in Vygotsky's sociocultural theory, dynamic assessment, as a diagnostic assessment, for example, aims to identify learners' potential for development through mediated teaching such as modeling during the process of completing tasks (Poehner and Infante, 2016). Self-assessment can be used effectively with young learners to assist them in reflecting on their progress and setting learning goals – as long as they are given sufficient guidance (Butler, 2016).

In order to make the assessment informative and diagnostic, the teachers' role is critical. Edelenbos and Kubanek-German (2004) have argued that teachers need to develop sufficient diagnostic competence, which is composed of a series of abilities and actions for capturing and interpreting students' learning growth, handling assessment material and procedures, and providing students with assistance that corresponds to diagnostic information provided by the assessment.

CHOOSE AN ASSESSMENT FORMAT THAT SUITS YOUR STUDENTS' LEARNING STYLES AND YOUR PEDAGOGICAL GOALS

Just as instructional tasks and strategies should be age-appropriate for learners, assessment tasks and formats also should align with learners' cognitive maturity and experiences. Individual students' characteristics and needs should be thoroughly considered when designing assessments. For example, in formative assessment, an individual-based assessment format (teacher–child dyad format) may be advantageous for young learners, in that it allows teachers to tailor the assessment content and scaffolding to children's individual proficiency levels, personalities, and learning styles; in other words, the format enables teachers to stretch children's abilities. But at the same time, the individual format tends to elicit limited types of interactive responses from children, and the elicited language often looks like an initiation–response–evaluation (IRE) response, which is a typical classroom interaction pattern between teachers and students. On the other hand, pair- or group-assessment formats, in which children work on assessment tasks in pairs or groups, has the potential to elicit wider ranges of interactional responses from children. However, teachers' careful oversight is necessary to ensure that children collaborate well (Butler and Zeng, 2011).

LINK L2 PROFICIENCY TO ACADEMIC CONTENT LEARNING

In L2 learning contexts where children learn subject-matter content in their L2, teachers are increasingly held accountable for assessing learners' language proficiency as it is embedded in their content knowledge. Language proficiency and content knowledge have traditionally been considered separate constructs; content knowledge is considered a construct-irrelevant variance in language proficiency assessments, and vice versa.

However, linking language proficiency and content learning is inevitable in L2 contexts; this may require redefining the construct of language ability in specific academic contexts (Llosa, 2011). In standard-based educational systems, sufficient guidance is necessary for teachers in order for them to be fully familiar with standards (both L2 standards and subject-matter content standards).

To assess young learners' L2 abilities while engaging in academic content learning, assessment tasks should be designed to elicit particular language functions that are associated with critical cognitive and metacognitive skills for completing the given academic task. Sufficient consideration needs to be paid to learners' affective factors, such as their interest in, and anxiety about, the assessment task.

CONCLUSION

While research on child L2 acquisition is still relatively limited, we do know that L2 learning by young learners differs in important ways from children's L1 acquisition and adult L2 acquisition. This chapter described the heterogeneity of child L2 learners and outlined major issues in child L2 acquisition, offering a number of implications for teaching and assessing young learners. Due to the variabilities of learning goals and contexts, educators need to take flexible and localized approaches to teaching and assessment that meet learners' needs.

Discussion Questions

1. Think about a couple of tasks that you often use in your L2 instruction. What are some ways you can increase or reduce the cognitive demands for these tasks?

2. Edelenbos and Kubanek-German (2004) made a list of teachers' diagnostic competencies, based on their observations of teachers' assessment practices. Based on your own experience, what skills and actions do teachers need for capturing their students' learning processes and outcomes in order to provide them with useful diagnostic assistance?

Key Readings

Murphy, V. A. (2014). *Second Language Learning in the Early School Years: Trends and Contexts*. Oxford: Oxford University Press.

Pinter, A. (2011). *Children Learning Second Languages*. New York: Palgrave Macmillan.

References

Bailey, A. L., & Huang, B. H. (2011). Do current English language development/proficiency standards reflect the English needed for success in school? *Language Testing*, 28(3), 343–365.

Bialystok, E. (2009). Bilingualism: The good, the bad, and the indifferent. *Bilingualism: Language and Cognition*, 12(1), 3–11.

Black, P. J., & Wiliam, D. (1998). Assessment and classroom learning. *Assessment in Education: Principles, Policy & Practice*, 5(1), 7–74.

Bland, J. (2015). *Teaching English to Young Learners: Critical Issues in Language Teaching with 3–12 year olds*. London: Bloomsbury.

Butler, Y. G. (2016). Self-assessment of and for young learners' foreign language learning. In M. Nikolov (Ed.), *Assessing Young Learners of English: Global and Local Perspectives* (pp. 291–315). New York: Springer.

Butler, Y. G., & Zeng, W. (2011). The roles that teachers play in paired-assessments for young learners. In D. Tsagari & I. Csépes (Eds.), *Classroom-based Language Assessment* (pp. 77–92). Frankfurt: Peter Lang.

Davison, C., & Leung, C. (2009). Current issues in English language teacher-based assessment. *TESOL Quarterly*, 43, 393–415.

DeKeyser, R. (2003). Implicit and explicit learning. In C. J. Doughty & M. H. Long (Eds.), *The Handbook of Second Language Acquisition* (pp. 313–348). Oxford: Blackwell.

Dulay, H., & Burt, M. (1974). Should we teach children syntax? *Language Learning*, 24, 245–258.

Edelenbos, P., & Kubanek-German, A. (2004). Teacher assessment: The concept of 'diagnostic competence'. *Language Testing*, 21, 259–283.

Ellis, R. (2005). Measuring implicit and explicit knowledge of a second language: A psychometric study. *Studies in Second Language Acquisition*, 27, 141–172.

Flege, J. E. (1999). Age of learning and second language speech. In D. Birdsong (Ed.), *Second Language Acquisition and the Critical Period Hypothesis* (pp. 101–131). Mahwah, NJ: Lawrence Erlbaum.

Flege, J. E., & Fletcher, K. (1992). Talker and listener effects on degree of perceived foreign accent. *Journal of Acoustical Society of America*, 91, 370–389.

García, O., & Wei, L. (2014). *Translanguaging: Language, Bilingualism and Education*. London: Palgrave.

García Mayo, M. P., & García Lecumberri, M. L. (2003). *Age and the Acquisition of English as a Foreign Language*. Clevedon, UK: Multilingual Matters.

Grosjean, F. (2010). *Bilingual: Life and Reality*. Cambridge, MA: Harvard University Press.

Lichtman, K. (2013). Developmental comparisons of implicit and explicit language learning. *Language Acquisition*, 20, 93–108.

Llosa, L. (2011). Standards-based classroom assessments of English proficiency: A review of issues, current developments, and future directions for research. *Language Testing*, 28, 367–382.

Mihaljević Djigunović, J. (2009). Individual differences in early language programmes. In M. Nikolov (Ed.), *The Age Factor and Early Language Learning* (pp. 199–225). Berlin: De Gruyter Mouton.

Muñoz, C. (2014). Contrasting effects of starting age and input on the oral performance of foreign language learners. *Applied Linguistics*, 35, 463–482.

Murphy, V. A. (2014). *Second Language Learning in the Early School Years: Trends and Contexts*. Oxford: Oxford University Press.

Paradis, J. (2005). Grammatical morphology in children learning English as a second language: Implications of similarities with specific language impairment. *Language, Speech, and Hearing Services in Schools*, 36, 172–187.

Pinter, A. (2015). Task-based learning with children. In J. Bland (Ed.), *Teaching English to Young Learners: Critical Issues in Language Teaching with 3–12 year olds* (pp. 113–127). London: Bloomsbury.

Poehner, M. E., & Infante, P. (2016). Dynamic Assessment in the language classroom. In D. Tsagari & J. Banerjee (Eds.), *Handbook of Second Language Assessment* (pp. 275–290). Boston: De Gruyter.

Prensky, M. (2001) *Digital Game-based Learning*. New York: McGraw-Hill.

Unsworth, S., & Blom, E. (2010). Comparing L1 children, L2 children and L2 adults. In E. Blom & S. Unsworth (Eds.), *Experimental Methods in Language Acquisition Research* (pp. 201–222). Amsterdam/Philadelphia: John Benjamins.

CHAPTER 2

Learning as an Adolescent

Tracey Costley

INTRODUCTION

Adolescence is often considered to be a challenging period in an individual's development and one in which significant physiological, cognitive and social change takes place. It is a period in time that is often synonymous with creativity and enthusiasm, as well as disaffection and disengagement (Ryan and Patrick, 2001). A 2012 United Nations world population monitoring report suggested that the world has approximately 721 million adolescents (United Nations, 2012). They define adolescence as being represented by young people aged 12–17 years old, which makes adolescents a very large and interesting group of learners to focus on.

This chapter seeks to present some of the key ideas and issues in relation to the impact of adolescence on language learning, with a specific interest in the learning of English. The chapter begins with an overview of the main assumptions about the relationship between age and language learning, before moving on to discuss the ways in which these assumptions may impact on teaching and assessment.

OVERVIEW

Much has been written about the way in which we acquire language, and within this research age is often a focus of interest, with studies seeking to establish whether there is an optimum time for language learning. Studies in this area often refer to a 'maturational period', which is considered to mark the point in age where an individual's language learning ability begins to halt and decline (Bialystok, 1997; Birdsong, 2006). It is considered to mark a period after which a learner is unlikely to achieve a 'native-like' mastery of the language they are trying to learn. Studies have shown that as we age our ability to process, produce and remember information, particularly language, decreases and that this decrease begins around puberty (see Birdsong, 2006, for a detailed overview of the literature). The maturational period is important here, as it is often regarded as coinciding with the beginning of adolescence and has had a powerful impact on the ways in which these learners, and language learning, is understood.

The concept of a maturational period is a powerful one and one that has moved beyond the research community into society more broadly. For example, the idea that if language learning is to be successful, it should be introduced into the curriculum as early as possible, is one that has had a significant impact on language learning policies worldwide (see Chapter 1). The last 10-20 years have seen increased interest in, and calls for, the introduction of English into primary schools and kindergartens in countries such as South Korea, China and Japan, as well as the introduction of foreign languages into the primary school curriculum in England (see Cable et al. 2010; Tragant 2006). The idea of a maturational period is also often cited as an explanation for why, in many contexts, language learning often declines during adolescence. It is also not uncommon to hear people discuss the idea of an 'ideal age' for learning a language, and whether or not they feel as though they started learning at the 'right' age or not. As more and more studies in the field of applied linguistics have shown, however, even though there is some evidence that a maturational period may have an impact on some aspects of language learning, it is by no means as black and white as saying younger means better.

In her research, Bialystok (1997) identifies certain limits to the impact of the maturational period. Whilst she recognises that there is evidence to suggest that younger children tend to be successful language learners, Bialystok suggests that this is more to do with the ways in which children go about acquiring language than a biological influence. For her, the flexibility and ability young learners display is a more convincing proposition for explaining language learning success than a biological one. As she says, "children would appear to be more successful language learners … not because of maturational limits on language learning but because of stylistic differences in learning at different times in life" (Bialystok 1997: 132).

Researchers such as Schmid (2014), for example, show how support for a maturational effect has often been drawn from comparisons between individuals learning the target language and monolingual speakers of the language, which she suggests may not be appropriate. Schmid (2014) discusses how such studies are potentially problematic, on account of not comparing similar learners or learning conditions. As a result, she suggests that the results may not be sufficiently reliable to draw firm conclusions, and also highlights the importance of context in understanding any impact of age on language learning.

Other research into the relationship between age and language learning success has shown that age, and in particular adolescence, is in fact a positive factor (Cook, 1996; Muñoz 2006, 2008; Ryan and Patrick, 2001; Tragant 2006; Tragant and Victori, 2006). Instead of being a hindrance, adolescence, and the co-occurring cognitive, emotional and psychological changes that take place at this time, have a positive impact on learning and are in fact beneficial, if classroom practices and learning opportunities are effectively designed and delivered (Muñoz, 2006, 2008; Ryan and Patrick, 2001; Tragant, 2006; Tragant and Victori, 2006).

These differences in approaches and findings highlight the need for us to ask questions both about how the period of adolescence impacts learning approaches and what the learning strategies of these young learners are. It is also important to discover more about other factors, such as the role of context, to develop a better understanding of how adolescence may impact the language learning process.

KEY LEARNING ISSUES

From the literature on adolescent language learners it is possible to identify three broad interrelated and interdependent themes. The three categories are: *Learning needs, strategies, and opportunities*; *Engagement, interest and motivation;* and *Learning contexts*, and these are used to organise the following discussion, with specific reference to the learning of English.

LEARNING NEEDS, STRATEGIES AND OPPORTUNITIES

Ryan and Patrick (2001) posit that the developmental changes that take place during adolescence are very significant in terms of how they impact on learners' attitudes towards, and preferences, for learning. Some of the key changes they identify are an "increased desire for autonomy, increased reflection on more abstract constructs (e.g., fairness), increased need for positive and supportive relationships with both peers and nonparental adults, and increased self-consciousness and sensitivity regarding social comparison" (p. 439). For Ryan and Patrick (2001) these changes are important in that they are not regarded as 'choices' that learners make, but rather they are developmental needs that have to be met. Classrooms that, therefore, work with these needs rather than against them are likely to be sites of more effective learning.

In their work with adolescent learners of English, Tragant and Victori (2006) looked at the types of strategies used by this group of learners to try and understand more about how age may be an influence on learning strategies, and to what extent the strategies are positive or negative in terms of the learners' potential for learning English. In their work the authors found that, as older learners moved into adolescence, they tended to make increased use of more autonomous and metacognitively demanding learning techniques in comparison to the younger learners in the study. They found that the adolescent learners tended to use more "demanding strategies, such as analysing, classifying, studying and using mnemotechniques, all of which require a higher degree of elaboration on the part of the learner than simple memorisation techniques" (Tragant and Victori, 2006: 223).

The findings from their study echo similar findings to those of Muñoz (2006, 2008), Oxford (1989) and Tragant (2006), and also speak clearly to Ryan and Patrick's (2001) claims that adolescence marks a distinctive phase in the ways that learners actually go about learning. The crucial point for this discussion, however, is that the techniques and strategies used by this group of adolescents are the same as those often highlighted as being adopted by the most successful language learners (see Cook, 1996; Richards and Lockhart, 1996).

Building on the idea of adolescence as representing a stage in which distinctive learning strategies and styles are developed, and drawing from work in psychology and second language acquisition, Muñoz's (2006, 2008) work looks at the different ways in which the activities that learners are asked to engage in may complement, or actually contradict, their learning needs and strategies. Her work explores the extent to which learning at different ages can be aided, or indeed hindered, by different types of activities designed to practise the language.

Muñoz (2008) highlights both the implications that different types of activities have for successful language learning at different ages and the different impact activities have on the cognitive development of learners, as well as on learners' aptitude for language learning. She also looks at the ways in which different activities can help foster the development of successful learning strategies (see Chapter 9), as well as how activities impact (positively and negatively) on learners' motivation and personal engagement with the language (see Chapter 6).

Muñoz highlights the importance of providing opportunities for language practice that complement the age of the learner, and suggests that there are distinct activities that are more effective learning activities for older learners. For example, she suggests that activities that involve logic, reasoning and analysis, and which encourage cooperation rather than competition, are more suitable and effective for the cognitive and social needs of older learners. In contrast, Muñoz suggests that activities that require some sort of physical involvement, which may be routinised and involve very familiar patterns and scenarios, and which may be more repetitive in nature, are more suitable for the needs of younger learners. She further suggests that activities which foster autonomy, and provide the learners with the agency to select materials and to also be involved in task design (see Chapter 29), are also very important for meeting the learning needs of adolescent learners.

What we see from this discussion is that understanding how learners are changing during the time of adolescence is crucial in identifying how learning may need to be organised and reorganised in order to foster optimum conditions for learning. Some salient points here are that, contrary to often-held opinions and stereotypes, adolescent learners, by virtue of the cognitive and psychological changes they may be experiencing, are likely to be developing approaches and attitudes to learning that match very well with the learning strategies and attitudes associated with 'good' language learners.

ENGAGEMENT, INTEREST AND MOTIVATION

As we can see from the discussion above, the changes that are taking place within adolescent learners are likely to have a significant impact on the ways in which learning is approached, taken up and, possibly, rejected. Although the previous discussion has shown that adolescent learners may naturally be well-placed to be successful language learners, adolescence is still a period in time during which interest in and motivation for language learning often decreases in school contexts (Cable et al., 2010; Tragant, 2006).

One of the key factors that is regarded as having a significant impact on motivation and engagement at this period of time is the nature of the learning that individuals are engaged in. A feature of the learning experiences for adolescents is that not only is this period characterised by internal changes, but it is also characterised by a significant change in the nature of the curriculum and types of learning that learners are engaged in. This is a period in which learning often moves away from lower-stakes, freer practice to higher-stakes, more examination-oriented, form-focused work. Instead of a focus on enjoyment, the goal is likely to shift towards a focus on outcomes and grades. As we know from the work of researchers such as Muñoz (2006, 2008) and Ryan and Patrick (2001), this might not be the most conducive of contexts for motivating adolescent learners. It is no surprise, then, that learners highlight the ways in which classes are organised, and what the content is, as being crucial in determining their interests in language learning (see Lo Bianco and Aliani, 2013 for an interesting account).

Much of the literature on adolescent language learners focuses on this period in a young person's life as being a time when they are most influenced by extrinsic factors such as their peers and social groups (Kissau and Wierzalis, 2008; Merga 2014). Research has found that adolescents tend to be very sensitive to what their friends do and/or think and that they are likely to engage, or disengage, with particular activities depending on how the activities are viewed by their peer and friendship groups (Kissau and Wierzalis, 2008; Merga 2014). Many learners are also motivated by more intrinsic factors, such as wanting to experience different cultures and cultural practices like music, film and literature.

Here the concept of capital, that is, the value that the learner places on the language, is crucial in terms of how a learner is likely to be motivated to take up and continue learning a language. For many learners, English is a language that they are likely to need for entrance into secondary schools, to university, and to the job market, and this need may be highly motivating (Lo Bianco and Aliani, 2013). For some, however, the relative dominance of English and the gatekeeping role it often serves can be highly demotivating. For others the sociopolitical history of English may be a barrier to taking up the language (Canagarajah, 1999, Harklau, 2007; Pennycook, 1994; Tragant, 2006).

LEARNING CONTEXTS

Any discussion of learning a language as an adolescent, particularly in relation to the learning of English, must recognise the many and varied contexts in which adolescent learners engage in the process of learning. When we think of these learners, we could be referring to young teenagers studying English as a required subject at school in classrooms for two to three hours a week in a broad range of different countries. Depending on where this learning is taking place, these learners may, in addition to their classroom study, be active users of English outside the classroom, whereas others may not. We may also be thinking of learners who are enrolled in language courses, sometimes within their home towns and countries. These may be young adults enrolled in a programme of general English classes at a language centre, or in courses designed specifically to help them pass particular examinations, or they may be learners attending summer schools or study trips in language centres during school holidays. The term also includes those adolescent learners who are learning English as an additional language as a result of their attending schools where English is the medium of instruction, but not necessarily the learner's first/home language. These may be learners in multilingual classrooms in urban (as well as rural) centres around the world. These may be learners who are newly arrived and/or temporary migrants, settled residents as well as refugees.

Whilst the contexts in which adolescents might be learning English are many and varied, there are key themes that crosscut the literature as impacting on the language learning process. In her work on adolescent English learners in the USA, Harklau (2007) makes the important point that, for these learners, judgements about their cognitive abilities, and therefore the activities and materials they are given to interact with, are often made based on the levels of their English rather than their age and experience of the world. This situation often results in learners being given material and activities that may be aimed at much younger learners and which, instead of engaging learners, actually have the potential to alienate and disengage them. Such findings are widespread and such ideas about these adolescent learners often have a very negative impact on the language learning trajectories of these young individuals (see, for example, Ajayi, 2006; Chun, 2009; Rubinstein-Avila, 2003; Safford and Costley, 2008).

Disengagement with the cultural context that is often present in language learning materials is also an issue that is widely discussed in the literature (e.g., Canagarajah, 1999; Gray, 2002, 2013; Pennycook, 1994). In these cases, learners do not necessarily identify with the ideas, values and practices put forward in textbooks and other classroom materials. For some, it may be that the values and attitudes being put forward in the materials run counter to their own personal and cultural ideologies. For others, it might be that there is no common experience to draw their attention and/or interest in the materials, and there may be little motivation to allow the learners to make sense of the materials in relation to their own daily lives. In all of these cases, what these examples show us is that issues of power, identity and the extent to which learners are afforded individual agency play a significant role in the learning experiences of adolescent language learners (see Chapter 10).

IMPLICATIONS FOR TEACHING AND ASSESSMENT

What the literature, and the discussion presented here, has shown is that in the context of adolescent learners, effective teaching and assessment needs to take account of the unique set of characteristics and dispositions that adolescent learners bring with them to their language learning. Effective teaching and assessment needs to provide adolescents with a range of activities that allow them to take advantage of the cognitive changes that they may be experiencing. This means trying to create supportive spaces, to design activities and to provide materials that challenge adolescent learners and which enhance their language learning strategies, so that they might move towards increasingly greater autonomy over their learning.

Effective teaching and assessment for adolescents should also take account of the types of activities that learners are asked to engage in and whether, and to what extent, these activities are likely to be the most effective ways to engage them. As discussed earlier, adolescent learners are likely to be sensitive to explicit evaluations and comparisons, as well as potentially disengaged by materials and activities that do not provide them with sufficient cognitive challenge.

Effective teaching and assessment of adolescent learners also needs to take into account the broader sociocultural and sociopolitical context in which the learning in taking place. Such a view of language learning requires us to consider classrooms not simply as sites in which teachers and learners are involved in transmitting and receiving knowledge, but rather as sites of power and identity, of contest and negotiation, and construction and deconstruction of knowledge and ideas (Leung and Street, 2012).

CONCLUSION

The primary aim of this chapter has been to provide an overview of the main ideas and issues that are commonly discussed in research in relation to adolescent language learners. The chapter began by exploring the idea of the maturational period and what impact this has on adolescent learners. The discussion highlighted that contrary to often commonly held beliefs, research has shown that adolescence may in fact be a very positive and highly favourable age in which to learn a language. The discussion then moved on to explore some of the ways in which these potential advantages play out in language learning classrooms. The chapter concluded with some recommendations for teaching and assessment that take account of, and work with, the particular needs of this group of learners, rather than working against them.

Discussion Questions

1. What are your own assumptions about the role of age in language learning? How do you think these assumptions impact on your own ideas and approaches to language learning and teaching?

2. Thinking about your own learning and teaching contexts, how is/was learning organised for adolescent learners? What are some of the ways in which these arrangements might complement, as well as contradict, adolescent language learners' needs?

3. What motivates you to learn/teach English, and how has this motivation changed over time and with age? Are there examples of activities or experiences that you have also found demotivating? Are these the same for your colleagues/learners?

Key Readings

Bialystok, E. (1997). The structure of age: in search of barriers to second language acquisition. *Second Language Research*, 13(2), 116–137.

Harklau, L. (2007). The adolescent English language learner: Identities lost and found. In J. Cummins & C. Davison (Eds.), *International Handbook of English Language Teaching, Part 1* (pp. 639–655). New York: Springer.

Muñoz, C. (Ed.) (2006). *Age and the Rate of Foreign Language Learning*. Clevedon, UK: Multilingual Matters.

Ryan, A. M., & Patrick, H. (2001). The classroom social environment and changes in adolescents' motivation and engagement during middle school. *American Educational Research Journal*, 38(2), 437–460.

References

Ajayi, L. J. (2006). Multiple voices, multiple realities: self-defined images of self among adolescent Hispanic English Language learners. *Education*, 126(3), 468–480.

Bialystok, E. (1997). The structure of age: in search of barriers to second language acquisition. *Second Language Research*, 13(2), 116–137.

Birdsong, D. (2006). Age and second language acquisition and processing: A selective overview. *Language Learning*, 56, 9–49.

Cable, C., Driscoll, P., Mitchell, R., Sing, S., Cremin, T., Earl, J., Eyres, I., Holmes, B., Martin, C., & Heins, B. (2010). *Languages and Learning at Key Stage 2: A Longitudinal Study Final Report*. Department for Children, Schools and Families, UK.

Canagarajah, A. S. (1999). *Resisting Linguistic Imperialism in English Teaching*. Oxford: Oxford University Press.

Chun, C. W. (2009). Critical literacies and graphic novels for English-language learners: Teaching *Maus*. *Journal of Adolescent & Adult Literacy*, 53(2), 144–153.

Cook, V. (1996). *Second Language Learning and Language Teaching* (2nd ed.). London and New York: Arnold.

Gray, J. (2002). The global coursebook in English language teaching. In D. Block & D. Cameron (Eds.), *Globalization and Language Teaching* (pp. 151–167). London: Routledge.

Gray, J. (2013). *Critical Perspective on Language Teaching Materials*. Basingstoke, UK: Palgrave Macmillan.

Harklau, L. (2007). The adolescent English language learner: Identities lost and found. In J. Cummins & C. Davison (Eds.), *International Handbook of English Language Teaching, Part 1* (pp. 639–655). New York: Springer.

Kissau, S., & Wierzalis, E., (2008). Gender identity and homophobia: The impact on adolescent males studying French. *The Modern Language Journal*, 92(3), 402–413.

Leung, C., & Street, B. V. (Eds.) (2012). *English – a Changing Medium for Education*. Bristol, UK: Multilingual Matters.

Lo Bianco, J., & Aliani, R. (2013). *Language Planning and Student Experiences: Intention, Rhetoric and Implementation*. Bristol, UK: Multilingual Matters.

Merga, M. (2014). Peer group and friend influences on the social acceptability of adolescent book reading. *Journal of Adolescent & Adult Literacy*, 57(6), 472–482.

Muñoz, C. (Ed.) (2006). *Age and the Rate of Foreign Language Learning*. Clevedon, UK: Multilingual Matters.

Muñoz, C. (2008). Age-related differences and second language learning practice. In R.M. DeKeyser (Ed.), *Practice in a Second Language: Perspectives from Applied Linguistics and Cognitive Psychology* (pp. 229–256). Cambridge: Cambridge University Press.

Oxford, R. L. (1989). Use of language learning strategies: A synthesis of studies with implications for strategy training. *System* 17(2), 235–247.

Pennycook, A. (1994). *The Cultural Politics of English as an International Language*. Harlow: Longman.

Richards, J. C., & Lockhart, C. (1996). *Reflective Teaching in Second Language Classrooms*. Cambridge: Cambridge University Press.

Rubinstein-Avila, E. (2003). Conversing with Miguel: An adolescent English language learner struggling with later literacy development. *Journal of Adolescent & Adult Literacy*, 47(4), 290–301.

Ryan, A. M., & Patrick, H. (2001). The classroom social environment and changes in adolescents' motivation and engagement during middle school. *American Educational Research Journal*, 38(2), 437–460.

Safford, K., & Costley, T. (2008). 'I didn't speak for the first year': silence, self-study and student stories of English language learning in mainstream education. *Innovation in Language Learning and Teaching*, 2(2),136–151.

Schmid, M. S. (2014). The debate on maturational constraints in bilingual development: A perspective from first-language attrition. *Language Acquisition*, 21(4), 386–410.

Tragant, E. (2006). Language learning motivation and age. In C. Muñoz (Ed.), *Age and the Rate of Foreign Language Learning* (pp. 237–267). Clevedon, UK: Multilingual Matters.

Tragant, E., & Victori, M. (2006). Reported strategy use and age. In C. Muñoz (Ed.), *Age and the Rate of Foreign Language Learning* (pp. 208–236). Clevedon, UK: Multilingual Matters.

United Nations (2012). *World Population Monitoring: Adolescents and Youth: A Concise Report*. New York: United Nations.

CHAPTER 3

Learning as an Adult

Carol Griffiths and Adem Soruç

INTRODUCTION

A number of well-known studies have presented a negative view of adults' ability to learn language, and various reasons have been suggested to explain why language learning might be more difficult for adults than for younger learners, including maturational factors (such as the Critical Period Hypothesis or myelination), identity issues (see Chapter 10), and affective variables (such as culture shock and language shock; see also Chapter 8). In more recent years, however, research evidence has been accumulating which indicates that motivated adults can manage to learn a new language to high levels of proficiency, sometimes to the point that they are indistinguishable from native speakers, especially if they are also exposed to an input-rich environment. In order to be able to learn language effectively, however, adults may need to be allowed to utilise their more highly developed cognitive abilities (somewhat out-of-fashion, according to a Communicative Approach), and to employ their familiar learning style (whether or not this accords with other classmates' styles). The commonly-employed 'native speaker' criterion for success may also need to be reconsidered, since learners may be able to communicate very effectively in their new language, but prefer to retain something of their old accent as an identity marker. This chapter aims to discuss these various aspects and to suggest implications for the facilitation of successful adult language learning.

OVERVIEW

Unfortunately for those who would like to adopt a 'can do' approach to adult language learning, much of the research has been quite negative. Several early studies (e.g., Harley, 1986; Oyama, 1976; Snow and Hoefnagel-Höhle, 1978) all concluded that, although adults made faster progress initially, younger learners were more successful than adults in the long run. Several well-known case studies painted a similarly pessimistic picture. For instance,

Schumann (1976) describes a ten-month study of Alberto, a 33-year-old Costa Rican living in the USA. Although test results indicated that Alberto was not lacking in cognitive ability, he appeared to lack motivation to learn English, did not socialise with English speakers, and made very little progress during the ten months of the study. Schmidt's (1983) subject, Wes, a Japanese artist living in Hawaii, also 33 years old, was very sociable and had a strong drive to communicate, and his oral competence developed considerably; but Wes showed little or no interest in formal study, so he remained unable to read or write in English and his grammatical control remained low after a three-year observation period. Another example of an unsuccessful adult, Burling (1981) recounts his own experience of trying to learn Swedish during a year as a guest professor at a university in Sweden. Burling was in his mid-50s, and he considered himself to have high motivation and positive attitudes. Nevertheless, he judged his own progress as "distinctly unsatisfactory" (p. 280).

Reasons which have been suggested for such negative results vary. The Critical Period Hypothesis has long been used to suggest that, past a certain age (often located around puberty), language learning becomes more difficult, or even impossible (see Chapter 2). Another possible maturational explanation is the process of myelination which, as Long (1990) explains, progressively wraps the nerves of the brain in myelin sheaths as the brain develops; like concrete pathways in a garden, myelin defines learning pathways, making it easier to get from one point to another, and removing the need to re-learn information or procedures every time they are encountered, but reducing flexibility. Maturational constraints are also suggested by Hyltenstam and Abrahamsson (2003) as the reason why successful adult language learners "deviate from the unspoken norm" (p. 539).

Viewing the question from a somewhat different angle, "the construction and reconstruction of learner identity" (Marx, 2002: 264) is noted as a potential issue for adults when trying to develop a new language (see Chapter 10). Although identity may not be an issue only for adults, our sense of who we are (and are not) tends to become more established as we mature, and this may result in our being less willing to accept change of any kind, including language, since most adults have already developed their own first language (L1). Indeed, according to Piller (2002), identity is actually more important than age when it comes to learning a language. The identity issue was also noted by the Turkish adult university students in a study by Soruç and Griffiths (2015): although there was some initial uptake of native-speaker features of spoken English in this study, by the time of the delayed post-test, most of these features were no longer being used. Several of the students attributed this attrition to conflict with their own identity, which created embarrassment and a sense of artificiality.

Other possible explanations which have been suggested in the literature include socio-affective factors such as culture shock, which leaves the learner feeling confused and excluded, and language shock, which leaves the learner feeling nervous and humiliated. Indeed, according to Schumann (1976), these may be the most important variables accounting for Alberto's failure to learn English in spite of living in an English-speaking environment, which might have been expected to facilitate his learning. Burling (1981) attributes his lack of success with learning Swedish mainly to social constraints, such as the need to maintain relationships among highly proficient English-speaking colleagues, which can erode motivation and mean that an adult is "likely to give up and conclude that he has lost the capacity to learn a language" (p. 284). And, according to Schmidt (1983), although his subject (Wes) was socially motivated to achieve a high level of oral communicative competence, he lacked the motivation to work hard to achieve equal competence in the more formal areas of the language (reading and writing).

Nevertheless, in spite of these negative views of adult language learners, there has been "growing evidence that some learners who start learning as adults can achieve a native-like competence" (Ellis, 2008: 31), leading Muñoz and Singleton (2011: 1) to recommend "a loosening of the association" between age and the ability to learn language. Examples of positive studies include a well-known case study by Ioup, Boustagui, El Tigi, and Moselle (1994) which documents a case of a successful adult language learner who achieved native-like performance in a new language (Arabic) within about two years, when her new husband was conscripted into the army and she was left in a situation of total immersion with her husband's relatives. This led Ioup et al. (ibid.) to re-examine the Critical Period Hypothesis, since, as Bialystok and Hakuta (1999) put it, "biological restrictions such as brain maturation should not be so easily overturned" (p. 177). A number of adult Dutch learners of English in a study by Bongaerts, van Summeren, Planken and Schils (1997) could not be distinguished from native speakers, suggesting that "it is not impossible to achieve an authentic, native like pronunciation of a second language after a specified biological period of time" (p. 447). Although they found that overall, target language attainment was negatively correlated with age, Birdsong and Molis (2001) nevertheless found "modest evidence of native like attainment among late learners" (p. 235). When Muñoz and Singleton (2007) asked L2 adult learners of English to re-tell the narrative of a movie, two of the students scored within the native speaker range, as judged by native speakers of English. High levels of native-like proficiency were discovered by Reichle (2010) among some of the adult participants in his study, leading him to conclude that "these results are incompatible with the traditional notion of a critical period for second language acquisition" (p. 53). And when Kinsella and Singleton (2014) investigated 20 adult Anglophone near-native users of French, 3 of the participants (all of whom were married to a French spouse, had either bilingual or French-speaking children, and strong links to the French community) scored within the native speaker range, and the authors concluded that "native-likeness remains attainable until quite late in life" (p. 458).

KEY LEARNING ISSUES

Given that evidence seems to be mounting that adults can become highly proficient in a language other than their first, it is useful to consider how successful learning is achieved by adults. Two factors which seem to be repeatedly in evidence with the adult language learning issue are motivation (see Chapter 6) and exposure (see Chapter 11).

MOTIVATION

Of course, motivation is well known to be a major predictor of success not only for adults, but also for learners of any age. However, if we look more closely, it is possible we may be able to identify different kinds of motivation. For younger students, motivation is often (though, of course, not always) extrinsic: they need to pass an examination, they are afraid of parental disapproval, or they feel some such other external pressure which drives them to be successful, or, at least, to avoid being unsuccessful. For adults, these kinds of pressures are largely behind them. Evidence from the literature suggests that what tends to drive an adult to learn another language is often the desire to integrate with a target person or group (such as a spouse, the spouse's family, or a target community), or the desire to use the language as an instrument to achieve a particular goal (such as a qualification or a job). In other words, in the case of an adult, motivation is more likely to be integrative and/or instrumental, and it is this that will drive an adult to invest time and energy in learning a new language.

We can see integrative motivation at work in the cases of Julie, who needed to integrate with her husband's family (Ioup et al., 1994), and Kinsella and Singleton's (2014) three very successful adult learners of French, who had strong ties to the target-language-speaking community. Examples of instrumental motivation might be the participants in a study by Bongaerts (1999), the most successful of whom were highly motivated for professional (instrumental) reasons. Other examples might be Kira and Kang, two of the most successful adult learners in a study reported by Griffiths (2013), who were both driven by the desire to improve themselves professionally and to achieve higher incomes and better lifestyles for themselves and their families. Kira (a 28-year-old Japanese man), and Kang (a 41-year-old Korean) were both very focused on their studies and they both invested a considerable amount of effort and out-of-class time in order to achieve much faster than average progress through the levels of the school – in fact, they progressed much more quickly than many of the much younger students with whom they studied. Compared with these two, Yuki (a 44-year-old Japanese woman) appeared to have minimal motivation to learn (she attended the school only as an immigration requirement, in order to be near her children who were studying at the school), and to invest little or no time or effort in her study. As a result, she made negligible progress over a two-year period, although she was quick to ascribe her lack of progress to her age: "my mind is blank", she said (Griffiths, 2013: 110).

EXPOSURE

As with motivation, exposure is not a factor only with adult language learning; for instance, study-abroad programmes aimed at giving students experience with a target language have become very popular among students of all ages (e.g., Freed, Dewey and Segalowitz, 2004; see also Chapter 11). But exposure does seem to be a factor which is commonly mentioned in connection with successful adult learners. Julie, for instance (Ioup et al., 1994), was totally immersed in her husband's family environment when he was called away soon after their marriage. Marinova-Todd (2003) found that out of 30 participants, the 6 most proficient students all lived with native speakers of the target language. Moyer (2009) also concluded that interactive experience in the target language was more important for target language development than instruction. Likewise, in a study involving 11 Spanish students, Muñoz and Singleton (2007) found that the most proficient learners were living with native speakers of English. Furthermore, the three most proficient participants in Kinsella and Singleton's (2014) study all participated actively in the target language community.

We might perhaps, suggest, then, that although merely living in an input-rich environment does not necessarily guarantee that a learner will be motivated to use the opportunity to learn (e.g., Yuki interviewed in Griffiths, 2008, 2013), there is evidence to suggest that such an environment maximises the opportunity for effective language development for those who are prepared to invest the time and the effort. Having said that, however, there are examples of adult learners who have achieved remarkable results with minimal exposure to the target language. One such case is described in Griffiths and Cansiz (2015). Gökhan was in his 40s when he decided he wanted to sit an international exam (IELTS). He describes his motivation as trying to avoid "being embarrassed in front of others" (p. 484). He worked hard, investing "as much time as possible" (p. 484), and he used many strategies, which are described in detail in the article. When he sat the IELTS exam he scored a Band 9 (reckoned to be native-speaker level). Yet he had never been out of Turkey (except for a brief holiday in the USA), and had had minimal contact with native speakers of English, whom he had found "not available at every corner or when you happen to find them they are usually too busy to offer a helping hand" (p. 484). In other words, we might suggest that, although there are studies which stress the importance of exposure to the target language (e.g., Kinsella and Singleton, 2014; Marinova Todd, 2003; Moyer, 2009; Muñoz and Singleton, 2007, see above) and although intuitively such exposure must be useful, it would seem that lack of this opportunity does not have to be a handicap for sufficiently motivated learners. This generalization probably applies to all learners irrespective of age, but Gökhan's case illustrates that it is no less applicable to adults than to younger learners.

IMPLICATIONS FOR TEACHING AND ASSESSMENT

However, if we accept that adults can learn a language, we must consider that they may not necessarily learn in the same way that younger learners do. They may, for instance, require more allowance to be made for familiar learning styles and established strategies which they have developed over many years (see Chapter 9). For instance, Hiro, a 64-year-old from Japan (Griffiths, 2013), tended to struggle with the kinds of communicative activities favoured by his teacher and enthusiastically enjoyed by his younger classmates. In order to cope with this situation, he would quietly withdraw to the back of the classroom and busy himself with reading or writing in his notebook. This troubled his teacher, however, who felt it interfered with classroom dynamics, and also was defensive about what she felt was an implied criticism of her teaching methods. After discussion with the Director of Studies, the teacher came to be more willing to allow Hiro to work according to the style with which he was comfortable, and, over the time they were together, they gradually negotiated a mutually satisfactory compromise, which included Hiro being progressively more willing to engage in the kinds of communicative activities that he had avoided in the beginning.

Cognitive differences between older and younger learners have also been hypothesised as an explanation of the results of several studies which have found that adults often make faster initial progress with language learning (e.g., Harley, 1986; Muñoz, 2006; Snow and Hoefnagel-Höhle, 1978). Krashen (1985) explains that older learners can achieve faster initial progress in terms of their ability to use more well-developed cognitive abilities to negotiate meaning. Ellis (2008) also acknowledges that "the greater cognitive development of older learners is advantageous where explicit learning is concerned" (p. 21). Given that cognition has tended to be downplayed in recent years in favour of communicative approaches, this may require some rethinking of contemporary teaching methodologies, and adults may need to be allowed more cognitive engagement with the language they want to learn in order to work out and apply the lexicon and the rules of the target language (e.g., Hiro interviewed in Griffiths, 2013).

When it comes to assessing what is 'successful' and what is not, the emphasis has traditionally been on the native-speaker norm, which is used as the criterion in many studies, (e.g., Birdsong and Molis, 2001; Bongaerts et al., 1997; Ioup et al., 1994; Muñoz and Singleton, 2007; Kinsella and Singleton, 2014). It is quite possible, however, that non-native speakers may get to be extremely effective communicators in a new language, but still retain an accent: indeed, this may be something they choose to do in order to preserve identity (Muñoz and Singleton, 2011). And when we add to this the difficulty (if not the impossibility) of defining what actually is the 'standard' accent, even within speakers of the same language, the use of native-speaker norms as a criterion gets to seem even more questionable. As Yates and Kozar (2015: 1) put it, "optimal proficiency development" according to the needs and preferences of the individual learner may actually be more important and useful than emphasizing native-speaker-like attainment. This does not, of course, apply only to adults, but it may be more applicable to adults, since they have had longer to establish the way they speak. They may, therefore, find it correspondingly more difficult to change, and they may be less willing to give up an accent which, as Muñoz and Singleton (2011) note, can be an identifying feature which they may wish to retain.

CONCLUSION

It is probably undeniable that the majority of successful language learners learn when they are younger (e.g., Birdsong and Molis, 2001; Harley, 1986; Oyama, 1976; Snow and Hoefnagel-Höhle, 1978). Even with the more positive studies, the highly successful adult students are usually a minority, amounting, for instance, to just 2 out of 12 in Muñoz and

Singleton's (2007) study or 3 out of 20 in the study by Kinsella and Singleton (2014). However, to go from this observation to conclude that adults cannot learn a language is not reasonable, since, there is evidence to indicate that under the right conditions, and given sufficient motivation, highly successful adult language learning is possible. And if it is possible for some, there is no logical reason why maturation per se should explain the fact that, in general, successful language learning is most likely to occur when the individual is pre-adult. There may be any number of reasons why adults, generally, do not learn a language as successfully as younger learners, including motivation, reconstruction of identity, time constraints, affective difficulties, social factors or lack of exposure and opportunity for practice. The fact that, in spite of these constraints, there are numerous examples of adults who do indeed manage to achieve high levels of competence in a new language, places the existence of a critical period for language learning in serious doubt. It would rather seem that motivated adults can learn to very high levels of proficiency. Some may even become indistinguishable from native-speakers, in as far as that is a valid comparison. And even though such learners may be the exception, the authors of this chapter would like to suggest it is time we adopted a positive 'can do' approach to adult language learning for those who wish to undertake it and who are prepared to invest sufficient time and effort in the endeavour.

Discussion Questions

1. How can adult learners manage their learning in order to achieve successful language learning outcomes? (For some possible ideas, see Griffiths and Cansiz, 2015.)

2. What can teachers do to facilitate successful language learning for their adult learners?

3. If you, as an adult, decided to try to learn a new language, what do you think your main constraints would be? What are some of the things you could do to try to manage these constraints?

Key Readings

Birdsong, D., & Molis, M. (2001). On the evidence for maturational effects in second language acquisition. *Journal of Memory and Language*, 44, 235–249.

Griffiths, C. (2008). Age and good language learners. In C. Griffiths (Ed.), *Lessons from Good Language Learners* (pp. 35–48). Cambridge: Cambridge University Press.

Kinsella, C., & Singleton, D. (2014). Much more than age. *Applied Linguistics*, 35(4), 441–462.

Marinova-Todd, S. H. (2003). Know your grammar: What the knowledge of syntax and morphology in an L2 reveals about the critical period for second/foreign language acquisition. In M. P. García Mayo & M. L. García Lecumberri (Eds.), *Age and the Acquisition of English as a Foreign Language* (pp. 59–73). Clevedon, UK: Multilingual Matters.

Moyer, A. (2009). Input as a critical means to an end: Quantity and quality of experience in L2 phonological attainment. In T. Piske & M. Young-Scholten (Eds.), *Input Matters in SLA* (pp. 159–174). Clevedon, UK: Multilingual Matters.

Muñoz, C., & Singleton, D. (2011). A critical review of age-related research on L2 ultimate attainment. *Language Teaching*, 44, 1–35.

References

Bialystok, E., & Hakuta, K. (1999). Confounded age: Linguistic and cognitive factors in age differences for second language acquisition. In D. Birdsong (Ed.), *Second*

Language Acquisition and the Critical Period Hypothesis (pp. 161–181). Mahwah, NJ: Lawrence Erlbaum.

Birdsong, D., & Molis, M. (2001). On the evidence for maturational effects in second language acquisition. *Journal of Memory and Language*, 44, 235–249.

Bongaerts, T. (1999). Ultimate attainment in L2 pronunciation: The case of very advanced late L2 learners. In D. Birdsong (Ed.), *Second Language Acquisition and the Critical Period Hypothesis* (pp. 133–159). Mahwah, NJ: Lawrence Erlbaum.

Bongaerts, T., van Summeren, C., Planken, B. & Schils, E. (1997). Age and ultimate attainment in the pronunciation of a foreign language. *Studies in Second Language Acquisition,* 19(4), 447–465.

Burling, R. (1981). Social constraints on adult language learning. In H. Winitz (Ed.), *Native Language and Foreign Language Acquisition* (pp. 279–290). New York: New York Academy of Sciences.

Ellis, R. (2008). *The Study of Second Language Acquisition*. Oxford: Oxford University Press.

Freed, B., Dewey, D. & Segalowitz, N. (2004). The language contact profile. *Studies in Second Language Acquisition,* 26(2), 349–356.

Griffiths, C. (2008). Age and good language learners. In C. Griffiths (Ed.), *Lessons from Good Language Learners* (pp. 35–48). Cambridge: Cambridge University Press.

Griffiths, C. (2013). *The Strategy Factor in Successful Language Learning*. Bristol, UK: Multilingual Matters.

Griffiths, C., & Cansiz, G. (2015). Language learning strategies: An holistic view. *Studies in Second Language Learning and Teaching*, 5(3), 475–495.

Harley, B. (1986). *Age in Second Language Acquisition*. Clevedon, UK: Multilingual Matters.

Hyltenstam, K, & Abrahamsson, N. (2003). Maturational constraints in SLA. In C. J. Doughty & M. H. Long (Eds.), *The Handbook of Second Language Acquisition* (pp. 539–588). Oxford: Blackwell.

Ioup, G., Boustagui, E., El Tigi, M., & Moselle, M. (1994). Reexamining the critical period hypothesis: A case study of successful adult SLA in a naturalistic environment. *Studies in Second Language Acquisition*, 16, 73–98.

Kinsella, C., & Singleton, D. (2014). Much more than age. *Applied Linguistics*, 35(4), 441–462.

Krashen, S. D. (1985). *The Input Hypothesis*. London: Longman.

Long, M. H. (1990). Maturational constraints on language development. *Studies in Second Language Acquisition*, 12, 251–285.

Marinova-Todd, S. H. (2003). Know your grammar: What the knowledge of syntax and morphology in an L2 reveals about the critical period for second/foreign language acquisition. In M. P. García Mayo & M. L. García Lecumberri (Eds.), *Age and the Acquisition of English as a Foreign Language* (pp. 59–73). Clevedon, UK: Multilingual Matters.

Marx, N. (2002). Never quite a 'native speaker': accent and identity in the L2 and the L1. *The Canadian Modern Language Review*, 59(2), 264–281.

Moyer, A. (2009). Input as a critical means to an end: Quantity and quality of experience in L2 phonological attainment. In T. Piske & M. Young-Scholten (Eds.), *Input Matters in SLA* (pp. 159–174). Clevedon, UK: Multilingual Matters.

Muñoz, C. (2006). The effects of age on foreign language learning: The BAF project. In C. Muñoz (Ed.), *Age and the Rate of Foreign Language Learning* (pp. 1–40). Clevedon, UK: Multilingual Matters.

Muñoz, C., & Singleton, D. (2007). Foreign accent in advanced learners: two successful profiles. *The EUROSLA Yearbook,* 7, 171–190.

Muñoz, C., & Singleton, D. (2011). A critical review of age-related research on L2 ultimate attainment. *Language Teaching*, 44, 1–35.

Oyama, S. (1976). A sensitive period for the acquisition of a nonnative phonological system. *Journal of Psycholinguistic Research*, 5, 261–285.

Piller, I. (2002). Passing for a native speaker: identity and success in second language learning. *Journal of Sociolinguistics,* 6(2), 179–206.

Reichle, R. (2010). Judgments of information structure in L2 French: Nativelike performance and the critical period hypothesis. *International Review of Applied Linguistics in Language Teaching*, 48(1), 53–85.

Schmidt, R. (1983). Interaction, acculturation, and the acquisition of communicative competence: A case study of an adult. In N. Wolfson & E. Judd (Eds.), *Sociolinguistics and Language Acquisition* (pp. 137–174). New York: Newbury House.

Schumann, J. H. (1976). Second language acquisition: The pidginization hypothesis. *Language Learning*, 26(2), 391–408.

Snow, C., & Hoefnagel-Höhle, M. (1978). The critical period for language acquisition: Evidence from language learning. *Child Development*, 49, 1119–1128.

Soruç, A., & Griffiths, C. (2015). Identity and the spoken grammar dilemma. *System*, 50, 32–42.

Yates, L., & Kozar, O. (2015). Expanding the horizons of age-related research: A response to the special issue 'Complexities and interactions of age in second language learning: Broadening the research agenda'. *Applied Linguistics*, 1–6.

CHAPTER 4

Learning with Learning Difficulties

Judit Kormos

INTRODUCTION

In many contexts today, being able to communicate in another language might be just as important as basic literacy and numeracy skills. The relevance of cognitive factors in influencing language learning outcomes has been widely recognized in the field of second language acquisition research, but it is only recently that the language learning processes of students with additional needs have received sufficient attention (see e.g., Kormos and Kontra, 2008; Kormos and Smith, 2012). Language learners with additional needs constitute between 5 and 15 % of the population of students in the European Union (Drabble, 2013). Specific learning difficulties (SpLDs) not only have an effect on the acquisition of oral and literacy skills in the first language, but also influence the processes of second language learning. In order to ensure that learners with SpLDs also attain the level of second language (L2) competence necessary to fulfil their potential, it is essential that language teachers are aware of how this diverse group of students acquires additional languages and become familiar with the techniques and intervention programs that can be used to assist their learning. In this chapter, I will focus on the language learning processes of one group of students with additional needs: those who have SpLDs. I will describe the challenges students with SpLDs face in learning additional languages, and outline ways in which language teachers can successfully meet the needs of these learners.

OVERVIEW

The terminology to describe and label learning difficulties varies greatly across disciplines and geographical contexts. The terms 'specific learning differences' and 'specific learning difficulties' are applied interchangeably in the United Kingdom, whereas in the USA the label 'specific learning disorder' is used. In this chapter I will adopt the term 'specific learning difficulties'. The American Psychiatric Association (APA, 2013) includes three subgroups under the umbrella term of SpLDs: specific learning difficulty with impairment in reading, in written expression and in mathematics. In the United Kingdom, SpLDs also include dyspraxia (difficulty in planning and coordinating movement) and attention deficit and hyperactivity disorder (ADHD).

Among SpLDs, dyslexia is the most commonly occurring literacy-related learning difficulty. The main cause of dyslexia is assumed to be an underlying phonological processing difficulty, namely, impaired phonological awareness (Snowling, 2008). Phonological awareness has two levels: syllabic and phonemic knowledge. Syllabic knowledge entails the ability to segment words into syllables and manipulate the syllables in words (e.g., deleting or adding syllables). Phonemic knowledge involves the ability to divide words into sounds, differentiate sounds from each other and manipulate them (e.g., deleting, adding and substituting sounds). These underlying processing problems usually result in word-level reading problems, but they can also affect global text comprehension (Snowling, 2008). Dyslexia, as well as other types of SpLDs, is often associated with a smaller capacity of working memory which is responsible for the temporary storage and manipulation of information before it is encoded in long-term memory (Baddeley, 2003). Another frequent correlate of SpLDs is a shorter phonological short-term memory span, which explains why people with SpLDs tend to find it difficult to keep several pieces of verbal information in their short-term memory (Jeffries and Everatt, 2004). Students with SpLDs commonly have difficulties with attention control and implicit learning (Snowling, 2008).

It is widely acknowledged that first language (L1) linguistic skills provide the main foundation for L2 learning (Cummins, 1991). Likewise, in their Linguistic Coding Differences Hypothesis, Ganschow and her colleagues argued that "the primary causal factors in successful or unsuccessful foreign learning are linguistic; that is, students who exhibit foreign learning problems have overt or subtle L1 deficiencies that affect their learning of a foreign language" (Ganschow, Sparks, and Javorsky, 1998: 248–9). While we have to acknowledge that there can be many other affective, social and educational reasons for unsuccessful L2 learning outcomes, not just underlying cognitive difficulties, the significant role played by cognitive factors in second language acquisition is certainly undeniable. To illustrate, phonological short-term memory and phonological awareness jointly assist in learning new words. These abilities are instrumental in decoding sequences of sounds, identifying words in the sound stream, and associating words with their meaning and written form. These skills and processes are essential in learning to read and spell, in both L1 and L2. Adequate attention control mechanisms need to be in place to help students attend to and process relevant features of the input and to coordinate their output processing mechanisms. Verbal reasoning skills are related to grammatical sensitivity, i.e., the ability to identify the grammatical role of words in context, and inductive language learning ability, both of which help learners in reading and assist in identifying linguistic regularities in the input. These latter two cognitive abilities are also constituents of language learning aptitude, which is a significant cognitive determinant of L2 learning success (Carroll, 1981). Empirical research does indeed show that students with SpLDs tend to score consistently lower on all components of tests of foreign language aptitude than their peers with no apparent signs of learning difficulties (e.g., Downey, Snyder, and Hill, 2000).

KEY LEARNING ISSUES

There is very little empirical research on the L2 learning processes of students with SpLDs, other than dyslexia. Students with dyscalculia (difficulty in making arithmetic calculations) were found to exhibit phonological processing difficulties which overlap with the profile of dyslexic students (Fletcher, Morris, and Lyon, 2003). Other types of SpLDs, such as dyspraxia and ADHD, also share many of the cognitive characteristics of dyslexia

(Jeffries and Everatt, 2004). Therefore, one can rightly assume that language learners with SpLDs in general might have lower than average language aptitude and, as a result, face challenges in language learning. It is important to note, however, that different types of SpLDs frequently co-occur and can have different degrees of severity. This can result in substantial variation with regard to the cognitive abilities underlying L2 learning, and hence in a continuum of language learning difficulties (Ganschow et al., 1998).

In addition to cognitive abilities, and often in a complex interaction with them, the affective characteristics and reactions of L2 learners also influence the processes of second language acquisition. Motivation, language learning anxiety, self-confidence and self-esteem are among the concepts that are particularly important to consider in relation to language learners with SpLDs (see Chapters 6 and 8). Students with SpLDs face considerable challenges in L2 learning and, consequently, they might be at a risk of losing their motivation (Kormos and Csizér, 2010), might experience foreign language anxiety (Piechurska-Kuciel, 2008) and often have low self-esteem and self-confidence. In a questionnaire survey, Kormos and Csizér (2010) found that Hungarian dyslexic learners of English and German displayed significantly less positive motivational characteristics than their non-dyslexic peers. The results of their study also revealed that the participants had a negative self-concept in the domain of language learning. SpLDs might cause anxiety in academic contexts and in the private sphere of life. Piechurska-Kuciel (2008) explored the English language learning anxiety of dyslexic students in a Polish secondary-school context and found that the participants exhibited significantly higher levels of anxiety throughout their language learning career than did their peers. The cognitive effects of anxiety might further aggravate the difficulties of language learners with SpLDs. If these feelings are not given sufficient attention, and if the instructional environment is not inclusive, given a choice, students with SpLDs might decide to opt out from learning an additional language altogether.

Many language teachers and education policymakers assume that students with SpLDs, especially those with dyslexia, only have difficulties in acquiring spelling and reading in another language. Contrary to this popular belief, students with SpLDs often fall behind their peers in many components of English language proficiency, including grammar, vocabulary, reading, writing and listening skills (Helland and Kaasa, 2005; Kormos and Mikó, 2010). In an interview study, Kormos and Kontra (2008) also asked language teachers with a broad range of expertise in teaching students with SpLDs what difficulties they noticed their students experience in language learning. The teachers mentioned writing and spelling with the highest frequency, but they also gave accounts of problems in acquiring reading and listening skills, as well as vocabulary and grammatical knowledge. A similar range of challenges was reported by Hungarian dyslexic learners of English, who experienced the most serious difficulties in writing and spelling as well as problems with learning how to read in an L2 and remembering words and understanding grammatical rules (Kormos and Mikó, 2010).

Both students with SpLDs and their teachers report that a very high number of encounters and many practice opportunities are needed for the successful memorization of words in the L2 (Kormos and Kontra, 2008). Language learners with SpLDs may also experience difficulties with the acquisition of L2 grammar, and they tend to find it challenging to extract the patterns and regularities of grammar without guidance from the input. Therefore, they often report that they prefer explicit explanations of syntax, morphology and spelling (Kormos and Mikó, 2010).

Students with SpLDs often face challenges in reading in an additional language, and this has been documented by a number of studies in a variety of language learning contexts. For example, in the cases of both Norwegian children (Helland and Kaasa, 2005) and Hungarian students learning English as an additional language (Kormos and Mikó, 2010), it was found that children with an official diagnosis of dyslexia scored significantly lower on a test of L2 word reading than their non-dyslexic peers. Similar findings were obtained in Canada in the case of young second language users of English as an additional language (Geva, Wade-Woolley, and Shany, 1993). Kormos and Mikó (2010) also reported that Hungarian schoolchildren with a formal diagnosis of dyslexia perceived that they had significantly more difficulties with reading comprehension in either L2 German or English than did their non-dyslexic peers. The findings of these studies show that even reading in L2 German and Spanish, with their relatively more transparent orthographies, causes considerable challenges for language learners with SpLDs.

With regard to understanding spoken L2 texts, the nature of the problems that students with SpLDs experience depends on their phonological processing skills, phonological short-term memory and oral language comprehension ability in their L1. Learners with an official diagnosis of dyslexia who showed less serious phonological processing problems, and no associated oral language processing difficulties, did not exhibit problems with L2 listening skills in a Norwegian context (Helland and Kaasa, 2005). Similar findings were obtained by Kormos and Mikó (2010) in the case of Hungarian school children with a formal assessment of dyslexia.

There also exist significant differences between the written production and writing processes of students with SpLDs and their peers with no SpLDs. Ndlovu and Geva (2008) compared the writing skills of L1 and L2 speaking children in Canada. They found that regardless of language background, the students with SpLDs had difficulty with spelling, punctuation and the monitoring of syntax. The results also indicated that these students struggled "with higher level aspects of writing such as sentence structure constraints and the generation and coordination of vocabulary, as well as with aspects of the overall structure of their compositions including the ability to compose stories with interesting plots and story lines" (p. 55). With regard to spelling, formally diagnosed dyslexic students were found to perform well below the level of non-dyslexic students in either a Norwegian or a Hungarian English language learning context (Helland and Kaasa, 2005; Kormos and Mikó, 2010). Interestingly, the spelling difficulties of L2 learners with SpLDs did not only manifest in languages with non-transparent orthographies. Hungarian dyslexic learners of L2 German perceived spelling to be just as difficult as those students who studied English (Kormos and Mikó, 2010).

IMPLICATIONS FOR TEACHING AND ASSESSMENT

The challenges described above that language learners with SpLDs face does not mean, however, that they cannot become successful multilingual speakers. The first step in any instructional context is to create an inclusive environment where every possible action is taken to meet the needs of the diversity of students, including those with SpLDs. Inclusion is a process and not an end state, and it begins with the analysis of the barriers within the school and the educational system, and policies that can hinder the participation of all students (UNESCO, 2012). The establishment of an inclusive school culture serves as a key foundation for inclusive teaching practice. In inclusive schools, diversity is welcome and seen as a resource rather than an obstacle to learning. In order to achieve this, there is a need for strong cooperation among all stakeholders, including teachers, parents, students and the local community. In inclusive classrooms, the participation of every student is encouraged and every learner is actively involved in the learning process. Learning often takes place collaboratively and assessment is adjusted to serve the needs of the students. In an inclusive context, the curriculum can be flexibly adapted and teachers are free to adjust and vary their teaching methods to meet the needs of all students (UNESCO, 2012). Inclusion cannot be successful if it is not based on relevant teacher knowledge and skills about diversity, and hence teacher education plays a key role in supporting inclusion.

Inclusion also entails attending to the specific needs of students and offering relevant accommodations in the classroom for learners with SpLDs. A key condition for successful inclusion is the accurate and reliable identification of students with SpLDs. Classroom teachers play a key role in identification, and in contexts where the students' first language has a transparent orthography, it is often the English language teacher who first spots the signs of SpLDs (Kormos and Kontra, 2008). Therefore, the identification process is frequently initiated by classroom teachers and is then continued by qualified specialist teachers or a team of school-based experts. Early detection is crucial, and an effective plan of action can only be put in place if teachers have a detailed understanding of the students' learning processes and difficulties. In many cases, especially if students' learning difficulties are not severe, minor adjustments in the language teaching process might be sufficient to ensure that these students also fulfil their potential. These adjustments can involve: providing classroom notes, word lists and key points in a written format for students; breaking down instructions into smaller steps; giving more explicit explanations; and offering additional practice tasks. Allowing students extended time and additional breaks in the completion of assessment tasks, giving them support when revising for tests and planning how to accomplish complex assignments are also helpful. Assistance in developing students' awareness of the learning process and their self-regulation and learning strategies are beneficial for students with SpLDs (for more details, see Kormos and Smith, 2012).

Specific methods that can be used successfully to develop the L2 skills of students with SpLDs include phonological awareness-raising programs in the early years of education, and phonics-based direct and explicit instruction in sound-letter correspondences to teach word-level reading skills (National Reading Panel, 2000; see also Chapters 17 and 23). Students who are speakers of additional languages, and receive an English language medium instruction in the target language environment, benefit considerably from reading intervention programs. These programs enhance awareness of the cognitive processes involved in reading, and provide explicit teaching of reading comprehension strategies and opportunities to practice and apply these strategies until they can use them autonomously (August and Shanahan, 2010).

In the teaching of additional languages, the most frequently recommended teaching method is the Multisensory Structured Learning (MSL) approach, in which sound-letter correspondences are also taught explicitly and which, as its name suggests, activates different sensory channels (e.g., Nijakowska, 2010; Schneider and Crombie, 2003; Sparks, Ganschow, Kenneweg, and Miller 1991). The MSL approach is highly structured, proceeds in small and cumulative steps, and provides L2 learners with SpLDs with sufficient practice and revision opportunities. Its aim is to develop students' phonological, morphological and syntactic awareness, and thereby help them to acquire L2 skills successfully. Schneider and Crombie (2003) highlight that because students with SpLDs tend to find it difficult to learn implicitly from input, they benefit from explicit explanation or from guided discovery activities. They also emphasize the role of the students' L1 as a resource and a supportive tool for L2 learning.

The MSL approach consists of numerous elements that facilitate learning for every student, not just those with SpLDs. Information can be learned more quickly, and can be better integrated into the existing knowledge system, if it is presented through several sensory channels. Limitations on verbal and visual attentional resource pools and working memory can also be overcome if information is presented in multiple modalities (Baddeley, 2003). This is especially helpful for students with SpLDs, because their weaknesses in phonological processing can be counterbalanced. Several recent research overviews also suggest that explicit instruction of grammatical constructions is more effective than implicit instruction, in which no explicit explanation of the grammatical construction or instruction to pay attention to specific constructions in the input is provided (Spada and Tomita, 2010).

CONCLUSION

Although students with SpLDs face particular challenges when learning additional languages, with appropriate support and teaching methods they can also become successful multilingual language users. While these specific techniques require some additional training, they are not substantially different from the language teaching techniques generally used in mainstream classrooms. Therefore, any language teacher with a basic understanding of SpLDs, a positive attitude to inclusion, and confidence in their ability to adapt teaching practices flexibly can meet the diverse needs of students.

Discussion Questions

1. Should students with specific learning differences learn additional languages? Explain why / why not.

2. What kind of barriers are there to inclusion in your teaching context, and how could these be overcome?

3. Think about one language learner with SpLD you have taught or observed. What kind of adjustments could you make in your teaching to help this student?

Key Readings

Kormos J., & Kontra, H. E. (Eds.) (2008). *Language Learners with Special Needs: An International Perspective*. Bristol, UK: Multilingual Matters.

Kormos, J., & Smith, A. M. (2012). *Teaching Languages to Learners with Specific Learning Differences*. Bristol, UK: Multilingual Matters.

Nijakowska, J. (2010). *Dyslexia in the Foreign Language Classroom*. Bristol, UK: Multilingual Matters.

References

American Psychiatric Association (2013). *Diagnostic and Statistical Manual of Mental Disorders* (5th ed.). Washington, D.C.: American Psychiatric Publishing.

August, D., & Shanahan, T. (2010). Response to a review and update on developing literacy in second-language learners: Report of the national literacy panel on language minority children and youth. *Journal of Literacy Research*, 42, 341–348.

Baddeley, A. D. (2003). Working memory: looking back and looking forward. *Nature Reviews Neuroscience*, 4, 829–839.

Carroll, J. B. (1981). Twenty-five years of research on foreign language aptitude. In K. C. Diller (Ed.), *Individual Differences & Universals in Language Learning Aptitude* (pp. 83–118). Rowley, MA: Newbury House.

Cummins, J. (1991). Conversational and academic language proficiency in bilingual contexts. In J. Hulstijn & J. F. Matter (Eds.), Reading in Two Languages, *AILA Review*, 8, 75–89.

Downey, D., Snyder, L., & Hill, B. (2000). College students with dyslexia: Persistent linguistic deficits and foreign language learning. *Dyslexia*, 6, 101–111.

Drabble, S. (2013). *Support for children with special educational needs (SEN)*. Santa Monica, CA: RAND Corporation. Online at: http://www.rand.org/pubs/research_reports/RR180.

Fletcher, J.M., Morris, R.D., & Lyon, G. R. (2003). Classification and definition of learning disabilities: An integrative perspective. In H.L. Swanson, K.R. Harris, & S. Graham (Eds.), *Handbook of Learning Disabilities* (1st ed., pp. 30–56). New York: Guilford Press.

Ganschow, L., Sparks, R.L., & Javorsky, J. (1998). Foreign language learning difficulties: An historical perspective. *Journal of Learning Disabilities*, 31, 248–258.

Geva, E., Wade-Woolley, L., & Shany, M. (1993). The concurrent development of spelling and decoding in two different orthographies. *Journal of Literacy Research*, 25, 383–406.

Helland, T., & Kaasa, R. (2005). Dyslexia in English as a second language. *Dyslexia*, 11, 41–60.

Jeffries, S., & Everatt, J. (2004). Working memory: Its role in dyslexia and other specific learning difficulties. *Dyslexia*, 10, 196–214.

Kormos, J., & Csizér, K. (2010). A comparison of the foreign language learning motivation of Hungarian dyslexic and non-dyslexic students. *International Journal of Applied Linguistics*, 20, 232–250.

Kormos J., & Kontra, H. E. (2008). Hungarian teachers' perceptions of dyslexic language learners. In J. Kormos & E. H. Kontra (Eds.), *Language Learners with Special Needs: An International Perspective* (pp. 189–213). Bristol, UK: Multilingual Matters.

Kormos, J., & Mikó, A. (2010). Diszlexia és az idegen-nyelvtanulás folyamata [Dyslexia and the process of second language acquisition]. In J. Kormos & K. Csizér (Eds.), *Rész-képességzavarok és idegen nyelvtanulás* [Learning disabilities and foreign language acquisition] (pp. 49–76). Budapest: Eötvös Kiadó.

Kormos, J., & Smith, A. M. (2012). *Teaching Languages to Learners with Specific Learning Differences*. Bristol, UK: Multilingual Matters.

National Institute of Child Health and Human Development. (2000). *Report of the National Reading Panel. Teaching Children to Read: An Evidence-based Assessment of the Scientific Research Literature on Reading and its Implications for Reading Instruction*. Available at: www.nichd.nih.gov/publications/pubs/nrp/Pages/smallbook.aspx [Accessed 9 August 2015].

Ndlovu, K., & Geva, E. (2008). Writing abilities in first and second language learners with and without reading disabilities. In J. Kormos & E. H Kontra (Eds.), *Language Learners with Special Needs: An International Perspective* (pp. 36–62). Bristol, UK: Multilingual Matters.

Nijakowska, J. (2010). *Dyslexia in the Foreign Language Classroom*. Bristol, UK: Multilingual Matters.

Piechurska-Kuciel, E. (2008). Input, processing and output anxiety in students with symptoms of developmental dyslexia. In J. Kormos & E. H Kontra (Eds.), *Language Learners with Special Needs: An International Perspective* (pp. 86–109). Bristol, UK: Multilingual Matters.

Schneider, E., & Crombie, M. (2003). *Dyslexia and Foreign Language Learning*. London: David Fulton.

Snowling, M. J. (2008). Specific disorders and broader phenotypes: The case of dyslexia. *The Quarterly Journal of Experimental Psychology*, 61, 142–156.

Spada, N., & Tomita, Y. (2010). Interactions between type of instruction and type of language feature: A meta-analysis. *Language Learning* 60, 263–308.

Sparks, R. L., Ganschow, L., Kenneweg, S., & Miller, K. (1991). Use of an Orton-Gillingham approach to teach a foreign language to dyslexic/learning-disabled students: Explicit teaching of phonology in a second language. *Annals of Dyslexia*, 41, 96–118.

UNESCO (2012). The Salamanca statement on principles, policy and practice in special needs education. Available at: www.unesco.org/education/pdf/SALAMA_E.PDF [Accessed 9 August 2015].

CHAPTER 5

Learning Two or More Languages

John Witney and Jean-Marc Dewaele

INTRODUCTION

Language learning does not take place in isolation. A monolingual speaker learning an L2 will necessarily make a number of conscious or unconscious assumptions about what may be similar to their first language (L1) during the acquisition process. An L3 learner will do the same, but has the advantage of two dynamic linguistic systems on which to draw, one of which, crucially, is a foreign language one. In this chapter, we examine the principal facets of multilingual learning and the psycholinguistic processes that inform learners' perceptions and assumptions during the acquisition of additional languages, as well as the various language-learning strategies at their disposal, and consider the extent to which these elements together may be exploited in the foreign language classroom. We begin with an overview of the topic.

OVERVIEW

At the initial stages of L3 acquisition, a multilingual learner will have already developed not only various strategies for learning a foreign language, but also an enhanced metalinguistic awareness, or knowledge about language. It is generally assumed, and has been empirically shown, that such cognitive benefits increase further, the more languages the learner acquires. This all sounds very straightforward but in practice, of course, the factors influencing the acquisition of a new language are multiple and the processes dynamic and non-linear, whether in the lifetime of a multilingual speaker or in the chronological acquisition of foreign languages during the initial stages of classroom-based instruction. Adding to this, research interests in the literature are broad and varied focussing, inter alia, on the role of Universal Grammar, typological relatedness, L1 influence, L2 status, L1 and L2 proficiency levels, recency of use and foreign language exposure. Regardless of specific research paradigms and approaches, let us attempt to establish a few key issues of relevance to all multiple language learners.

KEY LEARNING ISSUES

In this chapter we are concerned with learning two or more languages, so let us begin by looking at what this means in practice for the L3 learner, based on the principal factors outlined above. First, the multilingual learner will draw on their previous linguistic experiences at the initial stages of L3 acquisition, with the effects of cross-linguistic influence (Sharwood Smith, 1983) being of greater benefit, that is, resulting in positive transfer, if the languages are more closely related (e.g., Ringbom, 2007) or indeed perceived to be (e.g., Kellerman, 1979). Of course, not all learners share the same combination of languages, and not all who do will exhibit the same patterns and preferences when embarking on another (Jarvis, 2015) but, as we shall see in the sections that follow, what all learners do share is the attention they pay to cross-linguistic similarities – rather than differences – and of course typologically closer languages will present more opportunities. Secondly, the advantage that the L3 learner has over the L2 learner – and possibly over the L1/L2-bilingual L3 learner (see e.g., Le Pichon, de Swart, Vorstman, and van den Bergh, 2010) – concerns the acquisition of a further foreign language. It can be assumed, as Bardel and Falk note, that:

> L3 learners, especially those who have learned the L2 in a formal setting, have acquired metalinguistic awareness and learning strategies that may facilitate foreign language learning. They are familiar with at least some of the efforts and methods that are required from a learner in order to succeed. (Bardel and Falk, 2012: 69; see Figure 5.1 below)

Therefore, where there are fewer opportunities for identifying cross-linguistic similarities, for example where languages are more typologically distant, the learner will nevertheless have a number of cognitive mechanisms, if not linguistic typology, on which to draw; where languages within the learner's constellation are typologically close, this, alongside foreign language-learning strategies, will make for even greater benefits.

L1 acquisition

Prerequisites for language acquisition

L2 learning

Prerequisites for language acquisition

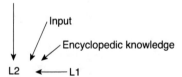

L3 learning

Prerequisites for language acquisition

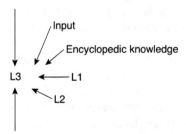

Experiences and strategies acquired during L2 learning

Figure 5.1   L1, L2, L3 (Bardel and Falk, 2012: 69)

In summary, the present chapter considers three key issues that concern the learning of two or more languages: cross-linguistic influence, metalinguistic awareness and language-learning strategies. These issues will, in turn, inform the implications for teaching in the final section, which are followed by some general questions for discussion at the end of the chapter.

CROSS-LINGUISTIC INFLUENCE

The main body of research into Third Language Acquisition (TLA) has investigated various aspects of cross-linguistic influence (CLI). Indeed, many volumes over the years have been dedicated to the concept and it remains prominent in the psycholinguistic field (e.g., Cenoz, Hufeisen, and Jessner, 2001; De Angelis and Dewaele, 2011; De Angelis, Jessner, and Kresić, 2015; Jarvis and Pavenko, 2008; Odlin, 1989; Tsang, 2016; Yu and Odlin, 2015). For the most part, these studies have highlighted the facilitative effects of CLI on L3 learning (e.g., Jarvis, 2015; Rivers and Golonka, 2009), especially when previously learned languages are more closely related to the target language, given that "consciously or not, [learners] do not look for differences, they look for similarities whenever they can find them" (Ringbom, 2007: 1). So, learners embarking on an L3 will logically draw on their previously learned languages to assist with the process, and if similarities exist – in either the L1 or L2 – this process will necessarily be facilitated. The question, of course, is what exactly constitutes similarity and to what extent is this, in practice, present in the mind of the learner acquiring a new language.

For the purposes of the present chapter, let us consider similarity in CLI as a basic subjective concept (see Ringbom (2007) for a full discussion of cross-linguistic similarity). Subjective similarity – as opposed to similarities (or differences) regarding actual or *objective* features of language (e.g., Linck, Micahel, Golonka, and Twist, 2014) – affects the degree to which learners rely on their prior linguistic knowledge when using the target language. These similarities have been further divided into two categories in the literature – *assumed* and *perceived*: assumed similarities are the conscious or unconscious hypotheses that a form in the learner's existing language(s) has a counterpart in the target language, regardless of whether the learner has encountered it or whether it exists; perceived similarities are conscious or unconscious judgements that a form encountered in the target language is similar to a corresponding feature from the learner's existing language(s). In addition, perceived similarities are more likely than assumed similarities to result in positive transfer (Jarvis and Pavlenko, 2008: 179; Ringbom, 2007: 24–26).

Applying this frame of reference to L3 learners in a study of identical placement in French and Spanish of two specific adverbs of manner, Witney (2015) showed that L1 English secondary school learners with prior knowledge of French performed more accurately than those without, not only when producing grammatical Spanish sentences that reflected Spanish and French word order, but also in rejecting English word order. As such, the L3 learners had a distinct advantage over the L2 learners in being able to perceive rather than merely assume similarity, at least with this particular feature in two typologically related foreign languages. We shall return to this in the section below on implications for teaching.

In another CLI study of Spanish and Catalan secondary school bilinguals learning German and English, Sanchez (2011) found that a significant proportion of her learners transferred verb-second (V2) word order constructions from German when narrating a picture story in English. Here, the most recently studied foreign language – but also perhaps the perception that German is typologically closer to English – appears to have overridden the influence of word order similarity in the L1s (Spanish and Catalan), which in this instance matched that of the L3 (English).

This leads us on to the so-called L2 status effect, which has been seen widely in the TLA literature at the lexical level (e.g., Dewaele, 1998; Williams and Hammarberg, 1998) – where the most recently acquired language may account for transfer effects – and also in syntax (e.g., Falk and Bardel, 2011), where it has been argued that "the L2 can supersede the L1 as a source of transfer, because of a higher degree of cognitive similarity between L2 and L3, than between L1 and L3" (p. 61). Elsewhere, however, (psycho)typological proximity has been shown to be more significant than the L2 status in determining sources of transfer at both lexical and syntactic levels (e.g., Ringbom, 2001; Rothman, 2010, 2011; Westergaard, Mitrofanova, Mykhaylyk, and Rodina, 2016). More research is therefore needed, testing a greater variety of properties across linguistic levels and in particular within and beyond the Indo-European family of languages (e.g., Jarvis, 2015; Tsang, 2016; Yu and Odlin, 2015), before any definitive conclusions may be drawn. Indeed, as Jaensch (2013) has already noted, "[a]lthough it would be empirically 'cleaner' if an L3A [TLA] model could be a type of 'one theory fits all' scenario, given the complexity of L3A, this might not be appropriate" (p. 85).

Cross-linguistic influence, however, remains one of the most important resources available to the multiple language learner – at least of typologically related languages – and one which, as we shall see in the following sections, interacts favourably with two other major areas of investigation in the TLA literature: metalinguistic awareness and language-learning strategies (see Chapter 9).

METALINGUISTIC AWARENESS

The facilitative effects of CLI on L3 learning are closely associated with an enhanced metalinguistic awareness (e.g., Bono, 2011; Jarvis, 2015; Jessner, 2006, 2008). In accumulating language-learning experience, the learner is able to draw on prior linguistic encounters in their development of a number of enhanced cognitive abilities including an "explicit knowledge of language" (Jarvis and Pavlenko, 2008). As such, the multilingual learner is equipped with a higher degree of metalinguistic awareness compared with that of the monolingual learner (e.g., Rivers and Golonka, 2009). Jessner defines metalinguistic awareness as:

> The ability to focus on linguistic form and to switch focus between form and meaning. Individuals who are metalinguistically aware are able to categorize words into parts of speech; switch focus between form, function, and meaning; and explain why a word has a particular function. (Jessner, 2008: 277)

Within a dynamic multilingual framework, the author extends and links two types of awareness: cross-linguistic and metalinguistic, whereby cross-linguistic awareness during L3 production is defined as "the awareness (tacit and explicit) of the interaction between the languages in a multilingual's mind; metalinguistic awareness adds to this by making objectification possible" (p. 279). Thus the relationship between cross-linguistic interaction and metalinguistic influence is a significant facet of the multilingual mind (Bono, 2011: 25).

Metalinguistic awareness is an important factor in an instructed environment, that has been shown to develop during the learning of a first foreign language and to increase during the learning of a third and subsequent language (e.g., Kemp, 2001). In an early L3 study, Thomas (1988) examined the role played by metalinguistic awareness in instructed second and third language learning. The study found that English speaking students with prior knowledge of Spanish had an advantage over monolinguals when performing those activities usually associated with learning French formally in the classroom, providing evidence that developing students' metalinguistic awareness may increase the potential advantage of knowing two languages when learning a third. Furthermore, the study revealed a distinction between those with formal L2 instruction in Spanish and those who used L2 Spanish actively or passively at home, with the former group outperforming the latter. In more recent studies, Bono (2011) and Witney (2015) found that multilingual learners were able to discuss options based on their prior linguistic knowledge and foreign language-learning experiences, making use of an analytical approach to the language-learning process unavailable to second language learners, demonstrating that they were equipped with a fine-tuned capacity to focus on the systemic features of the languages within their constellation. An increased exposure to L2 literacy afforded by formal instruction would therefore appear to be of benefit to the L3 learner (see Chapter 26). Furthermore, Falk, Lindqvist, and Bardel (2015) found that the degree of L1-explicit metalinguistic awareness also played a decisive role in the initial stages of L3 learning.

In short, we know that metalinguistic awareness is an asset for the instructed language learner in general, but it is significantly enhanced among multilingual learners, interacting favourably with cross-linguistic influences and with a further variable to which we now turn: language-learning strategies.

LANGUAGE-LEARNING STRATEGIES

A learner with enhanced metalinguistic awareness will, as a result, be able to make judicious use of appropriate language-learning strategies during the acquisition process, in particular beyond the L2. Language learning strategies – whether cognitive, social or affective – may be conscious or semi-conscious, but the ultimate goal will be to increase target language knowledge and understanding, which may be purely linguistic, cultural or socially-motivated (see Cohen, 2003 for a distinction between strategies that relate to language learning and language use). According to Roehr (2004), a mature analytic ability at the cognitive level, reflected more generally in society at large, allows the language learner to think scientifically, thereby maximising efficiency and gaining a sense of order during the acquisition process in which a fine-tuned set of strategies will allow for greater success in the completion of language-learning tasks. Kemp (2007) found that learners knowing more languages (up to 12) used a greater number of grammar learning strategies and used them more frequently. Moreover, highly multilingual learners were more likely to have developed their own unique grammar learning strategies. Witney (2015) found that advanced L1 English learners of Spanish (level B2 on the Common European Framework of Reference for Languages (CEFR) scale) were able to turn their knowledge of L2 French to their advantage through language-learning strategies, combined with a heightened understanding of interlingual connections at play between two typologically similar foreign languages; they were equally conscious of, and able to identify, the grammatical differences and similarities between the languages known to them (L1(s), L2 and L3) through effective use of metalanguage and metalinguistic awareness, afforded to them in an instructed language-learning environment. Berthele (2011) showed that the advantage of multilingual learners extends to receptive competences, as they are more efficient in using a process of interlingual inferencing when confronted with previously unknown languages.

In sum, there is evidence that foreign language-learning strategies interact favourably with an enhanced metalinguistic awareness among instructed language learners in developing an overall understanding of cross-linguistic influences, which in turn has important pedagogical implications, as previously noted in the literature:

> For L2 influence to become a learning accelerator, CLIN [crosslinguistic interaction] needs to be coupled with metalinguistic awareness, which is known to be particularly enhanced in multilingual speakers. (Bono, 2011: 26)

IMPLICATIONS FOR TEACHING AND ASSESSMENT

Drawing together the various strands from the sections above, we now focus on the extent to which these elements together may be exploited in the classroom to the benefit of the multilingual learner. From what we have seen so far, the primary aim of the teacher should be to facilitate positive transfer and highlight incidences that may potentially lead to negative transfer, whilst making as much use as possible of learners' metalinguistic awareness and their language-learning strategies.

Clearly, not all teachers operate within the same environment. In terms of language instruction, TWI (Two-Way Immersion) programs in the United States, for example, and CLIL (Content and Language Integrated Learning) programs – favoured particularly by the European Commission and increasingly popular in the bilingual populations of Catalonia and the Basque Country – have for some time challenged the traditional methodologies of the foreign language classroom. However, a review of these programs (Jarvis, 2015) shows that no categorical claims can yet be made as to the overall effectiveness of one over the other based on research in the literature to date.

Let us therefore return to evidence from the literature on cross-linguistic influence outlined in the sections above, in order to further evaluate implications for teaching. We have seen that knowledge of previous languages (both L1(s) and foreign languages) impacts significantly on the learning of subsequent languages and, as such, new languages cannot be learned – nor should they be taught – in isolation. This has been addressed by Cook (2001, 2008) regarding the L2 classroom and the potential facilitative use of the L1, hitherto frequently seen as "the enemy of the L2" (Jarvis and Pavlenko, 2008: 217); beyond the L2 classroom, multilingual learners are necessarily drawing not only on knowledge of their L1 and previously learned foreign languages, but also on specific foreign language-learning strategies, which will to a greater or lesser extent be active during the process. Furthermore, as Linck et al. (2014) note, it is essentially counter-productive to ignore what is ultimately a powerful resource for the teacher in promoting positive transfer from prior linguistic knowledge and "efforts to completely ignore the L1 and L2 may be futile" (p. 6). As we have seen, in promoting this positive transfer Ringbom (2007) argues that language learners are drawn naturally towards similarities to – rather than differences from – their previously acquired languages. However, this does not, of course, preclude teachers from focusing on both: whilst drawing the learner's attention to similarities will necessarily facilitate positive transfer, active highlighting and explicit teaching of differences will equally reduce the likelihood of negative transfer.

More specifically, we have seen evidence of cross-linguistic interaction at a number of levels including lexis, phonology and (morpho)syntax which, combined with an instructed learner's enhanced metalinguistic awareness, may be exploited by the teacher to maximize the effects of L3 processing. At the level of lexis, for example, focusing on cognates – both true and false – where possible across multiple languages, especially in the early stages of instruction, will bring substantial benefits in terms of effective L3 lexical processing (e.g., Linck et al., 2014). The same of course applies at the level of syntax, as we have seen above in the examples of cross-linguistic similarities and differences regarding adverbial placement across three languages, and teachers will come across numerous others, whether lexical, phonological, syntactic or morphological. Encouraging the multilingual learner to be aware of grammatical structures that overlap – or providing explicit instruction of those that do not – between either or both the L1 and L2 will significantly help with L3 (morpho) syntactic processing (e.g., Linck et al., 2014).

The ultimate goal of the L3 teacher, therefore, is to make full use of the tools available, encouraging pupils to reflect on their previously acquired linguistic systems through a discussion of objective similarities and differences, turning assumed similarities into perceived similarities, thereby increasing the opportunity for positive transfer.

The fact remains, of course, that not all teachers will be proficient in the languages known by the L3 learner and, as such, may feel that from a practical point of view it is more useful to focus on cognitive processes rather than structures within specific language combinations, thereby allowing the learner to facilitate the process more automatically. This is certainly reflected in research that seeks to define a comprehensive TLA framework (e.g., Rivers and Golonka, 2009).

CONCLUSION

Learners of two or more languages are in a unique position: they have the benefit of prior foreign language-learning experiences, during which they develop a heightened sense of what language is about in general and how specific languages interact within one multilingual mind. Instructed multilinguals, in particular, are in a strong position to draw on a range of language-learning strategies that interact favourably with enhanced cognitive abilities in developing an overall understanding of cross-linguistic influences.

The aim of all teachers, regardless of any specific program of instruction that they may be required to follow, should be to encourage multilingual language learners to make use of the cognitive and linguistic tools at their disposal, primarily by drawing attention to similarities between languages and by explicitly teaching differences where these elements exist.

Discussion Questions

1. To what extent may multiple language learners be considered better linguists?

2. Can metalinguistic awareness develop fully without knowledge of metalanguage?

3. Do multilingual language learners need to be made aware of cross-linguistic interactions to become proficient users?

4. What are the main challenges facing the teacher in a multilingual classroom?

Key Readings

Cook, V. (2008). *Second Language Learning and Language Teaching*. London: Hodder.

De Angelis, G., & Dewaele, J.-M. (2011). *New Trends in Crosslinguistic Influence and Multilingualism Research*. Bristol, UK: Multilingual Matters.

Jarvis, S., & Pavlenko, A. (2008). *Crosslinguistic Influence in Language and Cognition*. London: Routledge.

Jessner, U. (2006). *Linguistic Awareness in Multilinguals*. Edinburgh: Edinburgh University Press.

Ringbom, H. (2007). *Cross-linguistic Similarity in Foreign Language Learning*. Bristol, UK: Multilingual Matters.

References

Bardel, C., & Falk, Y. (2012). The L2 status factor and the declarative/procedural distinction. In J. Cabrelli Amaro, S. Flynn, & J. Rothman (Eds.), *Third Language Acquisition in Adulthood*. Amsterdam/Philadelphia: John Benjamins.

Berthele, R. (2011). On abduction in receptive multilingualism: Evidence from cognate guessing tasks. *Applied Linguistics Review*, 2, 191–220.

Bono, M. (2011). Crosslinguistic interaction and metalinguistic awareness in third language acquisition. In G. De Angelis & J.-M. Dewaele (Eds.), *New Trends in Crosslinguistic Influence and Multilingualism Research*. Bristol, UK: Multilingual Matters.

Cenoz, J., Hufeisen, B., & Jessner, U. (2001). *Cross-linguistic Influence in Third Language Acquisition: Psycholinguistic Perspectives*. Bristol, UK: Multilingual Matters.

Cohen, A. (2003). The learner's side of foreign language learning: Where do styles, strategies, and tasks meet? *International Review of Applied Linguistics*, 41, 279–291.

Cook, V. (2001). Using the first language in the classroom. *Canadian Modern Language Review*, 57, 402–423.

Cook, V. (2008). *Second Language Learning and Language Teaching*. London: Hodder.

De Angelis, G., & Dewaele, J.-M. (2011). *New Trends in Crosslinguistic Influence and Multilingualism Research*. Bristol, UK: Multilingual Matters.

De Angelis, G., Jessner, U., & Kresić, M. (2015). *Crosslinguistic Influence and Crosslinguistic Interaction in Multilingual Language Learning*. London: Bloomsbury.

Dewaele, J.-M. (1998). Lexical inventions: French interlanguage as L2 versus L3. *Applied Linguistics*, 19(4), 471–490.

Falk, Y., & Bardel, C. (2011). Object pronouns in German L3 syntax: Evidence for the L2 status factor. *Second Language Research*, 27(1), 59–82.

Falk, Y., Lindqvist, C., & Bardel, C. (2015). The role of L1 explicit metalinguistic knowledge in L3 oral production at the initial state. *Bilingualism: Language and Cognition*, 18, 227–235.

Jaensch, C. (2013). Third language acquisition: Where are we now? *Linguistic Approaches to Bilingualism*, 3(1), 73–93.

Jarvis, S. (2015). Influences of previously learned languages on the learning and use of additional languages. In M. Juan-Garau & J. Salazar-Noguera (Eds.), *Content-based Language Learning in Multilingual Educational Environments* (pp. 69–86). Berlin: Springer.

Jarvis, S., & Pavlenko, A. (2008). *Crosslinguistic Influence in Language and Cognition*. London: Routledge.

Jessner, U. (2006). *Linguistic Awareness in Multilinguals*. Edinburgh: Edinburgh University Press.

Jessner, U. (2008). A DST model of multilingualism and the role of metalinguistic awareness. *The Modern Language Journal*, 2, 270–283.

Kellerman, E. (1979). Transfer and non-transfer: Where we are now. *Studies in Second Language Acquisition*, 2(1), 37–57.

Kemp, C. (2001). *Metalinguistic Awareness in Multilinguals: Implicit and Explicit Grammatical Awareness and its Relationship with Language Experience and Language Attainment*. Unpublished doctoral thesis, University of Edinburgh.

Kemp, C. (2007). Strategic processing in grammar learning: Do multilinguals use more strategies? *International Journal of Multilingualism*, 4(4), 241–261.

Le Pichon, E., de Swart, H., Vorstman, J., & van den Bergh, H. (2010). Influence of the context of learning a language on the strategic competence of children. *International Journal of Bilingualism*, 14(4), 447–465.

Linck, J., Micahel, E., Golonka, E., & Twist, A. (2014). *Moving beyond two languages: The effects of multilingualism on language processing and language learning*. Technical Report, Center for Advanced Study of Language, University of Maryland.

Odlin, T. (1989). *Language Transfer: Cross-linguistic Influence in Language Learning*. Cambridge: Cambridge University Press.

Ringbom, H. (2001). Lexical transfer in L3 production. In J. Cenoz, B. Hufeisen, & U. Jessner (Eds.), *Cross-linguistic Influence in Third Language Acquisition: Psycholinguistic Perspectives* (pp. 59–68). Bristol, UK: Multilingual Matters.

Ringbom, H. (2007). *Cross-Linguistic Similarity in Foreign Language Learning*. Bristol, UK: Multilingual Matters.

Rivers, W., & Golonka, E. (2009). Third language acquisition theory and practice. In M. H. Long & C. J. Doughty (Eds.), *The Handbook of Language Teaching*. Oxford: Wiley-Blackwell.

Roehr, K. (2004). Exploring the role of explicit knowledge in adult second language learning: Language proficiency, pedagogical grammar and language learning strategies. *Lancaster University CRILE Working Papers*, 59.

Rothman, J. (2010). On the typological economy of syntactic transfer: Word order and relative clause high/low attachment preference in L3 Brazilian Portuguese. *International Review of Applied Linguistics*, 48, 245–273.

Rothman, J. (2011). L3 syntactic transfer selectivity and typological determinacy: The typological primacy model. *Second Language Research*, 27(1), 107–127.

Sanchez, L. (2011). 'Luisa and Pedrito's dog will the breakfast eat': Interlanguage transfer and the role of the second language factor. In G. De Angelis & J.-M. Dewaele (Eds.), *New Trends in Crosslinguistic Influence and Multilingualism Research* (pp. 86–104). Bristol, UK: Multilingual Matters.

Sharwood Smith, M. (1983). Cross-linguistic aspects of second language acquisition. *Applied Linguistics*, 4, 192–199.

Thomas, J. (1988). The role played by metalinguistic awareness in second and third language learning. *Journal of Multilingual and Multicultural Development*, 9(3), 235–241.

Tsang, W. L. (2016). *Crosslinguistic Influence in Multilinguals: an Examination of Chinese-English-French Speakers*. Bristol, UK: Multilingual Matters.

Westergaard, M., Mitrofanova, N., Mykhaylyk, R., & Rodina, Y. (2016). Crosslinguistic influence in the acquisition of a third language: The Linguistic Proximity Model. *The International Journal of Bilingualism*, http://journals.sagepub.com/doi/abs/10.1177/1367006916648859

Williams, S., & Hammarberg, B. (1998). Language switches in L3 production: Implications for a polyglot speaking model. *Applied Linguistics*, 19(3), 295–333.

Witney, J. (2015). *Lateral (morpho)syntactic transfer: An Empirical Investigation into the Positive and Negative Influences of French on L1 English Learners of Spanish Within an Instructed Language-learning Environment*. Unpublished doctoral thesis, Birkbeck College, University of London.

Yu, L., & Odlin, T. (2015). *New Perspectives on Transfer in Second Language Learning*. Bristol, UK: Multilingual Matters.

SECTION 2

INDIVIDUAL, SOCIAL AND AFFECTIVE DIMENSIONS OF LEARNING ENGLISH

The chapters in this section consider areas that have perhaps been more 'traditionally' associated with second language acquisition (SLA) research – the dimensions of learning that relate to individual, social and affective factors. While these areas are also integrated into other chapters in this guide, as they relate to the particular domain or construct being considered, these chapters acknowledge the importance of considering these variables in the language learning process.

The first chapter, by **Stephen Ryan**, discusses the complex and highly unpredictable dimension of motivation, an aspect of language learning which is often central in many teachers' minds. He stresses that motivation is influenced by numerous internal and external individual factors, as well as by cultural, social, affective and cognitive dimensions surrounding any given learner's learning situation and experiences. He argues that motivation for learning, and success in learning, can fluctuate over time and place and that teachers need to abandon their roles as 'external controlling motivators' and seek to view their students more from a whole-person perspective.

Next, the chapter by **Shaofeng Li** discusses language aptitude and considers to what extent it is predictive of language achievements. He argues that in general what is considered as 'traditional aptitude', that is, phonetic coding ability, language analytic ability and rote memory, is a strong predictor of language ability. He provides a comprehensive review of research covering the issues of the predictive power of aptitude, the relationship of aptitude to type of instruction, and aptitude and age. He recommends that aptitude be considered in the selection and placement of students in language programs, in decisions about inductive or deductive approaches to learning, and in relation to student age. He advocates an eclectic approach, especially in teaching large groups where assessment of learners' aptitude may be difficult.

Elaine K. Horwitz and **Lama Nassif** focus on language anxiety, noting that it is a type of 'situation-specific' anxiety, in that it relates to a particular phenomenon or situation. Their review of the research on language-learning anxiety focuses on studies that have mainly investigated college-age foreign-language learners, and in their chapter they stress the need for more extensive research on K-12 students. One notable research finding, from the point of view of classroom teaching, is that between 30 and 40% of learners from a variety of backgrounds experience language anxiety. The authors note that while this figure does not represent a majority, it still warrants considerable empathy from English language teaching educators.

In the next chapter, **Rebecca L. Oxford** considers how learners regulate their learning through the use of language learning strategies (LLS). She stresses that the concept of LLS is not easily definable and the use of LLS is highly complex, as it is dependent on a wide range of cultural, social, political and personal factors. Moreover, it is not confined to the classroom, which raises issues of how teachers can promote flexible and fluid ways to help promote their learners' self-regulation in learning a language. Using two case study examples, she illustrates and identifies dimensions that are 'the soul' of language learning strategies, and draws out the implications for a range of practices that can be incorporated into English language teaching and assessment.

In the final chapter in this section, **Martha C. Pennington** argues that identity is central to learning a second language (L2). Taking the position that identity is not a fixed entity that one is 'born with', she argues that language-learner identity is constructed through dialogic interactions within communities of learning practice. Language thus needs to be conceived of as central to the formation of different manifestations of learner identity. She poses a number of crucial questions relating to self-concept, self-esteem and self-confidence that should be central considerations in English language teaching and learning. In so doing, she points to the crucial role played by the teacher in learners' language identity formation.

These chapters reflect the complexity of the cognitive, cultural, social and affective factors that need to be taken into account in L2 learning. It is clear that a one-size-fits-all or generalized account of what it means to learn an L2 falls far short of the complex realities and varying conditions that exist for different learners in different learning environments. The discussions also reflect how the 'social turn' in the field of SLA research has greatly expanded the theoretical and practical lenses through which the learning of English as a second language can be viewed.

CHAPTER 6

Motivation

Stephen Ryan

INTRODUCTION

The broad course of thinking about language education over the past fifty years or so can be characterised as a move away from a focus on language and teaching to a greater interest in learners and their learning. A growing awareness of the importance of motivation in successful language learning has been central to that shift. As researchers and teachers have become interested in what makes some learners more successful than others, and the various contributions learners make to their own learning, motivation has risen to a position of prominence unimaginable only two decades ago.

In this chapter, I want to first step back and think carefully about what we mean by the word motivation, before going on to discuss the particular motivation to study a foreign language. Following on from this, I will explore how an understanding of motivation connects and contributes to both learning and teaching. In doing so, I hope to highlight the immense sweep covered by the term motivation and some of the risks associated with a narrow, simplistic view of the concept.

OVERVIEW

The scope of motivation research is neatly captured in the title of Deci and Flaste's (1996) popular and highly accessible book, *Why We Do What We Do.* And if we throw in the supplementary questions of *how long* and *how strong,* we start to get some idea of the scale of what motivation studies investigate. In effect, motivation attempts to explain the almost countless factors that influence human behaviour. Unsurprisingly, such a vast area of investigation has attracted diverse approaches and any account of motivation is inevitably selective.

One of the reasons that the topic of motivation can be so attractive and appealing to teachers is that 'motivation' is a term people readily use in their everyday lives. The term is a familiar one we use in connection with all kinds of topics, such as sport, business, and, yes, the classroom. It is a concept we all understand in some way, and it is something about which we all have our own individual lay theories. Perhaps the most pervasive of these lay theories of motivation is the 'carrot and stick' model, in which people are motivated by either the fear of punishment or the promise of some reward. This is a familiar framework across a wide range of cultures, and one that was supported by early motivation research in psychology, which presented human behaviour solely in terms of responses to rewards and punishments. In the latter half of the twentieth century, this view of motivation was vigorously challenged from various directions, but the main thrust of these challenges was that human motives are far more complicated – and more interesting – than a simple impulse to avoid pain or approach pleasure. Although something of a simplification, the various challenges to the simplistic rewards and punishment view of motivation can be seen as part of a general move towards looking at motivation as being internally driven, as coming from within the individual.

The move to a more internally directed conceptualisation of motivation is one, as I discuss in more detail later in the chapter, that has significant implications for teaching and learning, as it changes how we regard the motivational dynamic between teachers and learners. It is a move that was part of a broader shift within psychology to look at how people's own thinking shaped their behaviour. In its early days, the field of psychology was dominated by experiments on animals – often isolated and starved – and from these experiments the findings were extrapolated to explain human behaviour. However, the field gradually began to change with a realisation that the human experience, with its complex interactions of social relationships, hopes, dreams, obligations, memories and regrets, was very different from that of a starving rat in a box.

The cognitive shift in thinking about motivation that occurred in the latter decades of the twentieth century introduced a range of new concepts, and many of these have changed how we discuss language learning motivation. One of the most important of these is how individuals set and pursue goals for themselves. Understanding the different types of goals people set offers an insight into how they direct their efforts. A number of key distinctions in the way people set goals have been identified, and one distinction of particular relevance to language learning is that between what are known as mastery and performance goals (Dweck, 1999). Individuals with a mastery goal orientation engage in tasks in order to experience the satisfaction of successfully performing that task well. On the other hand, individuals with a performance goal orientation are motivated to show their worth in relation to other people. In the case of language learning, a mastery goal orientation might be observed in a learner setting a particular challenge, say being able to comprehend a short news report in English, with little regard to the relative performance of others; an example of a performance goal orientation could be someone working hard in order to outperform his or her classmates on an important test. In the literature, the general consensus is that mastery goal orientations are more facilitative of long-term motivation, yet in many educational contexts the focus of English language teaching is still very much on performance.

It is important to remain aware that people do not set goals in a vacuum; they set goals based on their own experience, their past successes and failures. Or perhaps it is more accurate to say, their interpretations of those successes and failures. One concept that helps us understand people's interpretations of their various successes and failures is known as attribution theory (Weiner, 2007). Put simply, attributions represent our own internal explanations of success and failure, and these explanations affect our future behaviour. A key concern in attribution theory is how much control the individual believes he or she has over these successes and failures (Locus of Control is the technical term). If we attribute success or failure to factors beyond our control, such as luck, a great teacher, or innate ability, we have little control over our own destiny and there is little we can do to achieve future success. However, if we attribute success to factors within our own control, such as effort or persistence – or failure to a lack of effort – then we are more likely to believe in our capacity to achieve future success and make the required efforts to do so.

The above discussion barely skims the surface of the fascinating range of explanations for learning behaviour ushered in by the cognitive shift in educational psychology. There are so many other concepts that could be considered of equal relevance to a discussion of language learner motivation, but I have chosen to focus on goals and attributions, because they highlight the dynamic nature of motivation. Motivation connects our current self to a desired future state based on interpretations of past efforts. Motivation is constantly changing – we have motivational highs and motivational lows – and it is changing in response to events, and how we process those events.

In more recent years, thinking about motivation has begun to shift once again. Researchers have started to think more about the role of emotion (Ryan, 2007) and its influence on behaviour. The cognitive shift of the late twentieth century made a huge contribution to our understanding of motivation, yet it was largely based on the assumption that people's behaviour is based on rational decisions. There are times when this is the case, but there are also times when emotion is a significant feature in our decision-making. Referring back to the discussions of goals and attributions, there is an assumption that individuals are rationally evaluating past events and, based on this rational analysis, constructing well-thought-out goals for themselves. However, let us imagine an English learner attempting to order a meal at a restaurant in English. The order is not successfully communicated, which prompts the busy person taking the order to switch to the learner's L1, in order to speed up the process. This is a clear failure, and logically the learner might analyse the situation, coming to the conclusion that it is a useful learning experience and that more persistence is required. However, on an emotional level, the feelings of failure and rejection may run counter to, or even override, the broadly positive motivational cognitive decisions.

Summarising the development of motivation theory, we can say that early thinking about motivation was very simple: people made efforts to get rewards or to avoid punishment or pain. Over time, thinking has developed in a way that positions individuals as agents of their own actions. As a result of these changes, discussions have inevitably become more complex, taking into account the dynamic nature and the emotional base of many of our motivational decisions and impulses.

MOTIVATION IN FOREIGN LANGUAGE LEARNING

Serious research into language learner motivation began in Canada in the 1960s, and this body of research is most closely associated with the social psychologist, Robert Gardner (1985). Though somewhat out of fashion these days, Gardner's work represented a major breakthrough in thinking about language learning, as it stressed the role learners play in their own learning: learners are more than passive receptacles of knowledge and their attitudes to learning affect learning outcomes. However, it is fair to say that despite the insights this approach brought, its relevance to teachers trying to understand what was occurring in their own classrooms was limited (Ushioda, 2008). From the 1990s onwards, influenced by the cognitive shift in mainstream psychology, there was a marked moved to more 'education-friendly' explanations of language learner motivation, seeking to make research more accessible to practising teachers.

Bearing in mind the earlier discussion of attributions and goals, an important development in thinking about language learner motivation was Williams and Burden's (1997) distinction between initiating motivation and sustaining it. A useful working definition of language learning motivation is that it "provides the primary impetus to initiate L2 learning and later the driving force to sustain the long, often tedious learning process" (Dörnyei and Ryan, 2015: 72). Williams and Burden made the point that the things that initially attract us to learning a language can be very different to those that encourage us to pursue and persist with that learning over the long term.

Explorations of this temporal dimension have been an important part of discussions of language learner motivation in recent years. Of all the attempts to explain the dynamic nature of language learning motivation, the most important and the most successful has been Dörnyei's L2 Motivational Self System (Dörnyei, 2005, 2009), the currently dominant theoretical model. This model proposes three core components:

1. An ideal L2 self, which is based on the individual's future aspirations and visions as an L2 user.

2. An ought-to L2 self, which is based on the individual's perceived responsibilities and obligations to others as an L2 learner.

3. The L2 learning experience, which represents individuals' internal narrative interpretation of past successes and failures as a language learner.

It is important to point out that this is conceived as a system and that motivation emerges from the interaction of the component parts; when the various components are in harmony, motivation should be higher and sustained, as long as that state of harmony or balance exists.

KEY LEARNING ISSUES

One of the main factors behind the recent surge in interest in learner motivation is the simplistic belief that increased motivation leads to more successful learning outcomes. However, some caution is required here, as in any long-term undertaking, such as learning English, where there are so many possible variables affecting success, it is impossible to identify any single cause. The data identifying a strong correlation between motivation and successful learning is convincing, yet we have to take great care in interpreting this as evidence of motivation as the cause of successful learning; after all, it is highly plausible that success in learning, and the accompanying feelings of satisfaction and achievement, could lead to higher levels of motivation. In some learner-centred discussions of English language learning, motivation has come to represent something of a panacea, with the belief that understanding what motivates learners offers a guaranteed route to successful learning. However, this is something of a simplification, or distortion even, of the research findings, which tell us nothing more than a strong connection exists between motivation and successful learning. Nevertheless, while it is important to advise caution against overstating the role of motivation in successful language learning, it is safe to say that many of the concepts and processes discussed in the other chapters of this book are dependent on learner motivation; motivation does not necessarily lead to language learning success but this success does not occur without motivation.

If we explore the connections between motivation and English language learning with reference to the earlier theoretical discussion, then it should be immediately clear that we cannot talk in terms of precise, causal relationships between motivation and learning outcomes. Learners and their motivation are unpredictable, changing over time, encountering various ebbs and flows. Rather than discussing the effect of motivation on learning, it makes more sense to discuss the relationships between motivation and learning. This was the thinking behind Dörnyei and Otto's (1998) influential Process Model of Motivation. In this model, it was proposed that language learners make an initial decision to act in a certain way, they act upon this decision, and they plan future actions based on their evaluations of the initial round of action. Although the process model was a little problematic – for example, how does one make a clear distinction between where one set of actions end and the next begins? – it paved the way for more dynamic explanations of motivation, most notably the L2 Motivational Self System. Learning English requires motivation and the motivation to learn English, to a great degree, is dictated by the actual learning experience.

It may be more helpful to say that changes in motivation are at the core of the motivation-learning relationship. In understanding these changes in motivation, it is once again essential that we do not oversimplify by implying simplistic cause-effect relationships, for example, by saying that negative learning experiences, such as a failure to communicate in English, lead to falls in motivation. People can do the most unpredictable things and respond to events in unexpected ways. Let us imagine a young person observing a classmate do something impressive in English – perhaps having a lively conversation, laughing and joking with a group of young people. How would this young person respond? On the one hand, this could be inspirational: sharing in a peer's success could lead to a belief that such rewarding social experiences using English are achievable, and this could form the basis of an empowering, highly motivating vision. On the other hand, some people may feel envious or even resentful of their classmate's success, resulting in demotivation, frustration, and a possible resistance to learning the language. We cannot predict how any specific individual is going to react to a particular experience; instead, it makes sense to understand the processes of change and the range of motivational contingencies connected to key events associated with learning a language.

In the same way that we cannot know how any particular individual will respond to any specific event, we cannot really make any absolute claims as to how motivation will contribute to the success of any individual learner. After all, there are cases of highly motivated learners who are not successful English learners, and, conversely, there are even cases of successful learners who claim not to have been highly motivated to learn the language. Success is contingent on so many other factors, such as quality of instruction, opportunities to use the language outside the classroom, and, often ignored, other things going on in the learner's life. There is a temptation for both researchers and teachers to isolate the language learning experience from other aspects of the individual's life. In order to better understand motivation in a meaningful pedagogic way, it makes sense to look at the whole person, not just the language learner (Ushioda, 2009). As an illustration, we can imagine an, apparently highly motivated girl learning English at school. She takes a very important English test and gets a very good score. Everybody is pleased: the young person herself, her parents, her friends, her teachers. Looking at the language learner in isolation, it would be reasonable to assume that the test success should serve as a reinforcement for motivation. However, what if the same girl achieves even better scores in physics and chemistry, which also happen to be the subjects her close friends enjoy and discuss studying at university in the future? It is highly plausible that in such a case, the success in physics and chemistry may negate the English success, possibly leading to a fall in the motivation to learn English. The point here is that we cannot understand motivation or how it will impact on learning English without considering the whole person and what goes on outside the language classroom.

The example of the young girl and the influence of her friends raises a further point to consider when discussing language learning motivation: the role of other people. Using a language is essentially a social activity (see Chapter 11), yet much of the thinking about learning a language focuses solely on the individual. Other people are a key factor in language learner motivation, and this is especially the case in formal learning contexts, where group motivation is so important. Groups in classrooms are constantly evolving and an individual's motivation and opportunities to learn are influenced by their attitudes towards the groups they are a part of, their sense of belonging to those groups, and their own roles within those groups (Williams, Mercer and Ryan, 2015). Groups go through various stages of development. Some groups can be maladaptive, perhaps enforcing a harmful norm of mediocrity that denies members the opportunity to push beyond this level. Other groups can be highly productive and empowering, with members working together and supporting each other in pursuit of a common goal. When discussing motivation and learning, it is impossible to separate the individual from the social context in which learning is taking place. A key aspect of this social context are the various groups that are a part of every classroom, and to which every learner belongs in some way. We need to think not only in terms of individual motivation but also of group motivation.

In summary, we cannot make any absolute claims about the effect of motivation on learning: both motivation and learning are too complex for that. However, we can observe and understand broad patterns, we can prepare for a range of possible, likely outcomes. We can say that, in general, higher levels of motivation lead to more adaptive approaches to learning, but the motivation of any individual is constantly changing. We can say that it is impossible to know everything about every learner, but the more we are able to understand learners as people, as opposed to mere language learners, the more we are able to understand their motivation to learn. We can say that highly personal, individual visions of possible future states lie at the heart of language learner motivation, but we cannot separate the individual from the social context, and in particular the motivational influence of the various groups to which she or he belongs.

IMPLICATIONS FOR TEACHING AND ASSESSMENT

The shift from a view of motivation as external, resulting from the rewards and punishments of others, to one that presents motivation as coming from within a person, has far-reaching implications for teachers and teaching. If we refer to a dictionary definition of motivation, such as the following from The New Oxford English Dictionary (1998), the verb 'motivate' is presented as to "Stimulate (someone's) interest in or enthusiasm for doing something: it is the teacher's job to motivate the child at school." This definition forcefully articulates a common view of the role of teachers in the motivation of learners. Going back to the earlier image of the carrot and stick being used to direct a stubborn donkey may help here. Applied to an educational context, the learner is the donkey – a lazy, stupid animal – and the teacher is the person attempting to force that donkey to go somewhere it does not want to go. If we unpack this metaphor a little further, a highly negative, pessimistic view of motivation emerges, in which learners are inherently unmotivated – perhaps lazy and stupid? – and motivation can only come from the direction of a controlling teacher. Fortunately, more recent thinking about motivation challenges this view and offers an altogether more optimistic outlook.

Bearing in mind the earlier discussion of the importance of groups, perhaps a more productive way for teachers to understand their own motivational role would be through their participation in the various groups forming in a class. As Csikszentmihalyi (1997) points out, the most motivating teachers, the ones who make a difference, tend to be those who show the most dedication and enthusiasm. Teachers' own enthusiastic participation as members of various groups within the classroom, rather than as an external, controlling motivator, may be a more effective way to model approaches to learning and stimulate motivation.

For many teachers, abandoning their central role as motivator goes against much of their training and their own life experience. Perhaps it even goes against some of their own emotional attachment to being a teacher; after all, the image of the life-changing, inspirational teacher can be a highly alluring one. Recent thinking on motivation suggests that teachers can best serve their learners by loosening their controlling motivational grip, perhaps through the use of rewards (for an excellent discussion of the futility of rewards, see Kohn, 1993) and stepping back to understand, rather than direct, motivation.

At an abstract level, understanding learner motivation requires teachers to be aware of the self-concept of learners, their sense of who they are and who they would like to become (see Chapter 10), and the degree to which it is compatible with the current learning experience. More specifically, this might involve teachers learning more about learners' goals and perhaps helping them to make those goals more realistic, specific or achievable. Another possibility is helping learners to re-evaluate their past learning experiences in a way that may encourage more adaptive approaches to learning.

One of the great joys of teaching, and especially language teaching, is that it can be so unpredictable. What works in one case may not work in another. Teachers need to bear this in mind when developing learning materials; an activity that may be motivating in one class may be demotivating in another. There is no guarantee of motivational success and teachers will never get it right every time. Nevertheless, teachers can make efforts to understand the individual learners in their classes, resisting the urge to direct or control, and to understand the dynamics of the various groups existing within these classes.

CONCLUSION

I began this chapter by referring to the shift from a language- and teaching-based approach to a more learner-centred one. It may be the case that we are now entering a new phase, in which the emphasis is not so much on the learner as on the person as a whole, and in this chapter I have attempted to show how important an understanding of the whole person is when discussing learner motivation. I have also tried to capture something of the scope of motivation, and the impossibility of describing motivation from any single perspective or attributing any specific learning outcomes solely to motivation. The topic of motivation is so huge that this chapter could quite easily have been based on any one of several concepts, such as *flow* (Csikszentmihalyi, 1990) or *vision* (Dörnyei and Kubanyiova, 2014), that have not even been mentioned. Instead, I have focused on the dynamic and unpredictable nature of language learning motivation, as I believe this represents the most pedagogically relevant approach. There is an understandable temptation for teachers to want order, stability and predictability in their classrooms. However, a view of learners and their motivation that emphasises change and unpredictability is likely to be a more productive one, more consistent with the reality of most teachers' experience.

Discussion Questions

1. What can a teacher do with a learner in a class who is clearly not motivated to learn English?

2. What can be done in a situation where some apparently highly motivated individuals have formed a motivationally inhibiting group in a class?

3. What are some of the advantages and disadvantages associated with the use of rewards and incentives to motivate English learners?

Key Readings

Dörnyei, Z., Henry, A., & Muir, C. (2016). *Motivational Currents in Language Learning: Frameworks for Focused Interventions*. New York: Routledge.

Dörnyei, Z., & Kubanyiova, M. (2014). *Motivating Learners, Motivating Teachers: Building Vision in the Language Classroom*. Cambridge: Cambridge University Press.

Dörnyei, Z., & Ushioda, E. (2011). *Teaching and Researching Motivation* (2nd ed.). Harlow: Longman.

Schunk, D.H., Pintrich, P.R., & Meece, J. (2007). *Motivation in Education: Theory, Research, and Applications* (3rd ed.). Upper Saddle River, NJ: Merrill.

Williams, M., Mercer, S., & Ryan, S. (2015). *Exploring Psychology in Language Learning and Teaching*. Oxford: Oxford University Press.

References

Csikszentmihalyi, M. (1990). *Flow: The Psychology of Optimal Experience*. New York: Harper and Row.

Csikszentmihalyi, M. (1997). Intrinsic motivation and effective teaching: A flow analysis. In J.L. Bess (Ed.), *Teaching Well and Liking it: Motivating Faculty to Teach Effectively* (pp. 72–89). Baltimore, MA: Johns Hopkins University Press.

Deci, E. L., & Flaste, R. (1996). *Why We Do What We Do: Understanding Self-motivation*. New York: Penguin.

Dörnyei, Z. (2005). *The Psychology of the Language Learner: Individual Differences in Second Language Acquisition*. Mahwah, NJ: Lawrence Erlbaum.

Dörnyei, Z. (2009). The L2 motivational self system. In Z. Dörnyei and E. Ushioda (Eds.), *Motivation, Language Identity and the L2 Self* (pp. 9–42). Bristol, UK: Multilingual Matters.

Dörnyei, Z., & Kubanyiova, M. (2014). *Motivating Learners, Motivating Teachers: Building Vision in the Language Classroom*. Cambridge: Cambridge University Press.

Dörnyei, Z., & Otto, I. (1998). Motivation in action: a process model of L2 motivation. *Working Papers in Applied Linguistics*, 4, 43–69.

Dörnyei, Z., & Ryan, S. (2015). *The Psychology of the Language Learner Revisited*. New York: Routledge.

Dweck, C. S. (1999). *Self-theories: Their Role in Motivation, Personality, and Development*. Hove: Psychology Press.

Gardner, R. C. (1985). *Social Psychology and Second Language Learning: The Role of Attitudes and Motivation*. London: E. Arnold.

Kohn, A. (1993). *Punished by Rewards: The Trouble with Gold Stars, Incentive plans, A's, Praise and Other Bribes*. Boston: Houghton Mifflin Company.

Ryan, R. M. (2007). Motivation and emotion: A new look and approach for two re-emerging fields. *Motivation and Emotion*, 31(1), 1–3.

Ushioda, E. (2008). Motivation and good language learners. In C. Griffiths (Ed.), *Lessons from Good Language Learners* (pp. 19–34). Cambridge: Cambridge University Press.

Ushioda, E. (2009). A person-in-context relational view of emergent motivation, self and identity. In Z. Dörnyei and E. Ushioda (Eds.), *Motivation, Language Identity and the L2 Self* (pp. 215–228). Bristol, UK: Multilingual Matters.

Weiner, B. (2007). Motivation from an attributional perspective and the social psychology of perceived competence. In A. J. Elliot & C. S. Dweck (Eds.), *Handbook of Competence and Motivation* (pp. 73–84). New York: Guilford Press.

Williams, M., & Burden, R. L. (1997). *Psychology for Language Teachers: A Social Constructivist Approach*. Cambridge: Cambridge University Press.

Williams, M., Mercer, S., & Ryan, S. (2015). *Exploring Psychology in Language Learning and Teaching*. Oxford: Oxford University Press.

CHAPTER 7

Language Aptitude

Shaofeng Li

INTRODUCTION

Language learning is subject to the intricate interplay between learner-external and learner-internal factors, with the former referring to the resources and constraints existing in the social and instructional settings and the latter to the cognitive (e.g., aptitude), conative (e.g., motivation), and affective (e.g., anxiety) variation among learners. The focus of this chapter is on one learner-internal factor – language aptitude, which refers to a set of cognitive abilities posited to be predictive of second language (L2) achievements. Interest in language aptitude commenced in the 1950s, when state-funded language programs in the U.S. and Canada used scores on aptitude tests to select learners with the potential to master a foreign language within a short period through intensive training. Driven by the interest in using aptitude scores to select elite learners, early research centred on the predictive validity of aptitude, that is, whether learners' aptitude scores were correlated with learning success gauged through course grades or scores on proficiency tests. Subsequently, researchers started to take a more fine-tuned approach, examining how aptitude and different aptitude components interfaced with different instructional settings and with age. In general, aptitude has been found to be a consistent, strong predictor of learning outcomes, and the influence of aptitude varies as a function of learning condition and maturation effects. The research on aptitude has contributed significantly to second language pedagogy and theory construction. In the following, I introduce the construct, report the research findings, and discuss ways practitioners may benefit from the findings.

OVERVIEW

Language aptitude consists of three components: phonetic coding ability, language analytic ability, and rote memory, which seem to match the learning of the three aspects of the linguistic system respectively, namely pronunciation, grammar, and vocabulary (see Chapters 17–20). Phonetic coding refers to the ability to distinguish sounds and establish connections between sounds and symbols; language analytic ability has been operationalized as the ability to identify the grammatical functions of sentence elements and to induce rules from given linguistic materials; and rote memory is the ability to learn and retain the associations between sounds and meaning (Carroll, 1990). Recently, there has been a call to include working memory as a component of aptitude on the grounds that:

- traditional aptitude measures were validated in audiolingual classes emphasizing rote memory and mechanical practice; and
- working memory is a device for simultaneous information storage and processing, and is therefore essential for meaning-oriented approaches where learners constantly shift between meaning and form, conducting online information integration and synthesis.

However, in light of the finding that traditional aptitude was separate from working memory (Yalçın, Çeçen, and Erçetin, 2016), and the fact that there have been parallel streams of research on the two variables, this chapter only deals with traditional aptitude.

The three components of traditional aptitude were identified by first observing what happened in language classes, and then developing and validating tests to measure the abilities postulated to be important for L2 achievements. Therefore, the validity of the concept of language aptitude has been primarily empirical (not theoretical) and, to a certain extent, aptitude has been defined in terms of what is measured in aptitude tests. Popular aptitude tests include the Modern Language Aptitude Test (MLAT), the Professional and Linguistic Assessments Board (PLAB) test, the Cognitive Ability for Novelty in Acquisition of Language-Foreign (CANAL-F) test, the LLAMA Language Aptitude Tests, the High-Level Language Aptitude Battery (Hi-LAB) test, and so on – among which the MLAT, validated in the 1950s (Carroll and Sapon, 1959), has been the most influential, due to the strong correlations identified in the research between learners' performance on the test and their second language attainment. However, the LLAMA test has recently replaced the MLAT as researchers' favourite aptitude measure because:

- it is predictive of learning outcomes;
- it is economical (free) and efficient (20 minutes); and
- other tests are not publically available.

The Hi-LAB, which is a recent initiative aiming to predict high proficiency, has a heavy focus on working memory and implicit learning abilities (Linck et al., 2013). Interestingly, rote memory, a traditional aptitude component included in the Hi-Lab, was found to be one of the three significant predictors of advanced learning, despite the criticism of traditional aptitude in the literature. The Hi-LAB did not include analytic ability and phonetic coding, the other two components of traditional aptitude, so it is unclear how they would have fared in Linck et al.'s (2013) validation study.

What is the nature of language aptitude? First, it is domain-specific in the sense that it is only drawn on in language learning and that it is dissociable from general academic abilities such as intelligence. However, Li (2016) found a large overlap between aptitude and intelligence ($r = .64$), which was probably due to the similarity between the measures of the two variables: both include subtests of memory and vocabulary. Li argued that despite the overlap, the two variables seemed separable because the correlation was not perfect and it did not reach the threshold ($r = .75$) that would have caused one to wonder whether they were distinct. Second, it is uncorrelated with motivation (see Chapter 6) and negatively correlated with anxiety (see Chapter 8), and when examined together with these two variables, aptitude often demonstrates stronger associations with learning outcomes (Li, 2016). Carroll (1990) also argued that as a cognitive trait, aptitude is not subject to external influence and should remain stable for a relatively long period of time. Although this argument sounds theoretically valid, there has been a lack of research on whether aptitude changes as a result of language learning experience. However, as Carroll suspected, even if aptitude improves with experience, whether the improvement affects learning outcomes is uncertain.

To be clear, so far the discussion concerns only traditional aptitude, which has recently been called explicit aptitude, that is, it is important in conscious learning. A group of researchers at the University of Maryland (Suzuki and DeKeyser, 2015) have attempted to identify abilities implicated in unconscious learning, which are termed 'implicit aptitude' – a concept that deviates from, and significantly complements, traditional aptitude.

KEY LEARNING ISSUES

The primary concern is whether language aptitude is important for language learning, and this overarching question has been examined in distinct streams of research. In general, aptitude researchers have sought to answer the following three questions:

1. How does aptitude affect learning outcomes (regardless of instruction type)?
2. How does aptitude interface with different types of instruction?
3. How does aptitude relate to maturation/age effects?

THE PREDICTIVE POWER OF APTITUDE

Researchers investigating the first question are interested to know how predictive aptitude is of learning rate. Typically, these studies include measures of aptitude and learning attainment, and analyses of correlational nature are conducted to see whether learners' aptitude scores are significantly correlated with their language proficiency. In these studies, instruction is not manipulated, and the primary concern is the significance (indexed by the p value) and strength of the correlation (the r value) between aptitude and proficiency scores. This constitutes what Li (2015a) referred to as a product-oriented, static approach, where aptitude is a determinant of ultimate attainment irrespective of the nature of the instruction; it contrasts with the treatment studies to be discussed in later sections.

Li (2016) aggregated the results of 53 such studies and found that overall aptitude measured by whole test batteries was significantly correlated with general L2 proficiency: $r = .50$, which means 25% of the variance of second language learning is accounted for by aptitude. The correlation is strong, based on Cohen's benchmarks for interpreting the magnitude of an effect, and it is the strongest when compared with the correlations of other individual difference variables with learning outcomes, such as motivation ($r = .37$) and working memory ($r = .25$). Furthermore, the magnitude of the correlation is comparable to that of intelligence ($r = .50$) with general academic learning (see Li, 2016 for a summary). It must be pointed out that most of the studies involve foreign language classes in North America dominated by traditional form-based instruction featuring heavy doses of grammar instruction, mechanical practice, and rote learning, which may predispose learners to exploit the kinds of abilities tapped by traditional aptitude tests. The importance of aptitude in more meaning-oriented settings remains unclear.

The aggregated results by Li (2015a, 2016) also showed that high school students were more likely to draw on aptitude than university students, in terms of both grammar learning and general proficiency. There are two possible explanations for this finding. One is that aptitude is likely to be more important in initial than later stages of learning, given that high school learners necessarily have less language learning experience than their university counterparts. If this is true, then Carroll's conceptualization of aptitude as initial readiness for learning or as something important for learning "from scratch" (Carroll, 1990: 24) would be confirmed. Carroll integrated this idea in his validation research on the MLAT, where learners with any previous language learning experience were excluded. However, Li's meta-analytic findings, albeit thought-provoking, cannot serve as direct evidence supporting the hypothesis that aptitude is more important for beginners, because the findings are synthesis-based; that is, the relevant variable was created based on a methodological feature, by dividing the included studies into two groups according to the level of the learners the studies involved. To date, there have been only a few studies on the influence of learner proficiency as a moderating variable for aptitude-achievement associations, and the results are mixed. The studies operationalized proficiency in different ways, used different aptitude and outcome measures, and were therefore unable to provide an unequivocal answer to the question in point (Li, 2017).

Despite the lack of robust empirical evidence, there is theoretical justification for the importance of aptitude for initial learning. It has been theorized in both cognitive psychology and second language acquisition (SLA) research that initial learning draws on explicit or conscious learning abilities, such as memory, reasoning, and analytic abilities, which are assessed through intelligence tests in psychology and aptitude tests in SLA. Learners utilize these cognitive resources to attend to, and glean information from, the input available in the environment that serves as fodder for unconscious or implicit learning that happens in subsequent, more advanced stages. In other words, if we assume that traditional aptitude is a set of abilities to learn consciously, then it should be more important for beginners than advanced learners, who likely draw more on implicit or unconscious learning abilities. While there has been some evidence for this hypothesis in psychology, whether or not it is true of language learning awaits empirical investigation.

Up to now, we have been discussing the associations between aptitude (measured through whole test batteries) and learning (represented by course grades or scores on tests of general proficiency) as unitary concepts. However, given that aptitude consists of three components – analytic ability, phonetic coding, and rote memory – and learning can be decomposed into specific aspects, such as knowledge about the linguistic system (vocabulary and grammar) and skills in applying the knowledge (listening, reading, speaking, and writing), it is important to know how aptitude and aptitude components correlate with specific aspects of learning. The following noticeable patterns were observed, based on Li's (2016) synthesis of the relevant literature. First, while aptitude as a holistic construct (composite aptitude scores) has demonstrated significant correlations with grammar, listening, and speaking, its correlations with vocabulary learning were weak. Second, phonetic coding was most predictive of vocabulary, and least of listening comprehension. Third, language analytic ability showed stronger links with grammar learning than with other aspects of learning. Fourth, rote memory was consistently less predictive than the other two aptitude components. Fifth, the correlations between aptitude and aptitude components on the one hand, and L2 writing on the other, were consistently weak and non-significant. These findings suggest that while aptitude has been discussed as a unitary construct, different aptitude components may have differential effects on different aspects of learning. This, together with the possibility that different abilities are drawn on at different stages (Skehan, 2012) and different learning conditions (Robinson, 2011), points to the need for a more fine-grained approach to language aptitude.

As pointed out earlier, the studies reviewed above are carried out in foreign language classes that are predominantly form-focused, and whether aptitude is correlated with the learning that happens in more meaning-oriented classes remains little known. One study that has frequently been cited as evidence for the importance of aptitude in communicative teaching is by Ranta (2002). The study showed that aptitude was significantly correlated with all measures of achievements of more than a hundred sixth graders in an intensive ESL program, where the classes were considered to be communicative, based on the Communicative Orientation of Language Teaching (COLT) observation scheme. However, in this study, aptitude was measured through an L1 metalinguistic test instead of a validated measure of analytic ability. Harley and Hart (1997) reported a study conducted with 11th graders in French immersion classes that were primarily meaning-focused. The study demonstrated that the learning outcomes of early immersion learners who started to be exposed to the L2 from Grade 1 were correlated with rote memory, and those of the late immersion learners starting from Grade 7 were correlated with analytic ability. These studies provide preliminary evidence for the relevance of language aptitude in meaning-focused classes, and for the possible differential effects of different aptitude components on learners with different experiences: whereas early immersion drew on memory, late immersion implicated analytic ability.

APTITUDE-TREATMENT INTERACTION

While the above section concerns studies that take an absolute approach, examining the associations between aptitude and learning rate regardless of instruction type, this section focuses on studies investigating how aptitude interfaces with instruction type. Studies in this paradigm are often labelled as Aptitude-Treatment Interaction (ATI) research, which is premised on the assumption that different aptitude components may play different roles under different learning conditions, depending on whether the processing demands of a learning condition require the application of a certain cognitive ability or whether a learning condition triggers or inhibits the function of a particular ability. In this view, the role of aptitude or aptitude components is not fixed, and whether a certain type of instruction works depends on whether there is a fit between instruction and learners' aptitude profiles. The findings of this line of research are more revealing about the process than the product of learning, and have valuable implications for L2 theory construction and pedagogy.

Several studies have examined the relation of aptitude to the effectiveness of deductive and inductive instruction. The distinction between deduction and induction was initially made in philosophy to refer to two methods of reasoning, with deduction referring to a process moving from general to specific and induction to a process from specific to general. Applied to language instruction, in deductive teaching, learners are typically presented with a grammar rule followed by practice activities requiring learners to apply the rule, while in inductive teaching, learners are presented with examples or materials and asked to induce the rule. Erlam (2005) found that language analytic ability was predictive of the effects of inductive instruction but not the effects of deductive instruction. Hwu and Sun (2012) reported that deductive instruction was significantly more effective than inductive instruction for learners with low language aptitude, but inductive instruction was more effective for learners with high aptitude, although the difference for inductive instruction was statistically nonsignificant. These studies seem to show that aptitude is important in situations where learners receive less external assistance, and that the two types of instruction have differential effects on learners with different aptitude profiles: low-aptitude learners benefit more from instruction imposing less burden on aptitude, and high-aptitude learners more from instruction requiring more use of aptitude.

There has been a considerable body of research on how aptitude is implicated when learners receive corrective feedback (CF). CF, which refers to the teacher's response to errors learners make in communicative tasks, has received much attention in SLA research over the past two decades, because of its advantage in directing learners' attention to linguistic forms during meaning-primary interaction – a practice called 'focus on form' by Long (2015). In their seminal research, Lyster and Ranta (1997) identified six types of feedback, among which recasts (reformulation of a wrong utterance such as "He kissed her" in response to "He kiss her") and metalinguistic feedback (comment on the well-formedness of an utterance such as "You need past tense") have been most studied. In a research synthesis on the role of cognitive abilities in mediating the process and product of L2 interaction, Li (in press) identified seven studies that investigated aptitude as a moderating variable for the effects of interactional feedback. Li aggregated the results of the studies and found that overall aptitude was significantly correlated with the immediate ($r = .42$) and delayed ($r = .32$) effects of CF. However, when feedback was coded as explicit (e.g., metalinguistic feedback) and implicit (e.g., recasts), based on whether learners' attention was overtly drawn to errors, the effects of explicit feedback were significantly more correlated with aptitude (composite scores) than implicit feedback: $r = .59$ versus $r = .32$; and the gap was wider for language analytic ability: $r = .51, .09$, for explicit and implicit feedback respectively.

It would seem that explicit feedback requires learners to exploit their analytic abilities to process the linguistic input they were prompted to attend to; hence its stronger correlations with aptitude. Implicit feedback, in contrast, encourages unconscious learning and therefore does not draw heavily on aptitude. However, it must be pointed out that in most of the studies Li aggregated, implicit feedback such as recasts was not entirely implicit, on the grounds that the feedback was intensively provided and targeted a particular linguistic structure, which made the corrective force easily noticeable (Li, 2015b). Nevertheless, noticeable as it might be, the feedback was perhaps not salient enough to reach the threshold of imposing heavy processing demands on learners' cognitive abilities.

Further evidence for aptitude's stronger associations with explicit learning than implicit learning comes from a group of studies characterized by consistent manipulation of explicit and implicit instructional treatments delivered via the computer. Carpenter (2008) found that aptitude measured via the MLAT was only predictive of the effects of explicit instruction requiring learners to learn the grammar rules of an artificial language, but not of the effects of implicit instruction where learners were only exposed to some examples of the language without receiving any rule explanation. De Graaff (1997) reported significant correlations between aptitude and both explicit and implicit instruction. However, the implicit instruction, which consisted of form-focused activities such as gap-filling, target structure comprehension, etc., may have encouraged explicit learning. Robinson (1997, 2002) demonstrated that explicit treatments such as rule explanation and rule search were more likely to draw on aptitude than implicit treatments such as memory (asking learners to memorize linguistic stimuli) and incidental learning (comprehension activities) tasks.

APTITUDE AND AGE

Age has been found to be a significant predictor of ultimate L2 attainment: the earlier one starts to learn a second language, the more likely it is for the learner to achieve native-like proficiency. While there has been abundant evidence for age effects, the reason behind this phenomenon remains to be unearthed (Granena and Long, 2012). One speculation is that children and adults learn differently – whereas children have access to domain-specific language learning abilities that enable them to learn a second language effortlessly and unconsciously, adults have lost that kind of ability and have to rely on alternative abilities such as language aptitude, which is essential for conscious and analytic learning (see Chapters 1 and 3). This explanation forms the core of Bley-Vroman's Fundamental Difference Hypothesis (1990), from which two predictions can be generated:

1. Language aptitude is only correlated with adult learning but not child SLA.
2. Adult learners with high attainment have high language aptitude.

In general, the two predictions have been confirmed by the research that has been carried out to date, despite some mixed results for (1) and some methodological variations across existing studies. DeKeyser (2000) is the first to investigate the relation of aptitude to age effects. He reported that the analytic ability component of aptitude was significantly correlated with adult learners' L2 achievements (measured through a grammaticality judgement test, or GJT) but not with child learners', and that four out of the five with exceptional L2 attainment also had exceptional aptitude. Abrahamsson and Hyltenstam (2008) investigated how aptitude was drawn upon by learners who were perceived as native speakers of the target language in terms of oral communication skills, but who started to learn the language at different ages. The results revealed that whereas the early starters' aptitude scores were varied and spread out, all the late starters had high aptitude. This finding suggests that in order to achieve native-like oral proficiency, aptitude is not important if one starts to learn a second language at a young age, but it is essential if one starts late. However, unlike DeKeyser, Abrahamsson and Hyltenstam detected a significant correlation between early starters' GJT scores and their aptitude scores, but no such correlation was found for late starters. A third study, conducted by Granena and Long (2012), demonstrated that aptitude was relevant only to adult learners' achievements in lexis and collocation, but not to any of the two other, younger groups' achievements in any aspect of proficiency.

Methodological commonalities and disparities exist between the above studies. They all examined the relationship between aptitude and ultimate L2 attainment, involved learners who started to learn a second language in naturalistic environments (that is, they are exposed to the language in their daily life, not simply in language classes), and divided learners into different age groups. However, the studies differ in a number of aspects. For example, aptitude was measured through the LLAMA test in Abrahamsson and Hyltenstam (2008) and Granena and Long (2012), but through the Words in Sentences subtest of a Hungarian aptitude battery in DeKeyser (2000). L2 proficiency was measured via an aural GJT in DeKeyser (2000), through both an aural and a written GJT in Abrahamsson and Hyltenstam (2008), and by means of a number of tests targeting different aspects of L2 learning including morphosyntax, lexis, and pronunciation in Granena and Long (2012). Also, learners were split into age groups based on different criteria: two groups were formed in Abrahamsson and Hyltenstam (2008), depending on whether they started to learn the L2 before or after 12 years; in DeKeyser (2000) the cutoff point was 16 years; and Granena and Long (2012) divided learners into three groups: 3–6, 7–15, and 16–29.

IMPLICATIONS FOR TEACHING AND ASSESSMENT

The findings of the different streams of aptitude research have valuable pedagogical implications. To begin with, aptitude has been found to be a strong predictor of learning success, which led Carroll (1990) to suggest several ways learners' aptitude scores can be used, including selecting learners for language programs where learners are expected to master a foreign language within a short period; ensuring equivalence of aptitude when placing learners into different classes; and diagnosing learning difficulties for the purpose of waiving foreign language requirements. Teachers and practitioners can also provide advice on what strategies learners should adopt, based on their aptitude profiles. For example, for learners with high analytic ability, it might be advisable to engage in activities that require analysing the structure of language; for those strong in memory, they may benefit more from memorizing chunks of text.

The research shows that high-aptitude learners benefit more from inductive instruction and low-aptitude learners more from deductive instruction. In order not to disadvantage either group of learners, teachers may combine these two approaches.

For example, they may start by asking learners to induce a grammar rule, then provide feedback and rule explanation, and finally follow up with practice activities involving rule application. Teachers may also assign deductive or inductive tasks depending on learners' aptitude levels, either in class when students work in groups or after class for homework. For instance, they may provide input materials – listening or reading – to high-aptitude learners and ask them to extrapolate linguistic patterns or regularities, and ask low-aptitude learners to work on the same material but provide an *a priori* explanation on the patterns and regularities.

The finding that aptitude is more likely to be implicated in explicit than implicit instruction suggests that learners with low aptitude may be disadvantaged in explicit instruction. However, the research on the effectiveness of instruction type (e.g., Li, 2010; Norris and Orgega, 2000) has demonstrated a superior effect for explicit instruction in comparison with implicit instruction, at least in terms of immediate or short-term effects. Therefore, it would seem advisable to utilize more explicit instruction. However, given the caveats that instructional treatments in SLA research tend to be short, which favours explicit learning, and that SLA researchers tend to assess treatment effects using measures of explicit knowledge, the superior effects of explicit instruction are not unequivocal. The solution at the moment seems to be striking a balance between the two instruction types by integrating explicit and implicit instruction and mixing awareness-raising, form-focused tasks with meaning-primary, communicative tasks.

The above recommendations lead to another perspective on how to cater to learners' individual differences in language aptitude, that is, embracing an eclectic approach that encompasses a variety of instructional devices and classroom tasks, so that learners of diverse aptitude profiles can all benefit to a certain extent. An eclectic approach is of particular value in settings where teachers face large groups and/or it is difficult to have an accurate assessment of learners' aptitude strengths or weaknesses.

The studies on age and aptitude interaction showed that aptitude is only relevant for adult learners, not child learners. In other words, adults learn a second language by drawing on a set of abilities essential for conscious learning, but children learn differently, most probably by drawing on abilities important for unconscious learning. It follows that teachers of child language classes should avoid instruction that contains or requires a large amount of metalinguistic knowledge, or instruction that predisposes learners to engage in conscious processing of linguistic forms. They do not rely on, and have not developed, the analytic learning abilities that characterize adult learning. Children benefit most from meaning-oriented instruction where they learn a language incidentally through exposure to the language and unconscious computation of linguistic input.

CONCLUSION

This chapter has provided an up-to-date, comprehensive synthesis of the research on the associations between language aptitude and L2 attainment. Most of the research, however, is predictive, in that it examines the correlations between aptitude and the final learning outcome. There needs to be more interactional research that explores what aptitude components are important in what learning conditions. There is also a lack of research on whether aptitude and aptitude components have differential effects on learners at different stages of L2 development. Finally, it has become clear that traditional aptitude is a set of explicit/conscious learning abilities, and the need arises to explore implicit language learning abilities. This area of research is in its infancy, and its potential and value is inestimable.

Discussion Questions

1. Does the influence of aptitude decline with the increase of learner proficiency?

2. Do different aptitude components play different roles at different stages of learning?

3. Is there a set of abilities central to implicit learning that is different from those measured by traditional aptitude tests?

Key Readings

DeKeyser, R., & Koeth, J. (2011). Cognitive aptitudes for second language learning. In E. Hinkel (Ed.), *Handbook of Research in Second Language Teaching and Learning, Volume II* (pp. 395–406). New York: Routledge.

Li, S. (2016). The construct validity of language aptitude. *Studies in Second Language Acquisition, 38*, 801–842.

Linck, J., Hughes, M. M., Campbell, S. G., Silbert, N. H., Tare, M., Jackson, S. R., Smith, B. K., Bunting, M. F. & Doughty, C.J. (2013). Hi-LAB: A new measure of aptitude for high-level language proficiency. *Language Learning*, 63(3), 530–566.

Robinson, P. (2001). Individual differences, cognitive abilities, aptitude complexes and learning conditions in second language acquisition. *Second Language Research*, 17(4), 368–392.

Skehan, P. (2012). Language aptitude. In S. Gass & A. Mackey (Eds.), *The Routledge Handbook of Second Language Acquisition* (pp. 381–395). New York: Routledge.

References

Abrahamsson, N., & Hyltenstam, K. (2008). The robustness of aptitude effects in near-native second language acquisition. *Studies in Second Language Acquisition*, 30, 481–509.

Bley-Vroman, R. (1990). The logical problem of foreign language learning. *Linguistic Analysis*, 20, 3–49.

Carpenter, H. S. (2008). *A Behavioural and Electrophysiological Investigation of Different Aptitudes for L2 Grammar in Learners Equated for Proficiency Level*. Unpublished doctoral dissertation, Georgetown University.

Carroll, J. B. (1990). Cognitive abilities in foreign language aptitude: Then and now. In T. Parry & C. Stansfield (Eds.), *Language Aptitude Reconsidered* (pp. 11–29). Englewood Cliffs, NJ: Prentice Hall Regents.

Carroll, J. B., & Sapon, S. (1959). *Modern Language Aptitude Test*. New York: The Psychological Corporation / Harcourt Brace Jovanovich.

De Graaff, R. (1997). The *experanto* experiment: Effects of explicit instruction on second language acquisition. *Studies in Second Language Acquisition*, 19, 249–276.

DeKeyser, R. M. (2000). The robustness of critical period effects in second language acquisition. *Studies in Second Language Acquisition*, 22(4), 499–533.

Erlam, R. (2005). Language aptitude and its relationship to instructional effectiveness in second language acquisition. *Language Teaching Research*, 9(2), 147–171.

Granena, G., & Long, M. H. (2012). Age of onset, length of residence, language aptitude, and ultimate L2 attainment in three linguistic domains. *Second Language Research*, 29(3), 311–343.

Harley, B., & Hart, D. (1997). Language aptitude and second language proficiency in classroom learners of different starting ages. *Studies in Second Language Acquisition*, 19(3), 379–400.

Hwu, F., & Sun, S. (2012). The aptitude-treatment interaction effects on the learning of grammar rules. *System*, 40, 505–521.

Li, S. (2010). The effectiveness of corrective feedback in SLA: A meta-analysis. *Language Learning*, 60, 309–365.

Li, S. (2015a). The associations between language aptitude and second language grammar acquisition: A meta-analytic review of five decades of research. *Applied Linguistics*, 36, 385–408.

Li, S. (2015b). The differential roles of language analytic ability and working memory in mediating the effects of two types of feedback on the acquisition of an opaque linguistic structure. In C. Sanz & B. Lado (Eds.), *Individual Differences, L2 Development and Language Program Administration: From Theory to Application* (pp. 32–52). Stamford, CT: Cengage Learning.

Li, S. (2016). The construct validity of language aptitude. *Studies in Second Language Acquisition*, 38, 801–842.

Li, S. (2017). Cognitive differences and ISLA. In S. Loewen & M. Sato (Eds.), *The Routledge Handbook of Instructed Second Language Acquisition* (pp. 396–417). New York: Routledge.

Li, S. (in press). The effects of cognitive aptitudes on the process and product of L2 interaction: A synthetic review. In L. Gurzynski-Weiss (Ed.), *Expanding Individual Difference Research in the Interaction Approach: Investigating Learners, Instructors, and Other Interlocutors*. Amsterdam/Philadelphia: John Benjamins.

Linck, J., Hughes, M. M., Campbell, S. G., Silbert, N. H., Tare, M., Jackson, S. R., Smith, B. K., Bunting, M. F. and Doughty, C.J. (2013). Hi-LAB: A new measure of aptitude for high-level language proficiency. *Language Learning*, 63(3), 530–566.

Long, M. (2015). *Second Language Acquisition and Task-Based Language Teaching*. Oxford: Wiley-Blackwell.

Lyster, R., & Ranta, L. (1997). Corrective feedback and learner uptake. *Studies in Second Language Acquisition*, 19, 37–66.

Norris, J., & Ortega, L. (2000). Effectiveness of L2 instruction: A research synthesis and quantitative meta-analysis. *Language Learning*, 50, 417–528.

Ranta, L. (2002). The role of learners' language analytic ability in the communicative classroom. In P. Robinson (Ed.), *Individual Differences and Instructed Language Learning* (pp. 159–180). Amsterdam: John Benjamins.

Robinson, P. (1997). Individual differences and the fundamental similarity of implicit and explicit adult second language learning. *Language Learning*, 47, 45–99.

Robinson, P (2002). Effects of individual differences in intelligence, aptitude and working memory on adult incidental SLA. In P. Robinson (Ed.), *Individual Differences and Instructed Language Learning* (pp. 212–266). Amsterdam: John Benjamins.

Robinson, P. (Ed.) (2011). *Second Language Task Complexity*. Philadelphia: John Benjamins.

Skehan, P. (2012). Language aptitude. In S. Gass & A. Mackey (Eds.), *The Routledge Handbook of Second Language Acquisition* (pp. 381–395). New York: Routledge.

Suzuki, Y., & DeKeyser, R. (2015). Comparing elicited imitation and word monitoring as measures of implicit knowledge. *Language Learning*, 65, 860–895.

Yalçın, Ş., Çeçen, S., & Erçetin, G. (2016). The relationship between aptitude and working memory: an instructed SLA context. *Language Awareness*. https://doi.org/10.1080/09658416.2015.1122026

Language Anxiety

Elaine K. Horwitz and Lama Nassif

INTRODUCTION

Most people have experienced anxiety at some time in their lives, and, unfortunately, some people experience anxiety on a daily basis. Many things can be the source of anxiety: some people react very negatively to small spaces, many people worry about tests, and some people are just more generally anxious than others. When people consistently have an anxiety reaction to a particular thing like small spaces or tests, psychologists call that type of anxiety a "situation-specific anxiety". Individuals who experience situation-specific anxieties do not generally have anxious personalities; that is, they are not simply anxious by nature, but they experience anxiety with respect to a particular object. With respect to the focus of this guide, second/foreign language learning has been found to be a situation-specific anxiety for some people.

Learning and using a new language can be an unsettling experience for many people. Many language learners, and even language teachers, report that learning or using their second language causes them to feel uncomfortable, and sometimes more severely, like an inauthentic version of themselves. In addition to the uncomfortable feelings that some learners may experience, a number of studies have found that language learners who report higher levels of second language anxiety tend to achieve lower levels of language proficiency and get lower grades in their language classes. Some anxious learners discontinue language study as soon as they can, or avoid using the language, even when they have the opportunity. Less is known about the influence of anxiety on learners who must do all their learning through their second language. For those second language learners, anxiety about language learning can not only limit their language progress, but also their achievement in content learning, and ultimately their entire academic experience.

Since the recognition of a situation-specific language learning anxiety, studies on the influence of anxiety on L2 learning have generally found moderate negative associations between anxiety and second language achievement. Some studies have also found negative associations between anxiety and various aspects of second language learning, such as listening or reading. This chapter describes how anxiety relates to language learning, offers suggestions for alleviating anxiety, and raises questions for future language teaching approaches and research.

OVERVIEW

Second language teachers and researchers have been interested in the role of anxiety in language learning for at least 50 years. Language learners have probably been interested in the issue since people began learning second languages! A number of studies in the 1960s and 1970s examined the possibility that anxiety would inhibit L2 learning, but contrary to expectations, these studies did not find a consistent negative association between anxiety and second language achievement. In fact, sometimes higher anxiety levels were found to be associated with higher levels of second language achievement. These results were considered puzzling until 1978, when Thomas Scovel pointed out that there are many kinds and sources of anxiety and that the various studies up until that time had focused on different types of anxiety. In 1986, Horwitz, Horwitz, and Cope further explained the discrepant findings by introducing the prospect of a situation-specific reaction to language learning. They originally used the term Foreign Language Anxiety (FLA), but went on to use the term Language Anxiety (LA) to encompass both foreign and second language learning (Horwitz and Young, 1991). Importantly, Horwitz, Horwitz, and Cope described LA as a distinct type of anxiety and not simply a combination of other seemingly related specific anxieties such as (first language) communication apprehension (McCroskey, 1970), test anxiety (Sarason, 1978), or fear of negative evaluation (Watson and Friend, 1969), transferred to language learning. To them, LA was an assembly of "self-perceptions, beliefs, feeling, and behaviors related to classroom language learning arising from the uniqueness of the language learning process" (p. 128). They attributed LA to the discomfort some learners experience when they perceive a disparity between their true selves and the more limited self they are able to communicate through the second language (Horwitz, 1996; Horwitz, Horwitz, and Cope 1986).

Once LA was recognized as a situation-specific anxiety, researchers were naturally interested in examining how anxious language learners performed in language classes. Since that time, a great number of studies concluded that LA is negatively associated with final grades in language courses as well as other measures of language proficiency. Such negative relationships have been found in a variety of languages including: Arabic (Elkhafaifi, 2005); Chinese (Luo, 2013; Zhao, Dynia, and Guo, 2013); English (Cheng, Horwitz, and Schallert, 1999; Kim, 2009); French and Spanish (Horwitz, 1986); Japanese (Aida, 1994; Saito and Samimy, 1996); and Spanish, Russian, and Japanese (Saito, Horwitz, and Garza, 1999).

It appears that some student groups tend to have higher levels of LA than others. For example, Aida (1994) and Koul, Roy, Kaewkuekool, and Ploisawaschai (2009) found that females tended to have higher levels of anxiety than males. Aida also found, perhaps not surprisingly, that students in required classes were more anxious than students in elective classes. Marcos-Llinás and Garau (2009) found that the advanced Spanish students had higher levels of anxiety than either the beginner or the intermediate students in their study. They suggested that the advanced students, who were taking Spanish as a major or minor, felt more pressure to do well, as they were more likely to actually interact with Spanish speakers. Saito and Samimy (1996) also found anxiety differences according to the level of instruction. The advanced Japanese students in their study had the highest anxiety levels, followed by the beginner students, while the intermediate students had the lowest anxiety levels. In contrast to these findings, with the exception of first-semester distance learners,

Pichette (2009) did not find differences in LA across instructional levels. Cultural expectations may contribute to LA (Horwitz, 2001). Horwitz (1986), Aida (1994), and Saito, et al., (1999) reported similar anxiety scores for American learners of various foreign languages, but Truitt (1995) found higher anxiety levels among Korean learners of English, and Kunt (1997) found lower levels of LA in Turkish EFL students.

It is important to note the frequency of LA. In general, studies have found that between 30 and 40% of learners from a variety of cultural backgrounds experience language anxiety. Thus, while many learners experience anxiety at some point in the course of language learning, it is important to recognize that the majority of learners do not identify as language-anxious. At the same time, 30 to 40% of learners represent a substantial population that requires the sincere consideration of the language teaching profession. We also want to point out that this percentage of anxious language learners, as well as the majority of research that we report in this chapter, describes college-age foreign language learners and not K-12 second language learners.

KEY LEARNING ISSUES

SOURCES OF LANGUAGE ANXIETY

Anxious language learners report a number of reasons for their anxiety. Price (1991) asked anxious language learners what it was like to be anxious, and their responses were sometimes heartbreaking, even likening language classes to prisons. Several reported that their greatest source of anxiety was speaking the language in front of their peers and expressed frustration with their inability to communicate effectively, despite seeing themselves as intelligent adults. More anxious language learners may also have low perceptions of their intellectual ability, as well as of their overall scholastic and foreign language competence (Bailey, Onwuegbuzie, and Daley, 2000). Students' negative perceptions of their grammatical accuracy, and of their classmates' 'superior' language ability, have also been reported as sources of anxiety (Ewald, 2007). In terms of classroom learning, Gregersen (2003) reported that anxious students made more errors, corrected themselves more often, recognized fewer errors in a stimulated recall situation, overestimated the number of errors that they made, and resorted to their native language more frequently.

Several studies have documented a number of factors associated with higher or lower levels of LA. Matsuda and Gobel (2004) found that EFL students with overseas experience were less anxious speaking English than students without overseas experience, but it is also possible that more confident students chose to participate in overseas experiences. The latter interpretation would be supported by Lui and Jackson's (2008) finding that willingness to communicate in the second language was associated with lower levels of LA. Gregersen and Horwitz (2002) reported a link between perfectionism and LA in pre-service English teachers in Chile. On an optimistic note, Dewaele, Petrides and Furnham (2008) concluded that larger social circumstances, such as the availability of supportive conversational partners and L2 role models, may help people overcome LA (see also Chapter 11).

Only a small number of studies have compared student anxiety levels under different instructional conditions. Pichette (2009) did not find differences in either general LA or reading anxiety in students enrolled in distance-learning and regular language classes, but Kim (2009) found higher levels of anxiety in students in a conversation class than in a reading class. (Pichette found somewhat higher levels of writing anxiety in the distance learners, but the difference did not reach significance.) In two studies in the USA, middle school English learners reported lower levels of anxiety in their ESL classes than in their mainstream content classes (Pappamihiel, 2001, 2002). This difference was more pronounced in females.

ANXIETIES ASSOCIATED WITH LISTENING, READING, AND WRITING

It appears that some students may only experience anxiety, or experience more pronounced anxiety, during some aspects of language learning. As noted throughout this chapter, speaking is often cited by students as the most anxiety-provoking aspect of second language learning (see also Chapter 22), but some students seem to be especially anxious during the development of other aspects of language learning, specifically listening, reading, and writing. Interestingly, these skill-specific anxieties seem to be reasonably independent of general LA.

Saito et al., (1999) hypothesized the existence of an anxiety response to second language reading and found that reading anxiety was negatively associated with final course grades in Russian, Japanese, and Spanish. Zhao et al. (2013) found that reading anxiety was negatively associated with actual reading performance in Chinese. Both studies suggested a role for unfamiliar scripts in reading anxiety, but Sellers (2000) reported that more anxious English-speaking students of Spanish recalled less passage content and fewer main ideas than low-anxiety participants. The more anxious learners also experienced more off-task thoughts. Thus, reading anxiety does not seem to be restricted to situations when learners are dealing with unfamiliar scripts.

In terms of listening and writing, Elkhafaifi (2005) reported a negative association between listening anxiety and both listening comprehension and final course grades in Arabic learners. Since Arabic is a less commonly taught language in the USA, Elkhafaifi thought that the unfamiliar writing and phonological systems, as well as the unfamiliar cultural context of Arabic, played roles in inducing anxiety. Cheng et al., (1999) investigated general LA and L2 writing anxiety in relation to speaking and writing achievement. Interestingly, writing anxiety had negative correlations with both speaking and writing achievement, and low self-confidence in speaking and writing in English were the strongest predictors of speaking and writing course grades.

IMPLICATIONS FOR TEACHING AND ASSESSMENT

A number of studies have investigated how anxiety impacts L2 speech. Steinberg and Horwitz (1986) found a qualitative difference in how language learners experiencing anxiety-inducing and standard conditions approached second language speaking. The anxious participants described pictures in a less interpretive and more objective manner than their low-anxiety counterparts, suggesting that anxiety causes students to be less adventurous and creative in their language use. Similarly, several participants in Gregersen and Horwitz's (2002) study reported that they were able to hear and speak more easily when they were not feeling anxious. Other studies have suggested negative effects on cognitive processing in the production of second language speech. For example, Sheen (2008) found that the effectiveness of teacher recasts varied based on students' levels of LA. Low-anxiety participants showed more attention to the target form (English articles) in the teacher feedback and increased more their use of articles in their later speech than high-anxiety participants.

When considering the role of anxiety in any kind of learning, it is important to recognize the possibility that anxiety is a result of poor learning rather than its cause. In a series of papers, Lenore Ganschow and Richard Sparks and their colleagues proposed that people with subtle language learning disabilities do more poorly in language learning and naturally feel anxious as a result of their poor learning. While we agree that it is possible that some people have cognitive disadvantages in language learning (see Chapter 4), we think it is unlikely that the 30 to 40 percent of learners who report LA, many from highly selective universities, all have such disabilities (see MacIntyre, 1995a,1995b and Horwitz, 2000 for responses, and Sparks and Ganschow, 2007 for a review of this literature). It is also possible that anxiety interferes with language production but not language learning itself. That would mean that anxious and non-anxious students learn equally well, but anxiety inhibits the ability of anxious learners to demonstrate what they have learned. This explanation also seems unlikely, since MacIntyre and Gardner (1994) found that anxiety interfered with language encoding, processing, and retrieval processes in second language learners of French. Regardless of any complications in the relationship between LA and second language learning, the essential consideration in dealing with anxious language learners is their feelings of discomfort and even distress in the course of language learning.

It appears that the learning environment and, particularly, the instructor are key in reducing LA. Language learners at different levels of instruction and in different learning contexts cite the teacher as one of the most, if not the most, important factors in creating a positive classroom atmosphere (Ewald, 2007; Frantzen and Magnan, 2005). MacIntyre and Gregersen (2012) suggest that teachers may "approach influencing students' emotions in at least two ways: (a) set up conditions to provoke a reaction; and (b) work with the cognition that modifies the emotional schema" (p. 200). Teachers could, therefore, provide stimulating, enjoyable, and positively challenging class activities within a collaborative and friendly classroom environment that promotes learners' strengths. Nassif (2014) found that within such a learning environment, moderate levels of LA were associated with higher levels of noticing and production of L2 forms. In addition, promoting learners' self-esteem and empowering them to take control of their learning through the use of successful learning strategies is also expected to help them manage their anxieties. Affective strategies that help learners regulate their emotions, and social strategies that direct them on how to learn with others (Oxford, 1990), are no less important than cognitive and metacognitive strategies that regulate the L2 learning process (see Horwitz, 2013 for more suggestions for alleviating student and teacher LA.)

It is especially important that future research addresses the impact of LA on K-12 second language learners, since these learners are especially vulnerable to negative outcomes from anxiety. In one of the few studies that have addressed this population, Mejias, Applbaum, Applbaum, and Trotter (1991) found that bilingual Hispanic high school and college students in the USA felt uncomfortable speaking either English or Spanish, and speculated that LA contributes to high school drop-out rates in this population. With more children across the world undergoing schooling in a new language, it is essential that the impact of anxiety on both language and academic learning be better understood.

CONCLUSION

This chapter has presented an overview of the literature on LA, especially research findings on how LA is related to other learner characteristics and various aspects of the language learning process. It described sources of LA, as well as several related anxieties that some learners experience in the development of specific language skills.

Although this chapter has identified a number of reasons that students feel anxious in the course of language learning, it is important to recognize that anxieties are fears that are, at least, somewhat out of proportion to any real impact of the anxiety source. This reality implies that some people will feel anxious, no matter what instructional modifications are made. We, therefore, return to Horwitz, Horwitz, and Cope's (1986) original conceptualization that LA results from people's discomfort with the discrepancy they perceive between their authentic selves and the 'self' they are able to present to the world through the new language. For these individuals, the most effective response to anxiety is probably caring teachers who acknowledge the existence of LA and listen empathetically to their students' feelings and concerns.

Discussion Questions

1. Have you experienced anxiety when learning or using a second language?

2. What did you do to make yourself feel more comfortable?

3. Why do you think language learning makes some people feel anxious?

4. How does anxiety impact second language learners who must learn content through their new language?

Key Readings

Horwitz, E. K. (1996). Even teachers get the blues: Recognizing and alleviating language teachers' feelings of foreign language anxiety. *Foreign Language Annals,* 29(3), 365–372.

Horwitz, E. K. (2013). *Becoming a Language Teacher: A Practical Guide to Second Language Learning and Teaching* (2nd ed.). Upper Saddle River, NJ: Pearson.

Horwitz, E. K., Horwitz, M. B., & Cope, J. (1986). Foreign language classroom anxiety. *The Modern Language Journal,* 70(2), 125–132.

Horwitz, E. K., Tallon, M., & Luo, H., (2010). Foreign language anxiety. In J. Cassady (Ed.), *Anxiety in Schools: The Causes, Consequences, and Solutions for Academic Anxieties* (pp. 96–115). New York: Peter Lang.

MacIntyre, P., & Gregersen, T. (2012). Emotions that facilitate language learning: The positive-broadening power of the imagination. *Studies in Second Language Learning and Teaching,* 2(2), 193–213.

References

Aida, Y. (1994). Examination of Horwitz & Cope's construct of foreign language anxiety: The case of students of Japanese. *The Modern Language Journal,* 78(2), 155–168.

Bailey, P., Onwuegbuzie, A., & Daley, C. (2000). Correlates of anxiety at three stages of the foreign language learning process. *Journal of Language and Social Psychology,* 19(4), 474–490.

Cheng, Y. S., Horwitz, E. K., & Schallert, D. L. (1999). Language anxiety: Differentiating writing and speaking components. *Language Learning,* 49(1), 417–446.

Dewaele, J. M., Petrides, K. V., & Furnham, A. (2008). Effects of trait emotional intelligence and sociobiographical variables on communicative anxiety and foreign language anxiety among adult multilinguals: A review and empirical investigation. *Language Learning,* 58(4), 911–960.

Elkhafaifi, H. (2005). Listening comprehension and anxiety in the Arabic language classroom. *The Modern Language Journal,* 89(2), 206–220.

Ewald, J. D. (2007). Foreign language learning anxiety in upper-level classes: Involving students as researchers. *Foreign Language Annals,* 40(1), 122–142.

Frantzen, D., & Magnan, S. S. (2005). Anxiety and the true beginner–false beginner dynamic in beginning French and Spanish classes. *Foreign Language Annals,* 38(2), 171–186.

Gregersen, T. (2003). To err is human: A reminder to teachers of language-anxious students. *Foreign Language Annals,* 36(1), 25–32.

Gregersen, T., & Horwitz, E. K. (2002). Language learning and perfectionism: Anxious and non-anxious language learners' reactions to their own oral performance. *The Modern Language Journal,* 86(4), 562–570.

Horwitz, E. K. (1986). Preliminary evidence for the reliability and validity of a foreign language anxiety scale. *TESOL Quarterly*, 20(3), 559–56.

Horwitz, E. K. (1996). Even teachers get the blues: Recognizing and alleviating language teachers' feelings of foreign language anxiety. *Foreign Language Annals*, 29(3), 365–372.

Horwitz, E. K. (2000). It ain't over 'til it's over: On foreign language anxiety, first language deficits, and the confounding of variables. *The Modern Language Journal*, 84(2), 256–259.

Horwitz, E. K. (2001). Language anxiety and achievement. *Annual Review of Applied Linguistics*, 21, 112–126.

Horwitz, E. K. (2013). *Becoming a Language Teacher: A Practical Guide to Second Language Learning and Teaching* (2nd ed.). Upper Saddle River, NJ: Pearson.

Horwitz, E. K., Horwitz, M. B., & Cope, J. (1986). Foreign language classroom anxiety. *The Modern Language Journal*, 70(2), 125–132.

Horwitz, E. K., & Young, D.J. (1991). Preface. In E. K. Horwitz & D. J. Young (Eds.), *Language Anxiety: From Theory and Research to Classroom Implications* (pp. xii–xiv). Englewood Cliffs, NJ: Prentice Hall.

Kim, S. (2009). Questioning the stability of foreign language classroom anxiety and motivation across different classroom contexts. *Foreign Language Annals*, 42(1), 138–157.

Koul, R., Roy, L., Kaewkuekool, S., & Ploisawaschai, S. (2009). Multiple goal orientations and foreign language anxiety. *System*, 37(4), 676–688.

Kunt, N. (1997). Anxiety and beliefs about language learning: A study of Turkish-speaking university students learning English in North Cyprus. *Applied Psycholinguistics*, 20, 217–239.

Lui, M., & Jackson, J. (2008). An exploration of Chinese EFL learners' unwillingness to communicate and foreign language anxiety. *The Modern Language Journal*, 92(1), 71–86.

Luo, H. (2013). Foreign language anxiety: past and future. *Chinese Journal of Applied Linguistics*, 36, 442–464.

MacIntyre, P. D. (1995a). How does anxiety affect second language learning? A reply to Sparks and Ganschow. *The Modern Language Journal*, 79(1), 90–99.

MacIntyre, P. D. (1995b). On seeing the forest and the trees: A rejoinder to Sparks and Ganschow. *The Modern Language Journal*, 79(2), 245–248.

MacIntyre, P. D., & Gardner, R. C. (1994). The subtle effects of language anxiety on cognitive processing in the second language. *Language Learning*, 44(2), 283–305.

MacIntyre, P., & Gregersen, T. (2012). Emotions that facilitate language learning: The positive-broadening power of the imagination. *Studies in Second Language Learning and Teaching*, 2(2), 193–213.

Marcos-Llinás, M., & Garau, M. J. (2009). Effects of language anxiety on three proficiency-level courses of Spanish as a foreign language. *Foreign Language Annals*, 42(1), 94–111.

Matsuda, S., & Gobel, P. (2004). Anxiety and predictors of performance in the foreign language classroom. *System*, 32(1), 21–36.

McCroskey, J. C. (1970). Measures of communication-bound anxiety. *Speech Monographs*, 37, 269–277.

Mejias, H., Applbaum, R. L., Applbaum, S. J., & Trotter, R. T. (1991). Oral communication apprehension and Hispanics: An exploration of oral communication apprehension of Mexican American students in Texas. In E. K. Horwitz & D. J. Young (Eds.), *Language Anxiety: From Theory and Research to Classroom Implications.* Englewood Cliffs, NJ: Prentice Hall.

Nassif, L. (2014). *Anxiety in the Noticing and Production of L2 Forms: A Study of Beginning Learners of Arabic.* Unpublished doctoral dissertation, University of Texas at Austin.

Oxford, R. L. (1990). *Language Learning Strategies: What Every Teacher Should Know.* Boston, MA: Heinle & Heinle.

Pappamihiel, N. E. (2001). Moving from the ESL classroom into the mainstream: An investigation of English language anxiety in Mexican girls. *Bilingual Research Journal*, 25(1-2), 31–38.

Pappamihiel, N. E. (2002). English as a second language students and English language anxiety: Issues in the mainstream classroom. *Research in the Teaching of English*, 36(3), 327–355.

Pichette, F. (2009). Second language anxiety and distance language learning. *Foreign Language Annals*, 42(1), 77–93.

Price, M. L. (1991). The subjective experience of foreign language anxiety: Interviews with highly anxious students. In E. K. Horwitz & D. J. Young (Eds.), *Language Anxiety: From Theory and Research to Classroom Implications* (pp. 101–108). Englewood Cliffs, NJ: Prentice Hall.

Saito, Y., Horwitz, E. K., & Garza, T. J. (1999). Foreign language reading anxiety. *The Modern Language Journal*, 83(2), 202–218.

Saito, Y., & Samimy, K. (1996). Foreign language anxiety and language performance: A study of learner anxiety in beginning, intermediate, and advanced-level college students of Japanese. *Foreign Language Annals*, 29(2), 239–251.

Sarason, I. G. (1978). The test anxiety scale: Concept and research. In C. D. Spielberger & I. G. Sarason (Eds.), *Stress and Anxiety, Volume 5* (pp. 193–216). New York: John Wiley & Sons.

Scovel, T. (1978). The effect of affect on foreign language learning: A review of the anxiety research. *Language Learning*, 28(1), 129–142.

Sellers, V. D. (2000). Anxiety and reading comprehension in Spanish as a foreign language. *Foreign Language Annals*, 33(5), 512–521.

Sheen, Y. (2008). Recasts, language anxiety, modified output, and L2 learning. *Language Learning*, 58(4), 835–874.

Sparks, R. L., & Ganschow, L. (2007). Is the foreign language classroom anxiety scale measuring anxiety or language skills? *Foreign Language Annals*, 40(2), 260–287.

Steinberg, F., & Horwitz, E. K. (1986). The effect of induced anxiety on the denotative and interpretive content of second language speech. *TESOL Quarterly*, 20(1), 131–136.

Truitt, S.N. (1995). Beliefs about language learning: A study of Korean university students' learning beliefs. *Texas Papers in Foreign Language Education*, 2(1), 1–14. (ERIC Document Reproduction Service No. ED416703)

Watson, D., & Friend, R. (1969). Measurement of social-evaluative anxiety. *Journal of Consulting and Clinical Psychology*, 33(4), 448–457.

Zhao. A., Dynia, J., & Guo. Y. (2013). Foreign language reading anxiety: Chinese as a foreign language in the United States. *The Modern Language Journal*, 97(3), 764–778.

CHAPTER 9

Language Learning Strategies

Rebecca L. Oxford

INTRODUCTION

Simply stated, language learning strategies (LLS; in this chapter, LLS refers to the plural form) are purposeful mental actions (sometimes accompanied by observable behaviors) used by a learner to regulate his or her second or foreign language (L2) learning. I offer a more formal definition of LLS later. Cohen (2017) and Cohen and Macaro (2007) used the term 'language *learner* strategies' to emphasize that a learner might use strategies without having the purpose of learning, but the present chapter focuses on strategies for learning.

In this chapter, the overview mentions complexity in relation to LLS, offers a brief picture of strategy-linked controversies, presents an encompassing definition of LLS, and discusses strategy flexibility. The section on key learning issues portrays two LLS of two highly strategic L2 learners, and presents the innovative concept of 'the soul of strategies', with components ranging from agency to hope. The rest of the chapter provides implications for teaching and assessing LLS, raises questions for further discussion, and offers key readings.

OVERVIEW

This overview begins with the issues of complexity and controversy, offers a formal definition of LLS, and paints a portrait of strategy flexibility.

COMPLEXITY

Learners employ LLS in many complex contexts: in classrooms, at home, at the gym, at the library, online, on the bus, and sometimes in the synagogue, temple, mosque, or church. The choice of LLS is influenced by complex factors such as cultural beliefs and expectations, educational policies, local influences, task requirements, personal preferences, learning opportunities, and individual differences in age, gender, education level, and social class. LLS complexity is exponentiated by numerous, often conflicting LLS definitions, theories, policies, procedures (e.g., strategy instruction and assessment), and data sources, as well as by the people involved (e.g., teachers, administrators, learners, and family members). These factors and more contribute to an immense, complex, multifaceted, diverse prism of LLS. Gu (2012) noted that although certain L2 scholars derided the LLS construct for lack of centeredness on a single theory or definition, conceptual diversity is a clear and meaningful reality. After all, he argued, the educational psychology field happily accepted diverse definitions of learning strategies and different theoretical perspectives for strategies.

CONTROVERSIES

Repeated calls for greater definitional clarity and true coordination of LLS definitions have often occurred (e.g., Cohen, 2014; Cohen and Macaro, 2007; Dörnyei, 2005; Dörnyei and Skehan, 2003; Macaro, 2006; Oxford, 1990, 2011, 2017; Oxford and Cohen, 1992), but the response of the LLS field has been slow. In my view, the first unified, theoretically integrated LLS definition arrived only recently (Oxford, 2017), based on my in-depth, solo investigation of 33 strategy definitions in 2016.

Certain criticisms of LLS have been oblique, abstract, or unsupported by evidence. For instance, Dörnyei and Skehan (2003) mentioned LLS in the same breath as 'superordinate magic tools' (p. 610). Dörnyei (2005) wrote that LLS are not strategic, that LLS are 'products' instead of processes (thus clashing with works by O'Malley and Chamot, 1990, and Oxford, 1990), that LLS were sidelined by educational psychologists in favor of self-regulation (several major reviews of research and theory contradict this; see Oxford, 2017), and, finally, that LLS do not even exist, although thousands of LLS dissertations, articles, chapters, and books, as well as countless learners' lives, suggest otherwise. Dörnyei and Ryan (2015) showed a gentler, kinder approach to LLS, but still seemed to assert that LLS are not suitable for research exploration. Some of these issues might have been obviated or resolved by having a consensus-based LLS definition. To move in the direction of consensus (i.e., general though not necessarily total agreement), intensive meetings of key researchers, theorists, teachers, and learners would be very useful.

AN ENCOMPASSING DEFINITION

The following is a short form of an encompassing definition of LLS, showing key characteristics, based on my intensive content-analysis of 33 strategy definitions, mentioned above (see details in Oxford, 2017):

> LLS are purposeful, conscious (or at least partially conscious), mental actions that the learner uses to meet one or more self-chosen goals, such as (a) overcoming a learning barrier, (b) accomplishing an L2 task, (c) enhancing long-term L2 proficiency, and (d) developing greater self-regulation (ability to guide one's own learning). Like most aspects of L2 learning, LLS occur in real contexts (specific settings), are complex (with multiple, interacting factors), and are dynamic (flexible, usable in different ways, and changeable along with learners' changing needs). LLS can be learned with help from a teacher, a friend, a book, or the internet, although many learners creatively and effectively generate their own LLS.

Though LLS are mental actions, some of them can also become observable. For instance, a mental action might be organizing information to remember it, and this action in the mind can become visible when the learner takes notes on paper or online in an organized way.

SETTING LLS FREE: RECOGNIZING THEIR FLEXIBILITY AND FLUIDITY

This definition accords well with a very new perspective on LLS: the idea of *strategy functions*. In this case, the word *function* means an *active* purpose or role for which a strategy is flexibly employed by a given person in a particular context to meet a certain aim. For decades each strategy, such as guessing from the context or relaxing, was carefully nudged into one, and only one, strategy *category*, such as cognitive or affective (emotion-related) (see e.g., O'Malley and Chamot, 1990; Oxford, 1990). These categories came to be interpreted rigidly. The old saying, 'hardening of the categories,' was apt for LLS categorization schemes.

However, Cohen (2017) and Oxford (2017) urged other scholars to set LLS free from their cages, i.e., the rigid, don't-cross-this-line categories such as cognitive, metacognitive, affective, and social strategies. Oxford and Cohen encouraged a greater focus on strategy functions than on categories. The functions (such as cognitive, emotional or affective, motivational, social, and metastrategic) might sound just like the old categories, but that is not quite true. In the new perspective, the strategies of planning, organizing, monitoring, and evaluating are broadly part of the metastrategic function and can move freely across cognitive, affective, motivational, and social functions. For instance, the monitoring strategy (i.e., checking) can be used along with other functions for a given task. The L2 learner can monitor his or her linguistic errors (cognitive function), feelings (affective), interest level (motivational), or group interactions (social) and, if needed, use this information to make a quick plan for improvement. Old LLS categories would never have supported such creative flexibility and fluidity, because monitoring was categorized only as metacognitive and was hence limited.

In this new view of LLS, a given strategy can be used flexibly to serve multiple functions in an environment. The fluid use of the strategy of *analyzing* for different functions is a perfect example. Analyzing means separating something into constituent parts or elements, or studying something closely. Tammy, a learner of German, often breaks down German grammar, words, or sentences into understandable parts, and this action represents the familiar, *cognitive* function of the analyzing strategy. She discovers that the analyzing strategy also has *emotional and social functions*, enabling her to analyze her emotions, specifically sadness and anxiety, which keep her from interacting in German under certain classroom conditions. Using analyzing, she figures out what is holding her back and making her feel bad in the classroom. The analyzing strategy can be applied in still another functional way. Tammy learns that she can use analyzing to help herself outline a simple plan to pull herself out of anxiety and grief and enable herself to interact effectively in German. For her, the analyzing strategy is no longer merely cognitive; it has been set free to play many roles that can alter with new tasks, contexts, and needs. Many strategies have such fluidity (see Cohen, 2017; Oxford, 2017).

KEY LEARNING ISSUES

The key learning issues discussed below are (a) LLS in action and (b) 'the soul of strategies,' comprised of agency, autonomy, hope, self-regulation, and other factors.

LLS IN ACTION: TWO EXAMPLES

Below are two highly strategic learners, Barry and Mikako. Notice their creative uses of LLS in distinctly different contexts.

Barry, a native English speaker from the UK, is a journalist who has a new job: reporting on news and culture from Greece for a major British newspaper. He recently moved to Greece but still has a UK flat. Years ago, he took a Basic Greek course at his university but remembers little from it. Now he needs to dramatically expand and sharpen his Greek reading skills, because his new job causes him to read difficult material in Greek as one foundation for reporting in English. He might need to read almost anything in Greek, such as: a published biography or interview in a magazine; a history of an ancient Greek city; a newspaper article about a political conflict; a script for a play; or a review of a book, a film, or a sporting event. Sometimes he can find reliable, published English translations, but sometimes not. Barry creates his own strategies for learning to read in Greek. One of his favorites is *guessing the meaning of a Greek reading passage based on his background knowledge of the topic*. He is good at this strategy because he has a lot of personal and professional background knowledge to draw on. Another strategy he employs is *associating newly encountered Greek words with relevant English words and with other already-learned Greek words*. If he is unable to understand something important, he occasionally resorts to using an electronic translator (though this can cause lots of errors) or to searching an online Greek-English dictionary. If it is essential for him to comprehend the Greek sentences and phrases very closely, Barry uses the strategy of *consulting a bilingual Greek person* for help. If a reading gap does not seem too important, he decides on *moving ahead without fully understanding* and eventually gets the gist anyway.

Mikako, a student of French at a Japanese university, sometimes becomes anxious while preparing for French-speaking sessions with other Japanese students in the same class. At times of anxiety, she typically employs *deep-breathing and progressive relaxation*, two emotion-regulation (affective) strategies that were useful to her in the past when studying English. Mikako has also taught herself to use the strategy of *outlining on paper useful, interesting conversational information* – specifically, timely topics along with relevant vocabulary, sentences, and question points – and the strategy of *practicing this information in writing and aloud until it is internalized*. These two strategies help her to speak conversational French confidently and without much hesitation. She also employs the strategy of *monitoring her errors during speaking, and using this information to improve*. Recognizing errors as a source of helpful feedback enables Mikako to avoid feeling discouraged about not being perfect. She is proud of her growing competence in speaking and realizes that she can help others, not just herself, to use relevant strategies for speaking.

Are all L2 learners as capable and resourceful as Barry and Mikako, who create and implement their own strategies without help? The answer is no: many learners need more help than those two highly strategic learners (see strategy instruction later in this chapter).

'THE SOUL OF STRATEGIES' AS A SET OF LEARNING ISSUES

Agency, autonomy, growth mindsets, self-efficacy, resilience, internal attributions for success, hope, and self-regulation are the 'the soul of strategies' and 'the learner's strength factors' (Oxford, 2017, Chapter 2). Due to space limitations, I discuss only the first two and the last two of these phenomena.

'Agency [is] the sense of knowing and having what it takes to achieve one's goals' (Little, Hawley, Henrich, and Marsland, 2002: 390) – the capability to act with the aim of influencing outcomes. Mercer (2015) stated that three elements contribute to a learner's agency:

1. The learner's (cognitive) belief that improvement is possible and that the learner has the capacity to face the task.

2. The learner's (affective) willingness to invest in the learning process and take significant action for learning.

3. The learner's strategy knowledge, which allows him or her to manage and organize learning.

Agency is often viewed as a starting-point for autonomy development (see Oxford, 2017 for more on this.) Like agency, autonomy is also linked to LLS (Griffiths, 2013; Oxford, 1999, 2011, 2017).

Autonomy has many definitions, all of which involve taking responsibility for one's own learning. For example, Benson (2011: 40) defined autonomy as the 'capacity to control or take charge of one's learning.' In the twenty-first century, most L2 scholars seem to agree that autonomy is not just a Western, individualist, cultural construct; autonomy can also thrive in a social, collaborative form in collectivist societies (see Oxford, 2017).

Hope is 'a desire accompanied by a reasonable chance of fulfillment' (Oxford, 2017: 88). To use two metaphors, hope is the soul's oxygen and the foundation of human development (Oxford, 2017). Based on many observations, I argue that L2 learners employ LLS strategies effectively *only* if they have some hope that LLS will be useful, and if they know how to use them. Desperate, hopeless L2 learners often fail to know how to use LLS and/or are too demoralized to employ them. This area of inquiry deserves a closer look.

Effective L2 learning involves recognizing the importance of learner self-regulation, or regulating (guiding, taking control over) one's learning by using helpful LLS. Notice the similarity between self-regulation and autonomy, both of which are based in agency and involve strategies. Many researchers (e.g., Chamot, 2014; Donato and McCormick, 1994; Griffiths, 2013; Oxford, 1999, 2011, 2017; Oxford and Amerstorfer, 2017) have shown the linkages between LLS and self-regulation. The next section of this chapter shows the teaching of LLS (strategy instruction), often aimed at self-regulation.

IMPLICATIONS FOR TEACHING AND ASSESSMENT

This section is comprised of implications for teaching LLS and implications for assessing LLS.

IMPLICATIONS FOR TEACHING LLS (KNOWN AS STRATEGY INSTRUCTION)

Below I discuss strategy instruction from various viewpoints: three stages of teaching LLS for self-regulation (Vygotsky, 1978); the three-phase task cycle in which strategy instruction can occur (Zimmerman and Schunk, 2011); the need for differentiation to meet students' needs in strategy instruction; and an important, overarching study of strategy instruction.

In Vygotsky's (1978) theory, the more capable person, such as the teacher, a parent, or a more advanced peer, provides mediation (support, assistance) to the learner through interactions (dialogues). In these interactions with the teacher, the learner internalizes what many scholars today would call learning strategies (Oxford, 1999, 2011), such as analyzing, synthesizing, planning, summarizing, and monitoring. In this example of interactions, the teacher, Mr. Brown, guides the learner, Ana, across an expansive area of further knowledge and understanding where she can go only with assistance (the zone of proximal development). With this assistance, Ana passes through three transformative stages.

- The first stage is 'social speech,' in which Mr. Brown has great control over the learning of his student Ana, with whom he interacts. The form of learner regulation occurring at this stage is other-regulation, meaning that the more capable person is in charge.

- At the stage of 'egocentric speech,' Ana talks orally to herself to provide some degree of self-guidance. For example, while doing an L2 task (reading a story and answering questions), she quietly says to herself, 'I'd better look for the main idea and focus on words I already know.' She goes on to suggest to herself a couple more strategies, but she is far from fully regulating her learning. She remains partially or largely dependent on Mr. Brown to tell her what to do and which LLS to try.

- By the third stage, called 'inner speech,' Ana has become increasingly able to guide her own learning through instructions that she gives herself. She readily uses a range of LLS and mentally talks herself through them as necessary. At this stage, to accomplish the task of reading a story and answering questions Ana uses a range of very sophisticated strategies, such as identifying her emotions regarding each part of the story, and asking each character in the story to 'talk to her' and give her personal insights in response to the questions. By now, Ana is a self-regulated learner, and her self-regulation is likely to continue deepening and widening.

In contrast to Vygotsky's three stages, Zimmerman and Schunk's (2011) social cognitive model (see also Panadero and Alonso-Tapia, 2014) focuses on learners using strategies throughout the task cycle. The cycle has three phases: forethought (before the task), performance (during task implementation), and self-reflection (after the task). Below are basic descriptions of the task phases and examples of some LLS that might go with each phase. This model lends itself to having a skilled person who conducts strategy instruction. Strategy instruction might include explaining the task cycle and mentioning (or better yet, leading students in practicing) possible strategies that would be useful for each phase.

- Learners start with the *forethought phase*, where they use strategies to set goals, identify barriers, and make plans. Before or during the forethought phase, the teacher might teach a goal-setting strategy, combined with a barrier-identifying strategy for each element of a goal, and might also teach learners to make a plan for getting past their self-identified barriers.
- At the *performance phase*, learners solve immediate learning problems, monitor the situation and specific errors, and decide whether to change the strategies they are now using. A problem-solving strategy (many are available) and the strategy of monitoring are very valuable to teach immediately before the performance phase. Reminding students of their freedom to change strategies is helpful to many learners, especially those who tend to stay in one groove all the time.
- At the *self-reflection phase*, learners evaluate their performance, their progress, and their strategy use after the task is done. As noted earlier, self-reflection is the last phase. The teacher can introduce a self-evaluation strategy (of performance and progress) and an evaluation strategy to decide the effectiveness of the strategies used during the task.

As described in the three task phases above, strategy instruction is teacher-led. For a different, more learner-centered mode of strategy instruction, teachers could encourage learners in small groups and in the whole class to brainstorm strategies that they could try for each phase.

Success in strategy instruction depends on addressing students' diverse needs and desires. First, some learners prefer strategy instruction that is visual, others seek auditory, still others desire tactile or kinesthetic, and the rest hope for various combinations of senses. Second, some learners need LLS to take them to high proficiency levels, while others want just enough strategy help to reach a low rung on the proficiency ladder without falling off entirely. Third, some want LLS for reading and writing, others want LLS for speaking and listening, and still others need LLS for all skills. Fourth, students differ in their main L2 learning purposes (e.g., professional purposes, personal enjoyment, friendship, integrating into another culture, and others). Due to this diversity, scholars and teachers are now thinking of differentiating strategy instruction by paying attention to learners' sensory preferences, proficiency aims, preferred L2 skill areas, and L2 learning purposes, all mentioned in this paragraph. Other differentiating factors for strategy instruction might be current strategy use, specific strategies already in use, strategy knowledge, current L2 proficiency, interests and motivation, background (socioeconomic, educational, and cultural), personality, age, and gender (Chamot and Harris, 2017; Oxford, 2017). It would be an immense task to adapt (differentiate) strategy instruction to meet many different needs in a class. It is probably better to focus on a few differentiating factors at a time and gather data (qualitative and quantitative) to discern what factors make a difference in strategy use, strategy effectiveness, improved task-performance, and proficiency. Chamot's (2009) other exceptional contribution to strategy instruction is the Cognitive Academic Language Learning Approach (CALLA), which focuses on teaching LLS, the L2, and subject matter (content) together, while attending to the specific needs of the learner.

Finally, Plonsky (2011) conducted an excellent meta-analysis, or what I call a master study of studies, concerning 61 strategy instruction studies in the L2 field. Results showed a small to medium effect of strategy instruction on learning across the studies. Various factors such as age, proficiency, education level, and duration of strategy instruction, made a difference in the effectiveness of strategy instruction.

IMPLICATIONS FOR ASSESSING LLS

This interesting point might catch your eye: political-technical currents, sometimes condemnatory, keep flowing around LLS assessment in the form of rigid statements about quantitative LLS questionnaire design and analysis. Simultaneously, countercurrents move to defend against condemnation, maintain progress, and gather creative LLS assessment ideas. Some LLS scholars are happy to realize that expert professional statisticians have stated that blanket prohibitions (e.g., against any use of parametric statistics with Likert-scale items) do not fit statistical or research reality. Parametric and nonparametric statistics have nearly identical outcomes under certain circumstances, and some statisticians encourage using parametrics with varied scales (see Oxford, 2011; for additional information, see Mizumoto and Takeuchi, 2017). The LLS quantitative assessment saga goes on: currents and countercurrents, offense and defense, with the hope that the L2 learner does not get lost in the waters.

Fortunately, other options also exist for LLS assessment. For example, narratives (e.g., diaries, stories, and auto-ethnographies) help learners identify their LLS, explore their related thoughts and feelings, and provide rich data for assessment specialists and researchers. An exciting, scenario-based, emotion-regulation questionnaire, *Managing Your Emotions for Language Learning (MYE)* (Gkonou and Oxford, 2017), is in international field testing now. The MYE gives short scenarios of classroom situations that can cause emotions to arise, and it allows learners to (a) indicate their emotions related to the scenarios and (b) identify the strategies they would use for emotional self-management. In a typical MYE assessment session, L2 learners would react to ten scenarios.

Feuerstein's Instrumental Enrichment Program, or FIE (Feuerstein, Falik, Rand, and Feuerstein, 2006; Feuerstein, Feuerstein, Falik, and Rand, 1979/2002; Oxford, 2011, 2017) offers an assessment approach built partly on Vygotsky's mediated learning, as described earlier. This approach is known as *dynamic assessment*, a 'test-teach-test' mode involving strategies (called 'operations' in the model). Dynamic assessment proceeds in three steps:

- *The first test step*: The more capable person, such as the teacher, has a dialogue with the learner while testing the learner's performance. During this dialogue, the more capable person identifies the learner's strengths, weaknesses, and operations/strategies.

- *The teach step*: In this step, the more capable person teaches additional operations/ strategies for enhancing the learner's performance based on the prior dialogue, all the while encouraging the learner to use those new strategies with pertinent tasks.
- *The second test step (retesting)*: At this step, the more capable person retests the strategy-enriched performance of the learner. Tested performance is likely to improve after students have had the opportunity to learn and use strategies/operations.

CONCLUSION

The overview dived immediately into LLS complexity and controversies, followed by a new, empirically- and theoretically-founded definition of LLS and an innovative perspective on strategy flexibility. We looked at the strategies of L2 learners Barry and Mikako and examined special factors, such as agency and hope, that comprise the 'soul of strategies'. The section on implications for teaching LLS highlighted several themes: three stages of mediated learning, three phases of the task cycle, differentiation of strategy instruction, and a meta-analysis of strategy instruction studies. Strategy assessment implications involved quantitative LLS assessment via questionnaires; narrative tools, such as diaries; an innovative, scenario-based questionnaire; and the strategy-rich, test-teach-test process called dynamic assessment.

Discussion Questions

1. What examples of LLS that you have personally used? Try and think of at least five examples. If you have taught languages, make a list of LLS that you have noticed your students using frequently. Try for ten LLS based on your students' learning.

2. Why is the link between self-regulation and LLS important to learners and teachers? How does it relate to you?

3. Culture does not *determine* the use of specific types of LLS used by a given learner for a certain task in a particular setting. Nevertheless, cultural systems, such as idiocentric (individualist) and allocentric (collectivist), influence a learner's beliefs and strategies. Give three to five examples from your experience.

Key Readings

Chamot, A. U., & Harris, V. (Eds.) (2017). *Learning Strategy Instruction in the Language Classroom: Issues and Implementation*. Bristol, UK: Multilingual Matters.

Cohen, A. D. (2014). *Strategies in Learning and Using a Second Language* (2nd ed.). New York: Routledge.

O'Malley, J. M., & Chamot, A. U. (1990). *Learning Strategies in Second Language Acquisition*. Cambridge: Cambridge University Press.

Oxford, R. L. (2017). *Teaching and Researching Language Learning Strategies: Self-Regulation in Context* (2nd ed.). New York: Routledge.

Oxford, R. L., & Amerstorfer, C. M. (Eds.) (2017). *Language Learning Strategies and Individual Learner Characteristics: Situating Strategy Use in Diverse Contexts*. London: Bloomsbury.

References

Benson, P. (2011). *Teaching and Researching Autonomy in Language Learning*. Harlow, UK: Pearson Longman.

Chamot, A. U. (2009). *The CALLA Handbook: Implementing the Cognitive Academic Language Learning Approach* (2nd ed.). White Plains, NY: Pearson Education/Longman.

Chamot, A. U. (2014). Developing self-regulated learning in the language classroom. *Knowledge, Skills and Competencies in Foreign Language Education* (pp. 78–88). Singapore: Proceedings of the Sixth International CLS Conference (CLaSIC).

Chamot, A., & Harris, V. (Eds.) (2017). *Learning Strategy Instruction in the Language Classroom: Issues and Implementation.* Bristol, UK: Multilingual Matters.

Cohen, A. D. (2014). *Strategies in Learning and Using a Second Language* (2nd ed.). New York: Routledge.

Cohen, A. D. (2017). Moving from theory to practice: a closer look at situated language learner strategies. In R. L. Oxford & C. M. Amerstorfer (Eds.), *Language Learning Strategies and Individual Learner Characteristics: Situating Strategy Use in Diverse Contexts.* London: Bloomsbury.

Cohen, A. D., & Macaro, E. (Eds.) (2007). *Language Learner Strategies: Thirty Years of Research and Practice.* Oxford: Oxford University Press.

Donato, R., & McCormick, D. E. (1994) A sociocultural perspective on language learning strategies: the role of mediation. *Modern Language Journal*, 78, 453–464.

Dörnyei, Z. (2005). *The Psychology of the Language Learner: Individual Differences in Second Language Acquisition.* Mahwah, NJ: Lawrence Erlbaum.

Dörnyei, Z., & Ryan, S. (2015). *The Psychology of the Language Learner – Revisited* (2nd ed.). New York: Routledge.

Dörnyei, Z., & Skehan, P. (2003). Individual differences in second language learning. In C. J. Doughty & M. H. Long (Eds.), *The Handbook of Second Language Acquisition* (pp 589–630). Oxford: Blackwell.

Feuerstein, R., Falik, L., Rand, Y., & Feuerstein, R. S. (2006). *Creating and Enhancing Cognitive Modifiability: The Feuerstein Instrumental Enrichment Program.* Jerusalem: ICELP Press.

Feuerstein, R., Feuerstein, R. S., Falik, L. H., & Rand, Y. (1979/2002). *The Dynamic Assessment of Cognitive Modifiability.* Jerusalem: ICELP Press.

Gkonou, C. & Oxford, R. L. (2017). Questionnaire: Managing your emotions for language learning (MYE). In R. L. Oxford, *Teaching and Researching Language Learning Strategies: Self-Regulation in Context*, (2nd ed., pp. 317–333). New York: Routledge.

Griffiths, C. (2013). *The Strategy Factor in Successful Language Learning.* Bristol, UK: Multilingual Matters.

Gu, P. (2012). Learning strategies: Prototypical core and dimensions of variation. *Studies in Self-Access Learning (SiSAL) Journal*, 3(4), 330–356.

Little, T. D., Hawley, P. H., Henrich, C. C., & Marsland, K. (2002). Three views of the agentic self: Developmental synthesis. In E. L. Deci & R. M. Ryan (Eds.), *Handbook of Self-Determination Research* (pp. 389–404). Rochester, NY: University of Rochester Press.

Macaro, E. (2006). Strategies for language learning and for language use: Revising the theoretical framework. *Modern Language Journal*, 90(3), 320–337.

Mercer, S. (2015). Learner agency and engagement: Believing you can, wanting to, and knowing how to. *Humanizing Language Teaching*, 17(4). Retrieved from www.hltmag.co.uk/aug15/mart01.rtf

Mizumoto, A., & Takeuchi, O. (2017). Modeling a prototypical use of language learning strategies: Decision tree-based methods in multiple contexts. In R. L. Oxford & C. M. Amerstorfer (Eds.), *Language Learning Strategies and Individual Learner Characteristics: Situating Strategy Use in Diverse Contexts*. London: Bloomsbury.

O'Malley, J. M., & Chamot, A. U. (1990). *Learning Strategies in Second Language Acquisition*. Cambridge: Cambridge University Press.

Oxford, R. L. (1990). *Language Learning Strategies: What Every Teacher Should Know*. Boston: Heinle.

Oxford, R. L. (1999). Relationships between second language learning strategies and language proficiency in the context of learner autonomy and self-regulation. *Revista Canaria de Estudios Ingleses*, 38, 108–126.

Oxford, R. L. (2011). *Teaching and Researching Language Learning Strategies: Self-Regulation in Context* (1st ed.) Harlow, UK: Pearson Longman.

Oxford, R. L. (2017). *Teaching and Researching Language Learning Strategies: Self-Regulation in Context* (2nd ed.) New York: Routledge.

Oxford, R. L., and Amerstorfer, C. M. (Eds.) (2017). *Language Learning Strategies and Individual Learner Characteristics: Situating Strategy Use in Diverse Contexts*. London: Bloomsbury.

Oxford, R. L., & Cohen, A. D. (1992). Language learning strategies: Crucial issues in concept and classification. *Applied Language Learning*, 3(1-2), 1–35.

Panadero, E., & Alonso-Tapia, J. (2014). How do students self-regulate? Review of Zimmerman's cyclical model of self-regulated learning. *Anales de Psicología / Annals of Psychology,* 30(2). Available at: http://revistas.um.es/analesps/article/view/analesps.30.2.167221

Plonsky, L. (2011). Systematic review article: The effectiveness of second language strategy instruction: A meta-analysis. *Language Learning*, 61(4), 993–1038.

Vygotsky, L. S. (1978). *Mind in Society: The Development of Higher Psychological Processes* Cambridge, MA: Harvard University Press.

Zimmerman, B. J., & Schunk, D. H. (Eds.) (2011). *Handbook of Self-Regulation of Learning and Performance*. New York: Routledge.

CHAPTER 10

Identity and Language Learning

Martha C. Pennington

INTRODUCTION

Identity is both an internally and an externally defined characteristic of the self, in part the product of a person's genetics and long-term history, but is also shaped in ongoing development during everyday interactions. As Norton and Toohey observe:

> A great deal of language learning research in the 1970s and 1980s conceptualized 'identities' of language learners as their fixed personalities, learning styles, and motivation. In contrast, more recent work on language learner identities adopts poststructural understandings of identities as fluid, context-dependent, and context-producing, in particular historical and cultural circumstances. From this perspective, personalities, learning styles, motivations, and so on are not fixed, unitary, or decontextualized, and while context 'pushes back' on individuals' claims to identity, individuals also struggle to assume identities that they wish to claim. Constructs of investment and imagined communities/imagined identities have been particularly important in these debates. (Norton and Toohey, 2011: 419–420)

"[I]n educational practice as in other facets of social life, identities and beliefs are co-constructed, negotiated, and transformed on an ongoing basis" (Duff and Uchida, 1997: 452) through interaction with others and, specifically, "by means of language" (ibid.), as the primary vehicle that humans use for creating meaning and making sense of experience (see Chapter 11). A person's linguistic identity and other facets of identity are always implicated, to a greater or lesser degree, in learning a second language.

In this chapter, starting from the position that identity is a central aspect of language learning, I explore a number of propositions about identity:

- Identity is not something you're born with.
- Identity is created dialogically.

- Identity is formed in communities of practice.
- Language is a central aspect of identity.
- Identity is implicated in language learning.

I then discuss identity issues that can arise with language learners, and offer suggestions as to how identity may be addressed in teaching and assessment.

OVERVIEW

IDENTITY IS NOT SOMETHING YOU'RE BORN WITH

A person's identity is a complex construct that combines individual characteristics and social categorization. Identity used to be considered in terms of relatively stable traits or unalterable categories, such as gender, race, and other biological characteristics. One's individual nature and social categorization are now recognized as malleable, subject both to outside influences and to people's will and specific actions, that is, their agency in constructing their identity and the meaning of different attributes of their identity. Even genetically inherited characteristics are now recognized as socially alterable in deliberate actions by people to change their identity, both situationally – such as assuming a different gender as an online identity – and permanently – such as self-identifying as a gender different from one's primary biological sexual characteristics. Also, it is increasingly possible for a person to change physical characteristics associated with identity, to align with a desired social identity. Thus, identity has come to be recognized as socially constructed and as subject to a person's will and deliberate actions, and therefore as open to change at any time of life.

People shape identity in an attempt to be the kind of person they want to be and imagine themselves being. Identity therefore has an aspirational aspect, an image of the self that a person wishes to project to others through word and deed, and a performed identity, which may diverge from that person's aspirational identity. The failure to perform a desired identity may be because of lack of competence or experience – the person is not skilled enough (yet) to be able to talk and act in the desired way – or lack of attention – the person is tired or distressed and so is not monitoring words and actions. There may be times when a person tries out or experiments with an alternate identity in a certain situation or with a certain audience. Over time, an alternate identity may become a more dominant part of a person's character and take on aspirational or core status.

IDENTITY IS CREATED DIALOGICALLY

"Life is by its very nature dialogic" (Bakhtin, 1929/1984: 293), in that a person's voice is formed in childhood and throughout life in dialogue – whether in concert or disagreement – with the voices of others. More broadly, a person's entire identity is formed and continually reformed in a give-and-take, dialogic process with the words, the ideas, and the actions of others. In this process, a person imitates and forms alignments with certain other individuals and groups, while at the same time seeking to differentiate themselves in word and deed from certain other individuals and groups. The process of identity formation is also a dialectic process, in which differing and even contrary traits and behaviors are synthesized into new characteristics and modes of action that represent a unique individual.

People of all ages make decisions about their self-definition as deliberate "acts of identity" (Le Page and Tabouret-Keller, 1985: 14) in which they construct an internal image of the self as a composite of characteristics, their imagined or aspirational identity, and attempt to present it to others, as their performed identity. One's identity image and characteristics draw on and synthesize the perceived characteristics of many other people, including those whom one associates with daily or on a regular basis – such as caregivers and other family members, friends and other peers in the neighborhood or in school, and authority figures in institutional settings (e.g., teachers, coaches, and other leaders) – as well as others known or viewed at a distance – such as heroes and role models known from print and mass media sources (including fantasy characters), or from personal experience and history (including family lore and stories about influential ancestors or living relatives). One's identity is open to change as the people one associates with, or aspires to be like, change. Identity change may also result from changes in context or circumstances that provoke reflection on core values and behaviors.

IDENTITY IS FORMED IN COMMUNITIES OF PRACTICE

Wenger (1998) describes identity as constructed within different communities of practice in which people participate. Having a place in a community of practice means possessing knowledge relevant to that community of practice and exhibiting behaviors appropriate to the roles and membership in that community. The relevant knowledge and behaviors are developed through the dual processes of identification and negotiation with the people, values, and activities of the community in order to "belong" to that community and thus have the right to "contribute to, take responsibility for and shape the meanings that matter within [that] social configuration" (Wenger, 1998: 197). People may be on different "trajectories," as Wenger describes them, in terms of how centrally they "belong" to a community at a given point in time. They may be on an "inbound" trajectory, as relatively central members or "insiders"; a "peripheral" trajectory, as marginal members; an "outbound" trajectory leading out of one group and into another; or a "boundary" trajectory linking between different groups.

People's identities can incorporate the practices of multiple communities within which they have some claim to membership. Thus, language learners can maintain a strong identity in one or more communities of practice where their primary language is dominant, even as they also aspire to and cultivate status in one or more communities of practice in which a second language is dominant, such as a school, a language class, a web community, or a multicultural group of friends.

LANGUAGE IS A CENTRAL ASPECT OF IDENTITY

Language is a main vehicle for achieving and enacting individual and social identity. Much can be inferred about a person's identity through the person's language, since "identity is represented by language use, with language seen as a window into identity" (Trent, 2015: 45). What a person talks about, and how a person talks, identify that person as an individual and a member of various groups. The language a person speaks, the specific variety or dialect, and the person's unique voice and way of speaking (idiolect), is one of the defining features of identity. A person's linguistic identity is moreover tied to many other facets of identity related to ethnicity, culture, and primary activities such as school and profession. Language has not just practical communicative value, but also symbolic value. As observed by Fishman, language serves as:

> A referent for loyalties and animosities, an indicator of social status and personal relationships, a marker of situations and topics as well as of the societal goals and the large-scale value-laden arenas of the interaction that typify every speech community. (Fishman, 1972: 4)

A person's primary language is part of the person's core identity, though identity may be tied to more than one language, and which language is primary at a given point in time may change. Like all aspects of identity, linguistic identity is multifaceted and dynamic, responsive to others and to context and situation. It is thus dialogic and potentially shifting and changeable in terms of its characteristics. Also like other aspects of identity, it may be composed of inconsistent features. "As language references the multiple layers of contexts in which a speaker resides, it is normal that these contextual spheres are overlapping, and, at times, conflicting with each other" (Hallman, 2015: 7).

Language is the main means through which identity is negotiated and performed (Norton, 2000), within a larger context of culture and discourse that forms the backdrop of a person's lifelong dialogic and dialectic process of absorbing the words, ideas, and actions of others and then negotiating one's own words, ideas, and actions into an individual identity. In Gee's (2008) definition, "Discourses are ways of behaving, interacting, valuing, thinking, believing, speaking, and often reading and writing, that are accepted as instantiations of particular identities (or 'types of people') by specific groups" (p. 3). Gee observed that people are brought up with a primary discourse, and develop secondary discourses through education and participation in the larger society. Discourses are important communicational currency, defining insiders and outsiders as well as peripheral or marginal members of social groups or communities of practice.

IDENTITY IS IMPLICATED IN LANGUAGE LEARNING

Learning a second or additional language means acquiring a new way of communicating and presenting oneself that can open a person's identity to change, making identity more malleable and offering opportunities to experiment with new communicative features, such as accent or prosody, and with the social and cultural attributes of the new language and its associated discourses. It also means gaining access to new groups and communities of practice, where new knowledge and behaviors can be developed that make it possible to participate in new discourses and to have a role in shaping those communities and discourses, thus enhancing a person's social and communicative power. Learning a new language can confer social status and can widen opportunities for education, employment, and new experiences that can impact identity.

Referencing identity in relation to more than one group and community of practice makes it possible for people "to enjoy multiple identities" (Canagarajah, 2006: 10) that can be expressed "in a contextually relevant manner in shifting relationships" (ibid.) and shifting use of languages, including in mixed varieties. On the other hand, since language is so closely tied to a person's sense of self in relation to other people, acquiring and using a new language and its associated discourses may raise issues of identity and community loyalty that may be stressful for the learner. The learner's new communicative modes and behaviors may also raise issues for others, as they are seen by some in the primary discourse community as acting out of character or changing allegiances.

KEY LEARNING ISSUES

Since a language is a communicative vehicle and also a repository of culture, learning a new language makes it possible to expand oneself by developing a new communicative and cultural repertoire and gaining an insider trajectory into new and potentially highly valued communities of practice. At the same time, language learners carry along aspects of their core cultural and ethnic identity that may provide valuable stabilizing influences, but may also cause them to resist referencing their identity to new linguistic practices and their associated discourses, cultural attributes, and communities. In addition, students from some cultures or backgrounds may find it harder to experiment with the new identities made possible by acquiring a second language and its associated discourses. As Schwartz, Donnellan, Ravert, Luyckx, and Zamboanga (2012) remark, "Personal identity development in non-Western contexts may be framed more around clearly prescribed social roles and responsibilities than around individually chosen goals, values, and beliefs" (p. 350). Those coming from such cultures may choose a peripheral, or even an outsider, trajectory in relation to the community of second language speakers that limits their language acquisition goal or motivation.

In Norton's (2000) view, students need to invest their identity into their language learning, though this is not always a straightforward matter, given the potential conflicts and the fact that identity must be negotiated and may be contested in a new context. Moreover, students risk discouragement and loss of confidence when their aspirational identity is not realized in performance and they fall short of their language learning target. Identity work can be face-threatening and can raise sensitive psychological issues of relationship, community loyalty and affiliation, who a person is, and where a person belongs. Like those learning how to teach a language, as described by Pennington and Richards (2016: 3), those learning a language may experience "identity stress" or even an "identity crisis" when they feel unsure about their identity, such as when they face questions raised by others about their identity or major contextual changes that make them rethink their values and change their behavior. The more immersed a learner is in a second language environment, the greater the potential for identity issues to arise that require reflection on the self and others, and that may present welcome opportunities or unwelcome pressure for change. The result may be a period of stress and struggle that has some transforming effects, while also serving to reaffirm and strengthen core characteristics, or a major transformation of identity in which the person gains insider status in the second language community or a new bilingual-bicultural or translingual-transcultural identity (see also Chapter 5).

IMPLICATIONS FOR TEACHING AND ASSESSMENT

As Costley (2015) points out, "schools and classrooms are dynamic living organisms within which identities and power relations are constructed, (in)formed and played out" (p. 76). Norton and Toohey comment that language learners:

> Need not be locked forever in particular positions. ... [A]lthough some contexts and practices may limit or constrain opportunities for learners to listen, speak, read, or write, other contexts and practices may offer enhanced sets of possibilities for social interaction and human agency. Thus, pedagogical practices have the potential to be transformative in offering language learners more powerful positions than those they may occupy either inside or outside the classroom. (Norton and Toohey, 2011: 417)

Teachers need to be aware of their own and learners' language-related identity and cultural characteristics, and the power relations that are linked to the language the students are aiming to learn and the access and power they can gain in learning it. This can be seen as an aspect of the "[c]ultural awareness and understanding" which Duff and Uchida (1997) maintain "are essential for language teachers, whether they are working with relatively homogeneous populations in certain EFL settings abroad or with students from diverse cultural backgrounds in ESL settings" (p. 476).

Abendroth-Timmer and Hennig (2014) define identity according to Krewer and Eckensberger (1991) as a "construct consisting of the individual's self-concept, his or her self-esteem and his or her self-confidence" (Abendroth-Timmer and Hennig 2014: 27) and describe cultural and plurilingual identities on the basis of these three dimensions, which I have adapted and revised as follows:

SELF-CONCEPT
- "What languages does the individual speak in which contexts and in which situations?" To what degree does the person feel these practices match his or her aspirational identity?

- "How does the individual define him- or herself as a linguistic and cultural person?"
- To what extent does the person's self-concept link language to ethnicity, home culture, or country of origin?

SELF-ESTEEM
- "What value and prestige does the individual assign to his or her languages", and does the person's status vary in different contexts?
- How does the perceived status of those languages affect the person's self-esteem?
- "How is the individual viewed by people having more/less access to power in society?"

SELF-CONFIDENCE
- "How does the individual perceive and evaluate his or her competences with regard to his or her different languages?"
- How confident is the person in the identity he or she projects and the power and status he or she conveys through use of those languages?
- To what degree does the person feel able to use his or her languages to accomplish desired ends, to participate fully in any context or situation, and to "contribute to changes in society"?

(Adapted and revised from Abendroth-Timmer and Hennig, 2014: 28)

These questions can be suggested for assessing the language-related identity and sense of empowerment and status of language learners, either for purposes of testing or as topics for classroom discussion and learning tasks such as storytelling, peer interviews, or community surveys. The same set of questions can be considered by the teacher for purposes of self-reflection as well as comparison and contrast with the students.

Cummins (2011) stresses the teacher's role in students' identity work, noting that "students will engage academically only to the extent that classroom interactions and academic effort are identity-affirming" (Abstract, p. 189). Cummins (2011) recommends building lessons around "identity texts" (Cummins and Early, 2011), in which students who are second language learners, or otherwise non-insiders in the secondary discourse of the school, tell and write about their own lives and experiences, potentially including use of their primary language. In so doing, they create representations of themselves that give them a chance to make their own discourse, language, and identity primary, thereby empowering them and helping them develop a coherent and comfortable identity in a new culture. Culturally responsive pedagogy (Taylor and Sobel, 2011) is another approach that incorporates the students' culture, experience, and language(s) in instruction, by bringing learners' home and community cultures and languages into the classroom, affirming their backgrounds, and treating the learners and their home and community cultures and languages as resources for class content and process (see also Chapter 28). The goal is to reinforce and develop positive student identity in the classroom so that learners can gain the maximum benefit from education.

Abendroth-Timmer and Hennig (2014) recommend using "[t]asks based on literature, films and music…in order to make students reflect upon their cultural and linguistic identity, …not only cognitively but also emotionally" (p. 34). They also suggest (p. 32) the value of foreign exchange and using class time for students to reflect on experiences of living in another culture. Online cross-cultural interaction with conversation partners or sister classes, and reflection on that experience, can be another way to highlight identity and culture. In addition, teachers can encourage students to experiment with alternate or new identities through role-playing, drama, and simulations. On the basis of such experimentation, students can be guided to form an aspirational identity in terms of their desired language competence, and can gain experience and perspectives about the time and personal investment required to develop the skills needed to achieve their aspirational identity as a user of the second language.

Instruction can initiate and foster talk about changes in perceptions, values, and behaviors related to language learning, and students' feelings about these. Teachers need to realize the risks, the stress, and the possible confusion that may be part of the identity work tied to language. They may be able to help learners in times of identity stress or crisis, by leading them to reflect on their situation and their feelings, examine their options, and make choices about how they want to respond. Rather than insisting on cultural adaptation or acculturation, teachers are advised to allow students to be critical, and to accept a wide range of responses and adaptations – from resistance and maintenance of outsider status, to assimilation and full insider status.

CONCLUSION

Identity is the cumulative product of a person's genetic and cultural inheritance, filtered through a lifetime of experiences observing and interacting with other people in communities of practice. As the main means of communicating with other human beings and of functioning in communities of practice, language is a key component and expression of identity. Learning a second or additional language involves the core identity, and may also involve alternate and new identities.

Educational contexts and pedagogical practices offer language learners new, transformative opportunities in identity development and expression. Language teaching practices can raise students' awareness of the ways in which culture and identity are embodied in language, and of the identity issues surrounding learning a language, and can connect students' lives and experiences to class work and the curriculum. In so doing, language teachers will be encouraging and enabling students to maximize their identity investment in language learning, thereby gaining the maximum effect of that learning in terms of their self-development and opportunities for the future.

Discussion Questions

1. How do the identity issues raised in this chapter apply to the specific group of students you teach?

2. To what extent and in what way(s) is your teacher identity interrelated with the identities of your students?

3. What can you do to continue developing your own aspirational identity as a teacher in relation to your students' aspirational identities?

Key Readings

Cheung, Y. L., Ben Said, S., & Park, K. (Eds.) (2015). *Advances and Current Trends in Language Teacher Identity Research*. London and New York: Routledge.

Cummins, J. (2001). *Negotiating Identities: Education for Empowerment in a Diverse Society* (2nd ed.). Los Angeles: California Association for Bilingual Education.

Norton, B. (2000). *Identity and Language Learning: Gender, Ethnicity and Educational Change*. London: Pearson Longman.

Taylor, S. K., & Cummins, J. (Eds.) (2011). Identity Texts, Literacy Engagement, and Multilingual Classrooms: Special Topic Issue of *Writing & Pedagogy*, 3(2).

Wenger, E. (1998). *Communities of Practice: Learning, Meaning, and Identity*. Cambridge: Cambridge University Press.

References

Abendroth-Timmer, D., & Hennig, E.-M. (2014). Plurilingualism and multiliteracies: Identity construction in language education. In D. Abendroth-Timmer & E.-M Hennig (Eds.), *Plurilingualism and Multiliteracies: International Research on Identity Construction in Language Education* (pp. 23–37). Frankfurt am Main: Peter Lang.

Bakhtin, M. M. (1984/1929) *Problems of Dostoevsky's Poetics*. C. Emerson (ed. and trans.). Minneapolis, MN: University of Minnesota Press.

Canagarajah, A. S. (2006). Constructing a diaspora identity in English: The case of the Sri Lankan Tamils. In J. Brutt-Griffler & C. E. Davis (Eds.), *English and Ethnicity* (pp. 191–216). London: Palgrave.

Costley, T. (2015). What's in a name? Power, space and the negotiation of identities. In Y. L. Cheung, S. Ben Said, & K. Park (Eds.), *Advances and Current Trends in Language Teacher Identity Research* (pp. 74–85). London and New York: Routledge.

Cummins J. (2011). Identity matters: From evidence-free to evidence-based policies for promoting achievement among students from marginalized social groups. *Writing & Pedagogy*, 3(2), 189–216.

Cummins, J., & Early, M. (2011). *Identity texts: The Collaborative Creation of Power in Multilingual Schools*. Stoke-on-Trent, UK: Trentham Books.

Duff, P. A., & Uchida, Y. (1997). The negotiation of teachers' sociocultural identities and practices in postsecondary EFL classrooms. *TESOL Quarterly*, 31(3), 451–486.

Fishman, J. (1972). *The Sociology of Language: An Interdisciplinary Social Science Approach to Language in Society*. Rowley, MA: Newbury House.

Gee, J. P. (2008) *Social Linguistics and Literacies: Ideology in Discourses* (3rd ed.). London and New York: Routledge.

Hallman, H. L. (2015). Teacher identity as dialogic response: A Bakhtinian perspective. In Y. L. Cheung, S. Ben Said, & K. Park (Eds.), *Advances and Current Trends in Language Teacher Identity Research* (pp. 3–15). London and New York: Routledge.

Le Page, R. B., & Tabouret-Keller, A. (1985). *Acts of Identity: Creole-based Approaches to Language and Ethnicity*. Cambridge: Cambridge University Press.

Norton, B. (2000). *Identity and Language Learning: Gender, Ethnicity and Educational Change*. London: Pearson Longman.

Norton, B., & Toohey, K. (2011). Identity, language learning, and social change. *Language Teaching*, 44(4): 412–46.

Pennington, M. C., & Richards, J. C. (2016). Teacher identity in language teaching: Integrating personal, contextual, and professional factors. *RELC Journal*, 47(1), 1–19.

Schwartz, S. J., Donnellan, M. B., Ravert, R. D., Luyckx, K., & Zamboanga, B. L. (2012). Identity development, personality, and well-being in adolescence and emerging adulthood. In R. M. Lerner, M. A. Easterbrooks, & J. Mistry, (Eds.), *Handbook of Psychology* (2nd ed.), *Volume 6: Developmental Psychology* (pp. 339–364). Hoboken, NJ: John Wiley & Sons.

Taylor, S. V., & Sobel, D. M. (2011). *Culturally Responsive Pedagogy: Teaching Like Our Students' Lives Matter*. Leiden: Brill.

Trent, J. (2015). Towards a multifaceted, multidimensional framework for understanding teacher identity. In Y. L. Cheung, S. Ben Said, & K. Park (Eds.), *Advances and Current Trends in Language Teacher Identity Research* (pp. 44–58). London and New York: Routledge.

Wenger, E. (1998). *Communities of Practice: Learning, Meaning, and Identity*. Cambridge: Cambridge University Press.

SECTION 3

CONTEXTS OF LEARNING ENGLISH

In this section, the chapters explore the role of language-learning contexts, both in and outside the classroom, and consider the affordances, and also the constraints, in facilitating second language development. While these chapters also touch on the use of technology for learning in both actual and virtual contexts, the main attention is on the types of learning interactions offered by these contexts. Because technology is a vast and growing field for learning in its own right, the more specific dimensions and affordances of technology are further considered in Section 9.

First, **Patricia A. Duff** and **Victoria Surtees** consider the concept of socialization in English language learning, and discuss the nature of social interaction and its role in classroom-based learning, as well as in learning in other contexts. They conceptualize social interaction as spontaneous talk, and consider a range of theoretical positions that have contributed to a deeper understanding of how interaction contributes to language learning. They refer to the opportunities provided by technology, as well as to other initiatives such as studying abroad, to mediate new forms of social interaction that can facilitate language development. They suggest a variety of ways that teachers can promote interaction beyond the classroom and engage students in interactive assessment approaches.

In the next chapter, **Martin East** discusses the limitations of classroom-based language teaching encounters in attempts to implement a communicative or task-based methodology. He looks at the difference between language as an object of study and language as a resource for authentic communication and use in the real world. In order to address the mismatch between these two contexts for language use, he proposes a 'flipped-classroom' approach, where the classroom serves as a preparation for out-of-class English language use.

The chapter by **Alice Chik** further examines the nature of out-of-class learning. She offers a categorization of the features of out-of-class learning opportunities, and suggests that such learning activities prompt both a redefinition of traditional understandings of 'language learning' and a repositioning of the role of the learner in this process. She concludes that learning another language is a life-long process and that, increasingly, the majority of learning is likely to take place outside the classroom.

Teaching a second language in any given situation means fine-tuning one's knowledge of the contextual factors that operate for different kinds of learners, and of the affordances that may, or may not, be incurred in these various learning contexts. What becomes very clear is that creative and well-informed teaching solutions are needed that harness the needs and learning preferences of different types of students to the multiple opportunities that are offered through combinations of in-class, out-of-class, and virtual spaces.

CHAPTER 11

Learning Through Social Interaction

Patricia A. Duff and Victoria Surtees

INTRODUCTION

Most contemporary theories of second language (L2) learning place considerable emphasis on the role of social interaction, joint activity, or socialization in learning. In this chapter, we present some of the core features shared by these social-interactional approaches, discuss relevant research findings, and then consider some implications for L2 education and assessment.

OVERVIEW

Intuitively, when we think of social interaction, we imagine familiar scenes of friends chatting over coffee, children playing with their parents, or students gossiping before class. In a formal language learning context, those interactions might include spontaneous talk produced for classroom tasks, such as information-gap activities (where students must share information to solve a problem or complete an activity), debates, or peer-feedback sessions on writing. Outside of class, learners might speak with servers at a lunch counter or with friends, roommates, or coworkers for a variety of purposes. Each situation presents an opportunity for language practice and, potentially, development (i.e., greater fluency, accuracy, pragmatic effectiveness, clearer pronunciation, and also growing confidence as an L2 user, among other potential measures of development). Social interactions can also foster mutual attention and language use that is both personally relevant and linguistically accessible, and thus can be especially rewarding for language learners.

We tend to associate social interaction with face-to-face discourse such as conversation. Indeed, that is how interaction has traditionally been viewed in the field of second language acquisition (SLA). However, in today's increasingly technology-enabled society, social interaction encompasses a much broader spectrum of language practices, actions, and semiotic forms (that is, not just language but other visual and auditory information;

see Chapter 34). People of all ages are now using smartphones and tablets or computers to communicate via text messages, audio messages, or video chat with peers, relatives, strangers, and even teachers. L2 interaction research, pedagogy, and assessment are also turning towards these new forms of communication and investigating both face-to-face and technologically-mediated discourse, some of which is written but shares features with oral discourse. While some researchers have investigated asynchronous social interaction (i.e., exchanges that do not take place in real time), such as email messages (e.g., Stockwell and Harrington, 2013), we aim here to represent the primary focus of SLA literature for the past four decades, which investigates synchronous (real-time) talk amongst small groups of learners, or between learners and expert speakers, in a variety of face-to-face and online settings (see, for example, Ellis, 2008; Mackey, 2013; McDonough and Mackey, 2013).

For the purposes of this chapter, we consider social interaction to be relatively unscripted, spontaneous talk in a particular context that occurs between two or more interlocutors who are actively engaged in the verbal activity. This interaction offers L2 practice for at least one of the interlocutors (if not all), and thus, potential opportunities for L2 development. Of course, not all forms of social interaction are created equal: each presents different opportunities and challenges for language learning, depending on formality, the relationship between interlocutors, the purpose and nature of the talk, and the mode of communication.

In the following section, we review key insights from two different clusters of SLA theories regarding the role of social interaction in the language learning process.

Key Learning Issues

Since the early 1980s, L2 learning and teaching have emphasized the role of social interaction in language development and in education more generally (e.g., Ellis, 2008; Markee, 2015; Mitchell, Myles, and Marsden, 2013; Ortega, 2009). Not only does interaction provide opportunities for language practice, it also allows interlocutors to question one another, or to alter their utterances to ensure that their intended meanings are understood. This process of negotiating for meaning, according to decades of SLA research, facilitates L2 learning. Applied linguists and teachers recognize that ample exposure to another language without social engagement, interactivity, or the negotiation of forms and meanings, is, for most learners, inadequate if they wish to become proficient, communicatively competent users – and especially speakers – of another language.

In what follows, we consider how different theories of L2 learning have conceptualized the role of social interaction. We group the approaches as firstly, cognitive-interactionist and secondly, sociocultural. Each represents a much wider and more diverse set of approaches to learning, but space precludes a detailed discussion of all of the distinctions within and across these groupings. Of central importance here is their shared emphasis on an individual's active interaction or engagement with others – and with language – as part of the SLA process. Differences lie in their relative emphasis on cognitive or linguistic aspects versus the social-relational and cultural aspects of mutual engagement in language activity. Both consider mental processes, but in different ways and using different metaphors.

COGNITIVE-INTERACTIONIST THEORIES: INPUT–INTERACTION–OUTPUT

Researchers adopting a cognitive-interactionist approach investigate how external environmental factors, such as type of linguistic input, interact with cognitive processes – such as attention, memory, and syntactic processing – to foster acquisition. Long's Interaction Hypothesis (Long 1980, 1996) posited that social interaction, typically involving pairs of speakers, facilitates connections between external input the language learners see and hear and internal representations of language by focusing learners' attention on linguistic structure (or form) through the negotiation of meaning. According to Long, social interaction can provide learners with opportunities to:

- notice new forms in personally meaningful communication;
- request clarification of unfamiliar or unclear meanings or usage;
- receive explicit or implicit feedback; and
- experiment with new forms in authentic contexts.

These opportunities afforded by social interactions typically entail brief breakdowns in communication that are subsequently negotiated and resolved. For example, when one learner says to another "I go to football game" and the response is: "When? Yesterday or today?", these questions might help the first speaker realize that the time- or tense-marking in the initial utterance was not adequate (i.e., that if it is a past event, *go* should be *went*, or if a future event, then *am going* or *will be going*). The clarification requests might also signal that adding a temporal adverb (e.g., *yesterday, tonight*) would help.

Thus, cognitive interactionists view social interaction as an essential factor in SLA characterized (ideally) by:

- modified input targeted at the level of the speaker;
- negotiation for meaning to ensure mutual understanding; and
- opportunities for output, or the production of speech.

Interaction provides not only practice, but an occasion for speakers to hear their own output and consider how it compares with their own intended production or with others' ways of saying the same thing. These three components indicated by the bullet points above are sometimes referred to as 'input–interaction–output', a phrase associated with an information-processing, computational metaphor. Positive outcomes of negotiated interaction are, in this line of research, expected to include higher rates of comprehension by learners and evidence of having learned the negotiated forms (usually based on immediate responses, or tests soon after the original negotiation or even much later).

Early investigations of Long's (1980) Interaction Hypothesis focused on the acquisition of morphology and syntax in tasks in which learners negotiated meaning in interaction with more proficient speakers (see Ortega, 2009). Two pioneering studies found that adult learners of English who interacted spontaneously with English native-speakers during structured tasks were able to use target forms (e.g., certain kinds of questions) more accurately in later tasks than those who did not interact in the same manner (Gass and Varonis, 1994; Mackey, 1999). Current research is examining how different elements of the interaction, such as the purpose (task-type), interlocutor (learner vs. expert speaker), and communication mode (online vs. face-to-face), shape opportunities for negotiating meaning or form. Adams (2007), for example, investigated the development of past-tense forms, locative constructions (e.g., *to the right of*), and question formation for 25 adult ESL learners, following three learner–learner interactive tasks. She found that when tested on the language forms that were negotiated in interaction, learners demonstrated development for about 60% of the test items, a proportion similar to other research involving learner–native speaker interactions. She therefore concluded that learner–learner interaction may be as beneficial as interaction with native speakers for the learning of certain forms.

Rouhshad, Wigglesworth, and Storch (2016) also investigated adult ESL learner–learner interactions, but compared face-to-face and online text-chat interactions for 12 dyads during particular decision-making tasks. They found that the online context produced substantially fewer negotiations despite the task instructions, which explicitly encouraged peer feedback. These findings indicate that negotiation is not present in all forms of social interaction and may be a function of the talk's purpose and mode, rather than the interaction itself.

Research from this general cognitive-interactionist orientation reveals that the variety of social interactions in which learners engage provides a rich tapestry of distributed opportunities for processing, practicing, and internalizing linguistic forms. These studies also show that interaction with native speakers of the L2 as the ultimate learning configuration should not be over-emphasized, knowing that learners can gain a great deal from interacting with other learners from their own and other linguistic backgrounds.

SOCIOCULTURAL THEORIES

A growing body of research places much more emphasis on the social and cultural dimensions of learning, in addition to mental ones. This work also underscores participants' roles, relationships, interactions and goals when taking part in various kinds of linguistic activity (e.g., Lantolf, 2000, 2014; Swain and Deters, 2007). Sociocultural approaches draw heavily upon the early work of Vygotsky (1978) and consider social interaction (often described as mediation, involving language and other means of communication), scaffolding (or calibrated support from more proficient mentors), and joint goal-focused activity as key factors in language development and learning more generally. The broader learning context or ecology (such as curriculum, ideologies, linguistic environment) is also taken into account. Additional dimensions of interaction may also be examined, such as learners' emotional states or sense of identity or self (see Chapters 8 and 10), as well as how learners gain access to, or are positioned in and through, interactions as capable or incapable speakers, for example, or as native vs. non-native speakers, and how that positioning affects their learning. The linguistic (L2) communities of practice (Lave and Wenger, 1991) or social networks learners participate in (or wish to participate in) are also examined, as well as their changing modes and degrees of participation in them (Swain and Deters, 2007; Zappa-Hollman and Duff, 2015). Given this focus on the socially-situated nature of interaction and participation, sociocultural research tends to examine language activity in naturally occurring contexts (including classrooms and communities) rather than in experimentally designed interactions in laboratory-like settings.

Recent sociocultural SLA studies reveal that social contexts which are assumed to be conducive to considerable amounts of interaction (e.g., immersion or study-abroad programs) may not be as effective as expected, depending on the kinds of relationships learners have access to (e.g., Kinginger, 2009). Furthermore, for some learners it is precisely those relational and cultural aspects of learning or using another language that are considered more important than linguistic accuracy. In study-abroad research contexts, the interactions between students and their homestay hosts, or between roommates in university dormitory settings, or other interlocutors, are often studied to examine how learners improve in their L2 pragmatics (see Chapter 27), fluency, register variation, and culturally and linguistically appropriate ways of expressing affect or emotion (Kinginger, 2009). Some of these aspects of everyday language use may not be addressed in more formal learning contexts or textbooks.

Socioculturally-oriented study-abroad research often takes a language socialization perspective, which examines processes of linguistic and cultural development (see Chapter 28). Language socialization foregrounds the roles of (co-)participation and mentorship, or apprenticeship, within social groups that enable novices/learners and peers to observe, internalize, and increasingly use language in normative ways in a given culture or discourse community (Duff and Talmy, 2011).

Pragmatics (i.e., using language in appropriate ways in different social contexts) is one of several traditional foci of L1 and L2 socialization and other SLA research. For example, if a person (A) wanted to end an interaction with others and leave the premises, the utterance "I go now!" might be corrected by an interlocutor (B) through a recast: "You're *going* now? So soon? See you later!" B's response to A attends to both the grammatical and pragmatic attributes of the utterance. Mentors such as teachers or tutors might be quite explicit in pointing out pragmatic conventions connected with leave-taking in different situations (i.e., announcing that you are leaving is not a substitute for some kind of salutation, such as *Goodbye* or *See you later!,* depending on the context). Usually, through extended experience involving observation and social interaction within a particular community, newcomers become sensitive to such normative, highly situated linguistic/cultural practices and begin to approximate and internalize the linguistic behaviors, cultural dispositions and values of more experienced group members. However, as seen in the previous section, without explicit feedback (a form of socialization), learners might not notice differences between their language use and that of others, or might not be aware of the underlying values or cultural meanings associated with particular routine forms.

Sociocognitive approaches to L1 and L2 learning and interaction (e.g., Atkinson, 2011, 2014), highlight how interlocutors align with each other physically, affectively, and cognitively in their face-to-face interactions as part of the communication and learning process. Atkinson's work, for example, explores how the physical movements of interlocutors – their gestures or their eye gaze – become subconsciously synchronized (i.e., aligned with or attuned to one another) as they jointly focus their attention on certain linguistic tasks or structures. In this view, learning by means of social interaction is a kind of mutual adaptation and not simply the processing and storage of linguistic information. For this reason, sociocognition is more closely associated with the second approach (sociocultural SLA) than the first (cognitive-interactionism).

Much of this socioculturally-oriented L2 research (and the learning it is based on) takes place outside of formal second-language instructional settings, such as in informal tutorials. To gain an understanding of the out-of-class contexts (see Chapter 13) in which learners interact with others, researchers and teachers can examine the strength, type and number of their connections with others in the learning milieu. They can then discern how interactions with members of their social networks facilitate or mediate their L2 learning (e.g., Zappa-Hollman and Duff, 2015). In addition, learners can reflect on how such associations and interactions affirm their identities or provide emotional, linguistic, and other forms of support (e.g., academic, cultural) that contribute to their learning and social integration.

IMPLICATIONS FOR TEACHING AND ASSESSMENT

If social interaction is indeed a crucial feature of becoming more communicatively competent in an L2, then teachers need to devise ways of optimizing instructional activities and assessments to allow students to use language with others to accomplish learning and performance objectives. Many curricular approaches, such as task-based language teaching (see Chapter 29) and service learning, emphasize students' active engagement with others in the learning process (see Celce-Murcia, Brinton, and Snow, 2014). In these approaches, social interaction is fostered through students' mutual interest in working collaboratively to accomplish group tasks or projects or to achieve other kinds of shared goals. The instructor carefully designs and manages the learning activities to ensure maximal participation and benefits for all. In what follows, we highlight some of the innovative ways in which instructors and program designers are encouraging L2 interaction beyond the classroom, or are incorporating interactive tasks into assessment practices.

PROMOTING INTERACTION BEYOND THE CLASSROOM

It has never been easier to put learners in contact with other L2 speakers, either through out-of-class projects involving a local L2 community or through telecollaboration projects that connect students in different parts of the world via email and chat. For example, taking advantage of the multicultural urban environment in Japanese cities, Strong (2009) reported a project in which university students of English participated in a field trip to an English-dominant synagogue, where they interviewed English speakers in order to complete a cultural project. In another study, Bower and Kawaguchi (2011) took advantage of students' access to new technologies and created an online language exchange between English learners in Japan and Japanese learners in the United States. Using a chat application, students were able to chat informally via text with similarly-aged peers. In these ways, even in contexts with few L2 speakers, the researchers created meaningful opportunities for social interaction and learning.

In contexts where students are surrounded by L2 speakers (as in study abroad), it would seem a simple task to encourage students to interact informally with locals. However, students with low language proficiency, or those who are shy, or who travel to a new country as part of a group, may have difficulties finding opportunities for sustained L2 interaction and relationships. Program designers may want to incorporate mentorship or language exchange programs (sometimes called tandem learning), where a session is split so that an English-speaking learner of Japanese, for example, can practice speaking Japanese with a Japanese speaker; in return, in the other half of the session, the pair speaks English. Similarly, interview activities could be assigned for those in homestay situations, to foster longer and more complex interactions with their host families. Knight and Schmidt-Rinehart (2010) created a *Family Interactive Journal*, in which American students sojourning in either Mexico or Spain completed two interactive tasks of their choice per week on cultural topics such as the news, food, or local customs. Students who completed the journal tasks reported more interaction and a better understanding of their host family.

INTERACTIVE ASSESSMENTS AND THE ASSESSMENT OF INTERACTION

Increasingly, language assessment incorporates an interactional approach as well. In one approach, for example, pairs of test-takers might be matched to do oral tasks together (e.g., compare and contrast pictures) with an assessor present. This format is found in the spoken component of the Cambridge English: Advanced (CAE) exam http://www.cambridgeenglish.org/exams/advanced/exam-format/). In another interactive approach to assessment, peers take part in group-based oral activities; the individuals within the groups are then assessed individually (Gan, 2010; Winke, 2013). For example, the groups might be asked to decide which items from a large set of possible items they would take with them to a deserted island, and why those items and not others. The participants in both of these test formats are assessed based on how well they perform linguistically in interaction with others (e.g., by not monopolizing talk, but contributing to it in constructive, effective, comprehensible and appropriate ways). The information from such assessments can then be used to evaluate student learning for summative purposes (showing what they have learned in a course), for placement purposes (to determine the level of class they should be placed in), or as part of a general measure of proficiency.

Another approach to assessment, known as 'Dynamic Assessment', which draws on sociocultural theory, provides individuals being assessed some assistance from their assessors or others (e.g., peers) in order to demonstrate what the learners are capable of doing – and learning – when particular forms of support are provided (Antón, 2015; Lantolf and Poehner, 2011; Poehner, 2009). It is felt that these interactive approaches to assessment better mirror the ways in which language is used in communication-oriented classroom instruction, as well as in optimal extracurricular social encounters. Furthermore, these approaches, it is claimed, provide a better representation of people's ability to speak with others than traditional (more monologic) forms of assessment. In addition, particularly with Dynamic Assessment, students learn from engaging in the assessment activities themselves.

CONCLUSION

In this chapter, we have highlighted some of the contemporary approaches to second language learning theory that view social interaction as a fundamental dimension of learning. Taken together, these approaches are quite distinct from teaching/learning approaches that are more heavily scripted and recitative, with little opportunity for extemporaneous speech by students.

We have also suggested applications of social-interactionist approaches to language learning, both inside and outside of classrooms, for teaching and assessment. Finally, our focus here has been interaction in the learners' L2 primarily for the purposes of L2 learning. For many learners, however, their L1 and additional languages (and other tools for expressing meanings) may be used very effectively to help support their L2 learning; these aspects, particularly in multilingual contexts, are likely to receive even more attention in future theoretical accounts of language learning in global contexts.

Discussion Questions

1. Consider your own past or present experience of learning (or teaching) a second language. To what extent were you expected to – and able to – interact in the L2 as part of the learning process? With whom and how? What kind of activity or task was the most conducive to productive interaction, in your view? Was this social interaction part of your classroom instruction or did the interaction take place outside of class? What did you learn (in terms of language, culture, or other content) from those interactions?
2. Imagine that you are required to take an L2 proficiency test, either:
   a) as a student, to demonstrate your level of proficiency for placement purposes; or
   b) as a teacher, to demonstrate that you are proficient enough to be a teacher of that L2.

Instead of doing the oral component of the test with just a tester/interviewer, you have been assigned to do some oral tasks together with another unknown test-taker or two instead. What might be some of the advantages and disadvantages of this interactive approach to assessment for you, as a test-taker, on the one hand, or for the teachers or testers involved, on the other hand?
3. A group of students in your second or foreign language class seek additional out-of-class opportunities to practice their L2 with others. What kinds of interactions, resources, or contexts would you recommend? Why? What might be some of the challenges in trying to set up these interactions?

Key Readings

The Douglas Fir Group (2016). A transdisciplinary framework for SLA in a multilingual world. *Modern Language Journal*, 100, Supplement S1.

Mackey, A., & Polio, C. (Eds.) (2009). *Multiple Perspectives on Interaction: Second Language Research in Honor of Susan M. Gass.* New York: Taylor & Francis / Routledge.

Markee, N. (Ed.) (2015). *The Handbook of Classroom Discourse and Interaction.* Malden, MA: Wiley-Blackwell.

Mitchell, R., Tracy-Venture, N., & McManus, K. (Eds.) (2015). *Social Interaction, Identity and Language learning During Residence Abroad*. European Second Language Association. Available at: http://www.eurosla.org/eurosla-monograph-series-2/

References

Adams, R. (2007). Do second language learners benefit from interacting with each other? In A. Mackey (Ed.), *Conversational Interaction in Second Language Acquisition: A Series of Empirical Studies* (pp. 29–51). Oxford: Oxford University Press.

Antón, M. (2015). Shifting trends in the assessment of classroom interaction. In N. Markee (Ed.), *The Handbook of Classroom Discourse and Interaction* (pp. 74–89). Malden, MA: Wiley-Blackwell.

Atkinson, D. (Ed.) (2011). *Alternative Approaches to Second Language Acquisition*. New York: Routledge.

Atkinson, D. (2014). Language learning in mindbodyworld: A sociocognitive approach to second language acquisition. *Language Teaching*, 47(4), 467–483.

Bower, J., & Kawaguchi, S. (2011). Negotiation of meaning and corrective feedback in Japanese–English etandem. *Language Learning & Technology*, 15(1), 41–71.

Celce-Murcia, M., Brinton, D., & Snow, M. A. (Eds.) (2014). *Teaching English as a Second or Foreign Language* (4th ed.). Boston, MA: National Geographic / Heinle Cengage.

Duff, P., & Talmy, S. (2011). Second language socialization: Beyond language acquisition in SLA. In D. Atkinson (Ed.), *Alternative Approaches to Second Language Acquisition* (pp. 95–116). London: Routledge.

Ellis, R. (2008). *The Study of Second Language Acquisition* (2nd ed.). Oxford: Oxford University Press.

Gan, Z. (2010). Interaction in group oral assessment: A case study of higher- and lower-scoring students. *Language Testing*, 27, 585–602.

Gass, S. & Varonis, E. (1994). Input, interaction, and second language production. *Studies in Second Language Acquisition*, 16, 283–302.

Kinginger, C. (2009). *Language Learning and Study Abroad*. London: Palgrave Macmillan.

Knight, S. M., & Schmidt-Rinehart, B. C. (2010). Exploring conditions to enhance student/host family interaction abroad. *Foreign Language Annals*, 43(1), 64–71.

Lantolf, J. P. (Ed.) (2000). *Sociocultural Theory and Second Language Learning*. Oxford: Oxford University Press.

Lantolf, J. P. (2014). The sociocultural perspective. *Studies in Second Language Acquisition*, 36, 368–374.

Lantolf, J. P. & Poehner, M. E. (2011). *Dynamic Assessment in the Foreign Language Classroom: A Teacher's Guide* (2nd ed.). State College, PA: The Pennsylvania State University Center for Advanced Language Proficiency Education and Research.

Lave, J., & Wenger, E. (1991). *Situated Learning: Legitimate Peripheral Participation*. Cambridge: Cambridge University Press.

Long, M. H. (1980). *Input, Interaction, and Second Language Acquisition*. Unpublished doctoral dissertation, University of California, Los Angeles.

Long, M. H. (1996). The role of the linguistic environment in second language acquisition. In W. C. Ritchie & T. K. Bhatia (Eds.), *Handbook of Second Language Acquisition* (pp. 413–468). San Diego: Academic Press.

Mackey, A. (1999). Input, interaction, and second language development: An empirical study of question formation in ESL. *Studies in Second Language Acquisition*, 22, 471–497.

Mackey, A. (Ed.) (2013). *Conversational Interaction in Second Language Acquisition*. Oxford: Oxford University Press.

Markee, N. (Ed.) (2015). *The Handbook of Classroom Discourse and Interaction*. Malden, MA: Wiley-Blackwell.

McDonough, K., & Mackey, A. (Eds.) (2013). *Second Language Interaction in Diverse Educational Contexts*. Amsterdam/Philadelphia: John Benjamins.

Mitchell, R., Myles, F., & Marsden, E. (2013). *Second Language Learning Theories* (2nd ed.). London: Routledge.

Ortega, L. (2009). *Understanding Second Language Acquisition*. New York: Hodder/Routledge.

Poehner, M. E. (2009). Group Dynamic Assessment: Mediation for the L2 classroom. *TESOL Quarterly*, 43(3), 471–491.

Rouhshad, A., Wigglesworth, G., & Storch, N. (2016). The nature of negotiations in face-to-face versus computer-mediated communication in pair interactions. *Language Teaching Research*, 20, 514–534.

Stockwell, G., & Harrington, M. (2013). The incidental development of L2 proficiency in NS–NNS email interactions. *CALICO journal*, 20(2), 337–359.

Strong, G. (2009). Fieldtrips with Japanese student ethnographers. In A. Smith & G. Strong (Eds.), *Adult Language Learners: Context and Innovation* (pp. 117–125). Alexandria, VA: TESOL.

Swain, M., & Deters, P. (2007). "New" mainstream SLA theory: Expanded and enriched. *Modern Language Journal*, 91, 820–836.

Vygotsky, L. S. (1978). *Mind in Society: The Development of Higher Psychological Processes* Cambridge, MA: Harvard University Press.

Winke, P. (2013). The effectiveness of interactive group orals for placement testing. In K. McDonough & A. Mackey (Eds.), *Second Language Interaction in Diverse Educational Contexts* (pp. 247–268). Amsterdam/Philadelphia: John Benjamins.

Zappa-Hollman, S., & Duff, P. (2015). Academic English socialization through individual networks of practice. *TESOL Quarterly*, 49, 333–368.

CHAPTER 12

Learning in the Classroom

Martin East

INTRODUCTION

The classroom is an important locus for language learning. On that basis, it is important to maximise language learners' learning experiences and opportunities in the classroom so that they can gain the most from what happens in class. Since around the 1970s, a fundamental goal of many English as an additional language programmes across the world has been to help learners to acquire the ability to communicate effectively in the target language (TL), whether in an 'immersion' context (learning English in an English-speaking country, hereafter referred to as second language or L2), or in a foreign language context (learning English in a non-English speaking country, hereafter FL). In both L2 and FL contexts, the goal of communicative proficiency has influenced structures of classroom learning in a range of ways, with some structures more successful than others.

When the fundamental goal is effective communication, Brown (2007: 218) notes a "new wave of interest" in language classrooms in "language as interactive communication among individuals, each with a sociocultural identity". This 'new wave' makes the focus of language learning "the creation of meaning through interpersonal negotiation among learners", with teachers setting up their classrooms to become spaces that facilitate learners' engagement in "meaningful, authentic exchanges". This interactionist approach is central to many contemporary theories of second language learning (see Chapter 11).

In this chapter, I present some core considerations regarding enhancing language learning opportunities in the classroom, and discuss relevant theoretical perspectives against the backdrop of an interactionist approach. In particular, and guided by the central goal of effective communication, I consider a fundamental tension for language learners, the tension between fluency and accuracy. Initially I discuss the strengths and limitations of three different scenarios for classroom learning based on Michael Long's forms/meaning/form trichotomy (e.g., Long, 2000). I go on to propose one model for classroom learning that may help learners, whatever their level of proficiency and whatever their personal learning style, to move towards the goal of enhanced interactional proficiency in ways that pay due attention to both fluency and accuracy. I conclude with a brief discussion of the implications of the proposed model for teaching and assessment practices.

OVERVIEW

The introduction of Communicative Language Teaching (CLT) in the early 1970s in the UK precipitated an emphasis on language in actual use, with a view to helping learners meet their needs in genuine and concrete situations beyond the classroom. CLT heralded a significant pedagogical shift away from the structural and grammatical emphases found in approaches such as grammar-translation and audio-lingualism. The learning intentions became "what it means to *know* a language and to be able to *put that knowledge to use* in communicating with people in a variety of settings and situations [emphases added]" (Hedge, 2000: 45).

The beginnings of a similar shift were in evidence in the USA with the advent of the 'proficiency movement' and the 'proficiency-oriented curriculum' at the start of the 1980s. This shift found its genesis in the argument that language learning essentially has a functional communicative purpose, with the principal and overarching goal of enabling learners to become "interactionally competent on the international scene" (Kramsch, 1986: 367). This competence would be developed by focusing on learners' ability to operate successfully in the TL in real-world contexts (Higgs, 1984).

In essence, and seen from the above perspectives, a fundamental objective of communicatively oriented classrooms, in the broader context of enhancing competence across a range of skills, is the development of learners' interactional ability. The end-goal is automaticity in language use (DeKeyser, 2001; Segalowitz, 2005). Essentially, automaticity is the ability of language learners to draw on their growing knowledge of the TL automatically and spontaneously.

Interactional automaticity may be evidenced at a range of levels of proficiency, from the most basic social interactions to the most complex discussions that approach first language (L1) competence. The Common European Framework of Reference for Languages or CEFR (Council of Europe, 2001), a framework that has its roots in the early days of CLT, represents one significant step towards articulating what learners 'can do' with the language at levels of increasing complexity across a variety of skills – the receptive skills of listening and reading, and the productive skills of writing and speaking. Speaking is further differentiated between spoken production and spoken interaction.

At whatever level, for interactional proficiency to be effective, account must be taken of both fluency and accuracy. In the language learning classroom, the balance between fluency and accuracy is enacted in a range of ways which are presented in the following section.

KEY LEARNING ISSUES

FORMS, MEANING OR FORM?

Emerging from more structural and behaviourist (grammar-oriented) pedagogical approaches, and mindful of a more communicative and utilitarian emphasis, early proponents of CLT began to wrestle with the relationship between communicative proficiency and grammatical competence, or between fluency and accuracy. A key question became how fluency and accuracy were to be interconnected. The contributions of these intersecting components were conceptualised in different ways that, from a theoretical perspective, became most clearly articulated by Long (e.g., 2000) as a trichotomy: focus on forms, focus on meaning, and focus on form. Long introduced these labels as means to describe three entirely different approaches to grammar that have significant implications for learning in classrooms where a key objective is developing communicative proficiency.

Focus on forms is essentially a 'teach them the grammar' approach. In communicatively oriented classrooms, the learning is operationalised through what has become an established and familiar lesson structure of present/practise/produce or PPP. Teachers first present a grammatical rule in an explicit way. Then the learners practise the rule in some formal way through a grammar drill such as a gap-fill or transformation exercise. Finally, learners proceduralise or produce the rule in some kind of communicative activity, such as a role-play. The theory is that, through explicit teaching followed by practice and production, learners will both learn the rules and be able to use them correctly in communicative contexts.

Focus on forms brings to our attention that direct grammar teaching has a role to play in developing learners' knowledge of the language. This teacher-led 'deductive' approach helps learners to develop explicit grammatical knowledge. However, seen from the perspective of communicative proficiency, the approach has been found wanting. Long's (2000) argument against focus on forms is essentially that it leads to boring lessons and student attrition. Another challenge is that the production stage is often so constrained to practice of the targeted forms that learners do not develop the ability to use language beyond limited confines.

In English as L2 contexts where there may be extensive opportunities for authentic interactions with L1 speakers outside the classroom, there may arguably be a case for significant attention to form in class, but effectiveness may be limited by multilingual classrooms in which the medium of instruction will necessarily be English. Theoretically this may be useful for acquisition, but it is potentially cognitively too demanding, and therefore off-putting, especially for lower-proficiency learners. In English as FL contexts, the benefits of a shared L1 may reduce the cognitive load because L1 scaffolding can be added where necessary (Philp and Tognini, 2009), but where there are limited opportunities to engage in authentic interactions outside the classroom, the development of interactional proficiency will be hindered.

Focus on meaning, in contrast to forms, is a 'don't teach them the grammar' approach that avoids formal grammar teaching altogether. From this perspective, all that is considered necessary is learners' internal processing. As learners engage in language in actual use, it is considered that they will derive the rules implicitly for themselves. This approach means that learners can devote maximum time to language use in class.

Focus on meaning brings to our attention that opportunities for putting language to use have a significant role to play in developing learners' interactional proficiency. However, Long's (2000) argument against focus on meaning derives from studies that show advantages in rate of language acquisition for those who receive some level of formal instruction in the grammar. Once more, the L2 context potentially provides adequate scope for authentic interactional opportunities outside of class, leaving room for greater attention to form in class and thereby allowing the limitation of a pure focus on meaning to be addressed. In FL contexts, exclusion of grammar instruction is likely to prove ineffective. Swan (2005), for example, argues that learners in such contexts require a carefully planned and explicit focus on central linguistic elements and core grammatical structures and ample opportunities to practise and use, and thereby learn and acquire, these elements. In his view, learners at the very least need to know and be able to draw on basic grammatical concepts if they are to communicate with others with any degree of success.

Long's concept of focus on form aims to reconcile the limitations of both teacher-led explicit grammar explanations and a zero-grammar approach. Focus on form is based on the principle that language use comes first (the learners will do something meaningful with language input, and will experiment with language through output and interaction). Attention to the grammar is contingent on learners first noticing grammatical rules as they put language to use. Once noticed, more explicit attention to the rules can follow. There can still be a place for grammar explanation and grammar practice, but these build on what learners have first noticed for themselves. Focus on form has become the dominant theoretical model in so-called Task-Based Language Teaching or TBLT (see Chapter 29).

Focus on form brings to our attention that "what students can find out for themselves is better remembered than what they are simply told" (Ellis, 2003: 163). This learner-focused 'inductive' approach supports learners to develop their implicit knowledge of the grammar. However, focus on form (which requires learners first to have noticed a particular form in the input before it is attended to more explicitly) may also be challenging in classrooms. What if the learners just do not notice?

Each of Long's three theoretical positions has implications for classroom learning, and these implications differ, depending on whether the learning context is L2 or FL. As a consequence, the most beneficial interface between fluency and accuracy in the classroom is elusive, or, as Mitchell (2000: 296) argues, "much remains to be done before the most 'effective' mixes and sequences of instruction and use can be identified." Added to this, individual learner differences will play a part in what is likely to be most effective for different learners. Some learners really value having the rules carefully explained to them, followed by systematic practice. Others are not interested in such an approach and would prefer to throw themselves into language use. Limitations notwithstanding, each of the theoretical positions presented by Long do have something to say to us about learning in the classroom, and will influence teachers' decision-making about what (and where) instruction is necessary, and how (and when) use is to be encouraged.

Building on these three approaches to learning in the classroom, in what follows I propose one model for setting up learning that both maximises interactional language use and gives scope for valuable instruction and teacher input that can take account of learner differences.

FLIPPING THE CLASSROOM

As Brown (2007) makes clear, with the end-goal of real-world communicative language use in mind, what we are seeing in many language classrooms is an enhanced understanding and appreciation of the valuable learning potential of peer-to-peer interactions. Philp, Adams, and Iwashita (2014) argue that this learning potential is informed and supported by both a cognitive viewpoint (e.g., Long's (1996) interaction hypothesis) and a socio-cultural viewpoint through which learning is co-constructed and built into the process of interaction. For Philp et al. (ibid.), peer interaction is "any communicative activity carried out *between learners*, where there is minimal or no participation from the teacher" (p. 3). It is collaborative and interactive because learners are required to work together towards a specified outcome. It enhances opportunities for learners to speak, practise communication patterns, partake in negotiation of meaning, and take up new interactional roles. Automaticity in language use is the ultimate goal.

Increased emphasis on peer-to-peer interaction has strong theoretical appeal as a means to foster learners' communicative proficiency with actual and future real-world language needs in mind. However, if peer-to-peer interaction is to be encouraged as a central component of learning in the classroom, several principles of operation may be helpful in terms of addressing due attention to grammatical form and individual learner differences.

One means of enabling learners to process the key material required for effective interactions (e.g., important vocabulary, essential grammatical concepts), whilst also allowing ample classroom time for meaningful interactions to take place, is to follow a 'flipped classroom' model. In the flipped classroom, learners are required to "take more responsibility for their own learning and study core content either individually or in groups before class and then apply knowledge and skills to a range of [in class] activities using higher order thinking" (Sanchez, 2015: Slide 6). Under this model, preparation and learning of key vocabulary and initial processing of relevant grammatical structures can take place outside of, and prior to, class. The classroom then becomes the locus for learners' active and collaborative interaction with others, drawing on and making use of the material they have prepared outside class. Groups can be established to facilitate peer-to-peer interaction and language in actual use.

Under a flipped model, learners are not left entirely to their own devices, however. Prior to class, the teacher will need to expend time to locate or produce resources that will help learners to access and process the necessary key material. For example, this may require finding or creating short instructional videos that carefully introduce relevant grammatical principles, coupled with practice material that helps learners to consolidate their learning. In one sense, this replicates the present and practise components of a traditional PPP lesson structure, but its essential difference is that both presentation and practice take place outside of, and prior to, the lesson. Furthermore, individual learner differences can be taken into account. The crucial objective is to come prepared to class. However, in reaching that objective, learners can access the material they need at their own pace, for as long as is necessary for them to have been exposed to, and to have had an opportunity to practise, the target material.

In class, the teacher's role moves from expert to facilitator. Important occasions for learning can be exploited through "facilitating active learning, engaging students, guiding learning, correcting misunderstandings and providing timely feedback using a variety of pedagogical strategies" (Sanchez, 2015: Slide 7). This may include feedback to learners that focuses on use, and misuse, of the target structures as they engage in interaction (Philp and Tognini, 2009). Where necessary, there is room for specific grammar instruction (see Chapter 20). The emphasis, however, is on the learners' active engagement in the learning process through language use in class.

With fundamental preparatory work having taken place outside the classroom, there are all kinds of interactional activities in which learners can engage in the classroom. The kinds of tasks encouraged in TBLT models are apposite here, that is, "discussions, problems, games and so on" that "require learners to use language for themselves" (Willis and Willis, 2007: 1). Essentially, it is important to engage learners in authentic language use in class, however that is achieved. Thus, anything that is likely to promote genuine (rather than artificial or constrained) language use, and that will contribute to developing what learners can do with the language, can be of value. Although primary emphasis is on what the learners do together, teachers can, as required, adopt the role of "crucial interactional partner" – motivating, organising, supporting and providing feedback as "the more proficient, knowledgeable interlocutor" (Van den Branden, 2009: 284).

IMPLICATIONS FOR TEACHING AND ASSESSMENT

In essence, the flipped classroom model achieves the following goals for learning in the classroom. The flipped model:

- minimises teacher-dominated instructional time;
- maximises learner-focused interactional time;
- sets up ample opportunities for genuine peer-to-peer communicative interaction in class;
- aims for maximum exposure to the TL in class;
- builds in opportunities for feedback (and instruction where necessary); and

- encourages the learners to take ownership for a good deal of the preparation for what will happen in class (e.g., learning vocabulary or studying relevant grammar principles beforehand).

In a flipped classroom model, when it comes to learning in preparation for the classroom, some learners will rise to the expectations and challenges more than others, and local contexts will dictate the resources that can be made available. The greater the range of resources at learners' disposal, the more likely material relevant to different learners will be accessed. Richards (2015) outlines several different sources for out-of-class preparation including videos, the internet, chat rooms, mobile apps and self-access centres. Richards also reminds us that out-of-class learning requires "careful preparation and follow up on the part of the teacher" (p. 21). Its success in a flipped classroom model depends on learners seeing the value and importance of their own prior preparation so that they can take part meaningfully in classroom activities. As a consequence, "good *teaching* means preparing *learners* for learning both inside and outside of the classroom [emphases added]" (ibid.).

Richards (2015) also acknowledges several dimensions that may impact on a strong focus on peer-to-peer interactions for in-class learning. These include large class sizes, limited English proficiency on the part of teachers, and negative washback from assessment systems that are not conducive to encouraging interactional proficiency. Whilst larger class sizes and teacher proficiency may present some management challenges for in-class peer-to-peer interactions, one potential workaround is to arrange learners into peer groups in which learners of different proficiencies work together, with the more proficient peers taking on the 'crucial interactional partner' role, scaffolding and providing support for weaker proficiency peers. If, as Philp et al. (2014) suggest, peer interactions are principally activities undertaken between learners, valuable classroom learning experiences may still be achievable.

It is also important to recognise that the flipped classroom model and peer-to-peer interactional principles are not limited to speaking. Learners can be given opportunities to integrate different skills, for example, working together on collaborative reading or writing activities that are built on prior out-of-class preparation. The ultimate objectives of automaticity and communicative proficiency remain the same.

With regard to assessment regimes, learners inevitably want to do as well as possible on examinations, and teachers naturally want the same. Additionally, accountability can loom large in the minds of teachers who may be required to report on learner outcomes as measured through high-stakes assessment results. Teachers and learners will therefore inevitably tailor programmes to the purposes of assessment, and where these do not match with interactional proficiency, the learning potential of peer-to-peer interactions will be hindered. Fortunately, several high-stakes assessment systems are embracing practices that are in line with peer-to-peer interactions. For example, the speaking assessments that contribute to the suite of international Cambridge examinations of English as an additional language, provided at a range of levels benchmarked against the CEFR, are generally modelled on a paired-speaking format and aim to measure communicative interactional skills (Cambridge English Language Assessment, 2016). Where such examinations are in use, the washback potential (the effect of the assessment on teaching and learning practices) is arguably positive.

CONCLUSION

Making the most of learning in the classroom will require balancing instruction with language use. As previously stated, individual learners vary in their preferred learning styles, aptitude, attitudes and motivations (see Chapters 6–9). What works for some does not work for others, and therefore "[t]here can be no 'one best method' … which applies at all times and in all situations, with every type of learner" (Mitchell, Myles, and Marsden, 2013: 290). There is something to be learnt from each of Long's (2000) foci.

A flipped classroom model which places ownership on the learners to prepare in advance, in tandem with ample in-class interactional opportunities and appropriate teacher facilitation, may be a means of achieving the real-world communicative goals that are seen as important whilst still attending to learners' needs. This model does not negate the need, from time to time, for explicit instruction, but capitalises on opportunities for meaningful interaction by relegating much of the preparatory work to outside the class.

Discussion Questions

1. As a teacher, what kinds of learner-centred peer-to-peer interactional opportunities could you set up in the classroom to ensure maximum target language use? Try to come up with a couple of concrete examples.

2. Following on from Question 1, what is required, from you as the teacher and from your learners, both before these interactions, and after them? (That is, what preparatory work is needed, whether in class or at home, to get the most out of the interactions? What post-interaction support is needed to ensure that learners will have had the greatest opportunity to consolidate their knowledge and ability?)

3. Introducing a flipped classroom is not necessarily easy. What barriers do you perceive, and how might you address them?

Key Readings

Bergmann, J., & Sams, A. (2012). *Flip Your Classroom: Reach Every Student in Every Class Every Day*. Eugene, OR: International Society for Technology in Education.

Brown, H. D. (2007). *Principles of Language Learning and Teaching* (5th ed.). New York: Pearson.

Cunningham, U. (2016). Language pedagogy and non-transience in the flipped classroom. *Journal of Open, Flexible and Distance Learning*, 20(1), 44–58.

Philp, J., Adams, R., & Iwashita, N. (2014). *Peer Interaction and Second Language Learning*. London / New York: Routledge.

Richards, J. C., & Rodgers, T. S. (2014). *Approaches and Methods in Language Teaching* (3rd ed.). Cambridge: Cambridge University Press.

Willis, D., & Willis, J. (2007). *Doing Task-Based Teaching*. Oxford: Oxford University Press.

References

Brown, H. D. (2007). *Principles of Language Learning and Teaching* (5th ed.). New York: Pearson.

Cambridge English Language Assessment (2016). Available at: www.cambridgeenglish.org/exams/ [Accessed 9 August 2016].

Council of Europe (2001). *Common European Framework of Reference for Languages*. Cambridge: Cambridge University Press.

DeKeyser, R. M. (2001). Automaticity and automatization. In P. Robinson (Ed.), *Cognition and Second Language Instruction* (pp. 125–151). Cambridge: Cambridge University Press.

Ellis, R. (2003). *Task-based Language Teaching and Learning*. Oxford: Oxford University Press.

Hedge, T. (2000). *Teaching and Learning in the Language Classroom*. Oxford: Oxford University Press.

Higgs, T. V. (Ed.) (1984). *Teaching for Proficiency: The Organizing Principle*. Lincolnwood, IL: National Textbook Company.

Kramsch, C. (1986). From language proficiency to interactional competence. *The Modern Language Journal*, 70(4), 366–372.

Long, M. H. (1996). The role of the linguistic environment in second language acquisition. In W. C. Ritchie & T. K. Bhatia (Eds.), *Handbook of Second Language Acquisition* (pp. 413–468). San Diego: Academic Press.

Long, M. H. (2000). Focus on form in task-based language teaching. In R. D. Lambert & E. Shohamy (Eds.), *Language Policy and Pedagogy: Essays in Honor of A. Ronald Walton* (pp. 179–192). Amsterdam/Philadelphia: John Benjamins.

Mitchell, R. (2000). Applied linguistics and evidence-based classroom practice: The case of foreign language grammar pedagogy. *Applied Linguistics*, 21(3), 281–303.

Mitchell, R., Myles, F., & Marsden, E. (2013). *Second Language Learning Theories* (3rd ed.). London / New York: Routledge.

Philp, J., Adams, R., & Iwashita, N. (2014). *Peer Interaction and Second Language Learning*. London / New York: Routledge.

Philp, J., & Tognini, R. (2009). Language acquisition in foreign language contexts and the differential benefits of interaction. *International Review of Applied Linguistics in Language Teaching*, 47(3/4), 245–266.

Richards, J. C. (2015). The changing face of language learning: Learning beyond the classroom. *The RELC Journal*, 46(1), 5–22.

Sanchez, M. A. (2015). Flipped classrooms. Available at: https://prezi.com/_xgns_kcdiab/flipped-classrooms/ [Accessed 11 August 2016].

Segalowitz, N. (2005). Automaticity and second languages. In C. J. Doughty & M. H. Long (Eds.), *The Handbook of Second Language Acquisition* (pp. 381–408). Oxford: Blackwell.

Swan, M. (2005). Legislation by hypothesis: The case of task-based instruction. *Applied Linguistics*, 26(3), 376–401.

Van den Branden, K. (2009). Mediating between predetermined order and chaos: The role of the teacher in task-based language education. *International Journal of Applied Linguistics*, 19(3), 264–285.

Willis, D., & Willis, J. (2007). *Doing Task-based Teaching*. Oxford: Oxford University Press.

CHAPTER 13

Learning Beyond the Classroom

Alice Chik

INTRODUCTION

Successful language learners do not only learn in the classroom, they also do other things outside the classroom to enhance, supplement or complement their classroom learning (Richards, 2015). A classroom is conventionally understood as a room in which students are taught. Van Lier (1988: 47) offered an expanded definition of a language classroom as "the gathering, for a given period of time, of two or more persons (one of whom generally assumes the role of instructor) for the purposes of language learning". In a discussion of classrooms as research sites, Candlin (1988) added that a classroom is more than a specific locale with a teacher and students because it embodies broader issues of ideology, socio-cultural institution and society. In this chapter, we will limit our definition of a language classroom to a place within an institution where a class of students is taught by a language teacher; and describe learning events that happen outside as 'beyond the classroom'.

OVERVIEW

Classroom-based language learning research is a well-established field with diverse research methodologies – from classroom observations to controlled experiments. It is the 'other things' learners do outside the classrooms that we have limited information on and understanding of. Language learning beyond the classroom cannot easily be defined, because it can be a very messy process that stretches over time and space. Learning processes are less observable because they happen in a space, time or interaction in which a teacher is frequently, though not necessarily, absent: How does it happen? Where does it happen? What is being learned? Who controlled what is learned? How does the learning develop over time? These are often invisible to teachers. Language teachers are thus likely to see only the results of learning beyond the classroom when, for example, learners display more confident speech, improved writing, or expanded vocabulary in reading. Two recent edited volumes on this topic (Benson and Reinders, 2011; Nunan and Richards,

2015) highlight the diversity and versatility of the language learning activities beyond the classroom – involving online and offline environments, intentional and incidental learning, interest- and purpose-driven content, and autonomous and structured other-direction. Language learning beyond the classroom, then, implies not just a reconfiguration of learning, it also posits the learners as being in the centre of, and in control of, this learning process (Nunan and Richards, 2015).

To capture diverse learning experiences, early studies suggested the use of learner diaries to access learners' experiences beyond the classroom (Bailey and Nunan, 1996; Schumann and Schumann, 1977). Schumann and Schumann (1977) used diaries to record their own language learning and, in recording their learning experiences, they demonstrated how language learning is connected to learners' personal and social worlds, and how classroom learning only constituted one facet of the whole learning experience. The section *The Classroom and Beyond* in Bailey and Nunan (1996) further highlighted the benefits of using learner diaries to showcase diverse learning experiences. Using interviews and surveys, other studies have demonstrated that learners engaged in an array of learning activities beyond the classroom, and that the activities were frequently related to popular culture consumption (Hyland, 2004; Lai, 2015; Murray, 2008; Nikula and Pitkänen-Huhta, 2008; Pickard, 1996). In this chapter, we will discuss the key learning issues associated with out-of-class language learning by introducing a theoretical model (Benson 2011; Chik, 2014), and, lastly, the implications for teaching and assessment.

KEY LEARNING ISSUES

Language learning beyond the classroom is diverse and versatile. In order to define the scope of language learning beyond the classroom, Benson (2011) proposed a theoretical model that examines learning in four dimensions: location, formality, pedagogy, and locus of control. The four dimensions are derived from terminology frequently used in discussion of language learning beyond the classroom: out-of-class, informal, non-instructed and self-directed learning. In Chik (2014), trajectory, a temporal dimension, is added to indicate learner management over time. In the following sections, each dimension will be introduced and learning issues discussed.

LOCATION

Location refers to the place or space in which a learning activity takes place, which can be a physical or virtual space. In some educational contexts, learning beyond the classroom, ironically, refers to 'after-school' learning or support programs in schools. Bailly's (2011) study shows how a school may support autonomous language learning in an after-school program. As foreign language education provision was limited in a vocational high school for students who are not academically inclined, the school organized after-school language advising and support sessions on a range of foreign languages. Though students were supported, they were mostly learning on their own by setting their learning goals and schedules independently. Unsurprisingly, after-school language learning programs are popular in Asia and, in some cases, languages other than English are being offered (Chik, 2014).

Organized learning activities are not necessarily only hosted by schools. Gao (2009) investigated self-organized 'English corners' and 'English clubs' in China and found voluntary gatherings of complete strangers in tea houses and cafés to speak and learn English. While Gao (2009) shows that some learners are enthusiastic about speaking English in public, Hyland (2004) found many Hong Kong students were happier to pursue English learning in the private domain. Her study with pre- and in-service English teachers showed that learners' choices of location for out-of-class language learning were highly related to what they perceived as socially acceptable. Some participants considered speaking English in a predominantly Chinese-speaking environment as pretentious and inappropriate. Consequently, participants reported turning to receptive activities, such as reading and listening to pop music, in the private domain.

Of course, locations of learning are not limited to physical spaces. Second language digital gamers regularly use online games and gaming forums as virtual learning sites. While some gamers play alone at home, others meet in person to play games together (Chik, 2014), so while the learners are in the same physical space, their co-learning and interaction is in virtual space. In addition to gaming-related websites, online language learning social network sites (LLSNSs) are emerging new platforms for independent language learning and exchange (Kozar and Sweller, 2014). It should be noted that while some learners are reappropriating social network sites for learning purposes (e.g., using Skype to meet target language speakers, see Kozar and Sweller, 2014), many LLSNSs are dedicated language teaching websites.

FORMALITY

Formality is concerned with whether or not a learning activity is part of an institutional program, possibly leading to qualifications. Informal learning frequently involves pursuit of interests outside institutionalized learning contexts. However, any informal leisure activity can be turned into an intentional language learning event when a learner displays an explicit intention of learning and uses learning strategies. In converting leisure activities to learning events, vocabulary learning appears to be the most popular engagement. Pickard (1996) showed German students using English newspaper and radio programs to improve their English vocabulary by extensive reading and listening, and by making vocabulary lists. Similarly, Hyland (2004) found pre- and in-service English teachers doing the same with recreational reading and TV watching. In sports, Nikula and Pitkänen-Huhta (2008) found Finnish youth developed a rich English vocabulary by refusing to use Finnish translations of skateboarding jargon. Because all skateboarding terms were invented in English, the teenagers thought it would not be right to use the Finnish terms. Their deliberate efforts in rejecting the Finnish translation and in using the English terms turned skateboarding into an English learning and use activity for these Finnish youths.

In a study with eight adult English learners in Japan, Murray (2008) illustrates how learners turned leisure popular cultural activities into intentional learning events. One participant enjoyed watching American movies, so he took a part-time job at a movie theatre during his undergraduate study. During lunch hours, he would watch the same movie multiple times – first, just enjoying the movie; then, additional viewings to make sure he listened to the English dialogues and did not read the Japanese subtitles. In addition to movies, other participants reported using pop cultural texts such as bestselling books, TV shows and pop songs to enrich their cultural and pragmatic knowledge.

Making learning intention transparent can be a public event, as in Chik's (2014) study, which found enthusiastic gamers advocating the benefits of using English-language games as both recreational and learning tools. These gamers actively share learning strategies and learning texts such as vocabulary lists and transcribed in-game texts on discussion forums. Vocabulary acquisition through digital gaming is not only reserved for self-reporting among adult gamers. Sylvén and Sundqvist (2012) found positive correlation between digital gaming and English proficiency level among Swedish primary school students. The gamers were found to perform better than non-gamers in both vocabulary and comprehension tests, and frequent gamers also outperformed occasional gamers. Though the researchers were cautious in categorizing digital gameplay sessions as intentional learning events, they believe English language games provide repeated exposures for learning.

PEDAGOGY

Pedagogy involves instruction, structured progression of material, explicit explanation, and assessment. Mentioned earlier, Bailly (2011) studied French vocational school students learning additional foreign languages in an after-school program. Though supported by conversation groups and language advising sessions, students found it difficult to gather relevant and structured learning resources. Consequently, certificate-oriented students engaged in 'serious' activities such as completing grammar exercises, while the more socially-oriented students engaged in 'lighter' activities like watching TV programs in the target language.

Pedagogy is not just about learning materials and resources; it also extends to the learners' communities. Learners frequently rely on people around them, such as older siblings, relatives and schoolmates, to support their learning and act as social resources. This is especially important for learners in resource-deprived rural areas (Lamb, 2013). In most scenarios, speakers of the target languages can be great conversation partners, and many of the learning events may be opportunistic rather than planned, for instance, during travel abroad (Coffey and Street, 2008). Of course, the popularity of 'English corners' in China has shown that incidental language teachers do not have to come from a learner's immediate social circles. They could be complete strangers who also attend the learning events (Gao, 2009).

Emerging online interest-driven communities show that learning support can be actively sought in virtual environments (Chik, 2014; Lam, 2014). For instance, digital gamers seek language support and advice from other gamers in interest-driven forums and chatrooms. While the transactional language, in most cases, is English, many digital gamers also reported learning Japanese and Korean, based on interests in Japanese- and Korean-exclusive online gaming (Chik, 2014). While some gamers find virtual partners to learn a second or foreign language, some learners use transnational language exchange to maintain heritage languages. Lam (2014) demonstrates the different strategies that a Chinese American teenager used to learn Chinese while her friends in China learned English from their exchanges. Though they first met on a study-abroad program for the American student in China, the learning community developed and extended to an online environment after the American student returned home. This type of self-organized language exchange can also happen when learners meet online. As reported in Ricker Schreiber (2015), a Serbian university student utilized his Facebook page to promote his interest in hip-hop music and his own rap duo. And in the process of sharing his musical passion, he was translanguaging between English and Serbian to create a unique linguistic identity to connect hip-hop and rap communities in both languages.

LOCUS OF CONTROL

Locus of control is a matter of whether a learning activity is self- or other-directed, and how the decisions about learning and teaching are distributed. Self-directed learning can mean a learner actively makes decisions about his or her learning, but it is not equivalent to an absolute control of every aspect of the learning. Content learning can be limited by choice of materials, and digital gaming is a case in point. Many gamers acquire a specialist vocabulary knowledge by playing certain genres of games (e.g., sports, and strategy games). A rich specialist vocabulary, for instance a pilot's flight vocabulary and phrases acquired from playing flight simulation games, may not have an everyday application but it can still boost a learner's confidence and motivation (Chik, 2014).

In many contexts, decisions about learning are distributed when learners seek advice and support from more experienced learners, either socially or from other online interest groups. In a study of a group of French-speaking African migrant teenagers in Canada, Ibrahim (1999) exemplifies how migrant youth used rap and hip-hop music to learn Black Stylized English and to cultivate a stronger identification with black popular culture. The migrant youth self-directed their ESL learning by using rap and hip-hop, but the control was also distributed among different members of the group, with female members resisting some aspects of the identification because of sexist components in rap music. Controversial aspects of some leisure activities can provide insight on locus of control. Generally, digital *bishōjo* games (literally 'pretty girl' games) are viewed as morally compromised because the genre is about players interacting with fantasy virtual young women; in addition, many *bishōjo* games contain pornographic elements. When a gamer asked for English-language *bishōjo* games for learning purposes, many forum discussants weighed in with opinions and advice to try to 'reform' the gamer to other 'morally healthier' games. While this might be seen as an attempt to other-direct an otherwise autonomous learning practice, the gamer resisted by stating that he felt most comfortable with *bishōjo* games, and thus wanted to use the game genre to improve his English (Chik, 2014).

On the increasingly popular LLSNSs, the question about who has the control over learning can be ambiguous (Álvarez Valencia, 2016). LLSNSs are foreign language learning platforms that include social network features for online users to create personal profiles and make friends, and some LLSNSs feature language exchanges among members. Some LLSNSs provide highly structured courses (e.g., Duolingo and Rosetta Stone), others include spaces for unstructured member language exchange (e.g., busuu and Livemocha). Though a learner may voluntarily join the learning process, many of these learning sites create constraints through their platform designs and payment structures. The learner may intend to direct his or her own learning, but the designs and features of the learning websites may redistribute the decision making away from the learners (Kozar and Sweller, 2014).

TRAJECTORY

Trajectory is concerned with the management and development of learning over time. This dimension can be a trickier dimension to categorize, because it requires longitudinal observation or retrospective interviews which focus on changes over time. In a study with mature foreign language learners, Coffey and Street (2008) argue that many learners view foreign language learning as a lifelong project that links to life events. Interviews with two mature French and German learners showed that foreign language learning practices changed in response to changes in life stages and personal circumstances. When recounting learning that spanned over forty years, the learners linked changes in learning styles and strategies in adolescent and later years. Murray (2008) suggests that one way in which learners develop a series of strategies and manage their learning at different times is by referring to 'folk pedagogy', or understandings about how we and other people learn (Bruner, 1996).

Using interview and online discussion forum data, Chik (2014) showed that some digital gamers manage their learning through gaming by following all the game editions in a game series, settling on a preferred gaming language (e.g., Japanese), changing game genre, and graduating from one game to another in the same genre. When gaming in a foreign language, proficiency is one key to satisfactory gameplay, which in turn prompts changes in gaming and learning practices. However, it should be stated that the data were mostly collected from gamers in their early to late twenties, who were quite capable of articulating changes in their gaming and language learning practices. Lamb

(2013), in contrast, observed that though Indonesian adolescents in rural areas were creative in utilizing limited resources to access English learning opportunities beyond the classroom, most learning events were idiosyncratic and spontaneous. His observations suggest that the youths had yet to show any developmental path in their learning beyond the classroom.

IMPLICATIONS FOR TEACHING AND ASSESSMENT

Richards (2015) argues that the benefits of out-of-class learning are for both learners and teachers, especially in terms of creating learning opportunities that are not readily available in the classroom and bridging the gap between classroom and out-of-class learning. It is important for teachers to acknowledge these benefits, and begin to view both classroom and out-of-class learning activities as part of the learners' learning ecology (Lai, 2015). Acknowledgement should also be given to learners' autonomous learning initiatives. It is not enough to know that our students engage in a wide range of activities – what they do – it is important to know more about where, when, how, and who with. The model (Benson, 2011; Chik, 2014) introduced in this chapter can be a helpful guide for teachers by identifying settings (location), modes of practice (formality, pedagogy, and locus of control), and temporal development (trajectory). Teachers can start by using the model to reflect upon their prior language learning experiences outside the classroom, and to promote students' mapping of the model. Second, teachers can let students articulate what they believe about learning beyond the classroom, and share the practices they engage in. Students could be introduced to the model to map their own out-of-class learning activities, and reflect upon areas for further expansion (for instance, making a recreational activity into an intentional learning event). Students can share their mappings to cultivate a sense of community and to exchange learning strategies beyond the classroom (see Chapter 9). Teachers can introduce additional out-of-class learning strategies and provide hands-on advising to students (Nunan and Richards, 2015). The model may also be used at different points of time for reflection, and for tracking and assessing learner development.

CONCLUSION

As articulated by Coffey and Street (2008), second and foreign language learning is a lifelong project, and learners will spend more time outside the classroom than they will spend in it. Diversity and versatility are the two main characteristics of language learning beyond the classroom, but they also highlight key learning issues: the where, how, who, when, and what of the learning process. This chapter summarized a theoretical model (Benson, 2011; Chik, 2014) that defines the scope in five dimensions: location, formality, pedagogy, locus of control and trajectory. The model can be viewed as an initial platform for systematically unveiling the colourful, individualistic and messy learning process. The wider and globalized availability of digital tools and resources points to greater affordances. Further research will be needed on exploring available affordances to examine how learning is distributed over time and space, and across interests. Another possible line for further pursuit could be cultural differences: are learners from diverse cultural and linguistic backgrounds applying similar or different strategies? Are learners of different age groups doing the same or different things? Are certain types of learners more likely to recognize and capitalize learning opportunities beyond the classroom than others? As our understanding of language learning beyond the classroom expands, more questions need to be asked and answered.

Discussion Questions

1. As a language teacher, which dimension (i.e., location, formality, pedagogy, locus of control, trajectory) do you believe to be most important in helping learners to understand their out-of-classroom learning practices? Why?

2. If you ask your students to map their out-of-class learning activities according to the five dimensions mentioned above, what do you think the mappings will look like?

3. How can learners be encouraged to use this five-dimension framework to monitor and reflect upon their learning practices?

Key Readings

Benson, P. & Nunan, D. (Eds.) (2004). *Learners' Stories: Difference and Diversity in Language Learning*. Cambridge: Cambridge University Press.

Benson, P. & Reinders, H. (Eds.) (2011). *Beyond the Language Classroom*. Basingstoke, UK: Palgrave Macmillan.

Kalaja, P., Menezes, V., & Barcelos, A.M. (Eds.) (2008). *Narratives of Learning and Teaching EFL*. London: Palgrave Macmillan.

Nunan, D. & Richards, J. C. (2015). *Language Learning Beyond the Classroom*, New York: Routledge.

Reinders, H. & Benson, P. (2017). Research agenda: Language learning beyond the classroom. *Language Teaching* 50(4), 561–578.

Richards, J. C. (2015). The changing face of language learning: Learning beyond the classroom. *RELC*, 46, 5–22.

References

Álvarez Valencia, J. A. (2016). Language views on social networking sites for language learning: The case of Busuu. *Computer Assisted Language Learning*, 29(5), 853–867.

Bailey, K. M. & Nunan, D. (Eds.) (1996). *Voices from the Language Classroom: Qualitative Research in Second Language Education*. Cambridge: Cambridge University Press.

Bailly, S. (2011). Teenagers learning languages out of school: What, why and how do they learn? How can school help them? In P. Benson & H. Reinders (Eds.), *Beyond the Language Classroom* (pp. 119–130). Basingstoke, UK: Palgrave Macmillan.

Benson, P. (2011). Language learning and teaching beyond the classroom: An introduction. In P. Benson and H. Reinders (Eds.), *Beyond the Language Classroom* (pp. 7–16). Basingstoke, UK: Palgrave Macmillan.

Benson, P. & Reinders, H. (Eds.) (2011). *Beyond the Language Classroom*. Basingstoke, UK: Palgrave Macmillan.

Bruner, J. (1996). *The Culture of Education*. Cambridge, MA: Harvard University Press.

Candlin, C. N. (1988). Preface. In Allwright, D., *Observation in the Language Classroom* (pp. x–xiii). London: Addison Wesley Longman.

Chik, A. (2014). Digital gaming and language learning: Autonomy and community. *Language Learning and Technology*, 18, 85–100.

Coffey, S., & Street, B. (2008). Narrative and identity in the "Language Learning Project". *The Modern Language Journal*, 92, 452–464.

Gao, X. (2009). The 'English corner' as an out-of-class learning activity. *ELT Journal*, 63, 60–67.

Hyland, F. (2004). Learning autonomously: Contextualising out-of-class English language learning. *Language Awareness*, 13, 180–202.

Ibrahim, A. E. K. M. (1999). Becoming Black: Rap and hip-hop, race, gender, identity, and the politics of ESL learning. *TESOL Quarterly*, 33, 349–369.

Kozar, O., & Sweller, N. (2014). An exploratory study of demographics, goals and expectations of private online language learners in Russia. *System*, 45, 39–51.

Lai, C. (2015). Perceiving and traversing in-class and out-of-class learning: Accounts from foreign language learners in Hong Kong. *Innovation in Language Learning and Teaching*, 9, 265–284.

Lam, W. S. E. (2014). Literacy and capital in immigrant youths' online networks across countries. *Learning, Media and Technology*, 39, 488–506.

Lamb, M. (2013). 'Your mum and dad can't teach you!': Constraints on agency among rural learners of English in the developing world. *Journal of Multilingual and Multicultural Development*, 34, 14–29.

Murray, G. (2008). Pop culture and language learning: Learners' stories informing EFL. *Innovation in Language Learning and Teaching*, 2, 1–16.

Nikula, T., & Pitkänen-Huhta, A. (2008). Using photographs to access stories of learning English. In P. Kalaja, V Menezes & A. M. Barcelos (Eds.), *Narratives of Learning and Teaching EFL* (pp. 171–185). London: Palgrave Macmillan.

Nunan, D. & Richards, J. C. (2015). *Language Learning Beyond the Classroom*. New York: Routledge.

Pickard, N. (1996). Out-of-class language learning strategies. *ELT Journal*, 50, 150–159.

Richards, J. C. (2015). The changing face of language learning: Learning beyond the classroom. *RELC*, 46, 5–22.

Ricker Schreiber, B. (2015). "I am what I am": Multilingual identity and digital translanguaging. *Language Learning & Technology*, 19, 69–87.

Schumann, F. M. & Schumann, J. H. (1977). Diary of a language learner: An introspective study of second language learning. In H. D. Brown, C. A. Yorio & R. H. Crymes (Eds.), *On TESOL '77: Teaching and Learning English as a Second Language: Trends in Research and Practice* (pp. 241–249). Washington, D.C.: TESOL.

Sylvén, L. K. & Sundqvist, P. (2012). Gaming as extramural English L2 learning and L2 proficiency among young learners. *ReCALL*, 24, 302–321.

van Lier, L. (1988). *The Classroom and the Language Learner: Ethnography and Second-Language Classroom Research*. London: Longman.

SECTION 4

LEARNING ENGLISH FOR PARTICULAR PURPOSES

In Section 4, the focus is on some of the particularized purposes for which languages are learned, specifically for academic/disciplinary, specific/professional and workplace reasons. Research in these fields has grown dramatically over the last two decades, particularly since the rapid spread of English as a language used across the whole world and as more and more people find a need to use English to fulfil particular goals and purposes.

In the first chapter in this section, **Helen Basturkmen** addresses the learning of English for academic purposes. For learners, this involves understanding the assumptions and practices involved in the genres of academic English. Learning in this context involves mastering the use of specific text types, as well as cultural knowledge related to particular disciplines. Among the learning issues involved is the difference between the writing practices of novices and experts, as well as the transferability of skills acquired in the classroom context to contexts beyond the classroom.

Focusing on the learning of English for specific purposes, **Christoph A. Hafner** further clarifies the nature of genres and emphasizes the way that language use varies in different specialized domains, whether these be disciplinary domains, or professional or workplace contexts. Each of these domains makes up a different disciplinary community of practice, complete with its own culture, values, genres and systems of meaning making. Learning English for specific purposes involves developing the necessary genre knowledge in order to be able to achieve one's communicative purposes as a member of that disciplinary or professional community. Learning may involve explicit instruction, interaction between novices and experts, and participation in social practices.

In the final chapter in this section, **Jane Lockwood** focuses attention on the now globalized use of English in workplace contexts. She points out that while workplace interactions may take place between non-native and native speakers, multinational workplaces increasingly involve communication between non-native speakers of English. After outlining some of the challenges and shortcomings of language support currently offered to employees who need to communicate in English, she highlights two key strategies that contribute to improving learning opportunities – language auditing and workplace discourse analysis. She concludes by stressing that it is crucially important that businesses enable opportunities for employees to enhance their language skills for work.

In one way or another, all the chapters in this section point out the importance of context, social participation and meaning in the effective use of language for particular purposes. Learners must not only acquire the systems and skills of language, but also understand the potential impact of the social and disciplinary dimensions that may serve to enhance or impede meaning. Based on such understandings, learners also express their ability to act effectively to achieve their personal purposes. The notion of genre as a way of entering and engaging with different social and cultural contexts, and acquiring membership of desired communities of practice both within and beyond classrooms, is also foregrounded in this section as a significant area for learning development.

CHAPTER 14

Learning for Academic Purposes

Helen Basturkmen

INTRODUCTION

Many English language teachers work in higher education and teach English for academic purposes (EAP). Most teach English for study purposes, although some may act as advisors in English for instructional or research publication purposes. To date, EAP literature has largely aimed to develop descriptions of academic language use as "EAP linguistic enquiry" (Swales, 2001: 43) as well as proposals for EAP teaching. It has given relatively limited direct attention to the topic of learning. This chapter focuses on learning in EAP. First, it describes the nature of the domain and the various purposes for learning EAP. This is followed by an examination of key learning issues related to English for study purposes. The chapter continues with a section on implications for teaching and assessment, followed by a conclusion, discussion questions and key readings.

OVERVIEW

Two major groups of EAP learners are students and academic staff in higher education, including, but not restricted to, students and staff with English as an additional or second language. The purposes for learning of these groups is shown in Table 14.1 and discussed below. The Focus column in the figure refers to student, research and instructional discourses, which are terms taken from Hyland's (2009) classification of types of academic discourses.

Students in higher education are typically learners of EAP for study purposes. Some graduate students may also be learners of EAP for research publication purposes. It is generally understood that "student discourse, and in particular, writing are at the heart of teaching and learning" (Hyland, 2009: 123). The field of EAP originated largely as a response to the needs of English language teachers in higher education in supporting students, generally students with English as a second or additional language, to meet the linguistic

LEARNER GROUP	FOCUS	DOMAIN	COMPONENTS OF LEARNING	EXAMPLE COMMUNICATIVE EVENTS AND GENRES
Students	Student discourses	English for study purposes		
		General academic purposes	Formal academic English register (linguistic features, writing conventions, rhetorical styles and norms) Study skills and competencies	Lectures Presentations and seminars Textbooks (reading) Essays, assignments, theses (writing) Office-hour and supervisory meetings
		Specific academic purposes	Disciplinary uses of English Writing/Speaking practices and culture of a disciplinary discourse community	Depending on discipline: e.g., laboratory reports in sciences
Faculty and graduate students	Research discourses	English for research publication purposes	Expert writing and speaking practices in the academic discourse community	Research articles Conference presentations
Faculty and teaching assistants	Instructional discourses	English for instructional purposes	Monologic/Interactive speaking and listening skills	Lectures, seminars & tutorials Classes and labs Office-hour and supervisory meetings

Table 14.1   Components of EAP Learning in Higher Education, According to Group and Domain

demands of academic study. The field has given considerable interest to identifying and describing the types of communicative events (readings, writing tasks and spoken events, such as seminars and tutorials) encountered by the students in the higher education setting at hand. Analysis is made of the learners' linguistic skills, or competencies, benchmarked against the skills deemed to be necessary for successful participation in key communicative events and fulfilment of assessment tasks in their academic studies. Nesi and Gardner (2012), for example, identified the range of written genres students were required to submit for assessment in their disciplinary studies in UK universities, (for example, case studies, critiques and literature surveys).

A distinction is made between English for General Academic Purposes (EGAP) and English for Specific Academic Purposes (ESAP). The provision of EGAP instruction is fairly common, and tends to be offered to students before the commencement of, or during, the first and second year(s) of university study. The provision of ESAP instruction is not as common, and it is more likely to be offered in later years of undergraduate study and in postgraduate study, when students' majors or target disciplines have been determined. (ESAP is discussed further in *Key learning issues*, p.132.)

EGAP instruction conventionally targets study skills (such as listening to lectures, reading and note-taking, referencing skills and participating in seminars) and development of the "general academic English register incorporating a formal academic style" (Jordan, 1997: 5). In general, learners' ability to use planned genres rather than relatively unplanned genres is highlighted in the EAP literature (see Chapter 25). For example, more attention has been given to learning speaking skills for making presentations, rather than speaking skills for participating in class or lecture exchanges. Suggestions were made also (Waters and Waters, 2001: 378) to include study competencies, such as logical thinking and autonomy, the "underlying cognitive and affective attributes on which effective study is based".

The formal academic register is usually construed as academic prose, a complex and concise style of writing in which certain grammatical forms, word choices and discourse features are more frequent compared to other registers, such as conversation. Grammatically, for example, Academic English involves a high frequency of heavy nominal groups, indicating that learners need to learn to "pack meaning into the noun phrase, and to make the text nominally rather than clausally complex" (Parkinson and Musgrave, 2014: 48–49). Research by Coxhead (2000) shows a high frequency of certain word families, such as *analyse, concept* and *data*. The use of third person formulations, for instance *it was clear that* or *it is likely that* to mask opinions, is one of the many discourse features of scientific research articles (Hewings, Lillis, and Mayor, 2007: 231). Learners need to become proficient in using and/or understanding the meanings conveyed by such linguistic elements, as well as understanding the use of citations and other academic writing conventions that characterise this register.

In addition, learners studying in a second language education system may need to come to terms with new rhetorical structures and norms. Essays in English, for example, often employ a deductive style of argument (the main thesis is given before arguing the case), whereas students from some non-English speaking backgrounds may be more familiar with an inductive style (the case is given before the thesis) (Hewings et al., 2007). Li (2008) describes how she developed the literacy practices needed in writing a thesis with a strong argumentative style in a US university setting, a type of writing unlike that required in earlier experiences in writing a master's thesis in China.

As well as student discourses, EAP is concerned with research and instructional discourses. Research discourses are of interest to academics in both English and non-English speaking countries, as academics are generally keen to disseminate their research through journals published in English and to deliver presentations at international conferences. Globally, researchers are increasingly being required to publish in English for career development, although English is not the first language of many of these researchers (Flowerdew, 2013). Graduate students, especially doctoral candidates, too are increasingly required to publish in international journals published in English, and are likewise keen to develop their abilities in producing research discourses. English for research publication purposes has attracted considerable attention in the EAP literature. This is due in part to the fact that English has become the "unrivalled lingua franca of academia, the language in which most research articles are published, conferences held, reading is done and learning transmitted" and many academics go to considerable lengths to acquire English academic discourse (Bennet, 2015: 7).

Much research interest has been given to description of the rhetorical and linguistic features of the research article as a product of writing (Flowerdew, 2013). Investigation into the processes by which academic writers learn to write for publication has been more limited, although recent studies have investigated the problems and strategies of multilingual academics in preparing papers for publication (Martín, Rey-Rocha, Burgess, and Moreno, 2014).

Instructional discourses are of key interest to faculty staff (academics and teaching assistants). English may be used as a medium of instruction in higher education in settings where it is not the first language of the students and teaching staff. Teaching assistants and lecturers in such contexts may feel a particular need to develop the language they need to conduct classes and give lectures, tutorials and seminars in English. Developing the speaking and listening skills required for such events can be of interest to English L2 and English L1 faculty staff.

KEY LEARNING ISSUES

LEARNING GOALS

Arguably, there is no English for general academic purposes. Swales (1990) described academic life as a set of disciplinary discourse communities. Over time, each discipline comes to establish its own language conventions and practices. ESAP is centrally concerned with the ways English is conventionally used in particular disciplines, such as Engineering or Nursing. There has been considerable research in EAP into disciplinary variation in writing, which has been driven in part by pedagogical interests in how to help students understand the writing practices of their target disciplines (Hewings et al., 2007). According to ESAP perspectives, academic English should be understood as a set of disciplinary varieties, and learning goals should be understood as the development of features of language use, linguistic skills and cultural knowledge for study in particular disciplines. Components of ESAP language ability include: the written and spoken genres and linguistic skills/sub skills used in study of the target discipline; discipline-related uses of vocabulary and discourse; and development of an understanding of the culture of the academic discipline and departmental or disciplinary expectations for student writing.

ESAP goals for learning include developing an understanding of disciplinary practices of study genres, and the ability to comprehend and/or produce the variety of English used in the target discipline. Much research has investigated writing in different academic discourse communities in terms of the genres that students use in their disciplinary studies, and the kinds of knowledge of these genres that students would require to participate meaningfully in their academic studies. Genre-based perspectives of writing view writing not as a set of generic writing skills or rhetorical forms, but rather as a set of genres produced and reproduced in a particular academic discourse community, in response to the communicative needs of that community. Over time these genres have become conventionalised. Students in sciences are likely to need to learn to write the genre of the *laboratory report* and students in education or health care that of *practice notes* (Hewings et al., 2007: 232).

Increasingly, academic English is being viewed as a lingua franca and this leads to the questioning of the use of English academic native-speakers (or writers) as models for learning. The proficient non-native user of academic English may be a more appropriate model, especially in settings in which English is used as a foreign language. Nor might the writing of seasoned academics be an appropriate benchmark for assessing student academic writing. Students are novice academic writers and novice members of their academic discourse communities; proficient student writing or speaking may thus be more appropriate learning goals and models than the writing or speaking of expert members of the academic discourse community.

LEARNING NEEDS

The identification of learning needs is a key procedure in the development of instruction in English for study purposes. Findings from needs analysis are used to inform the development of the curriculum. Needs analysis is not always a straightforward procedure, however. Stakeholders (the institution, students and teachers) may have differing perceptions of learning needs and priorities. The institutional perspective may not match that of the learners or their teachers about what is needed, or what can feasibly be achieved in the time scale, for example.

Findings from needs analysis from one setting may not be very relevant to another setting. Learning needs can, for example, be regionally specific. Johns (2009) reports that in the North American context in which she works, EAP is generally delivered at first- and second-year undergraduate levels through freshman and sophomore composition (academic writing) courses, in which reading is an integral component. In the university context in which I work in New Zealand, EAP instruction is also delivered at first- and second-year levels through writing courses, but, in addition, through courses in other skill areas, such as speaking and comprehension (listening and reading). Learning needs can also be task-specific. Investigation of the EAP competencies required for a group case study project on a particular Business Studies programme (Smith and Thondhlana, 2015) suggested a number of competencies (such as ability to read a long, complex brief, participate in a group discussion, apply research recommendations to the design of an exhibit and prepare a written report and oral presentation), indicating areas in which some students might need EAP learning support. It is entirely possible that other group projects in Business Studies, or other disciplines, might require a somewhat different set of competencies.

The relevance of English for study purposes instruction depends on delineation of needs in the specific setting at hand. At present, relatively little is known about learner needs in secondary school settings. Do L2 students in such settings also sometimes face new rhetorical structures and norms? To what extent are secondary school students expected to use the linguistic features characteristic of the formal academic register? Relatively few published studies of learner needs in secondary school education have been evident in the EAP literature to date, although students' learning of academic writing and reading clearly begin long before commencement of university studies (see, however, the special issue, 'Academic English in secondary schools', of the *Journal of English for Academic Purposes*, edited by A.M. Johns and M.A. Snow, 2006).

DEVELOPMENTAL ASPECTS

The topic of how learners come to acquire academic language ability has received limited attention in the EAP literature. As described above, linguistic enquiry has led to advances in the description of academic English. Features of the academic register and patterns of organisation in key genres, such as sections of the research article, have been brought to light. Such descriptions, although useful for indicating goals for learning (what is to be learnt – the features of language use to be acquired or the kinds of texts to be produced or comprehended) do not shed light on how the features or texts come to be learnt, or the learning processes involved.

Learners may have particular difficulties in producing key text types. To identify such difficulties, researchers have compared the texts produced by different groups of learners. By comparing the use of linking adverbials in doctoral dissertations written by Chinese EFL students and published research articles, Lei (2012) identified areas of over and under-use by the student writers. Parkinson and Musgrave (2014) compared the use of noun modifiers in the writing of students on an EAP programme who were preparing for graduate study and students already enrolled in postgraduate study and who had a more advanced proficiency. Findings from the study enabled the researchers to suggest a developmental sequence in the learning of this particular linguistic feature of the academic register.

LEARNING TRANSFER

Instruction in the EGAP classroom often directly targets the kinds of components of academic language ability described above. It is expected that learners will transfer the study skills and knowledge of the academic register they gain from instruction to concurrent or later, subsequent, study in their disciplinary areas. This view of learning is based on two relatively untested assumptions: that transfer occurs (learners transfer the skills and knowledge from the EAP classroom to their disciplinary studies) and that the components of academic language ability (what is targeted in instruction) are relevant in study in the different disciplines to which the learners are headed. To illustrate, instruction in the EGAP classroom may focus on the development of a specific sub-skill of academic listening (helping learners recognise topic shifts in lectures). As the learners in the EGAP class are likely to be from a mix of disciplinary areas, practice listening material may be in the form of a lecture from a general interest subject, such as psychology. It is anticipated this sub-skill is important across study in different disciplines and that the students will be able, at a later point, to transfer their learning of topic shift recognition to listening to Business, History or Science lectures. The topic of learning transfer, or how learners apply or transfer what they learn from EGAP instruction to other academic contexts or activities, has only recently been subject to a systematic review, however (James, 2014).

SITUATED LEARNING

Situated learning of academic English, or learning English through academic (disciplinary) study is a topic of key importance for EAP as findings may be able to shed light on processes and products of the learning of academic English in situ. However, a limited number of studies have as yet appeared in the EAP literature. Studies include an investigation (Storch, 2009) into ways the academic writing of international students did and did not improve during one semester of immersion in a particular university setting in Australia, and a study (Green, 2013) examining changes in the processes used by three ESL learners in preparing written assignments over a year of university study. An observational study (Basturkmen and Shackleford, 2015) of university year-one accounting classes lectures in one New Zealand (English L1 setting) setting, revealed frequent time-outs from discussion of accounting to discuss language issues, especially vocabulary and accounting 'speak' (formulaic expressions). It thus appeared that the accounting lecturers in this setting supported their students (who were from a mix of English L1 and English L2 backgrounds) in learning disciplinary vocabulary during disciplinary teaching.

IMPLICATIONS FOR TEACHING AND ASSESSMENT

It has been argued that analysis of learning needs is a key procedure in developing instruction in English for study purposes, and that findings from needs analysis (even in a similar setting) may not be relevant to learners' needs in another setting. EAP teachers are often called on to develop or revise courses, materials and assessment tasks. It is important, therefore, for EAP teachers to be fully cognizant of the importance of basing the curriculum on an understanding of their learners' needs, and to have knowledge of the techniques and methods that can be used to identify needs.

As discussed above, academic English is increasingly construed as a lingua franca. Teachers can consider drawing on examples of academic language use by proficient L2 students as well as L1 students, in developing instructional materials and assessment schemes. Proficient L2 student users of academic English can be used as illustrative models.

Although there are differences in EGAP and ESAP's views of the nature of academic English and the goals of learning, this does not imply that the two orientations cannot be combined in practice. Within an overall EGAP-oriented type course, the teacher may target disciplinary uses of English at times. For example, instruction could be devised that focuses on a student genre that occurs across disciplinary areas, such as the argumentative essay. The instruction can highlight uses of the general academic register that occur in sample essays (such as, the use of hedging in making claims or the use of heavy nominal groups). By examining samples from different disciplines, instruction can also focus, in part, on disciplinary differences. For example, teaching may highlight how the introductions to the essays were constructed in the samples from different disciplinary areas.

CONCLUSION

In this chapter, I suggested that the topic of learning has been relatively neglected in the EAP literature and that the field's understanding of how learners acquire academic language skills and knowledge has been limited. The chapter described some recent thrusts of research enquiry into learning, such as enquiry into developmental sequences, learning transfer and situated learning. Findings from inquiry are beginning to shed light on the nature of learning in EAP, and it is expected that further research will continue to extend understanding of learning in this field.

Discussion Questions

1. How did you learn to write for study purposes or research publication purposes? Did you receive any formal instruction or were you self-taught? In either case, what seemed to work best in helping you develop your understanding of academic writing?

2. Do you think university students with English as a second language benefit from EGAP instruction before ESAP instruction? Do learners only need one of these types of instruction? If so, which?

3. What would you suggest to a group of new teaching assistants (mixed English L1 and L2) who ask you for ideas on how to improve their speaking and listening skills for teaching classes or interactive lectures in your university or school?

Key Readings

Bruce, I. (2011). *Theory and Concepts of English for Academic Purposes*. Basingstoke, UK: Palgrave Macmillan.

Charles, M., & Pecorari, D. (2016). *Introducing English for Academic Purposes*. Oxford: Routledge.

de Chazal, E. (2014). *English for Academic Purposes*. Oxford: Oxford University Press.

Hyland, K., & Shaw, P. (Eds.) (2016). *The Routledge Handbook of English for Academic Purposes*. London: Routledge.

Read, J. (2015). *Assessing English Proficiency for University Study*. Basingstoke, UK: Palgrave Macmillan.

References

Basturkmen, H., & Shackleford, N. (2015). How content lecturers help students with language: An observational study of language-related episodes in interaction in first year accounting classrooms. *English for Specific Purposes*, 37, 87–97.

Bennet, K. (2015). Towards an epistemological monoculture: Mechanisms of epistemicide in European research publication. In R. P. Alastrué & C. Pérez-Llantada (Eds.), *English as a Scientific and Research Language* (pp. 9–35). Berlin: De Gruyter Mouton.

Coxhead, A. (2000). A new academic word list. *Teaching English to Speakers of Other Languages Quarterly*, 34(2), 213–238.

Flowerdew, J. (2013). English for research publication purposes. In B. Paltridge & S. Starfield (Eds.), *The Handbook of English for Specific Purposes* (pp. 301–321). Oxford: Wiley-Blackwell.

Green, S. (2013). Novice ESL writers: A longitudinal case-study of the situated academic writing processes of three undergraduates in a TESOL context. *Journal of English for Academic Purposes*, 12, 180–191.

Hewings, A., Lillis, T., & Mayor, B. (2007). Academic writing in English. In N. Mercer, J. Swann & B. Mayor (Eds.), *Learning English* (pp. 227–252). Abingdon: Routledge.

Hyland, K. (2009). *Academic Discourse: English in a Global Context*. London / New York: Continuum.

James, M. A. (2014). Learning transfer in English-for-academic purposes contexts: A systematic review of research. *Journal of English for Academic Purposes*, 14, 1–13.

Johns, A. M. (2009). Tertiary undergraduate EAP: Problems and possibilities. In D. Belcher (Ed.), *English for Specific Purposes in Theory and Practice* (pp. 41–59). Ann Arbor, MI: The University of Michigan Press.

Johns, A. M., & Snow, M. A. (2006). Introduction to special issue: 'Academic English in secondary schools'. *Journal of English for Academic Purposes*, 5(4), 251–253.

Jordan, R. R. (1997). *English for Academic Purposes*. Cambridge: Cambridge University Press.

Lei, L. (2012). Linking adverbials in academic writing on applied linguistics by Chinese doctoral students. *Journal of English for Academic Purposes*, 11, 267–275.

Li, X. (2008). Learning to write a thesis with an argumentative edge. In C. P. Casanave & X. Li (Eds.), *Learning the Literacy Practices of Graduate School: Insiders' Reflections on Academic Enculturation* (pp. 46–57). Ann Arbor, MI: University of Michigan Press.

Martín, P., Rey-Rocha, J., Burgess, S., & Moreno, A. I. (2014). Publishing research in English-language journals: Attitudes, strategies and difficulties of multilingual scholars of medicine. *Journal of English for Academic Purposes*, 16, 57–67.

Nesi, H., & Gardner, S. (2012). *Genres across the Disciplines: Student Writing in Higher Education*. Cambridge: Cambridge University Press.

Parkinson, J., & Musgrave, J. (2014). Development of noun phrase complexity in the writing of English for academic purposes students. *Journal of English for Academic Purposes*, 14, 48–59.

Smith, F. V., & Thondhlana, J. (2015). The EAP competencies in a group case study project as revealed by task analysis. *Journal of English for Academic Purposes*, 20, 14–25.

Storch, N. (2009). The impact of studying in a second language (L2) medium university on the development of L2 writing. *Journal of Second Language Writing*, 18, 103–118.

Swales, J. M. (1990). *Genre Analysis: English in Academic and Research Settings*. Cambridge: Cambridge University Press.

Swales, J. M. (2001). EAP-related linguistic research: An intellectual history. In J. Flowerdew & M. Peacock (Eds.), *Research Perspectives on English for Academic Purposes* (pp. 42–54). Cambridge: Cambridge University Press.

Waters, A., & Waters, M. (2001). Designing tasks for developing study competence and study skills in English. In J. Flowerdew & M. Peacock (Eds.), *Research Perspectives on English for Academic Purposes* (pp. 375–389). Cambridge: Cambridge University Press.

CHAPTER 15

Learning for Specific Purposes

Christoph A. Hafner

INTRODUCTION

The field of English for specific purposes (ESP) emphasizes the way that language use varies in different specialized domains, whether these be disciplinary domains or professional or workplace contexts. For example, the specialized language skills and competencies required by lawyers to carry out their professional functions differ from those required by other professionals, whether they be engineers, architects, geologists, or nurses. Each of these domains makes up a different disciplinary community of practice, complete with its own culture, values, genres and systems of meaning making. Such disciplinary communities often straddle both academic and professional contexts and, as we shall see, there may be quite marked differences between practices in the academic and professional communities, even within the same discipline.

Learning English as a second language for specific purposes involves developing the necessary genre knowledge in order to be able to achieve one's communicative purposes as a member of that disciplinary community. Here, genre can be defined as staged, goal-oriented, social action that is designed to meet recurrent rhetorical situations (Martin, Christie, and Rothery, 1987; Miller, 1984). In other words, genres are communicative events that involve texts (spoken or written), which have been constructed with particular audiences in mind in order to achieve particular communicative purposes, usually related to typical goals of the community (see Chapters 14 and 25). For example, the genre of research article is written by academics for an audience of disciplinary specialists, with the goal of communicating research findings. As such, the genre meets a recurrent, communicative need of the academic community of practice.

This chapter is concerned with theories of language learning that explain how second language learners acquire competence in such genres, as these theories underlie and inform practices in English for specific purposes. The chapter begins by providing an overview of theoretical work on genre learning, considering theories that have been developed with both first language (L1) and second language (L2) learners in mind. It then addresses key learning issues as suggested by empirical studies. Finally, it suggests practical implications of these studies for the teaching and assessment of English for specific purposes.

OVERVIEW

Genre learning in English for specific purposes presents a challenge for both L1 and L2 learners, and has therefore attracted the attention of researchers in both contexts. Genre learning is usually seen as a social process, one that involves participation in the target community of practice, with a gradual progression from outsider to insider status. As a result, theories of learning in this area tend to adopt a sociocultural perspective, seeing learning as situated in social contexts. The process has variously been described as a process of 'socialization' or 'enculturation' in a 'discourse community' (Berkenkotter and Huckin, 1995; Swales, 1990); alternatively, as 'legitimate peripheral participation' in a 'community of practice' (Lave and Wenger, 1991).

The concept of socialization is a useful one for understanding the process of genre learning. According to Ochs (1988: 5), socialization is "the process by which one becomes a competent member of society". As such, socialization involves not only learning the ways of meaning, but also the ways of doing, being, and thinking of particular communities. Duff (2007: 310) focuses on the more specific notion of 'language socialization', which she defines as "the process by which novices or newcomers in a community or culture gain communicative competence, membership, and legitimacy in the group". As mentioned above, learning a genre is frequently seen in terms of such language socialization processes. It follows that learning a genre is not only about mastering the formal features of the genre – its generic structure, its lexical and grammatical realization – but also about learning the culture and values of the relevant community. For example, learning to write effectively for law involves developing the ability to 'think like a lawyer' by employing specialized modes of legal reasoning.

An essential element in the process of language socialization is interaction between experts and novices. Experts, 'old-timers' who are more proficient in the genres of the community and more familiar with its norms and values, provide novices, or 'newcomers', with implicit or explicit mentoring, helping them to develop necessary communicative and cultural competence (Duff, 2010). The idea is that learning takes place through interaction and collaboration with more knowledgeable individuals (see Chapter 11). This idea draws on Vygotsky's social theory of mind, in particular the concept of the Zone of Proximal Development (ZPD), which can broadly be defined as the learner's development potential (Vygotsky, 1978: 86). Vygotsky conceives of the ZPD as the difference between a learner's ability working independently, and a learner's ability working in collaboration with others (for example, a teacher, a parent). In terms of genre learning, when learners co-construct genres with more expert individuals, this gives rise to a series of learning opportunities that are realized through the guidance and scaffolding provided by the experts.

One influential theory that attempts to explain how such expert-novice interactions lead to learning is the theory of situated learning developed by Lave and Wenger (1991). According to this theory, learning is a process of 'legitimate peripheral participation', where newcomers learn by participating in the sociocultural practices of a community of practice. At first, they perform simple, low-stakes tasks, which nevertheless contribute meaningfully to community goals. In this, they may be working under the supervision of more expert members of the community. Gradually, as they themselves develop expertise, they are entrusted with more and more important tasks until they reach full participation in community practices. In this learning process, success depends on gaining access to various parts of the activity, so that the practice can be understood as a whole; access to interaction with experts, so that learning opportunities and feedback can be secured; and access to the technologies and structures of the community, so that these can be properly understood (Artemeva and Fox, 2014). In addition, learning is understood to be embedded in community practices and need not involve explicit instruction. It is therefore particularly useful for understanding how genres might be learned 'in the wild', that is, outside of academic classrooms (see Chapter 13).

Rogoff's (1990) theory of situated learning has also received considerable attention from scholars interested in genre learning. Rogoff characterizes learning as an 'apprenticeship in thinking' that involves interaction between experts and novices. She is particularly interested in the way that children are explicitly mentored in cultural practices by teachers and parents. She sees this as a process of 'guided participation', in which teachers and parents structure learning opportunities for children and guide them towards mastery of cultural practices. In terms of genre learning, this theory is useful to explain the kinds of classroom interactions that one might observe, in writing instruction in the academy, for example.

Such theoretical frameworks provide a useful starting point in understanding the processes of genre learning that occur in language socialization. However, these frameworks have been criticized for presenting an overly simplistic account of learning. The actual social processes involved appear to be much more complex. First, although Lave and Wenger's theory of situated learning presents the target community and its practices as unproblematically stable and uniform, they may in fact be highly variable, differing from one individual or context to another (Hyland, 2000). Second, while it is assumed that interactions between experts and novices provide plentiful opportunities for learning, e.g., 'modeling' and 'coaching' on the part of mentors, there is evidence that this is not always the case in practice (Belcher, 1994). Similarly, it has been noted that participants in the process, for example undergraduate university students, may not themselves perceive their learning in terms of an apprenticeship to a community of practice (Candlin and Plum, 1999). Finally, these models have been criticized for representing the learning process in a simplistic way, as a uni-directional process, with novices moving from peripheral to full participation. As Duff (2007) points out, it is in reality a bi-directional process, in which novices may also 'teach' experts about their particular communicative needs.

In spite of these critiques, the theoretical constructs of socialization, legitimate peripheral participation, and apprenticeship provide useful tools for understanding processes of genre learning. The next section considers empirical studies of actual socialization processes, in order to highlight the key issues that L2 learners might encounter.

KEY LEARNING ISSUES

Empirical work shows how the learning process involved in language socialization is mediated by a wide range of different interactions. Parks' studies (e.g., Parks, 2001) provide an in-depth description of the socialization processes of francophone nurses working in an English-medium hospital in Canada. Her participants included 11 L2 learners, novice nurses, who were followed over a period of 22 months. In order to facilitate the induction of these nurses, the hospital had created an orientation program, which was headed up by a Clinical Educator (a senior nurse) and included a three-week intensive English course followed by a two-week workplace orientation. Subsequently, the novice nurses were paired with an experienced nurse, called a Preceptor, whose role was to introduce the novices to the units that they were assigned to. This final phase lasted three weeks, and after that the nurses took up normal duties on the ward.

In this context, Parks (2001) investigated the nurses' development of communicative competence with respect to the 'care plan' genre, a collectively maintained text that records information about a given patient, such as diagnosis, objectives, intervention and evaluation. As a preliminary note, it was observed that the care plans that the nurses had learned to write at nursing school differed in important ways from those found on the ward. The study showed how, over time, the novice nurses' plans changed as they adapted to the writing practices of the ward. This learning process was facilitated by a range of community interactions and resources and involved both overt and covert forms of collaboration. Overt collaboration occurred during the actual process of writing up the text, as the novices received feedback from more expert peers, such as the Clinical Educator or the Preceptor. Covert collaboration occurred when the novices consulted prior texts, for example sample care plans, or care plan reference books. Another form of covert collaboration was talk and interaction with more expert peers that was only marginally related to the production of the documents. In this highly supportive environment, the novice nurses were able to gain access to:

- all stages of the care plan activity;
- feedback from a range of more expert peers; and
- samples of writing and other textual resources to support the writing activity.

In line with the theories described above, this research suggests that interaction with community members and community texts provides opportunities for situated learning and legitimate peripheral participation in community practices.

Other studies of genre learning in L2 contexts suggest that the process also involves the development of an expert disciplinary identity, as learners "build a sense of themselves as members of the … community" (Tardy, 2006: 88). Such an expert identity is indexed in the discursive choices that disciplinary writers make, as evidenced by a comparison of expert and novice texts. For example, working in the Hong Kong context, Hafner (2013) compared the writing of novice lawyers at the vocational stage of legal education with that of expert barristers. Both groups were provided with a simulated factual situation and asked to respond to it by writing a barrister's opinion – a common professional legal genre. When participants were interviewed about discursive choices observed in their work, it became clear that they saw their own writing as, at least in part, a representation of themselves as expert members of the legal community (see also Ivanič, 1998). However, an analysis of the writing produced showed a marked difference in approach between the expert and novice groups. Compared to the expert professionals, the novice lawyers tended to take an unnecessarily 'academic' approach, placing too much importance on the analysis of legal principles and not enough on the analysis of facts. Novices seemed to transfer strategies that had worked well for them in the academy but that were not appropriate to the professional context. Developing the appropriate 'discoursal identity' appears to require sustained engagement with community practices over a period of time (Dressen-Hammouda, 2008).

These studies draw attention to differences in disciplinary genres across academic and professional contexts. Indeed, researchers into genre learning point out that the underlying goals of writing in the academy and writing in the professional workplace are fundamentally different. According to Freedman, Adam, and Smart (1994), academic genres tend to fulfil an 'epistemic' purpose, that is, they aim to demonstrate disciplinary knowledge to the academic reader. In contrast, professional genres are more 'praxis-oriented', that is, they use disciplinary knowledge in order to solve real-world client problems. These researchers conclude that the activity of writing in the academy is profoundly different from the activity of writing in the profession. As a result, the same genre may look quite different, depending on whether it was written for academic or professional purposes. This raises an important issue: is it possible for students in academic contexts to practice writing professional genres in any meaningful way? What, ultimately, is the role of the academic writing course in promoting genre learning?

Bremner's (2012) case study of Sammi, an L2 intern in the Public Relations (PR) industry in Hong Kong, identifies various contributing factors in her language socialization process: learning by doing, inputs from colleagues, and inputs from the academy. Here 'learning by doing' refers to the situated learning process of participation in PR practices. 'Inputs from colleagues' includes both direct inputs, in the form of instructions, advice and feedback, and indirect inputs, in the form of encouragement. Finally, 'inputs from the academy' refers to Sammi's use of communication concepts that she had learned on her undergraduate English courses (she had graduated as an English major). These concepts came primarily from courses in intercultural communication, and organizational culture and communication, e.g., 'culture', 'power structure', 'division of labour', and so on. Drawing on these concepts helped Sammi to make sense of the communicative practices of the PR firm, as well as her own process of socialization into it. This study suggests that the academy does have a role to play in learning professional genres, a point which will be picked up again below.

Two remaining issues that are especially relevant to L2 learners are those of access to satisfactory mentoring and access to productive oral interactions. In her meta-analysis of 60 articles on genre learning, Tardy (2006) noted a clear difference between L1 and L2 studies of mentoring processes. While L1 studies were generally positive about the beneficial effects of mentoring, L2 studies tended to observe more difficulties, and these were not always resolved positively. Belcher (1994) conducted a multiple case study of three L2 graduate students and their supervisors in a university in the USA, in the areas of Chinese history, applied mathematics and applied science. She found that the students and their mentors sometimes had different cultural expectations of what the mentoring process involved, as well as different conceptions of the requirements of the target community of practice. For example, Li, a Chinese student of Chinese literature, was characterized by his supervisor as "still thinking too Chinese" (p. 27), writing like "traditional 'old-style' Chinese scholars who read to accumulate facts and wrote mainly to display them" (p. 27). In order to foster a more critical approach, the Chinese-American supervisor responded to Li's writings by marking them up with copious critical questions. However, rather than having the desired effect of pushing Li to adopt a more critical stance, these annotations were taken as a flat rejection of the student's writing. Ultimately, this student abandoned his studies, presumably, at least in part, because of the misunderstandings experienced with his supervisor.

Finally, as mentioned earlier, oral interaction has been shown to play a productive role in language socialization and genre learning. In the academic context, written genres are the product of a range of interactions, which may include interactions in lectures, tutorials, and group discussions (see Chapter 14). However, such oral interactions can pose particular challenges for L2 learners, because of the way that these interactions produce a kind of hybrid discourse, combining oral and literate practices. Duff's research into socialization processes in Hungarian and Canadian secondary schools is instructive. As Duff (2010: 179–180) notes, "for many of the English language learners in the mainstream social studies classes who were analysed, the vernacular discourse and pervasive extra-curricular references (to *The Simpsons* and other iconic pop culture TV programs) were especially perplexing". If L2 learners are unable to 'do' these kinds of oral interactions, then that has an effect on their access to certain community resources that they need for genre learning.

IMPLICATIONS FOR TEACHING AND ASSESSMENT

On the whole, empirical studies support the notion that genre learning involves participation in community practices, gradually moving towards full participation. For such situated learning to be effective, the learner must have:

- access to interaction with more knowledgeable peers;
- access to community resources, including prior texts, guidebooks and so on; and
- access to all stages of the process, along with relevant technologies and structures.

The studies also suggest that genre learning involves the development of an expert disciplinary identity, a 'discoursal identity' (Ivanič, 1998) that is indexed in expert writers' discursive choices. Having established these general principles, a number of practical implications for learners and their teachers can be suggested.

First, if learning occurs through participation in social practices, then one implication is that ESP courses should seek to engage closely with the social practices of the target discipline. This comment applies as equally to course design as it does to assessment, both of which should focus on the genres and practices of the target community. As we have seen, language socialization means developing both cultural and communicative competence with respect to a specialized community of practice. It therefore follows that courses in ESP should not confine themselves to linguistic aspects of competence, but should go beyond this to ask more probing questions: How do genres reflect the values of the community? How are genres situated in community activities and how, through strategic rhetorical choices, do they help to achieve community goals? Addressing such questions would link typical disciplinary ways of doing/thinking/being with the ways of meaning embodied by genres.

Practically, engaging with community practices can be achieved in a range of ways:

- **Needs analysis:** Instructors assess the specific needs of particular groups of learners (e.g., students of a specific discipline, members of a workplace, a group of professionals) by identifying and analysing key genres, in consultation with community stakeholders.
- **Project-based learning and simulations:** Students are given projects that simulate disciplinary activities, for example scientific investigation and report writing. Such projects can be designed in collaboration with specialists from the discipline, to enhance their authenticity.
- **Students as 'researchers':** Students interview members of the disciplinary community, asking them about the disciplinary culture and the expected conventions of particular genres, especially student assignments.
- **Data-driven learning:** In class, students consult a corpus of disciplinary texts, considering how functional lexical phrases are used to achieve generic goals of the disciplinary community.
- **Adjunct courses:** Disciplinary specialists and language specialists combine forces, linking a disciplinary content course with an 'adjunct' language course. On the adjunct course, students learn the disciplinary expectations and generic resources needed for their content course assignments.
- **Internships, real-world experiences:** The language course is designed to prepare students for a real-world internship. Students learn the values of the discipline and the features of specific genres that they will encounter as part of an actual internship.

- **Conceptual education:** Students learn principles of genre analysis and organizational communication, which they can use as tools to understand disciplinary and workplace contexts beyond the academy.

CONCLUSION

The approaches discussed in this chapter aim to target particular genres and practices of the given community, in as authentic a way as possible. However, they also go beyond genres and practices to focus on disciplinary culture and even, in the case of 'conceptual education', the generative, theoretical tools needed to understand and act in new communicative contexts. Although some scholars have raised questions about the possibility of teaching professional genres in academic contexts, others see a clear role for the academy (Artemeva, 2009; Bremner, 2012). The approaches listed above, grounded as they are in an understanding of genre learning as participation in disciplinary practices, provide a principled starting point for teachers interested in teaching English for specific purposes.

Discussion Questions

1. Think about your own experience of learning specialized disciplinary genres, for example, at university. Answer the following questions:
   a) As you went about learning, did you:
      i.   Interact with or get feedback from mentors or more knowledgeable peers?
      ii. Collaborate with others?
      iii. Use example texts or guidelines?
   b) How did such interactions, provision of feedback, and use of examples and guidelines support your genre learning?
2. How do the approaches suggested at the end of this chapter (e.g., project-based learning, adjunct courses, internships) work to engage with community practices? In learning a second language for specific purposes, which of these approaches do you think would be most effective, and why?

Key Readings

Artemeva, N., & Fox, J. (2014). The formation of a professional communicator: A socio-rhetorical approach. In V. Bhatia & S. Bremner (Eds.), *The Routledge Handbook of Language and Professional Communication* (pp. 461–485). Abingdon / New York: Routledge.

Duff, P. A. (2010). Language socialization into academic discourse communities. *Annual Review of Applied Linguistics*, 30, 169–192.

Lave, J., & Wenger, E. (1991). *Situated Learning: Legitimate Peripheral Participation*. Cambridge: Cambridge University Press.

Swales, J. M. (1990). *Genre Analysis: English in Academic and Research Settings*. Cambridge: Cambridge University Press.

Tardy, C. M. (2006). Researching first and second language genre learning: A comparative review and a look ahead. *Journal of Second Language Writing*, 15(2), 79–101. http://doi.org/10.1016/j.jslw.2006.04.003

References

Artemeva, N. (2009). Stories of becoming: A study of novice engineers learning genres of their profession. In C. Bazerman, A. Bonini, & D. Figueiredo (Eds.), *Genre in a Changing World* (pp. 158–178). Fort Collins, CO and West Lafayette, IN: The WAC Clearing House and Parlor Press.

Artemeva, N., & Fox, J. (2014). The formation of a professional communicator: A socio-rhetorical approach. In V. Bhatia & S. Bremner (Eds.), *The Routledge Handbook of Language and Professional Communication* (pp. 461–485). Abingdon / New York: Routledge.

Belcher, D. (1994). The apprenticeship approach to advanced academic literacy: Graduate students and their mentors. *English for Specific Purposes*, 13(1), 23–34.

Berkenkotter, C., & Huckin, T. N. (1995). *Genre Knowledge in Disciplinary Communication: Cognition/Culture/Power*. Mahwah, NJ: Lawrence Erlbaum.

Bremner, S. (2012). Socialization and the acquisition of professional discourse. *Written Communication*, 29(1), 7–32. http://doi.org/10.1177/0741088311424866

Candlin, C. N., & Plum, G. A. (1999). Engaging with the challenges of interdiscursivity in academic writing: Researchers, students and tutors. In C. N. Candlin & K. Hyland (Eds.), *Writing: Texts, Processes and Practices* (pp. 193–217). London: Longman.

Dressen-Hammouda, D. (2008). From novice to disciplinary expert: Disciplinary identity and genre mastery. *English for Specific Purposes*, 27(2), 233–252. http://doi.org/10.1016/j.esp.2007.07.006

Duff, P. A. (2007). Second language socialization as sociocultural theory: Insights and issues. *Language Teaching*, 40(4), 309–319.

Duff, P. A. (2010). Language socialization into academic discourse communities. *Annual Review of Applied Linguistics*, 30, 169–192.

Freedman, A., Adam, C., & Smart, G. (1994). Wearing suits to class: Simulating genres and simulations as genre. *Written Communication*, 11(2), 193–226. http://doi.org/10.1177/0741088394011002002

Hafner, C. A. (2013). The discursive construction of professional expertise: Appeals to authority in barrister's opinions. *English for Specific Purposes*, 32(3), 131–143. http://doi.org/10.1016/j.esp.2013.01.003

Hyland, K. (2000). *Disciplinary Discourses: Social Interactions in Academic Writing*. Harlow: Longman.

Ivanič, R. (1998). *Writing and Identity: The Discoursal Construction of Identity in Academic Writing*. Amsterdam/Philadelphia: John Benjamins.

Lave, J., & Wenger, E. (1991). *Situated Learning: Legitimate Peripheral Participation*. Cambridge: Cambridge University Press.

Martin, J. R., Christie, F., & Rothery, J. (1987). Social processes in education: A reply to Sawyer and Watson (and others). In I. Reid (Ed.), *The Place of Genre in Learning: Current Debates* (pp. 35–45). Geelong, VIC: Centre for Studies in Literary Education, Deakin University.

Miller, C. R. (1984). Genre as social action. *Quarterly Journal of Speech*, 70(2), 151–167.

Ochs, E. (1988). *Culture and Language Development: Language Acquisition and Language Socialization in a Samoan Village*. Cambridge: Cambridge University Press.

Parks, S. (2001). Moving from school to the workplace: Disciplinary innovation, border crossings, and the reshaping of a written genre. *Applied Linguistics*, 22(4), 405–438. http://doi.org/10.1093/applin/22.4.405

Rogoff, B. (1990). *Apprenticeship in Thinking: Cognitive Development in Social Context.* New York: Oxford University Press.

Swales, J. M. (1990). *Genre Analysis: English in Academic and Research Settings.* Cambridge: Cambridge University Press.

Tardy, C. M. (2006). Researching first and second language genre learning: A comparative review and a look ahead. *Journal of Second Language Writing*, 15(2), 79–101. http://doi.org/10.1016/j.jslw.2006.04.003

Vygotsky, L. S. (1978). *Mind in Society: The Development of Higher Psychological Processes.* Cambridge, MA: Harvard University Press.

CHAPTER 16

Learning for the Workplace

Jane Lockwood

INTRODUCTION

There have been a number of studies that have estimated that there are more non-native speakers (NNSs) than native speakers (NSs) of English worldwide, and that many of these use English for work purposes in the new globalized economy (Graddol, 2006). This chapter briefly overviews some of the work contexts where English is used between NSs/NNSs and between NNSs, with a particular focus on the business processing outsourcing (BPO) industry in Asia. This context provides many language learning challenges, described in the second part of this chapter, and I conclude with a discussion on the implications of these for training, coaching and assessing English in this business context. Whilst this context is a highly specific exemplar, there are generalizable principles and practices that can be applied to other workplace contexts.

OVERVIEW

There are many global contexts where English is used for work, but the specific language learning challenges are very different. For example, there have been many studies on how newly arrived immigrants in countries such as the USA, Canada, the UK, Australia and New Zealand learn English (see, for example, Mawer, 2014) to start their new lives at work. Typically, in this context, government-sponsored language learning programs are provided to these immigrants to adapt to their new environments, and to the expectations of employment. Essentially language learning requires an acculturalization process, where, for example, understanding humour in the New Zealand workplace (Holmes and Marra, 2002) is seen as an important factor in operating successfully with work colleagues.

However, there are numerous other global workplace examples where the contexts and purposes for learning English are very different. Take, for example, the use of English in European multinational firms, where, despite being European-owned, the firm may have acquired other companies and expanded its global operations. In this situation, the firm typically mandates English to be the lingua franca for the practical purpose of it being a shared language (Piekkari, Welch, and Welch, 2014). Such business English as the lingua franca (BELF) policies create very different language learning challenges from the one described above. For example, there may be resistance from some employees who do not speak English well and perceive a power shift within the firm, and a threat to identity, due to such a policy.

A further example of a globalized workforce which is not so obviously motivated instrumentally or integratively, is the BPO industry in Asia. This industry is relatively new and is currently worth about 18.9 billion USD in the Philippines alone (Mercado, 2015). It comprises all sorts of work, sent to overseas developing countries by mostly western multinational companies. Employees in this setting are keen to work and are cheaper; however, English is not the mother tongue of the workforce. The BPO industry comprises back office functions of multinationals, ranging from routine work such as keying in change of address information through to much more sophisticated work, such as writing legal summaries for British legal firms and transcribing medical consultations (now a legal requirement in the USA). One of the largest segments within the BPO industry in Asia is the emergence of call centres in the Philippines and India. In the Philippines alone, there are over one million young graduate employees working for English-speaking call centres serving western English-speaking customers in the USA, the UK, Australia and New Zealand.

The BPO industry, and call centres specifically, will provide us with an expanded discussion on learning English in the workplace, exemplifying how language learning decisions are made by the business and how such decisions impact learners, who are also the employees. This example is especially pertinent, given that good quality communication in customer service on the phones is a 'core commodity' of these businesses, and therefore how the customer services representatives (CSRs) learn to listen and speak well is not only a language learning concern, but also a key business one.

THE ASIAN-BASED CALL CENTRES

Call centres in Asia typically hire young graduates for a variety of customer service work in large Western English-speaking retail, finance and banking, insurance and telecommunications companies such as Citibank, Prudential, WalMart and TalkTalk. Most call centres employ hundreds of CSRs, who typically work through the night assisting American customers with their problems. In order to do this well, the CSRs need to have extremely good levels of English, particularly in understanding and speaking to NS customers, which necessarily involves a degree of acculturalization. They are typically trained in the product/process line and provided with 'communications training', emphasizing the ability to build customer relationships, prior to taking phone enquiries.

Teams of about 12 CSRs work together, and are overseen by a team leader who monitors them during work and provides communications support as required. Quality assurance specialists are also allotted to the CSRs to appraise the quality of their phone exchanges and provide regular scoring for monthly bonus payments and feedback in regular coaching sessions. The call centre, therefore, represents a kind of 'communications eco-system' where young graduates are provided with pre-employment language training, assessed at recruitment for account suitability, mentored and coached on the floor and provided with regular communications appraisal scores for quality assurance reasons. An ability to use English well in this workplace is the cornerstone of business quality.

In order to gain employment at the call centre, there are a series of language assessments administered by recruitment departments to select the best speakers of English. However, many of the assessment tools and practices lack validity and in one recruitment department, applicants are typically asked to read 'tongue twisters' with known consonant difficulties for Filipino and Indian speakers. If the applicants make a certain number of phonological mistakes, they are not hired. Other assessments include grammar and reading comprehension tests that bear little relation to the kind of skills CSRs need when talking to customers on the phones. Unfortunately, such high stakes recruitment practices wash back into intensive accent and grammar accuracy preparation for the recruitment process, and therefore at this stage, language learning bears no relation to communicative competence required on the phones. Unwittingly, many Asian call centres fail to recruit the best English language communicators (Lockwood, 2012a).

KEY LEARNING ISSUES

Many hopeful CSR applicants say at interview that one of the motivations for working in the call centre is to develop their own spoken communication for possible postgraduate study abroad and future promotions at work. One CSR worker described it as 'the best language school' in the world. It is interesting to unpack this comment and speculate why this is the case. Certainly, there are generous English language training programs on offer to ensure spoken standards are reached before CSRs 'go live'; however, it is perhaps the experience of working with NS customers on the phones for eight hours a day that promotes fast and effective language learning. This point is also certainly true of many English-speaking workplaces where employees are required to speak and write in English; this would be especially true of multinational companies.

Language learning in the call centres takes place at a number of levels. The first level, which can be characterized as unstructured, takes place on-the-job, where the CSR works with mostly NS customers on the phones. Here the 'doing' of work in English provides rich practice in listening and spoken skills. However, the effectiveness of learning through exposure on the phones may, to some extent, be affected by the linguistic readiness of the CSRs. It is notable that in the first month of work, there is often high attrition where new CSRs and/or quality managers cite poor English communication skills as the reason. In particular, CSRs and managers complain about the ability to relate well to customers and resolve their issues in an efficient and professional way. The second level, which can be described as semi-structured, relies on the CSR, as a self-directed and reflective learner, taking opportunities in peer exchange and observation of, and listening in to, colleagues as they work with customers on the phones. Informal exchanges at work for learning development are well-documented (see, for example, Boud and Garrick, 1999). Interestingly, these practices are institutionalized in the call centres through mentoring support structures, aptly called 'nesting' or 'incubation', in the first few weeks of work. The final level is through formal pre- and post- recruitment training and coaching on the floor, representing structured interventions specifically designed to accelerate and support communications improvement. It is this level that requires most investment in terms of time and resources, and is perhaps most affected by business perceptions of how best to improve CSR communication skills. I focus on this third level for the purposes of this chapter, but note the important contribution of this level in tandem with the first two.

BUSINESS MANAGERS' PERCEPTIONS OF ENGLISH LANGUAGE COMMUNICATION PROBLEMS

Resources provided for language communication development are often wasted in the call centre workplace context, because of business decisions where managers believe that the communication problems of CSRs relate to mother-tongue interference phonologically and grammatically. Assessment, training and coaching approaches are rarely informed by applied linguistics. Problematic assessment tools, as described above, result in a negative washback into communications training and coaching provided at the workplace, such as accent neutralization courses and grammar accuracy drilling; such approaches jeopardize successful language learning for work.

FINDINGS FROM APPLIED LINGUISTIC STUDIES ON COMMUNICATION BREAKDOWN

A number of recent linguistic studies have explored the nature of communication break-down when Indian and Filipino CSRs communicate with English-speaking customers on the phones. Authentic call centre exchanges were provided for these studies and different linguistic analyses have been carried out, including corpus studies, systemic functional linguistic analyses and conversational analyses (see, for example, Friginal, 2007; Forey and Lockwood, 2007). Contrary to the business beliefs, however, accent and grammatical inaccuracies did not feature as problems in communication; breakdown was found to relate to an inability to understand and profile the NS customer well, which in turn led to interactional and strategic problems in the exchange. In addition, it has been found that in certain types of accounts, such as technology and insurance claim accounts, CSRs were not able to structure their explanations in a way that made comprehension easy. For example, insurance claim customers were found to complain that CSRs were evasive and 'beating around the bush' when explaining, say, the reasons behind different payouts. The implications of these findings are discussed later in this chapter.

CURRENT SUPPORT FOR LANGUAGE LEARNING

The continued popularity of India and the Philippines as call centre destinations has resulted in a scarcity of very good speakers of English, because the industry has already employed the best English-speaking graduates from the best universities and the industry continues to grow rapidly. Generally, the approaches to language learning in the schools in many Asian countries promote rote learning of grammar and vocabulary, with the receptive skills of reading and listening generally being better than the productive skills of writing and speaking (Friginal, 2007). Businesses therefore bemoan the poor standards of English coming out of both the schools and universities, with one recent report produced by the Business Processing Association of the Philippines (BPAP) (BPAP, 2006) warning that poor spoken English-language skills is the single biggest threat to the continued development of the call centre industry in the Philippines. This language proficiency gap at graduation has meant that businesses now provide comprehensive language learning resources, called 'near hire' and 'pre-hire' training, for the call centres. This bridging of the proficiency gap between recruitment and starting the job is also common in other industry groups. The Hong Kong Workplace English Campaign (2000) was launched as a government initiative to enhance English communication skills.

'Near hire' training provides listening and spoken language development for applicants who still require substantial English language support before they are recruited. These intensive type programs usually run for four to six weeks to ensure proficiency gain in these two skills, and do not assume a knowledge of call centre work. Typically, students will be engaged in role-plays and listening exercises involving authentic exchanges, although the quality and content of such courses vary enormously. 'Pre-hire' communications training, on the other hand, relates to the typical two- to three-week 'communications course' provided to successful applicants at recruitment before they start to take calls. Over the years, the quality of such courses has varied enormously, with many companies doing little more than accent and grammar training. Communications training, in the view of the business, is typically fragmented into sub-sets of training, for example, language (meaning grammar); accent neutralization; culture training (meaning downloaded fact-learning from the internet); and 'soft skills' training (meaning customer service etiquette, often taught by American visiting trainers). It was observed that an American soft skills trainer visiting the Philippines took no account in her training for the fact that her group were second rather than first language speakers. She consequently made assumptions about the intercultural and linguistic knowledge of the participants, and in showing a slide that said 'never say sorry', the CSRs took her literally; in a subsequent insurance claims call, one of the CSRs was heard to say to a customer who had just lost her husband, "I do apologize for that"! Just as problematically, communication problems on the floor are poorly diagnosed, often focusing on accent, and resulting in inappropriate coaching. Most coaches are experienced CSRs, but have little understanding of the needs of second language learners and, therefore, the precise nature of the problems their coachees are having.

In applied linguistics, needs analysis or language auditing in the workplace requires an ethnographic approach, where language specialists are able to: listen to a sample of good and bad call centre exchanges as identified by the business; interview key stakeholders about what are perceived as good and bad calls; review customer feedback information; and, critically, transcribe call samples to analyse how language choices add or detract from the quality of the calls. Such processes and 'knowledge transfer', however, are rare. To date, no formal studies have been carried out to track the development of spoken performance levels over the first few months on the phones, although anecdotally CSRs and team leaders report big gains in language proficiency.

THE IMPACT OF TECHNOLOGICAL DEVELOPMENT IN LEARNING ENGLISH IN THE CALL CENTRES

Over the last two decades, advances in fibre optic cabling have opened up the possibility of establishing the BPO industry in developing countries. In addition, with recent developments in smartphone technology, chat (texting) exchanges for customer service are becoming popular with many companies. One of the main reasons is that smartphones do not allow toll-free call centre numbers, so texting is the only option; however, other customers, particularly younger ones, are reported to prefer chat to voice exchange, citing the ability to multi-task and save time when using the texting option (Telus International, 2012). Very little research has been carried out in this area and, again, businesses find themselves in the situation of having to make decisions about how to assess, train and coach for language exchange using this new media. For example, many companies now require that the chat exchange follows the same generic structure as a voice exchange, believing that this will safeguard interpersonal effectiveness and customer relationship building. Unsurprisingly perhaps, the chat exchanges are found to be very long, compared to voice. In order to mitigate this problem, businesses have enforced a further rule of multiple chats, where each CSR deals concurrently with up to six chat exchanges. Businesses also provide large databases of templates, from which CSRs are encouraged to paste in standard responses to customers. These business decisions result in employee language training and learning challenges, such as a consideration of whether chat is essentially a speaking or writing skill, whether it can be constructed effectively through the use of template responses, and what the pragmatic differences are between texting and voice exchange. No applied linguistic research has been done to date to evaluate the impact of such business decisions and resultant challenges for language learning.

Whilst these are interesting questions, the next section in this chapter will be concerned with spoken skills development in the call centres.

IMPLICATIONS FOR TEACHING AND ASSESSMENT

The effectiveness of language learning in this workplace eco-system relies on the high quality of assessment, training and coaching; the implications for language auditing, program and materials development and assessment products and processes are briefly discussed to conclude this chapter.

LANGUAGE AUDITING AS NEEDS ANALYSIS

In applied linguistics training and TESOL courses, syllabus planning processes promote needs analyses related to students and the broader context in which language learning is to take place (see, for example, Nation and Macalister, 2010). Most contexts are typically educational: program development for schools and universities where the educational purposes for language learning are, for example, passing entry and final examinations. However, in the workplace context, a much broader needs analyses process is required, where organizational and specific job requirement needs, along with post-holder language needs, are probed to locate communication gaps resulting in business problems. I call this 'language auditing' for the purposes of this chapter. Language auditing was a term first coined by Reeves and Wright (1996) in response to many multinationals, irrespective of ownership, requiring good levels of English for trade within the European Union. Businesses therefore wanted a detailed 'audit' of the language proficiency levels of all their employees, as well as indications as to whether such levels were sufficient for the posts held; thus, large scale testing was carried out to achieve this. The context described in this chapter is perhaps best characterized as language auditing 'end-to-end' in the call centre communications eco-system. In such worksites, where English language communication is a core competency, a language audit can help a company identify key processes for communications recruitment, training, coaching and quality assurance, and, just as importantly, how to develop products and processes to ensure the successfully recruited CSR applicants are the best English language communicators. A language audit ideally diagnoses the overall communication health of the worksite and makes recommendations for communications improvements.

IDENTIFYING THE PROBLEMS AND TRANSFERRING KNOWLEDGE

As described above, discourse analysis is a critical component of a language audit, where authentic instances of written and spoken exchange are examined to reveal the linguistic reasons for communication difficulty. In order to do this well, a language framework is required for analysis. For the purposes of this chapter, I will briefly discuss how systemic functional linguistics (SFL) (Halliday, 1985) has enhanced our understanding of where language choices impact a capacity to work in the call centres. This framework has also been used in other workplace settings (see, for example, Iedema, Feez, and White, 1994).

SFL is a context-sensitive language framework which explains language choices for meaning making, and two studies cited here have contributed to our understanding of what the communication gaps appear to be in customer exchanges. The first one (Forey and Lockwood, 2007) isolated the moves in the call where there was frequent occurrence of breakdown on the phones relating to problematic listening and profiling skills. The study revealed problematic interactional and strategic skills, and problematic discoursal skills, in situations where CSRS are often asked to explain policies and procedures clearly. This had a direct impact on training and coaching interventions in call centre training program development (Lockwood, 2012b). The second study (Forey and Lam, 2012) explored how good and poor calls in a specific Collections account revealed patterns of different linguistic choices, including phonological choices, in the exchanges. Again, the workplace used these findings to develop training and coaching tools and report quality improvements, linking these to amounts of money collected.

Implications of the research, however, have not only enhanced the learning of the specific language required for the workplace, but also the measurement of this language at recruitment and at work. Regular formative assessment practices, which provide targeted feedback and are based on criteria related to communication quality, will all have the desired washback into language learning.

CONCLUSION

The combination of applied linguistic research as described above, and the application of adult learning strategies in the workplace, together with the input of business stakeholders, can contribute to improved language learning. Lifelong language learning at work obviously relates to the nature of the specific work, the organization involved, the geographical location and even the technology available. In this chapter I have looked at just one workplace to demonstrate this complexity and the crucial role applied linguists and adult educationalists have in ensuring businesses and employees maximize language learning opportunities at work. As Boud and Garrick comment:

> There are few places left for employees at any level who do not continue to learn and improve their effectiveness throughout their working lives. There is no place for managers who do not appreciate their own vital role in fostering learning. The future of enterprises and the agenda of educational institutions are becoming intimately linked with the present reconceptualisation of work and learning. (Boud and Garrick, 1999: 1)

Discussion Questions

1. Apart from the workplace contexts described in the first section of this chapter, can you think of any other examples that may suggest different types of language learning approaches?

2. How would you define business English as a lingua franca (BELF) characteristics across different workplaces, and what implications do these differences have for language learning?

3. How would you seek to influence business decisions about communications problems in a work setting? How best could you support those employees to enhance their language learning?

4. What kinds of language learning activities do you think would be suitable for developing extensive speaking skills where a customer service representative may need to explain a refund policy or give instructions?

5. Draw a language learning pathway for an aspiring CSR from CEFR B1(near-hire) to C1 (coaching support). Insert as many details about appropriate language learning strategies and interventions along this pathway.

Key Readings

Forey, G., & Lockwood, J. (Eds.) (2010). *Globalization, Communication and the Workplace: Talking Across the World.* London / New York: Continuum.

Mawer, G. (2014). *Language and Literacy in Workplace Education: Learning at Work.* Harlow, UK: Longman.

Piekkari, R., Welch, D., & Welch, L. (2014). *Language in International Business: The Multilingual Reality of Global Business Expansion.* Cheltenham, UK: Edward Elgar.

References

Boud, D., & Garrick, J. (Eds.) (1999). *Understanding Learning at Work.* London: Routledge.

BPAP (2006). *English is not the Problem! Communication Skills in the BPO Industry.* Annual report.

Forey, G., & Lam, M. (2012). Applying systemic functional linguistics: Understanding choices of quality in the workplace. *Journal of Applied Linguistics and Professional Practice*, 9, 61–80.

Forey, G., & Lockwood, J. (2007). 'I'd love to put someone in jail for this': An initial investigation of English in the business processing outsourcing (BPO) industry. *English for Specific Purposes*, 26, 308–326.

Friginal, E. (2007). Outsourced call centres and English in the Philippines. *World Englishes,* 26, 331–345.

Graddol, D. (2006). *English Next: Why Global English May Mean the End of 'English as a Foreign Language'.* London: The British Council and The English Company (UK) Ltd.

Halliday, M. A. K. (1985). *An Introduction to Functional Grammar.* London: Edward Arnold.

Holmes, J., & Marra, M. (2002). Having a laugh at work: how humour contributes to workplace culture. *Journal of Pragmatics*, 34, 1683–1710.

Iedema, R., Feez, S., & White, P. (1994). *Literacy of Administration.* Disadvantaged Schools program, NSW Department of Schools Education.

Lockwood, J. (2012a). Are we getting the right people for the job? A study of English language recruitment assessment practices in the business processing outsourcing sector: India and the Philippines. *Journal of Business Communication*, 49(2), 107–127.

Lockwood, J. (2012b). Developing an English for specific purpose curriculum for Asian call centres: How theory can inform practice. *English for Specific Purposes*, 31, 14–24.

Mawer, G. (2014). *Language and Literacy in Workplace Education: Learning at Work.* Harlow, UK: Longman.

Mercado, J. (13 May, 2015). Presentation at BPAP entitled *The Philippine IT-BPM Industry Mid-Year Update.*

Nation, I. S. P., & Macalister, J. (2010). *Language Curriculum Design.* London: Routledge.

Piekkari, R., Welch, D., & Welch, L. (2014). *Language in International Business: The Multilingual Reality of Global Business Expansion.* Cheltenham, UK: Edward Elgar.

Reeves, N., & Wright, C. (1996). *Linguistic Auditing: A Guide to Identifying Foreign Language Communication Needs in Corporations.* Bristol, UK: Multilingual Matters.

Telus International (2012). White Paper. *Comparing Costs: Chat vs. Voice Customer Service.* Part of the *Best Practices Online Chat* series. https://www.telusinternational.com/landing/compare-chat-vs-voice-customer-service/

SECTION 5

LEARNING THE 'SYSTEMS' OF ENGLISH

The chapters in this section consider how the different 'systems' – pronunciation, word-level vocabulary, phrase-level features and grammar – of language knowledge and skills develop. These chapters provide a precursor to discussion of the learning of the four macro-skills of listening, speaking, reading, and writing considered in Section 6.

In the first chapter, **Ee Ling Low** focuses on the learning of pronunciation. She first discusses fundamental concepts of what can be considered to constitute pronunciation skills and the goals of pronunciation in learning English as a second language (L2). She then looks at factors that influence the development of such skills, such as age, aptitude, first language and motivation. She stresses that pedagogical goals in teaching pronunciation should focus on raising awareness of different varieties of English, comprehensibility, intelligibility and communicative competence.

David Hirsh outlines the nature of word knowledge, describes how understanding of word meanings develops and discusses factors that facilitate L2 vocabulary learning. He describes the lexical threshold needed to enable reading in English as an L2; identifies targets for receptive and productive vocabulary acquisition; suggests factors that enable learners to retain words they encounter; and considers the role of direct and indirect instruction, as well as autonomous learning, in L2 vocabulary development.

In the following chapter, **Frank Boers** extends the notion of lexical knowledge to include phrases and chunks – multiword units that contribute significantly to fluent and natural L2 use. For L2 learners, multiword units can pose problems both for comprehension and for production, and explicit instruction is often needed to offset the assumption that these features will be acquired implicitly through exposure.

In his chapter, **Scott Thornbury** notes the undue prominence of a focus on grammar in second language acquisition research, as compared to other dimensions of language. He points out that different theories of the nature of grammar focus on different aspects of L2 grammar acquisition, but have not resolved central questions concerning the role of the first language (L1), such as whether there is a natural sequence of grammatical development, and the role of instruction in developing the learner's knowledge and use of grammar.

In various ways, these chapters draw attention to the need for explicit attention to the systems of the language that underpin the ability to communicate in spoken and written language. While some aspects, such as grammar and vocabulary, have traditionally played a large (and some would argue, too large) role in language teaching and learning, it is clear that other systems, notably pronunciation, may be overlooked. Moreover, the relationship of learning these systems in an L2 to learners' repertoires and language awareness in L1 is an area that warrants much more investigation.

CHAPTER 17

Learning Pronunciation

Ee Ling Low

INTRODUCTION

This chapter presents a general discussion of English as a second language (ESL) pronunciation learning. It first considers fundamental concepts concerning pronunciation learning and provides an overview of the topics covered in the chapter. Secondly, it deals with issues surrounding the development of ESL pronunciation skills. Specifically, it focuses on: intelligibility and norms in pronunciation learning; development in segmentals (vowels and consonants) and suprasegmentals (rhythm, stress and intonation); features that influence the development of proficiency in ESL pronunciation; and strategies in ESL pronunciation learning. The final section considers pedagogical implications for ESL pronunciation teaching and assessment.

OVERVIEW

In general, surveys of the literature on pronunciation show that it is the area in second language acquisition (SLA) that has received the least attention, although researchers acknowledge that many factors influence the process of learning ESL pronunciation, such as motivational levels, gender differences, and transfer from one's first language (L1), to name a few (Çakir and Baytar, 2014). Of these factors, some scholars (e.g., Scovel, 1969; Krashen, 1973) have drawn on Lenneberg's (1967) Critical Period Hypothesis and consider age to be the most important variable determining whether one is able to acquire near-native proficiency in learning a second or foreign language (see Chapters 1–3).

Research focusing on instructors' and learners' attitudes to teaching pronunciation, albeit scarce, does exist. In relation to instructors, Burgess and Spencer (2000) found that instructors considered pronunciation instruction difficult; they perceived in particular that learners had problems pronouncing phonemes in the target language not found in their first language. Foote, Holtby, and Derwing's (2011) study, conducted in Canada, found that teachers deemed pronunciation instruction to be difficult, and 75% of the instructors they surveyed expressed the desire for further training in teaching pronunciation. In terms of learner attitudes towards the importance of pronunciation, Foote et al.'s (2011) research also showed that a majority of the subjects surveyed felt that achieving near-native pronunciation would win them more respect. An earlier study by Suter (1976), and another by Elliott (1995), suggest that learners who are concerned about their pronunciation developed better pronunciation. These findings fall in line with Gass and Selinker (2008), who purport that those who are motivated to learn another language will learn it faster and to a higher level (see Chapter 6).

The next section will focus on key issues in ESL pronunciation practice, learning and development.

KEY LEARNING ISSUES

INTELLIGIBILITY AND NORMS IN ESL PRONUNCIATION PRACTICE

In a context where English is now spoken by people from numerous different countries, with diverse language backgrounds and cultures, questions about who should one be intelligible to, and for what purpose, arise. Another emergent issue is about whose norms one should orient towards (see Low, 2015). Smith's (1992) study found major differences among concepts of intelligibility, comprehensibility and interpretability. Smith suggested that intelligibility of speech was easiest to perceive, and those who were more exposed to different varieties of English did better on the interpretability scale. Proficiency in English affected comprehensibility of the message most. Smith recommended exposure to different varieties of English in order to achieve greater levels of intelligibility, comprehensibility and interpretability.

Munro and Derwing (1995) showed that accentedness did not necessarily reduce the comprehensibility or intelligibility of speech produced by non-native speakers, while Derwing and Munro's (1997) study confirmed a correlation between familiarity with second language (L2) varieties of English and intelligibility scores. They suggested that in order to improve the comprehensibility of non-native speech for other listeners, there is a need to focus on grammatical and prosodic (suprasegmental) aspects rather than just phonemic errors.

Hahn (2004) investigated the impact of non-native lexical stress placement on native listeners, and found that appropriate primary stress positioning was important, as it affected the intelligibility of non-native speech to native American English listeners. Field (2005) showed that when stress shift was accompanied by changes to vowel quality, it affected intelligibility. Munro, Derwing, and Morton's (2006) study found that recognizable native English speech patterns ensured that intelligibility was not totally compromised, while Deterding and Kirkpatrick's (2006) study suggested that non-standard features of speech amongst different groups of speakers from countries belonging to the Association of Southeast Asian (ASEAN) nations enhanced rather than impeded intelligibility. In relation to future work on intelligibility, Rajadurai (2007) suggests that the role of the listener and the speaker in accommodating to their potential interlocutors in multicultural settings should be studied. Her views resonate with Low's (2015) suggestion about the importance of listener supremacy in dictating norms of pronunciation in the Inner, Outer and Expanding Circles of English (Kachru, 1982). What this research suggests is that the speaker should adhere to norms that depend on which variety of English the listener speaks.

DEVELOPMENT OF ESL PROFICIENCY

The effect of linguistic experience, that is, the length of learners' residence in the target country or the amount of use of the second language, has been reported to be an important factor affecting the development of segmental proficiency in English (Trofimovich and Baker, 2006). Flege, Bohn, and Jang (1997) showed that more experienced native Spanish, Mandarin and Korean learners of English who had resided in the USA between 5.4 and 9 years could pronounce the short vowel /ɪ/ (in *bit*) and identify the short vowels /æ/ (in *bat*) and /ɛ/ (in *bet*) more accurately than less experienced learners who had lived in the USA between 0.4 and 0.9 years. Another study by Flege and MacKay (2004) showed that native Italian ESL learners who rarely used their first language (i.e., more experienced users of English) were able to perceive English vowels more accurately than those who often used their first language (i.e., less experienced users of English).

Segmental accuracy alone, however, cannot guarantee communicative competence in a second or foreign language (Zarifi and Sayyadi, 2015), and scholars such as Morley (1991) and Jenkins (2002) have called for shifting the pedagogical focus of ESL pronunciation from segmentals to suprasegmentals. They and others argue that improvement in suprasegmental components contributes more efficiently to effective pronunciation competence (Jenkins, ibid.), as they are the main contributing features in achieving fluency acquisition in second language speech (Anderson-Hsieh and Vengartagiri, 1994; Trofimovich and Baker, 2006). These features include: pause duration (e.g., Anderson-Hsieh and Vengartagiri, 1994); rate of speaking (e.g., Derwing and Munro, 1997); fundamental frequency (F0) range (Mennen, 2006); peak alignment (Trofimovich and Baker, 2006); and intonation (Kang, Guion-Anderson, Rhee, and Ahn, 2012). The acquisition of these features is in turn affected by others mentioned earlier, including motivation (Conrad, 1991), the first language (Archibald, 1998), age (Guion, Flege, Liu, and Yeni-Komshian, 2000), and linguistic experience (Kang et al., 2012; Trofimovich and Baker, 2006).

FACTORS INFLUENCING THE DEVELOPMENT OF ESL PRONUNCIATION PROFICIENCY

Both intrinsic and extrinsic factors influence the learning of and development of proficiency in second language pronunciation.

AGE

As mentioned earlier, age plays an important role in the development of ESL pronunciation proficiency (see Chapters 1–3). However, scholars do not agree upon the best possible age for pronunciation acquisition. The Critical Period Hypothesis (Lenneberg, 1967) suggests that the period around puberty is critical for language learning, suggesting that the development of proficiency in ESL pronunciation should take place pre- rather than post-puberty. It is also argued that if ESL learners acquire a second language before the age of six, they are able to acquire near native-like pronunciation. However, if learning takes place between the ages of seven and eleven, a perceptible L2 accent may be detected and there will almost always be a perceptible L2 accent if learning of L2 takes place after the age of twelve (Nation and Newton, 2009: 78).

Recent works by Granena and Long (2012) and Abrahamsson (2012), however, contradict this proposition, and present a much more complicated relationship between age and pronunciation acquisition. Granena and Long (2012) conducted a study involving 65 Chinese learners of L2 Spanish and 12 L2 native speaker controls, with the learners divided into three groups based on age of onset (AO) (i.e., 3–6, 7–15 and 16–29 years), and concluded that there is a sensitive period for L2 phonological attainment which begins at

6 years old and ends by 12 years old. Abrahamsson's (2012) study involved 200 Spanish speakers of L2 Swedish and 20 native controls. Results showed that:

- for early learners (AO 1–15) "strong, negative correlations" (p. 210) between the AO and ultimate attainment occurred, whereas for the late learners (AO 16–30), ultimate attainment could no longer be predicted by AO;
- the possibility of L2 learners' performance within the native-speaker range was greatest among the early learners (AO 1–15), but nativelikeness ceased to occur at 13; and
- only the early learners (AO 1–15) "showed any sign of having developed both grammatical and phonetic aspects of L2 simultaneously" (Abrahamsson, 2012: 210).

Although controversy exists over the correlation between the exact age of acquisition and ESL pronunciation attainment, there seems to be some consensus that the younger an ESL learner is, the higher the possibility that they can master pronunciation well.

APTITUDE

Aptitude (see Chapter 7) has also been considered an important factor in ESL pronunciation learning. Phonemic coding ability has been proposed by Carroll (1981) to be one of the four components of language learning aptitude (the other three being grammatical sensitivity, rote-learning ability, and inductive language learning ability). Phonemic coding is defined as "an ability to identify distinct sounds, to form associations between those sounds and symbols representing them, and to retain these associations" (Carroll, 1981: 105). However, learners with a higher degree of aptitude may not be more successful in learning pronunciation, as there may be other factors at play, such as attitude and motivation. Scholars such as Celce-Murcia, Brinton, Goodwin and Griner (2010) hold that ESL learners with high phonemic coding ability are likely to experience less difficulty in attaining intelligible pronunciation. Instructors should therefore be aware of these learner differences that may affect levels of success in students' pronunciation learning.

ATTITUDE

Results from the Pronunciation Attitude Inventory show that learners who are more concerned about pronunciation are likely to achieve more accurate pronunciation of the target allophones (Elliot, 1995). In second language acquisition, it is common that different learners have different attitudes to the target language and the target language community. These attitudes can facilitate or hinder development of learners' proficiency in ESL pronunciation.

MOTIVATION

Motivation has been a subject of much debate (MacIntyre, 2002; see also Chapter 6). Gardner (1985) asserts that a definition of motivation must include four elements: having a goal, having the desire to attain the goal, having positive attitudes, and expending effort. Research suggests that motivation does affect pronunciation learning (see Derwing and Munro, 2015), and those with personal or professional goals for learning English will not just aspire towards, but become highly proficient in, their pronunciation of the target language (Marinova-Todd, Marshall, and Snow, 2000). Moyer's (2007) research found that those with a positive previous experience and orientation to language will develop greater authenticity in pronunciation. Derwing and Munro (2015: 45), however, express concerns over the motivation issue. These include determining appropriate ways to define and measure motivation, with problems arising from the interpretation of correlations between motivation and good pronunciation and other factors at play (e.g., a strong motivation for pronunciation attainment may not translate into desired outcomes without appropriate resources, learner aptitudes, talents, opportunities, etc.).

EXPOSURE TO THE TARGET LANGUAGE

One of the external factors affecting ESL pronunciation proficiency development is the degree of exposure to the target language. While it is difficult to give an exact definition of exposure, it may be said that it is associated with experiencing an environment where the target language (in this case, English) is used, and also to prior instruction. What matters is the frequency with which learners have the opportunity to listen to or speak the target language. The more frequent the exposure, the more proficient they may become in pronunciation.

Exposure entails more than just being in the environment or country where the target language is spoken. If learners choose to mix mainly with their peers from their home country, their exposure will be limited. Conversely, via technological affordances, exposure may go beyond the confines of the physical classroom (see Chapter 13), through multimedia platforms such as watching television programmes, movies, listening to music and surfing the internet for pronunciation instruction software.

More exposure may not always lead to higher proficiency in pronunciation, however, because the effect of greater exposure varies from learner to learner, due to individual differences – in motivation and attitude, for example. A learner who is less frequently exposed to the target language, but possesses more intrinsic learner attributes that have been shown to lead to successful ESL learning, may turn out to be more proficient in pronunciation than the learner who has more exposure but fewer intrinsic learner attributes.

LEARNERS' FIRST LANGUAGE

ESL learners' first language can be a major factor affecting the development of proficiency in their L2 pronunciation. Generally, the same patterns of pronunciation would typically be found in the speech of ESL learners who speak the same first language (Nation and Newton, 2009: 79). A learner's first language often contributes to the foreign-accentedness in their English pronunciation. This foreign-accentedness can be seen at both the segmental and suprasegmental levels. Beginning learners who are unfamiliar with the sound system of the English language tend to exploit the existing sound categories from their first languages. The difficulty arises when they come across English sounds that do not exist in their first languages. Therefore, the greater the differences in the sound systems between English and a learner's first language, the more difficulties the learner may encounter in the learning of ESL pronunciation.

Several other factors affect the acquisition of ESL pronunciation, such as personality, quality of instruction, individual efforts, and goal setting. These factors do not exist in isolation but are often interrelated, and they should therefore be viewed from an integrated language learning perspective.

STRATEGIES IN ESL PRONUNCIATION LEARNING

Table 17.1 provides a list of the major strategies (see also Chapter 9) for ESL pronunciation learning, adapted from Peterson (2000), Derwing and Rossiter (2002), and Osburne (2003).

According to Peterson (2000), the majority of strategies identified were related to cognitive strategies, followed by metacognitive and social strategies. Interestingly, only advanced learners reported using memory-related strategies. No compensatory strategies were reported by learners in Peterson (2000). In Derwing and Rossiter (2002), paraphrasing was reported to be the most popular strategy, followed by self-repetition and the other four strategies. It should be noted that Derwing and Rossiter's study focuses on communication strategies in relation to pronunciation, rather than pronunciation learning per se. Osburne (2003), however, reported memory or imitation as the most popular strategy adopted by the ESL learners in the study.

	PETERSON (2000)	DERWING AND ROSSITER (2002)	OSBURNE (2003)
Pronunciation Learning Strategies	• Practising naturalistically • Formally practising with sounds • Analysing the sound system • Setting goals and objectives • Planning for a language task • Self-evaluating • Representing sounds in memory • Cooperating with peers	• Paraphrase (56%) • Self-repetition (28%) • Writing/Spelling (7%) • Volume adjustment (5%) • Slowing speech rate (3%) • Speaking clearly (3%)	• Memory or imitation (17) • Paralanguage (14) • Individual words (13) • Local articulatory gesture or sing sound (13) • Global articulatory gesture (9) • Prosodic structure (6) • Individual syllables (3) • Clusters below syllable level (1)

Table 17.1 Some of the Major L2 Pronunciation Learning Strategies in Previous Studies. (Order of Strategies Rearranged According to the Degree of Popularity.)

Pronunciation learning strategies are likewise affected by other factors associated with attributes of good language learners (see Brown, 2008), and also tied to one's linguistic and cultural background.

IMPLICATIONS FOR TEACHING AND ASSESSMENT

Schaetzel and Low (2009) share a number of pedagogical strategies for teaching pronunciation that can help learners to fulfil their personal and professional needs. First, instructors should cultivate positive attitudes towards pronunciation accuracy by building respect for the different native languages spoken in the ESL classroom. Awareness must also be built about different varieties of English spoken internationally. Next, instructors need to identify specific pronunciation features that pose problems for ESL learners. Understanding the phonological patterning of the first language spoken by ESL learners can help instructors predict potential pronunciation problems for their listeners. Teachers can also observe learners in communication with each other, noting areas and features of speech causing miscommunications. As prosodic features affect comprehensibility, instructors need to pay attention to suprasegmental aspects of speech in ESL pronunciation teaching. These include teaching lexical stress and weak forms in unstressed syllables, for example.

Beyond pronunciation accuracy, the goal of ESL pronunciation learners should be to acquire communicative competence. In Low (2010), I argued that, moving beyond intelligibility, it is important for learners to acquire overall communicative competence, as defined by Canale and Swain (1980): that is, grammatical, sociolinguistic, discoursal and strategic competence. Research indicates that pronunciation contributes to the learning of other L2 skills such as listening comprehension and vocabulary. Some studies suggest that explicit phonetic instruction has a positive effect on L2 learners' listening comprehension performance (see, for example, Khaghaninejad and Maleki, 2015; Shimamune and Smith, 1995). De Jong, Seveke, and van Veen (2000) demonstrate that phonological sensitivity contributes to learners' acquisition of phonologically unfamiliar words. Hu's (2003) study investigated the effect of phonological memory on L2 word learning, and provided evidence supporting phonological memory as a strong predictor of EFL learners' ability to learn vocabulary. These findings point to a need for ESL teachers to incorporate pronunciation teaching (such as phonological sensitivity and phonological memory) into the teaching of listening comprehension and vocabulary.

In relation to assessment, tests of ESL pronunciation proficiency will also need to consider contexts where English is spoken around the world. Norms for English language proficiency cannot be centred on Inner Circle norms alone, but must consider the pluricentric norms offered by Outer and Expanding circle varieties as well. This affects the topics and materials selected for assessment. Low's (2015) suggestion of listener-oriented norms is a pragmatic way forward, and resonates with Tomlinson's (2010) suggestion that the ability to accommodate one's speech according to who our interlocutors are is an important criterion for testing pronunciation. The variety of English tested ought to be matched against where the test candidates are likely to use the language.

CONCLUSION

This chapter has discussed some key learning issues concerning ESL pronunciation, as well as implications for pronunciation teaching and assessment. It should be emphasized that these issues may influence both ESL pronunciation learning and teaching in different ways, according to learner and contextual differences. Future research needs to provide further empirical evidence to demonstrate how English pronunciation can facilitate or hinder ESL learners' language learning and use in this increasingly globalized world.

Discussion Questions

1. Based on your own English (or other) language learning experience, what are the factors that influenced your pronunciation learning? Are these factors similar to the ones mentioned in this chapter?

2. Interview three English language learners you know, and write down at least three strategies they use in their pronunciation learning. Compare them with your own answers and discuss which you think are the most effective.

3. What role could pronunciation play in the learning of other language skills such as listening, speaking, reading and vocabulary? List examples for each language skill.

Key Readings

Abrahamsson, N. (2012). Age of onset and nativelike L2 ultimate attainment of morphosyntactic and phonetic intuition. *Studies in Second Language Acquisition*, 34, 187–214.

Derwing, T. M., & Munro, M. J. (2015). *Pronunciation Fundamentals: Evidence-based Perspectives for L2 Teaching and Research*. Amsterdam/Philadelphia: John Benjamins Publishing Company.

Low, E. L. (2015). *Pronunciation for English as an International Language: From Research to Practice* (Chapter 10). UK: Routledge.

Osburne, A. G. (2003). Pronunciation strategies of advanced ESOL learners. *International Review of Applied Linguistics in Language Teaching*, 41, 131–143.

References

Abrahamsson, N. (2012). Age of onset and nativelike L2 ultimate attainment of morphosyntactic and phonetic intuition. *Studies in Second Language Acquisition*, 34, 187–214.

Anderson-Hsieh, J., & Vengartagiri, H. (1994). Syllable duration and pausing in the speech of Chinese ESL speakers. *TESOL Quarterly*, 28, 807–812.

Archibald, J. (1998). *Second Language Phonology*. Amsterdam/Philadelphia: John Benjamins.

Brown, A. (2008). Pronunciation and good language learners. In C. Griffiths (Ed.), *Lessons from Good Language Learners* (pp. 197–207). Cambridge: Cambridge University Press.

Burgess, J., & Spencer, S. (2000). Phonology and pronunciation in integrated language teaching and teacher education. *System*, 28, 191–215.

Çakir, I., & Baytar, B. (2014). Foreign language learners' views on the importance of learning the target language pronunciation. *Journal of Language and Linguistic Studies*, 10(1), 99–110.

Canale, M., & Swain, M. (1980). Theoretical bases of communicative approaches to second language teaching and testing. *Applied Linguistics*, 1, 1–47.

Carroll, J. B. (1981). Twenty-five years of research on foreign language aptitude. In K. C. Diller (Ed.), *Individual Differences & Universals in Language Learning Aptitude* (pp. 83–118). Rowley, MA: Newbury House.

Celce-Murcia, M., Brinton, D. M., Goodwin, J. M., & Griner, B. (2010). *Teaching Pronunciation: A Course Book and Reference Guide* (2nd ed.). Cambridge: Cambridge University Press.

Conrad, B. K. (1991). *The Relationship Between Empathy and Pronunciation Ability: A Study of Elementary-level College Students of German*. Unpublished doctoral dissertation, University of Texas at Austin.

de Jong, P. F., Seveke, M.-J., & van Veen, M. (2000). Phonological sensitivity and the acquisition of new words in children. *Journal of Experimental Child Psychology*, 76, 275–301.

Derwing, T. M., & Munro, M. J. (1997). Accent, intelligibility, and comprehensibility. *Studies in Second Language Acquisition*, 19, 1–15.

Derwing, T. M., & Munro, M. J. (2015). *Pronunciation Fundamentals: Evidence-based Perspectives for L2 Teaching and Research*. Amsterdam/Philadelphia: John Benjamins.

Derwing, T. M., & Rossiter, M. J. (2002). ESL learners' perceptions of their pronunciation needs and strategies. *System*, 30, 155–166.

Deterding, D., & Kirkpatrick, A. (2006). Emerging South-East Asian Englishes and intelligibility. *World Englishes*, 25(3), 391–409.

Elliott, A. R. (1995). Foreign language phonology: Field independence, attitude, and the success of formal instruction in Spanish pronunciation. *The Modern Language Journal*, 79(4), 530–542.

Field, J. (2005). Intelligibility and the listener: The role of lexical stress. *TESOL Quarterly*, 39, 399–423.

Flege, J. E., Bohn, O.-S., & Jang, S. (1997). The effect of experience on nonnative subjects' production and perception of English vowels. *Journal of Phonetics*, 25, 437–470.

Flege, J. E., & MacKay, I. R. A. (2004). Perceiving vowels in a second language. *Studies in Second Language Acquisition*, 26, 1–34.

Foote, J. A., Holtby, A. K., & Derwing, T. M. (2011). Survey of the teaching of pronunciation in adult ESL programs in Canada. *TESL Canada Journal*, 29(1), 1–22.

Gardner, R. C. (1985). *Social Psychology and Second Language Learning: The Role of Attitudes and Motivation*. London: E. Arnold.

Gass, S. M., & Selinker, L. (2008). *Second Language Acquisition: An Introductory Course* (3rd ed.). New York: Routledge.

Granena, G., & Long, M. H. (2012). Age of onset, length of residence, language aptitude, and ultimate L2 attainment in three linguistic domains. *Second Language Research*, 29(3), 311–343.

Guion, S. G., Flege, J. E., Liu, S. H., & Yeni-Komshian, G. H. (2000). Age of learning effects on the duration of sentences produced in a second language. *Applied Psycholinguistics*, 21, 205–228.

Hahn, L. D. (2004). Primary stress and intelligibility: Research to motivate the teaching of suprasegmentals. *TESOL Quarterly*, 38, 201–223.

Hu, C.-F. (2003). Phonological memory, phonological awareness and foreign language word learning. *Language Learning*, 53(3), 429–462.

Jenkins, J. (2002). A sociolinguistically based, empirically researched pronunciation syllabus for English as an international language. *Applied Linguistics*, 23, 83–103.

Kachru, B. B. (Ed.) (1982). *The Other Tongue: English Across Cultures*. Urbana, IIL.: University of Illinois Press.

Kang, S. H., Guion-Anderson, S., Rhee S.-C., & Ahn, H. K. (2012). The effect of language immersion on second language suprasegmentals. *Korean Journal of Applied Linguistics*, 28(1), 181–208.

Khaghaninejad, M. S., & Maleki, A. (2015). The effect of explicit pronunciation instruction on listening comprehension: Evidence from Iranian English learners. *Theory and Practice in Language Studies*, 5(6), 1249–1256.

Krashen, S. D. (1973). Lateralization, language learning, and the critical period: Some new evidence. *Language Learning*, 23, 63–74.

Lenneberg, E. H. (1967). *Biological Foundations of Language*. New York: Wiley.

Low, E. L. (2010). Sounding local and going global: Current research and implications for pronunciation teaching. In L. Lim, A. Pakir, & L. Wee (Eds.), *English in Singapore: Modernity and Management* (pp. 235–260). Hong Kong: Hong Kong University Press.

Low, E. L. (2015). *Pronunciation for English as an International Language: From Research to Practice*. London: Routledge.

MacIntyre, P. D. (2002). Motivation, anxiety and emotion in second language acquisition. In P. Robinson (Ed.), *Individual Differences and Instructed Language Learning* (pp. 45–68). Amsterdam/Philadelphia: John Benjamins.

Marinova-Todd, S. H., Marshall, D. B., & Snow, C. E. (2000). Three misconceptions about age and L2 learning. *TESOL Quarterly*, 34(1), 9–34.

Mennen, I. (2006). Phonetic and phonological influences in non-native intonation: An overview for language teachers. *QMUC Speech Science Research Centre Working Paper WP9*.

Morley, J. (1991). The pronunciation component in teaching English to speakers of other languages. *TESOL Quarterly*, 25(1), 51–74.

Moyer, A. (2007). Do language attitudes determine accent? A study of bilinguals in the USA. *Journal of Multilingual and Multicultural Development*, 28(6), 502–518.

Munro, M., & Derwing, T. (1995). Foreign accent, comprehensibility, and intelligibility in the speech of second language learners. *Language Learning*, 45, 73–97.

Munro, M. J., Derwing, T. M., & Morton, S. L. (2006). The mutual intelligibility of L2 speech. *Studies in Second Language Acquisition*, 28, 11–131.

Nation. I. S. P., & Newton, J. (2009). *Teaching ESL/EFL Listening and Speaking.* NY: Routledge.

Osburne, A. G. (2003). Pronunciation strategies of advanced ESOL learners. *International Review of Applied Linguistics in Language Teaching*, 41, 131–143.

Peterson, S. S. (2000). Pronunciation learning strategies: A first look. Retrieved from https://eric.ed.gov/?id=ED450599.

Rajadurai, J. (2007). Intelligibility studies: A consideration of empirical and ideological issues. *World Englishes*, 26(1), 87–98.

Schaetzel, K., & Low, E. L. (2009). Teaching pronunciation to adult English language learners. *CAELA Network Brief*, July 2009.

Scovel, T. (1969). Foreign accent: Language acquisition and cerebral dominance. *Language Learning*, 19, 245–254.

Shimamune, S., & Smith, S. L. (1995). The relationship between pronunciation and listening discrimination when Japanese natives are learning English. *Journal of Applied Behavior Analysis*, 28, 577–578.

Smith, L. E. (1992). Spread of English and issues of intelligibility. In B. B. Kachru (Ed.), *The Other Tongue: English Across Cultures* (2nd ed., pp. 75–90). Urbana, IL: University of Illinois Press.

Suter, R. W. (1976). Predictors of pronunciation accuracy in second language learning. *Language Learning*, 26, 233–253.

Tomlinson, B. (2010). Which test of which English and why? In A. Kirkpatrick (Ed.), *The Routledge Handbook of World Englishes* (pp. 599–616). Abingdon: Routledge.

Trofimovich, P., & Baker, W. (2006). Learning second language suprasegmentals: Effect of L2 experience on prosody and fluency characteristics of L2 speech. *Studies in Second Language Acquisition*, 28, 1–30.

Zarifi, A., & Sayyadi, A. (2015). How English suprasegmental features of pronunciation are viewed and treated by instructors in Iranian private language centers. *Theory and Practice in Language Studies*, 5(6), 1166–1172.

CHAPTER 8

Learning Vocabulary

David Hirsh

INTRODUCTION

Our understanding of the role of vocabulary in second language learning has been evolving over time, as a result of changing approaches to second language learning and as a result of research specifically into vocabulary learning. There has been a particular interest in identifying the most suitable words for vocabulary learning and in describing conditions favouring vocabulary learning and acquisition. This chapter explores the nature and process of second language vocabulary learning, and outlines implications for teaching and assessment, in light of the current understanding.

OVERVIEW

Before we look at how vocabulary is learned in a second language, it is useful to consider what we mean by vocabulary, and to consider different ways in which words have been categorized to assist language teachers with developing a vocabulary learning program for their learners.

WHAT IS A WORD?

A word can be thought of as a unit of language which conveys a meaning. Thus, the words *cat, sky, society* and *music* all generate different meanings, because of their recognisable forms. So we can think of words as form-meaning relationships. From a language learning point of view, some word forms convey a similar core meaning. The words *help, helps, helped, helping* and *helpful* can be regarded as members of the same word family, due to shared form and meaning. As learners improve their overall knowledge of a second language, they are more likely to recognize members of a word family, due to increasing familiarity with commonly used derivative forms (such as *-ed, -ing*), prefixes (*un-, re-*) and suffixes (*-able, -ment*) (see also Mochizuki and Aizawa, 2000). Aside from looking at individual words and word families, there has also been interest in identifying frequently occurring collocations, such as *best friend, arrived safely* and *population growth*. These collocations represent words that frequently appear together in the language, due to their close lexical associations (see Sonbul and Schmitt, 2013; see also Chapter 19).

CATEGORIES OF WORDS

There are an estimated 123,000 word families in the English language. Adult native speakers of English typically know around 20,000 of these, meaning that a large proportion of words are not widely used or widely known. The important point to make is that not all words are equally important.

High frequency words such as *animal, house* and *school* occur frequently in a broad range of communicative contexts. Academic words such as *data, domestic* and *analyze* are associated with tertiary level study. Technical words are related to a specialized domain such an area of employment (e.g., banking) or an area of study (e.g., science). Banking words include *deposit, withdrawal* and *investment*, while science words include *cell, oxygen* and *species*. Words which do not occur so frequently in the language, conveniently termed low frequency words, include some treasured and colourful words such as *omnipotent, ubiquitous* and *serendipity*.

Specialized words in academic and technical domains which have been borrowed into English from Greek and Latin (such as *philosophy, synchronous, alleviate*) can be both multisyllabic (i.e., have many syllables) and phonologically and/or morphologically complex (i.e., difficult to pronounce and/or spell). Corson (1985) talks of a lexical bar in the language facing native-speaking high school students as they meet and seek to master, not always successfully, certain Graeco-Latin words associated with and central to their academic studies.

WHAT IS REQUIRED TO KNOW AND USE A WORD?

Knowing a word involves learning its form, meaning and use. Form refers to a word's spelling and pronunciation. This can, in the case of word families, include learning the common parts of speech of a word, e.g., *succeed* (verb), *success* (noun), *successful* (adjective) and *successfully* (adverb), as well as learning common derivatives of the word, e.g., *succeeds, succeeded,* and *succeeding*.

Words can have more than one meaning. Aside from the core meaning(s) most commonly attached to the word form, there may be other meanings of the word listed in a dictionary. Some of these could be technical, or archaic, or infrequently used. The focus of learning should be on the meaning(s) of the word most likely to be met when using the target language.

Use refers to grammatical rules governing use of the word, common collocations of the word, and constraints governing its use in different contexts, including issues of formality (i.e., some words are more colloquial, while others are more formal) (see also Nation, 2001).

BREADTH VERSUS DEPTH OF KNOWLEDGE

Vocabulary knowledge is measured both in terms of breadth, meaning the number of words known, and in terms of depth, meaning the depth of the knowledge of individual words. The general rule is 'the more words the better', as a large vocabulary size enables comprehension and use of complex language. In addition, deep knowledge of words enables accuracy, precision, and sophistication of language comprehension and use. Learners need opportunities to develop their vocabulary knowledge in both quantitative and qualitative dimensions.

RECEPTIVE AND PRODUCTIVE DIMENSIONS

A clear distinction is made in vocabulary learning between receptive vocabulary knowledge, which allows for comprehension of written and spoken language when reading and listening, and productive vocabulary knowledge, which allows for production of language when speaking and writing. It is generally accepted that reception precedes production, and that a learner typically knows more words than they use, although the gap between receptive and productive vocabulary knowledge varies between individuals, and can change in an individual with time.

LEXICAL THRESHOLD

There are different lexical thresholds which have been proposed in second language vocabulary learning, to refer to the percentage of words that need to be known in a text for comprehension to occur. Research has suggested that learners with 95% lexical coverage of a text (i.e., familiarity with 19 in every 20 words) tend to display adequate reading comprehension of the text when compared with learners who fall below the 95% threshold. This 95% threshold is typically regarded as the minimum for adequate comprehension. A higher threshold of 98% lexical coverage (i.e., 49 familiar words in every 50) has been identified for more pleasurable reading. From a vocabulary learning perspective, above the 98% threshold, the focus is more on consolidating prior vocabulary learning than on learning new words, due to infrequent meetings with new words. Between 95% and 98% is a window in which incidental learning of new words could occur, due to the presence of meaningful and comprehensible contextual clues. Between 90% and 95% lexical coverage is a window in which vocabulary learning could occur, with direct involvement of the teacher and/or through provision of a glossary. In this threshold window, unassisted comprehension of texts would be less likely to occur, due to the high number of new words being met. Learners can determine their lexical coverage of a text by counting the number of unknown words in a 100-word sample of text while ignoring proper nouns (i.e., names of people, places, organisations), and converting this number into a percentage of known words (e.g., 8 unknown words represents 92% text coverage).

Research suggests that the 95% lexical threshold for a range of texts can be reached with knowledge of 4,000–5,000 words, while the 98% lexical threshold can be gained with knowledge of 8,000–9,000 words. This assumes that proper nouns do not present readers with a vocabulary learning burden (see also Laufer and Ravenhorst-Kalovski, 2010; Nation, 2006).

PARTIAL VERSUS PRECISE KNOWLEDGE

A learner's ability to store and later access knowledge of a word's form, meaning and use is incremental in nature, in that some learning can occur on the first meeting with a new word, while further meetings, and subsequent attempts at using the word, add to this initial learning experience. The partial-to-precise continuum, which describes the degree and pattern of vocabulary knowledge, is relatively poorly understood. What is understood is that developing word knowledge from partial to precise is a natural process of language acquisition; some learners will be more willing to take risks with using partially-known words, while others will be more cautious.

USE OF CORPORA

Attempts have been made to capture the core vocabulary of both general and specialized communicative contexts through the construction and analysis of corpora (see Chapter 33). Corpora, such as the British National Corpus, are a compilation of texts which can be used to investigate how language is used in certain contexts (e.g., in British English, in newspapers), or by select groups of users (e.g., native speakers, non-native speakers).

Corpora have been constructed and analyzed to provide us with a list of 2,000 high frequency words (Browne, 2013; West, 1953), a list of 570 academic words (Coxhead, 2000) and words for other specialised contexts, such as medicine and engineering. Corpora have also been used to examine how words typically appear in context, through concordance tables. These tables list the words appearing each side of a target word for multiple occurrences of the word in a corpus or section of a corpus, and can provide data on the most frequently occurring associates or collocations of a target word. Other word analysis data, such as frequency of occurrence of a target word in one million running words of written versus spoken language, are available due to the development of, and access provided to, large electronic corpora. Software has been developed to analyze the words appearing in a text or set of texts. This software, termed *vocabprofile* or *range*, compares the words appearing in a text with pre-prepared baseword lists, such as high frequency words and academic words, to generate a lexical profile of a text (see also Cobb, n.d.; Heatley, Nation, and Coxhead, 2002).

LINKS TO FRAMEWORKS

Vocabulary development can be mapped against language proficiency frameworks such as the Common European Framework of Reference for Languages (CEFR). Milton (2013) has looked at how vocabulary size increased at each level of the CEFR at six proficiency levels for 10,000 Greek learners of English, finding the following correspondences:

A1: Breakthrough (<1,500 words)

A2: Waystage (1,500–2,500 words)

B1: Threshold (2,500–3,250 words)

B2: Vantage (3,250–3,750 words)

C1: Effective Operational Proficiency (3,750–4,500 words)

C2: Mastery (4,500–5,000 words)

Aside from attempts to map vocabulary development across the six levels of the CEFR, tools have been developed to provide information on word use at the different levels. One such initiative is *English Vocabulary Profile,* which has been developed by a collection of organisations in Europe to provide information on word meanings, collocations, phrases and idioms used by language users at each level of the CEFR. This is an initiative designed to link vocabulary learning to independent language levels in the European context.

KEY LEARNING ISSUES

Having looked at the nature of vocabulary knowledge, we can now move on to explore the process of developing second language vocabulary knowledge, and identify key concerns associated with the development process.

GOALS OF VOCABULARY LEARNING

Vocabulary learning is generally embedded within a broader program of language learning, and such programs can be described in terms which reflect the language learning objectives of the learners. General Purpose programs would include a focus on developing knowledge of 2,000 high frequency words as a starting point, which would provide good return for learning effort. English for Academic Purposes (EAP) programs (see Chapter 14) would typically include a focus on learning academic vocabulary which features specifically language used in academic disciplines covering the arts, commerce, law and science. Technical vocabulary associated with a specific academic discipline can be acquired as part of the process of learning the content area, which occurs with commencement of tertiary studies. English for Specific Purposes (ESP) programs (see Chapter 15) can provide tailored vocabulary learning focusing on words widely used in the target situation (e.g., words for hospitality, words for aviation).

INTENTIONAL AND INCIDENTAL LEARNING

Vocabulary learning activities sit on an intentional–incidental continuum. While intentional vocabulary learning situations have an explicit focus on vocabulary learning as a goal, incidental learning situations do not explicitly set vocabulary learning as a goal or focus. The continuum thus represents the degree of intended engagement of learners in the vocabulary learning process. A learning activity may be typically regarded as suited to incidental vocabulary learning (such as extensive reading from graded readers), or suited to intentional vocabulary learning (such as developing a word association map for a given target word). A particular learner may choose to adopt an intentional orientation to a language learning activity, irrespective of the intent of the teacher (see also Barcroft, 2015a).

Learning becomes autonomous and self-directed when the learner seeks opportunities outside the classroom for vocabulary development, such as the case of a learner keeping an independent vocabulary learning log (with information on word form, meaning and use), adding entries based on meetings with new words while reading.

CONDITIONS FAVOURING VOCABULARY LEARNING

Conditions have been identified favouring vocabulary learning and retention. While learning refers to cognitive engagement with aspects of word knowledge, retention refers to the long-term storage of this knowledge for future use, and is measured by determining if a word learned can be recognized or retrieved two or more weeks following learning.

One condition favouring vocabulary learning is noticing a word. This can involve the learner pausing when they meet a new word, and may involve consulting a glossary or dictionary or seeking other forms of support. Input such as written texts can be modified to highlight target vocabulary as a way to promote the process of noticing. Examples of input enhancement techniques are use of bold, colored, enlarged or underlined font to draw learner attention to target words. In this vein, there is research interest in task manipulation techniques designed to increase the number of meetings of new words and to provide opportunities to meet a new word in different contexts, as well as the use of marginal glosses to provide meanings for target words. Another condition favoring vocabulary learning is retrieving a word, in which a learner recalls a word form and meaning at a later time. Repeated recall over an extended period is seen as a key to ensuring long-term retention. A third condition favouring vocabulary learning is using the word generatively. This involves the use of the new word in a newly created sentence or a new context. Generative use of newly acquired words assists in developing productive vocabulary knowledge, where knowledge of words acquired receptively can be applied in a speaking or writing context (see also Nation, 2001).

There is growing research interest in the role of task-induced involvement in vocabulary learning, in reference to the degree of learner involvement when meeting unknown words. This has given rise to an involvement load hypothesis, based on the components of need, search and evaluation. Need refers to the motivation to learn an unknown word. Search refers to the cognitive load attached to determining the form or meaning of an unknown word. Evaluation is the cognitive load attached to completing a task involving use of the new word in context. The involvement load in learning a new word reflects the combined strengths of the three components, in which greater involvement load corresponds with improved learning and retention (see also Hulstijn and Laufer, 2001).

Vocabulary learning outcomes can be enhanced if learners employ strategies at multiple levels, including: planning, involving selection for words for learning; sources, involving use of contextual clues, dictionaries, classmates and teachers; and processes, including noticing, retrieving and generating (see also Coxhead, 2014). One method of improving vocabulary learning outcomes which has attracted particular attention in the literature is the mnemonic keyword method. The method involves linking a target word to an acoustically similar word in the first language which has an independent meaning, and this linking provides a context for the learner to create a visual image to assist with future recall of the new word's meaning. As an example, to remember the Japanese word for *sunshine* (日光) pronounced as *nikkō*, which sounds rather like *nickel*, a learner could picture sunshine reflecting on a nickel coin.

FIRST LANGUAGE TRANSFER

Aside from the previous discussion of conditions shaping vocabulary learning, language learners can bring to the task of second language vocabulary learning varying degrees of existing knowledge about target words, based on their first language experience. When encountering a second language word with a known first language counterpart, learners can make assumptions regarding meaning and use of the word in the second language. This issue is particularly relevant in the case of true and false cognates. While true cognates represent words with a similar form and meaning in two languages (e.g., *fantastic* in English / *fantastique* in French), false cognates represent words with similar form but different meaning in two languages (e.g., *grape* in English / *grappe* in French, meaning *cluster* or *bunch*). The second language vocabulary learning program needs to include opportunities for learners to test their assumptions. If there is no known first language counterpart to a word being learned in the second language, as can occur when learning in new subject areas in the second language, there is less scope for first language transfer, and more dependence on the second language learning context to develop a deep and accurate understanding of the new word.

IMPLICATIONS FOR TEACHING AND ASSESSMENT

The discussion so far has viewed vocabulary knowledge and learning within the broader context of second language learning, and this approach to vocabulary also applies in teaching practice, where opportunities for vocabulary learning are ideally created from meaningful and comprehensible texts and communicative tasks. A key component of teaching practice should be maximising opportunities for learner engagement (i.e., task-induced involvement) with vocabulary. Teaching of second language vocabulary can be direct (i.e., with an explicit intent placed on learning new words), in a language-focused learning activity. Vocabulary teaching can also be indirect (i.e., opportunities for vocabulary learning arise during language learning without explicit intent or planning), in a meaning-focused learning activity. Vocabulary teaching can involve a combination of direct and indirect approaches, such as a Reading Plus treatment, where reading is followed by vocabulary learning activities such as gap-fill or original sentence-writing tasks with target words (see also Barcroft, 2015b). In addition, teaching of second language vocabulary can take place in the context of fluency tasks (such as ranking tasks and debates) designed to provide opportunities for learners to engage with previously acquired words in a meaningful communicative context.

From the perspective of language assessment, vocabulary can be explored as a construct, both in terms of how it is understood and in terms of how it is measured. Instruments have been developed which measure receptive and productive vocabulary knowledge. The Vocabulary Levels Test, in which learners match words with meanings, provides a rough indication of the vocabulary size of test takers, reporting at different levels based on word frequency (2,000/3,000/5,000/10,000) and specialisation (academic words) (see Nation, 1990). Beyond the 2,000-word list, the 3,000-, 5,000- and 10,000-word lists represent the third, fifth and tenth thousand list of words respectively, based on frequency of occurrence in the language. The Controlled Productive Vocabulary Levels Test, in which test-takers complete a partial word appearing in context, attempts to provide a picture of productive vocabulary knowledge at different vocabulary levels (see Laufer and Nation, 1999). There have been attempts to capture productive vocabulary use in a free way, through analysis of words used in a writing task. One such tool is the Vocabulary Frequency Profile, which compares word use appearing from and beyond the list of 2,000 high frequency words, to provide an indication of word complexity or diversity (see Laufer and Nation, 1995). In this profiling, increasing the proportion of distinct words used from outside the 2,000 high frequency word list increases the measure of lexical complexity. In addition, a Word Associates Format has been designed to measure aspects of depth of vocabulary knowledge, focusing on learner recognition of word associations and collocations (see Read, 1993).

These tools can be used at different stages of a language learning program, for different purposes. Placement tests can be used to place learners in classes based on language proficiency, where part of the overall measure is vocabulary size. Diagnostic tools can be used to assist with a needs analysis to tailor a vocabulary learning program for a group of learners. Achievement tests, which assess knowledge of form, meaning and use of words, can be used on a regular basis to provide feedback to learners and teachers on the success of learning target vocabulary.

CONCLUSION

This chapter has presented vocabulary knowledge in terms of:

1. form, meaning and use;
2. breadth and depth;
3. receptive and productive dimensions; and
4. the partial–precise continuum.

In this regard, vocabulary is viewed as a multidimensional construct. There is need for learners to develop vocabulary knowledge in the various dimensions. The process of second language vocabulary learning is incremental, and is shaped by the nature of language input, the quality and quantity of engagement with target words, and the opportunities provided for language production, with importance placed on intentional and incidental vocabulary learning, both in and beyond the language learning classroom.

Discussion Questions

1. What advice could we give learners asking if a certain text (e.g., a newspaper) was a suitable source text for independent vocabulary learning?

2. What types of vocabulary learning activities are most suited for autonomous or self-directed vocabulary learning?

3. How could vocabulary assessment tools be effectively integrated into a vocabulary learning program?

Key Readings

Bogaards, P., & Laufer, B. (Eds.) (2004). *Vocabulary in a Second Language: Selection, Acquisition and Testing*. Amsterdam/Philadelphia: John Benjamins.

Hirsh, D. (2015). Researching vocabulary. In B. Paltridge & A. Phakiti (Eds.), *Research Methods in Applied Linguistics: A Practical Resource* (pp. 369–386). London: Bloomsbury.

Milton, J., & Fitzpatrick, T. (Ed.) (2014). *Dimensions of Vocabulary Knowledge*. Basingstoke, UK: Palgrave Macmillan.

Nation, I. S. P. (2013). *Learning Vocabulary in Another Language* (2nd ed.). Cambridge: Cambridge University Press.

Read, J. (2000). *Assessing Vocabulary*. Cambridge: Cambridge University Press.

Schmitt, N. (2010). *Researching Vocabulary: A Vocabulary Research Manual*. Basingstoke, UK: Palgrave Macmillan.

References

Barcroft, J. (2015a). *Lexical Input Processing and Vocabulary Learning*. Amsterdam/Philadelphia: John Benjamins.

Barcroft, J. (2015b). Can retrieval opportunities increase vocabulary learning during reading? *Foreign Language Annals*, 48, 236–249.

Browne, C. (2013). The new general service list: Celebrating 60 years of vocabulary learning. *The Language Teacher*, 37, 13–16.

Cobb, T. (n.d.). *Compleat Lexical Tutor*. Université du Québec à Montréal. Available from www.lextutor.ca.

Corson, D. (1985). *The Lexical Bar*. Oxford: Pergamon.

Coxhead, A. (2000). A new academic word list. *TESOL Quarterly*, 34, 213–238.

Coxhead, A. (Ed.) (2014). *New Ways in Teaching Vocabulary* (revised ed.). Alexandria, VA: TESOL.

Heatley, A., Nation, I. S. P., & Coxhead, A. (2002). *Range Program*. Victoria University of Wellington. Available from: http://www.victoria.ac.nz/lals/about/staff/paul-nation

Hulstijn, J. H., & Laufer, B. (2001). Some empirical evidence for the involvement load hypothesis in vocabulary acquisition. *Language Learning*, 51, 539–558.

Laufer, B., & Nation, P. (1995). Vocabulary size and use: Lexical richness in L2 written production. *Applied Linguistics*, 16, 307–322.

Laufer, B., & Nation, P. (1999). A vocabulary size test of controlled productive ability. *Language Testing*, 16, 33–51.

Laufer, B., & Ravenhorst-Kalovski, G. C. (2010). Lexical threshold revisited: Lexical text coverage, learners' vocabulary size and reading comprehension. *Reading in a Foreign Language*, 22, 15–30.

Milton, J. (2013). Measuring the contribution of vocabulary knowledge to proficiency in the four skills. In C. Bardel, C. Lindqvist, & B. Laufer (Eds.), *L2 Vocabulary Acquisition, Knowledge and Use: New Perspectives on Assessment and Corpus Analysis* (pp. 57–78). Eurosla Monographs Series.

Mochizuki, M., & Aizawa, K. (2000). An affix acquisition order for EFL learners: An exploratory study. *System*, 28, 291-304.

Nation, I. S. P. (1990). *Teaching and Learning Vocabulary*. Boston, MA: Heinle & Heinle.

Nation, I. S. P. (2001). *Learning Vocabulary in Another Language*. Cambridge: Cambridge University Press.

Nation, I. S. P. (2006). How large a vocabulary is needed for reading and listening? *Canadian Modern Language Review*, 63, 59–82.

Read, J. (1993). The development of a new measure of L2 vocabulary knowledge. *Language Testing*, 10, 355–371.

Sonbul, S., & Schmitt, N. (2013). Explicit and implicit lexical knowledge: Acquisition of collocations under different input conditions. *Language Learning*, 63, 121–159.

West, M. (1953). *A General Service List of English Words*. London: Longman.

CHAPTER 19

Learning Lexical Phrases

Frank Boers

INTRODUCTION

This chapter looks at a facet of language that has received increasing attention from applied linguists in recent years – multiword expressions and word partnerships. Natural languages have extensive stocks of conventional fixed and semi-fixed expressions. Diverse terms have been used in the literature to refer to multiword expressions of various kinds, including such labels as formulaic sequences, phrasal expressions, multiword units, lexical bundles, prefabs, idioms, collocations, and chunks. Following Nattinger and DeCarrico (1992), in this chapter I will adopt 'lexical phrase' (or 'phrase', for short) as an umbrella term.

After presenting an overview of the importance of phrasal competence, I will describe the hurdles that learners face when it comes to mastering this dimension of language, and thus establish the need for pedagogic initiatives that help learners overcome these hurdles. I then turn to a discussion of such pedagogic initiatives and the desirability of further research in this area.

OVERVIEW

Lexical phrases perform a multitude of functions. They may be referential (e.g., *mow the lawn*) or expressive (e.g., *What the heck!*). They may signpost discourse organization (e.g., *on the other hand*), be part of interactional routines (e.g., *Nice to meet you.*), signal evaluation (e.g., *good as gold*), or simply help speakers to maintain their speech flow (e.g., *You know what I mean?*).

Given the abundance of lexical phrases in language, and their many referential and pragmatic functions, it is clear that language learners stand to gain a lot from building a sizeable phrasal repertoire. Learners who exhibit good knowledge of lexical phrases tend to come across as competent language users (Boers, Eyckmans, Kappel, Stengers, and Demecheleer, 2006; Crossley, Salsbury, and McNamara, 2015). Well-entrenched knowledge of phrases also aids fluency, both receptively and productively (see Boers and Lindstromberg, 2012, for a review of experimental evidence). It aids receptive fluency, because recognition of the onset of a phrase (e.g., *last but not __*) helps you anticipate what will follow (e.g., *least*). It aids productive fluency, because well-acquired phrases may be retrieved from the mental lexicon as though they were prefabricated units (which is also why conspicuous pauses are unlikely to occur inside such phrases).

Unfortunately, research suggests that – in the absence of vast amounts of exposure to the target language – the development of phrasal competence in a second language is a very slow process (e.g., Laufer and Waldman, 2011). It is well known, for example, that second language users tend to produce word strings that sound unconventional, and that this can often be attributed to transfer from their mother tongue (e.g., Yamashita and Jiang, 2010). For example, a Dutch learner of English may say 'do an effort' (instead of *make an effort*) and 'don't bite my nose off' (instead of *don't bite my head off*), because that is how the counterpart expressions in Dutch are worded. In the next section, I will propose a number of explanations for this generally slow development of phrasal competence.

KEY LEARNING ISSUES

Although language abounds with phrases in general, very few individual phrases are likely to occur multiple times in a short span of discourse. For example, Boers and Lindstromberg (2009) found only two instances of *tell the truth* in 120 pages of a crime novel – i.e., a text where the quest for truth is a central theme. If one does not meet the same phrase repeatedly, its chances of being acquired from mere exposure are very slim (Webb, Newton, and Chang, 2013). After all, how can one determine that, say, *take notice of* is a fixed phrase if one has not yet seen or heard – and taken notice of – this word sequence before?

A second explanation for the slow uptake of phrases lies with the limited salience of some types of phrases. There is now considerable agreement that attention is a crucial first step for language elements to leave an impression in the learner's memory. It is useful in this regard to make a distinction between phrases which are deemed semantically transparent (e.g., *make a distinction*; *fair play*) and phrases which are not (e.g., *cut corners*; *red tape*). If learners are familiar with *have* and *a dream*, for example, then encountering *I had a dream* is probably not going to prompt them to contemplate the precise lexical makeup of this phrase. This lexical makeup may not be congruent with the counterpart in their mother tongue, however, as would be the case if that mother tongue were French – 'j'ai fait un rêve' ('I made a dream'). Verb-noun expressions such as this constitute an area where even very advanced learners are known to use unorthodox word combinations. This may be due to the semantic vagueness of the verbs in many such expressions (e.g., *have an accident*). Owing to their lack of semantic distinctiveness, they seem particularly prone to being substituted by language learners (e.g., 'make an accident').

The above explanations focused on phrases that are experienced by the learner as semantically transparent, and that consequently tend to receive little spontaneous attention from the learner, beyond the content words that are perceived to carry most communicative value. The learning challenge, in such cases, lies with developing knowledge of the composition (or form) of the phrases – especially if 'accurate' (in the sense of native-like) production of phraseology is strived for, as is likely in EAP courses, for instance. However, as already mentioned, a language's phrasal repertoire also contains many expressions that are not semantically transparent, often called 'idioms' (e.g., *through thick and thin*). Idioms are phrases whose meaning does not follow straightforwardly from the meanings of their constituent composite parts. In that case, the learning challenge lies first and foremost with comprehension. Although few individual idioms are used with high frequency, it is now recognized that, as a class, idioms are common in everyday discourse and that they fulfill vital pragmatic functions (O'Keeffe, McCarthy, and Carter, 2007).

Most idioms are figurative expressions: their meaning can be traced back to the original or literal use of the expression (Grant and Bauer, 2004). If a learner recognizes this 'source', this may help interpretation of the idiomatic, figurative meaning of the phrase. For instance, recognition that *take a back seat* literally means taking the role of passenger in a car may help one infer that the expression denotes something along the lines of 'allowing others to take control'. Interestingly, second language learners have been found more inclined than native speakers to activate a literal reading of the words that make up figurative idioms (Cieślicka, 2006). This is not necessarily helpful, however: a single word may have various literal meanings, and learners' misinterpretation of the literal meaning can all too easily lead them astray as they try to figure out the idiom's meaning. For example, when encountering *to follow suit*, learners are likely to interpret *suit* as an article of clothing (rather than a type of card in card games) (Boers, Demecheleer, and Eyckmans, 2004). Learners may then wrongly infer that the expression means something like 'obeying authority' given their world knowledge that people with high status tend to wear suits. Often, a learner may not even be able to make any guesses at an idiom's meaning, due to a lack of familiarity with the source context from which the idiom is derived. For example, expressions derived from cricket (e.g., *off your own bat*) or from baseball (e.g., *touch base*) may be particularly obscure to learners without any familiarity with these sports.

One may, of course, be hopeful that the context in which a figurative expression is used will steer a learner towards an adequate interpretation. However, research suggests that even advanced learners often fail to adequately figure out the meaning of unfamiliar figurative expressions, despite the availability of contextual cues (Boers, Eyckmans, and Stengers, 2007). Native speakers' reliance on figurative expressions to communicate has indeed been found to be a source of considerable confusion for ESL learners (Littlemore, Chen, Koester, and Barnden, 2011). It is worth mentioning in this regard that many more expressions than those included in idiom dictionaries (which typically have about 5,000 entries) or in phrasal/ prepositional verb dictionaries (which due to space constraints will not be discussed in this chapter) can pose comprehension problems (Boers and Webb, 2015). Many phrases that are not included in idiom dictionaries, because the native-speaker dictionary maker assumes they are transparent, may actually be puzzling to second language learners. *To run a tight ship* is included in idiom dictionaries, because its meaning (to keep firm control of an organization) is obviously different from the meanings of *run*, *tight* and *ship* that come to mind most readily if one encounters these words in isolation. On the other hand, *to run a bath*, *to run a business*, and *to run for President* are absent from idiom dictionaries, although *run* is not used in its primary literal sense in these expressions either. As with the examples of idioms given above, a learner may activate the first meaning of a constituent word that springs to mind, but this may be misleading. For instance, a learner who associates *close* with the act of closing a door may misunderstand *close the meeting* as having a meeting behind closed doors. It must be hard for (native-speaker) teachers to put themselves in their students' shoes and anticipate comprehension problems of this nature.

IMPLICATIONS FOR TEACHING AND ASSESSMENT

Phraseology is clearly too vast a phenomenon to be learned through instruction alone. A lot of its acquisition will inevitably need to be relegated to chance encounters with phrases outside the realm of intentional vocabulary learning and teaching. The question, then, is what phrases among the many thousand candidates do merit a place in teaching initiatives or instructional materials. A primary criterion must be the usefulness of a phrase, and a proxy for usefulness is its frequency of occurrence (at least in the discourse genre of interest to the learners). This frequency criterion is also used for the prioritization of single words (see Chapter 18). However, operationalizing it is not straightforward, because a search for phrases in a corpus (see Chapter 33) may yield different results, depending on how one delineates 'phrase'. One approach has been to look for recurring, uninterrupted word strings and to stipulate a frequency threshold for their inclusion in a priority list. Such strings are often called 'lexical bundles' (e.g., Biber, Conrad, and Cortes, 2004). A potential problem with the outcome of this type of corpus search is that not all frequent word strings (e.g., *one of the*) are felt to be meaningful units in their own right (Liu, 2012). Another potential problem is that many phraseological patterns manifest variability (e.g., *play a part; played a part in; plays an important part in*), and tallies of only exact duplicates of uninterrupted word strings in a corpus will fail to do justice to these. Another approach, then, has been to examine how often particular lemmas co-occur within a certain (e.g., four-word) span, as a reflection of the strength of their partnership. This is commonly referred to as 'collocation' (Sinclair, 1991). The stronger the collocation, the less likely that a word in the phrase can be substituted by a synonym without the result sounding unconventional. In other words, some partnerships (e.g., *commit crimes; tell lies*) are more exclusive than others (e.g., *conduct / carry out / do research*).

Frequency cannot be the sole criterion to help teachers decide whether a given phrase merits attention from their students, however. As discussed above, not all phrases stand the same chance of being picked up by learners, despite similar frequencies of use. Due to non-congruence with counterpart phrases in their mother tongue, learners will produce 'malformed' collocations in the target language, unless their attention is drawn to the non-congruence (Laufer and Girsai, 2008). And learners will misinterpret certain idioms – especially when deceptively similar expressions exist in their mother tongue – unless steps are taken to clarify their meaning (Liu, 2008). Teachers' (and course-materials designers') efforts at determining what phrases merit explicit instruction therefore need to take such anticipated difficulties into consideration as well (Martinez and Schmitt, 2012). This naturally adds to the complexity of the task, because anticipating these difficulties adequately will require familiarity with the learners' linguistic (and cultural) background.

Let us now turn to interventions intended to accelerate learners' uptake of phrases. Given the aforementioned hindrances to second language learners' picking up phrases (beyond sufficiently frequent ones) 'incidentally', it is not surprising that pedagogy-minded applied linguists have called for interventions that direct learners' attention to the phrasal dimension of texts (e.g., Lewis, 1997). Learners can be guided by their teacher to identify phrases in the texts they are working with in the classroom (e.g, Boers, et al., 2006). Materials designers may also typographically enhance (e.g., by means of bold font or underlining) selected phrases in reading texts so as to attract the reader's attention (Boers, Demecheleer, He, Deconinck, Stengers, and Eyckmans, 2017). A practical concern inherent to text manipulations such as these is how many phrases in a text can be made perceptually salient without compromising the effectiveness of the intervention. After all, it stands to reason there must be a point where excessive use of typographic enhancement reduces the distinctiveness which the technique is meant to bestow on selected items.

Other initiatives concern the deliberate, explicitly phrase-focused learning and teaching. A growing number of lesson plans and teaching materials, as well as materials for independent study, with a distinct focus on lexical phrases have become available in recent years (e.g., Davis and Kryszewska, 2012; Lindstromberg and Boers, 2008; McCarthy and O'Dell, 2002, 2005). Also, many general-purpose EFL textbooks have started to incorporate exercises on lexical phrases. It needs to be acknowledged, however, that the effectiveness of many of these exercises and study procedures still needs to be put to the test in empirical research. An examination of textbook exercises on collocations reveals, for example, that many such exercises require learners to reassemble phrases by matching constituent parts or by choosing single words from jumbled lists to complete gapped phrases. And yet, research suggests that it is more judicious to engage learners in exercises where the phrases are kept intact from the start, because this reduces the risk of between-item confusion about which words pair up with one another (Boers, Dang, and Strong, 2017).

More research has examined the effectiveness of interventions intended to make phrases memorable. An effective procedure for making figurative idioms memorable, for instance, is to help learners to recognize how the meaning of an idiom 'makes sense', given the associations attached to its literal reading or original context of use (see Boers, 2013, for a review). For example, on encountering the idiom *out on a limb*, a learner can be informed that the literal reading of *limb* here would be a branch of a tree, asked to consider the perils of moving to the extremity of a branch, and then encouraged to infer the meaning of the expression in conjunction with any contextual cues. One explanation for the effectiveness of this procedure is that it evokes mental imagery, and imagery is known to benefit retention. The procedure also capitalizes on the aforementioned inclination of many second language learners to try and figure out idioms via a literal reading. Crucially, for the intervention to be helpful, the learner needs to be informed of the literal reading that is congruent with its figurative meaning – something which cannot be taken for granted if the learner is left unaided (as illustrated above). Raising learners' awareness of the literal underpinnings of idioms they encounter may also help them appreciate that the stock of idioms in the target language reflects the role played by certain domains of experience in the history of a community. For example, given the history of Britain as a seafaring nation, it is not surprising that many English idioms have their origin in the domain of sailing (e.g., *clear the decks; be on an even keel; give someone a wide berth; take something on board; be out of one's depth; learn the ropes; be blown off course; in the doldrums;* and *a leading light*).

Another intervention, with applicability to miscellaneous phrases, is to direct learners' attention to catchy sound patterns exhibited by a conspicuous fraction of the phrasal lexicon. In English, alliteration (e.g., *time will tell; cut corners; collision course; slippery slope; the gift of the gab; lifelong learning; good as gold; part and parcel; better safe than sorry*) is particularly common (see Boers and Lindstromberg, 2009: 106–125, for tallies in various sources). In addition, a non-negligible number of phrases manifest rhyme or near-rhyme (e.g., *brain drain; stranger danger; cook the books; small talk; high time*). The high incidence of this 'similarity attracts' factor in the formation of word partnerships is relevant, because classroom experiments have shown that the mere act of drawing learners' attention to the presence of alliteration and (near-) rhyme in target phrases renders these phrases more memorable (e.g., Eyckmans, Boers, and Lindstromberg, 2016).

With the growing recognition of the importance of phraseology have also come efforts to design instruments to gauge learners' phrasal competence. Given the diversity exhibited by a language's phrasal repertoire and given the multifaceted nature of phrasal knowledge, it is not surprising that test development in this realm has proven to be very intricate, even where it focuses 'narrowly' on collocational knowledge (e.g., Gyllstad, 2009).

CONCLUSION

While it remains undeniable that mastering second language phraseology is a formidable task, it is encouraging that steady progress is now being made in the development, validation and fine-tuning of pedagogic interventions to help learners tackle this challenge. Additional work will be needed, however, to ensure that the emerging research findings are translated into appropriate classroom procedures, learning materials, and assessment instruments.

Discussion Questions

1. Collocational accuracy (e.g., *The earthquake caused a lot of damage* rather than *The earthquake made a lot of damage*) has been shown to matter in contexts such as

proficiency exams and formal writing assignments; but should teachers give the same amount of attention to collocational accuracy when their students' purpose for learning the language is to engage in everyday communication?

2. While knowledge of figurative idioms (e.g., *below the belt*) is likely to be useful for learners in an immersion (e.g., ESL) setting, how relevant is it likely to be for those who are studying a foreign language (e.g., EFL) in their home country?

3. As the phrasal repertoire of a language is too vast to be 'covered' through classroom instruction, what effective steps can be taken to foster learner autonomy in this area?

4. How much guided practice do learners – and also (non-native) teachers – need to make optimal use of resources such as online corpora to verify the formulaic nature of word strings?

Key Readings

Barfield, A., & Gyllstad, S. (Eds.) (2009). *Researching Collocations in Another Language: Multiple Perspectives*. Basingstoke, UK: Palgrave Macmillan.

Boers, F., & Lindstromberg, S. (2009). *Optimizing a Lexical Approach to Instructed Second Language Acquisition*. Basingstoke, UK: Palgrave Macmillan.

Lewis, M. (Ed.) (2000). *Teaching Collocation*. Hove: LTP.

Schmitt, N. (Ed.) (2004). *Formulaic Sequences*. Amsterdam/Philadelphia: John Benjamins.

Wood, D. (Ed.) (2010). *Perspectives on Formulaic Language: Acquisition and Communication*. London / New York: Continuum.

References

Biber, D., Conrad, S., & Cortes, V. (2004). If you look at …: Lexical bundles in university teaching and textbooks. *Applied Linguistics*, 25, 371–505.

Boers, F. (2013). Cognitive linguistic approaches to second language vocabulary: Assessment and integration. *Language Teaching: Surveys and Studies*, 46, 208–224.

Boers, F., Dang, T. C. T., & Strong, B. (2017). Comparing the effectiveness of phrase-focused exercises: A partial replication of Boers, Demecheleer, Coxhead, and Webb (2014). *Language Teaching Research*, 21, 362–380.

Boers, F., Demecheleer, M., & Eyckmans, J. (2004). Etymological elaboration as a strategy for learning figurative idioms. In P. Bogaards & B. Laufer (Eds.), *Vocabulary in a Second Language: Selection, Acquisition and Testing* (pp. 53–78). Amsterdam/Philadelphia: John Benjamins.

Boers, F., Demecheleer, M., He, L., Deconinck, J., Stengers, H., & Eyckmans, J. (2017). Typographic enhancement of multiword units in second language text. *International Journal of Applied Linguistics*, 27, 448–469.

Boers, F., Eyckmans, J., Kappel, J., Stengers, H., & Demecheleer, M. (2006). Formulaic sequences and perceived oral proficiency: Putting a lexical approach to the test. *Language Teaching Research*, 10, 245–261.

Boers, F., Eyckmans, J., & Stengers, H. (2007). Presenting figurative idioms with a touch of etymology: More than mere mnemonics? *Language Teaching Research*, 11, 43–62.

Boers, F., & Lindstromberg, S. (2009). *Optimizing a Lexical Approach to Instructed Second Language Acquisition*. Basingstoke, UK: Palgrave Macmillan.

Boers, F., & Lindstromberg, S. (2012). Experimental and intervention studies on formulaic sequences in a second language. *Annual Review of Applied Linguistics*, 32, 83–110.

Boers, F., & Webb, S. (2015). Gauging the semantic transparency of idioms: Do natives and learners see eye to eye? In R. Heredia & A. Cieślicka (Eds.), *Bilingual Figurative Language Processing* (pp. 368–392). Cambridge: Cambridge University Press.

Cieślicka, A. (2006). Literal salience in on-line processing of idiomatic expressions by second language learners. *Second Language Research*, 22, 115–144.

Crossley, A.S., Salsbury, T., & McNamara, D.S. (2015). Assessing lexical proficiency using analytic ratings: A case for collocation accuracy. *Applied Linguistics*, 36, 570–590.

Davis, P., & Kryszewska, H. (2012). *The Company Words Keep: Lexical Chunks in Language Teaching*. Peaslake: Delta Publishing.

Eyckmans, J., Boers, F., & Lindstromberg, S. (2016). The impact of imposing processing strategies on L2 learners' deliberate study of lexical phrases. *System*, 56, 127–139.

Grant, L., & Bauer, L. (2004). Criteria for redefining idioms: Are we barking up the wrong tree? *Applied Linguistics*, 25, 38–61.

Gyllstad, H. (2009). Designing and evaluating tests of receptive collocation knowledge: COLLEX and COLLMATCH. In A Barfield & H. Gyllstad (Eds.), *Researching Collocations in Another Language: Multiple Perspectives* (pp. 153–170). Basingstoke, UK: Palgrave Macmillan.

Laufer, B., & Girsai, N. (2008). Form-focused instruction in second language vocabulary learning: A case for contrastive analysis and translation. *Applied Linguistics*, 29, 694–716.

Laufer, B., & Waldman, T. (2011). Verb-noun collocations in second language writing: A corpus analysis of learners' English. *Language Learning*, 61, 647–672.

Lewis, M. (1997). *Implementing the Lexical Approach*. Hove: Language Teaching Publications.

Lindstromberg, S., & Boers, F. (2008). *Teaching Chunks of Language*. Rum: Helbling Languages.

Littlemore, J., Chen, P. T., Koester, A., & Barnden, J. (2011). Difficulties in metaphor comprehension faced by international students whose first language is not English. *Applied Linguistics*, 32, 408–429.

Liu, D. (2008). *Idioms: Description, Comprehension, Acquisition, and Pedagogy*. New York: Routledge.

Liu, D. (2012). The most frequently-used multi-word constructions in academic written English: A multi-corpus study. *English For Specific Purposes*, 31, 25–35.

Martinez, R., & Schmitt, N. (2012). A phrasal expressions list. *Applied Linguistics*, 33, 299–320.

McCarthy, M., & O'Dell, F. (2002). *English Idioms in Use*. Cambridge: Cambridge University Press.

McCarthy, M., & O'Dell, F. (2005). *English Collocations in Use*. Cambridge: Cambridge University Press.

Nattinger, J. R., & DeCarrico J. S. (1992). *Lexical Phrases and Language Teaching*. Oxford: Oxford University Press.

O'Keeffe, A. M., McCarthy, M., & Carter, R. (2007). *From Corpus to Classroom: Language Use and Language Teaching*. Cambridge: Cambridge University Press.

Sinclair, J. (1991). *Corpus, Concordance and Collocation*. Oxford: Oxford University Press.

Webb, S., Newton, J., & Chang, A. C. S. (2013). Incidental learning of collocation. *Language Learning*, 63, 91–120.

Yamashita, J., & Jiang, N. (2010). L1 influence on the acquisition of L2 collocations: Japanese ESL users and EFL learners acquiring English collocations. *TESOL Quarterly*, 44, 647–668.

CHAPTER 20

Learning Grammar

Scott Thornbury

INTRODUCTION

Grammar is the linguistic system that has arguably received the most attention by researchers into second language acquisition (SLA). This may be due in part to the persistent belief that linguistic competence, and grammar in particular, is at the heart of language use, and that learning a language is a process of "accumulating entities", typically discrete grammatical items (Rutherford, 1988: 4). It may also owe to the pervasive influence of linguistics on SLA theory construction – theories, that, as Breen (2001: 173) puts it, account for "language acquisition as primarily the interface between learners' mental processes and the grammatical system of the target language." In this chapter I will challenge the centrality of grammar, but first I will address both the what and the how of grammar learning, before looking at the implications for teaching and assessment.

OVERVIEW

Depending on their theoretical perspective, linguists define grammar in a variety of different ways, which has meant that, for researchers into its acquisition, grammar has been a 'moving target'. Scholars committed to the generative grammar tradition, including Chomsky's (1981) Principles and Parameters framework, focus on those syntactic features, such as pro-drop or *wh*-movement, that might be indicative of parameter resetting. Those aligned with a functional tradition, on the other hand, are more interested in tracking, over the long term, the development of form-function relationships, such as those that express temporal or spatial relations. Cognitive linguistics has motivated a number of studies on the acquisition – or, better, *emergence* – of 'constructions', i.e., form-meaning mappings, such as exponents of futurity and such verb-argument constructions as ditransitives. Indeed, the term 'construction' has stretched the notion of grammar to include anything from individual morphemes, through lexical phrases, to clause-level or even discourse-level units (Goldberg, 2006).

For practical purposes such as teaching, however, grammar is taken to mean that subset of descriptive grammar items that have been selected as the 'scope and sequence' of language teaching syllabuses, and which typically consist of inflectional morphology and clause syntax, with a particular bias towards verb phrase structures (such as those that encode tense and aspect), even in relatively uninflected languages like English – a legacy perhaps, of the teaching of classical languages such as Greek and Latin. In fact, the findings of corpus linguistics (see Chapter 33) over the last three or four decades, especially in the area of spoken language (see, for example, Carter and McCarthy, 1995; Conrad and Biber, 2009) have challenged the weighting given to certain items in traditional grammar syllabuses, although the impact of these findings on materials design has been modest, to say the least.

Key Learning Issues

How, then, is this somewhat heterogeneous system acquired by second language learners? To answer this question we need to pose three more, which, to the present day, continue to engage teachers, methodology writers and researchers:

1. What is the role of the learner's first language (L1) in their acquisition of a second language (L2) grammar?
2. Does the acquisition of the L2 grammar follow a predetermined route, irrespective of the learner's L1?
3. If so, what role does instruction play?

L1 INFLUENCE

It is axiomatic that L2 learners' already have an L1 grammar partly or fully 'in place'. Unsurprisingly, therefore, the facilitative or inhibitory role of this grammar has long been a cause for speculation and debate. Conventional wisdom suggested that the L1 grammar was the cause of 'interference' or what Sweet (1899) called 'cross-associations': "These arise simply from the fact that each idea that comes into our minds instantly suggests the native expression of it" (1899 [1964]: 197). For Sweet, it was the *similarities* between two languages which encouraged cross-association and, hence, induced error.

Half a century later, and from the perspective of behaviorist learning theory, it was the differences that were held responsible, and a major preoccupation of researchers at that time was contrastive analysis, i.e., the contrasting of the L1 and L2 systems with a view to predicting areas of difficulty, so that teachers might take pre-emptive action. Contrastive analysis was also enlisted to explain the phenomenon of avoidance, where a grammatical feature, such as relative clauses, might be under-represented in a learner's output simply because there is no equivalent in their L1 (e.g., Chinese).

However, when researchers started paying closer attention to learners' output, and especially their 'errors', the predictions of contrastive analysis were not always – or even often – confirmed. For example[1], the Spanish-speaking learner of English who writes "I am 23 years old and I from Spain" would be expected to err on the first verb rather than on the second, since Spanish resembles English more in the second clause than in the first: *Tengo 23 años y soy de España* (literally 'I have 23 years and am from Spain').

Accordingly, error analysis studies from the 1970s onwards made a distinction between *interlingual* (or L1 transfer) errors and *intralingual* (or developmental) errors, prompting some researchers to make the (for many teachers, counterintuitive) claim that "*the majority of errors made by second language learners are not interlingual, but developmental* [original emphasis]" (Dulay, Burt, and Krashen 1982: 173).

Various reasons have been hypothesized as to the cause of these intralingual or developmental errors. Richards (1974) proposes at least four: over-generalization, ignorance of rule restrictions, incomplete application of rules, and the hypothesizing of false concepts. An example of an over-generalization error might be "I have an old table, I buyed it about ten years ago", where the past tense *-ed* suffix has been over-generalized to verbs that are in fact irregular.

Despite clear evidence of these developmental processes, the role of transfer has been reassessed over the years, now that it is less 'tainted' with behaviorism. For a start, the pre-occupation with learners' errors should not obscure the fact that *positive* transfer may play a role in the development of the learner's grammar. Studies of the acquisition of relative clauses, for example, (e.g., Hyltenstam, 1984) have shown that the target forms are learned more successfully when they 'match' those in the learner's L1. There is even evidence (e.g., Pavlenko and Jarvis, 2002) that the L2 can cause changes in the learner's L1: that is to say, transfer 'flows' both ways.

Crosslinguistic effects also underpin what is known as the 'competition model' (MacWhinney and Bates, 1989), which argues that particular meanings are encoded differently in different languages, and that their speakers are predisposed, therefore, to focus on specific 'cues', such as word order, rather than others, such as grammatical inflexion. L1 'cue strengths' have been shown to inhibit processing in the L2. This kind of transfer is less linguistic than conceptual, and has been the subject of recent research into the cognition of bilinguals, where studies that correlate language production with eye-tracking and gesture support the view that, in at least some domains, "the majority of L2 speakers think in the L1 when speaking in the L2" (Schmiedtová, von Stutterheim, and Caroll, 2011: 67).

Strengths – not of cues but of neural connections – feature in connectionist accounts of language acquisition (see N. Ellis, 2003). Using computer models of neural networks, researchers have demonstrated a correlation between frequency of exposure and connection strength. It follows, therefore, that the connections of the L1 system are already strengthened to the point that they will resist attempts to 'reset' them. Such a view argues that the effects of transfer are most acute at the early stages of learning, but become less apparent as L2 settings are gradually strengthened, a process that might be facilitated by directing learners' attention to form (see below).

'Resetting' is central to a Universal Grammar (UG) account of SLA, too – not of connection strengths, but of parameters. It is argued that those parameters such as the pro-drop one (which governs subject deletion) that are 'turned off' in the L1 may need to be reset for the target language: failure to do so would explain errors like "I like the bathroom because is very big", where the speaker is operating on the parameters of her L1 (in this case, Italian). The extent, however, to which the learner's UG is accessible, or even partly accessible, and hence amenable to resetting, is still a matter of debate, as is the nature and even existence of the UG itself. Nevertheless, the idea that learners might be 'hard-wired' for language acquisition provides a powerful explanation for the fact that many features of learners' grammar seem to be shared by all learners, irrespective of their L1: a finding that is captured in the concept of interlanguage, to which we now turn.

THE 'BUILT-IN SYLLABUS'

In order to account for errors that are both systematic and not obviously L1 induced, Corder (1967) hypothesized the existence of a 'built-in syllabus', a dynamic continuum along which the learner advances, independent of any externally-imposed syllabus. Subsequently,

Selinker (1972) coined the term *interlanguage* to encapsulate the notion of a transitional 'mental grammar' that is independent of both the L1 and the target language rule systems. At around the same time, researchers into the developmental stages of first language learning (e.g., Brown, 1973) had identified what they called an 'order of acquisition' of grammatical morphemes, which (following Chomsky) they attributed to an innate, age-constrained language acquisition device.

Meanwhile, research into the order of acquisition (also known as the 'natural order') of second languages, in both children and adults, produced similar results for the same or similar grammatical morphemes. Krashen (1981) summarizes the results of these early 'morpheme studies' (Figure 20.1), where the developmental order is represented as four successive stages, although the order within these stages is subject to some variation.

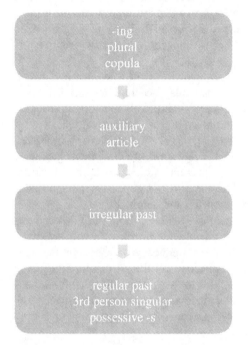

Figure 20.1   Proposed "Natural Order" for Second Language Acquisition and Agrammatics (adapted from Krashen, 1981)

Reviewing the findings of the (now largely discontinued) morpheme studies, R. Ellis (2008: 85) comments, "The picture that emerges from these studies is of a standard 'acquisition order' that is not rigidly invariant but is remarkably similar irrespective of the learners' language backgrounds, of their age, and of whether the medium is speech or writing."

Subsequently, researchers shifted their attention from individual morphemes to the developmental patterns of such syntactic structures as question forms, negation, and relative clauses. Their initial findings – replicated in a number of languages – led researchers to propose that the observed developmental sequences reflected the way learners overcome limitations in their processing capacity: the so-called 'processability theory' (Pienemann, 1998). Processing constraints determine that the 'hierarchy of acquisition' begins with single words or formulaic 'chunks', and progresses through stages of increasing syntactic complexity.

Meanwhile, a longitudinal study of untutored adult migrants in Europe (summarized in Perdue, 1993) identified a three-step sequence of 'learner varieties' that begins with a reliance on nouns (the 'pre-basic variety'), and evolves into the use of non-finite verb structures (the 'basic variety'), and thence to a finite utterance organization (the 'post-basic variety'). A similar progression from lexis to syntax was observed in a pioneering study of immigrant children in the USA (Wong Fillmore, 1979): in order to 'pass' as eligible group members in the playground, these children adopted the strategy of learning formulaic sequences, and then subsequently re-analyzed these 'chunks' into their constituents in order to create new utterances. More recently, studies of the acquisition of constructions by researchers aligned with usage-based theories of SLA show similar developmental trajectories, from item-learning to rule abstraction. As N. Ellis (2003: 67) claims, "The acquisition of grammar is the piecemeal learning of many thousands of constructions and the frequency-biased abstraction of regularities within them."

Coming from the same emergentist tradition, some scholars (such as Larsen-Freeman, 2006) have challenged the somewhat linear and incremental accounts of language acquisition that have been outlined thus far, and have focused their attention on the inherent variability of the process. Longitudinal studies of individual learners (as opposed to multi-participant studies) cast doubt on the view that there are uniform stages of development, and instead reveal a significant degree of instability, 'back-sliding' and sudden 'phase shifts'.

Nevertheless, one fact that is incontrovertible is that both group studies and single participant case studies demonstrate that grammatical development frequently stabilizes at a relatively ungrammaticized level, confirming the view that few adult learners achieve a native-like mastery of the target language grammar. Why this occurs has been attributed to a constellation of factors, including deficits in motivation, socialization, aptitude, affect, comprehensible input, 'pushed' output, practice, and focused attention (or 'noticing'). Space precludes a fuller discussion here (but see Chapters 6, 7 and 11 for discussion of some of these factors), except insofar as these factors might explain the effects of formal instruction, the subject of the next section.

THE EFFECTS OF INSTRUCTION

Since it is generally agreed that learners have a 'built-in' syllabus, even if there is considerable individual variation in both the route and the final destination, the question remains: to what extent – and how – does formal instruction affect the process? Can it be accelerated by the learning of explicit rules, for example, or by form-focussed corrective feedback, or by following a grammatical syllabus?

Doubts about the value of formal instruction – such as the learning and controlled practice of grammar rules – as opposed to naturalistic learning, have a very long history. They resurfaced in the 1970s in the wake of the morpheme studies, and were propelled in particular by Krashen's 'Monitor Theory' (1977). Essentially, Krashen claimed that knowledge learned from formal instruction (e.g., of grammar rules) serves only to monitor or edit output, and, even then, only under certain form-focused conditions. Otherwise, second languages are, like the L1, 'acquired', using subconscious learning mechanisms if, and only if, the learner is exposed to 'comprehensible input'. Moreover, Krashen insisted that there is no 'leakage' from the explicit 'learned system' into the implicit 'acquired' one.

This 'non-interface' position was lent support by studies that compared the order of acquisition in instructed and non-instructed learners (e.g., Pica, 1983), and found little significant difference, leading many scholars to conclude that, in the words of Skehan (1996: 19), "Second language acquisition (SLA) research … has established that teaching does not and cannot determine the way the learner's language will develop."

However, the instructed learners in these comparative studies did seem to achieve higher levels of grammatical competence, suggesting that instruction improves the *rate*, but not the *route*, of SLA (R. Ellis, 1990). A subsequent meta-analysis of nearly 50 studies (Norris and Ortega, 2000) provided confirmation that instructed learners progress at a faster rate, and achieve levels of accuracy and complexity that exceed those of uninstructed learners. These findings would seem to vindicate the need for explicit grammar instruction, and certainly for a 'focus on form' (Long, 1991), including corrective feedback. However, most of these and subsequent studies measured grammar learning by means of artificially-controlled exercises, such as gap-fills and sentence transformations, and not in real communication, and therefore did not necessarily disprove Krashen's argument that explicit knowledge is of use only in monitoring output. As Truscott (2015: 136), reviewing the evidence, concludes, "form-based instruction gave learners conscious knowledge that was very useful for tasks that could be done primarily with conscious knowledge but had only limited (and possibly no) value for tasks that required spontaneous communicative use of the forms."

Hence, the value of learning grammar explicitly (as opposed to simply picking it up incidentally while engaged in communicative tasks, for example), would seem to depend on whether – and the extent to which – explicit knowledge can become implicit. Truscott, above, takes the extreme 'non-interface' position, while others, like Ellis and Shintani (2014: 95) are more circumspect, arguing that explicit instruction can assist the learner "to achieve greater control over a feature that is *already partially acquired* [emphasis added]". Instruction may also have a 'priming' effect, that is, explicit teaching of a grammatical structure may make it more likely that learners will consciously attend to (or 'notice') the structure when they encounter it in naturalistic input, increasing the chance of the item being retained in long-term memory – a phenomenon reported by Schmidt and Frota (1986). Meanwhile, proponents of skill-learning theory take a 'strong interface' position, arguing that "slow, deliberate practice" (DeKeyser 2007: 107) can help 'proceduralize' explicit knowledge, lending support to the traditional 'present-practice-produce' (PPP) instructional sequence. Nevertheless, brain imaging studies have cast doubt on the inter-permeability of the explicit and implicit memory stores, leading at least one neuroscientist to argue that "acquisition is not a process of automatizing rules" (Paradis, 2004, quoted in Ellis, 2008: 754).

IMPLICATIONS FOR TEACHING AND ASSESSMENT

Given the range of divergent, even conflicting positions that I have reviewed, it is perhaps not surprising that teachers are often dismissive of research findings, and are resistant to the suggestion that, in the light of these findings, 'tried and tested' approaches should be re-evaluated, if not abandoned altogether. They have a point. As Larsen-Freeman (2015: 272) argues, "teaching and learning are complex and situated endeavours. Simple un-nuanced and decontextualized pronouncements for the interface or non-interface stances, or for and against focus on form, are likely to be wrong, or at least overstated."

Nevertheless, there now seems to be sufficient consensus among researchers on the following four issues to suggest that certain implications for teaching and assessment can safely be inferred.

THE GRAMMAR SYLLABUS

Despite attempts to 'unseat' it (notably with the advent of Communicative Language Teaching in the 1970s and 1980s), grammar is still the primary organizing principle of most general English syllabuses and textbooks. Yet, as we have seen, the 'route' of acquisition is largely impervious to external manipulation. Alternative instructional designs that replicate or complement more naturalistic or experiential learning processes, such as task-based and content-based instruction, have been proposed and empirically tested, and should be considered as viable pedagogical options, not least because they are grounded in psycholinguistic principles, rather than purely linguistic ones.

FOCUS ON FORM

Nevertheless, the research suggests that simply 'experiencing' language, as in immersion classrooms, is insufficient unless there is an intentional 'focus on form' in the form of pedagogical interventions, including corrective feedback. Moreover, these interventions seem to be most effective 'at the point of need' when learners are engaged in communicative activities (Lightbown, 1998). This view supports the case for equipping teachers with the skills both to set up and manage communicative activities and to provide reactive feedback on their students' performance.

EXPLICIT GRAMMAR TEACHING

At the same time, the case for explicit, proactive teaching of grammar has been argued on the grounds that:

- it may act as a kind of 'advance organizer' or 'acquisition facilitator' (Seliger 1979);
- it can counteract premature stabilization that might result from an exclusive focus on meaning (see Lyster, 2007); and
- explicit knowledge can become automated through practice.

There would seem to be no risks involved, therefore, in the occasional 'grammar lesson', so long as it targets those items for which the learners are optimally 'ready' and that it is not at the expense of plentiful practice opportunities.

THE PRIMACY OF GRAMMAR

Finally, the primacy – hegemony, even – of grammar needs to be challenged, along with the 'myth' that learning an L2 is essentially the acquisition of its grammar (Brown and Larson-Hall, 2012). "Grammar is fundamental to language. Without grammar, language does not exist" write Nassaji and Fotos (2011:1). But just as fundamental, surely, are phonemes, morphemes, words and phrases, not to mention pragmatics and discourse. The special, even iconic, status attached to grammar risks blinding teachers and course-planners to the totality and interdependence of language systems in use. It has an especially pernicious effect on assessment, where the measure of a learner's proficiency is often based almost entirely on discrete-point tests of grammatical knowledge rather than on, say, communicative competence. Integrative and performance tests, in which grammatical accuracy is measured only insofar as it impacts on communicative effectiveness, might go some way towards redressing the current grammar-centred mindset.

CONCLUSION

Grammar continues to occupy centre-stage, both in researching language acquisition and in designing curricula. What constitutes grammar, however, has become increasingly elusive, as the traditional separation between grammar and vocabulary, on the one hand, and grammar and discourse, on the other, has started to dissolve. This has had implications for how the learning of grammar is conceptualized: it is no longer so easy to separate the acquisition of the grammatical system from the acquisition of other systems, such as lexis, discourse or pragmatics. The situation is complicated by recognition of the fact that – like all areas of language – grammar is sensitive to contextual factors, and that the grammar of speech, for example, differs from the grammar of writing in many significant respects.

In turn, there are implications for how grammar might best be integrated into the curriculum, how it might best be taught, and how it might best be tested. Nevertheless, despite often strongly-voiced doubts as to the relation between traditional grammar syllabuses and the actual processes of acquiring grammar (e.g., Long 2015), curriculum design has been slow to respond to these new challenges. Research is needed, not only into how learners acquire grammar over time, but also into how changes in educational practice with regard to grammar teaching might be implemented with less resistance than they currently meet.

Discussion Questions

1. If L1 influence on the L2 is inevitable, how should this impact on pedagogy? For example, is there a case for incorporating translation activities into the teaching of grammar?

2. What are the arguments for and against teaching according to the 'natural order' of L2 grammar acquisition?

3. Why do you think that grammar has acquired such a central, even 'iconic', status, both in terms of SLA theory, and of curriculum design?

Key Readings

Ellis, R. (2006). Current issues in the teaching of grammar: An SLA perspective. *TESOL Quarterly*, 40(1), 83–108.

Swan, M. (2011). Grammar. In J. Simpson (Ed.), *The Routledge Handbook of Applied Linguistics* (pp. 557–570). London: Routledge.

Thornbury, S. (1999). *How to Teach Grammar.* Harlow: Pearson.

References

Breen, M. (2001). Postscript: new directions for research on learner contributions. In M. Breen (Ed.), *Learner Contributions to Language Learning: New Directions in Research* (pp. 172–182). Harlow: Pearson.

Brown, R. (1973). *A First Language: The Early Stages,* Cambridge, MA: Harvard University Press.

Brown, S., & Larson-Hall, J. (2012). *Second Language Acquisition Myths: Applying Second Language Research to Classroom Teaching.* Ann Arbor, MI: The University of Michigan Press.

Carter, R., & McCarthy, M. (1995). Grammar and the spoken language. *Applied Linguistics*, 16, 141–58.

Chomsky, N. (1981). Principles and parameters in syntactic theory. In N. Hornstein & D. Lightfoot (Eds.), *Explanation in Linguistics: The Logical Problem of Language Acquisition* (pp. 32–75). London: Longman.

Conrad, S., & Biber, D. (2009). *Real Grammar: A Corpus-based Approach to English.* White Plains, NY: Pearson Education.

Corder, S. P. (1967). The significance of learners' errors. *International Review of Applied Linguistics*, 5, 161–9.

DeKeyser, R. (2007). Skill acquisition theory. In B. VanPatten & J. Williams (Eds.), *Theories in Second Language Acquisition: An Introduction* (pp. 97–114). New York: Routledge.

Dulay, H., Burt, M., & Krashen, S. (1982). *Language Two.* New York: Oxford University Press.

Ellis, N. (2003). Constructions, chunking and connectionism. In C. J. Doughty & M. H. Long (Eds.), *The Handbook of Second Language Acquisition* (pp. 63–103). Oxford: Blackwell.

Ellis, R. (1990). *Instructed Second Language Acquisition.* Oxford: Blackwell.

Ellis, R. (2008). *The Study of Second Language Acquisition* (2nd ed.). Oxford: Oxford University Press.

Ellis, R. & Shintani, N. (2014). *Exploring Language Pedagogy through Second Language Acquisition Research*. London: Routledge.

Goldberg, A. (2006). *Constructions at Work: The Nature of Generalization in Language*. Oxford: Oxford University Press.

Hyltenstam, K. (1984). The use of typological markedness conditions as predictors in second language acquisition: The case of pronominal copies in relative clauses. In R. Andersen (Ed.), *Second Language: A Cross-Linguistic Perspective* (pp. 39–58). Rowley, MA: Newbury House.

Krashen, S. D. (1977). Some issues relating to the Monitor Model. In H. Brown, C. Yorio & R. Crymes (Eds.), *On TESOL '77* (pp. 144–148). Washington, D.C.: TESOL.

Krashen, S. D. (1981). *Second Language Acquisition and Second Language Learning*. Oxford: Pergamon.

Larsen-Freeman, D. (2006). The emergence of complexity, fluency, and accuracy in the oral and written production of five Chinese learners of English. *Applied Linguistics*, 27, 590–619.

Larsen-Freeman, D. (2015). Research into practice: Grammar learning and teaching. *Language Teaching*, 48(2), 263–280.

Lightbown, P. M. (1998). The importance of timing in focus on form. In C. Doughty & J. Williams (Eds.), *Focus on Form in Classroom Second Language Acquisition* (pp. 177–198). Cambridge: Cambridge University Press.

Long, M. H. (1991). Focus on form: A design feature in language teaching methodology. In K. de Bot, D. Coste, R. Ginsberg, & C. Kramsch (Eds.), *Foreign Language Research in Cross-cultural Perspectives* (pp. 39–52). Amsterdam/Philadelphia: John Benjamins.

Long, M. (2015). *Second Language Acquisition and Task-Based Language Teaching*. Oxford: Wiley-Blackwell.

Lyster, R. (2007). *Learning and Teaching Languages through Content: A counterbalanced approach*. Amsterdam/Philadelphia: John Benjamins.

MacWhinney, B., & Bates, E. (Eds.) (1989). *The Crosslinguistic Study of Sentence Processing*. Cambridge: Cambridge University Press.

Nassaji, H., & Fotos, S. (2011). *Teaching Grammar in Second Language Classrooms: Integrating Form-focused Instruction in Communicative Context*. London: Routledge.

Norris, J., & Ortega, L. (2000). Effectiveness of L2 instruction: A research synthesis and quantitative meta-analysis. *Language Learning*, 50, 417–528.

Pavlenko, A., & Jarvis, S. (2002). Bidirectional transfer. *Applied Linguistics*, 23, 190–214.

Perdue, C. (Ed.) (1993). *Adult Language Acquisition: Cross-Linguistic Perspectives, Volume II: The Results*. Cambridge: Cambridge University Press.

Pica, T. (1983). Adult acquisition of English as a second language under different conditions of exposure. *Language Learning*, 33, 465–97.

Pienemann, M. (1998). *Language Processing and Second Language Development*. Amsterdam: John Benjamins.

Richards, J. C. (1974). A non-contrastive approach to error analysis. In J. C. Richards (Ed.), *Error Analysis: Perspectives on Second Language Acquisition* (pp. 172–188). Harlow: Longman.

Rutherford, W.E. (1988). *Second Language Grammar: Learning and Teaching*. London: Longman.

Schmidt, R., & Frota, S. (1986). Developing basic conversational ability in a second language: A case study of the adult learner of Portuguese. In R. R. Day (Ed.), *Talking to learn: Conversation in Second Language Acquisition* (pp. 237–326). Rowley, MA: Newbury House.

Schmiedtová, B., von Stutterheim, C., & Carroll, M. (2011). Language-specific patterns in event construal of advanced second language speakers. In A. Pavlenko (Ed.), *Thinking and Speaking in Two Languages* (pp. 29–65). Bristol, UK: Multilingual Matters.

Seliger, H. (1979). On the nature and function of language rules in language teaching. *TESOL Quarterly*, 13, 359–69.

Selinker, L. (1972). Interlanguage. *International Review of Applied Linguistics*, 10, 209–31.

Skehan, P. (1996). Second language acquisition research and task-based instruction. In J. Willis & D. Willis (Eds.), *Challenge and Change in Language Teaching* (pp. 17–30). Oxford: Heinemann.

Sweet, H. ([1899] 1964). *The Practical Study of Languages: A Guide for Teachers and Learners*. London: Oxford University Press.

Truscott, J. (2015). *Consciousness and Second Language Learning*. Bristol, UK: Multilingual Matters.

Wong Fillmore, L. (1979). Individual differences in second language acquisition. In C. J. Fillmore, D. Kempler, & W. S.-Y Wang (Eds.), *Individual Differences in Language Ability and Language Behavior* (pp. 203–228). New York: Academic Press.

Note

[1] All examples are taken from the *Cambridge Learner Corpus*, a collection of exam scripts written by English language learners.

SECTION 6

LEARNING THE FOUR SKILLS OF ENGLISH

This set of chapters examines the learning of the macro-skills – aspects of language use, we would argue, that are not normally included in the second language acquisition literature on second language (L2) learning. For many learners and teachers, these skills constitute the 'core' of what language learning is about. Recent perspectives on these skills have considerably broadened understanding of what it means to learn to listen, speak, read and write another language, in this case English, as these chapters illuminate.

In the first chapter, on L2 listening, **Joseph Siegel** describes listening as an interactive process in which the listener draws on knowledge of the context and of speaker and listener intentions, and on language-related knowledge (vocabulary and syntax), as well as the ability to process rapid speech. Listening demands are often context- and task-specific, and the ability to engage in fluent listening will depend on exposure and practice, as well as on appropriate strategy choice. He suggests that the development of L2 listening involves gradual automatization of skills and processes, which can be facilitated both by direct instruction and by out-of-class extensive listening opportunities through the internet.

In her chapter, **Christine C. M. Goh** discusses the development of L2 speaking skills and notes that learning to speak has often not been distinguished from 'practising speaking'. She presents a model of the nature of L2 speaking skills that includes knowledge of rules and conventions at the levels of language and discourse, core speaking skills and communication strategies, and discusses the role of teachers, teaching materials and learners in the teaching and learning process.

The next chapter focuses on L2 reading in English. **Lawrence Jun Zhang** outlines the knowledge, skills and dispositions L2 readers bring to reading and the different dimensions involved in fluent reading. Successful L2 reading depends on both language ability and reading skills, and is influenced by metalinguistic and metacognitive knowledge, as well as by different culturally-based reading traditions. The differences between novice and expert readers serve to support recommendations for L2 reading instruction.

In discussing learning to write in an L2, **Neomy Storch** describes the sources learners make use of in producing a written text, pointing out that writing involves creating texts that reflect conventions of genres and that also acknowledge the contexts in which a text occurs, institutional and cultural conventions, and readers' expectations, as well as issues of identity and voice. Storch suggests the need for an explicit approach to the teaching of writing in English, involving analysis of texts, modeling and feedback. In addition, she recommends a need to move beyond the concept of texts as products and suggests a focus on the resources learners can make use of as multilingual writers.

As the chapters in this section demonstrate, a range of theories of learning is needed to account for the acquisition of the skills of language reception and production. Learners adopting another language must be able to acquire knowledge, skills and strategies that incorporate such diverse features of language learning as sensitivity to cultural and social contexts of use, the comprehension and inferencing of meaning, the production, management and negotiation of speech, and the development of reading and listening comprehension abilities.

Learning Listening

Joseph Siegel

INTRODUCTION

Listening is a deceptively complex ability. Although it seems almost effortless in one's first language (L1), learning to listen in a second language (L2) can be very challenging. Most people pay little attention to their ability to listen, except for situations in which they *cannot* hear well. Whereas the majority of people learn to listen in their L1 without any conscious attention, developing listening skills in an L2 requires explicit attention to the various processes and components that lead to successful aural comprehension. Among the most important of these elements is the complementary relationship between top-down and bottom-up processing, both of which contribute to listening competency in different ways. Listening strategies also impact the metacognitive, cognitive, affective, and interactional operations that aid aural comprehension. Ample exposure to L2 speech is also necessary for those skills to become increasingly more automatized. More recent thinking on L2 listening has also emphasized the roles of working memory, L2 vocabulary size, and the development of an aural vocabulary. This chapter aims to discuss the various aspects of listening, why they are important, and how they can be developed.

OVERVIEW

Before delving into L2 listening, it is important to have some understanding of how listening is viewed and treated in the L1. Most people develop the ability to listen in their L1 without any direct or explicit instruction. We usually become capable listeners through interaction with parents and family first, and then, in the early school years, through listening to our teachers and classmates. This all happens without any conscious thought or attention to aural development. Later, our other language skills (speaking, reading, and writing) gradually evolve, but we must remember that listening was (in most cases) established first and provided the foundation for our general L1 ability.

Listening in an L2, however, is far more complicated than in an L1, and many, including learners, teachers, and researchers, have expressed the viewpoint that high-level listening competency in an L2 is an extremely demanding task (e.g., Field, 2008; Rost, 2014a). Reasons for this sizable challenge are many. Two major concerns are typically the rapid speed of input (e.g., Brunfaut and Révész, 2015) and the ephemeral, 'you only get one chance' nature of listening (e.g., Renandya and Farrell, 2011). Other obstacles include a new sound system, unfamiliar lexicon, varying intonational patterns, and differing cultural norms. L2 learners aiming to achieve high levels of listening competency need to be aware of and address these, as well as several other aspects of listening in their L2, in order to achieve some comfort and confidence when unpacking meaning from incoming input.

In summarizing various definitions, Brunfaut and Révész (2015) describe listening as an interactive and cognitive event that draws on linguistic, contextual and pragmatic processing, while simultaneously activating the listener's background, world and linguistic knowledge. As L2 English listeners become increasingly more proficient in engaging these various elements, the automatization of listening increases, thereby bringing the L2 English listener closer and closer to the L1 listener's ability. While some listening behaviors operate internally and are therefore beyond direct observation (e.g., Flowerdew and Miller, 2005), others are more visible and occur in face-to-face interactive listening situations (e.g., Rost, 2014b).

One theory that has greatly impacted our understanding of listening comprehension involves the interaction of top-down (TD) and bottom-up (BU) processing. TD processing involves a listener's background and contextual knowledge, and likely varies from person to person. Specific elements of the TD view of listening include "topic, genre, culture, and other schema knowledge in long-term memory ... [which help] to build a conceptual framework for comprehension" (Vandergrift, 2004: 4). In other words, the basis for the TD view starts with a holistic interpretation of the situation, and from there, input is separated into smaller units of meaning. TD processing contributes essential elements to the listening process. For example, by incorporating background knowledge and previous experience, it allows listeners to eliminate unlikely interpretations and lexicon; in other words, listeners use their predictive abilities to limit options to only the most likely ones, an operation which frees up cognitive resources to focus on other aspects of the incoming message and/or to formulating a verbal or non-verbal response. TD processing also includes understanding of generic language patterns, such as lectures, transactional interactions, and informational announcements. Understanding these typical structures also lessens the burden on cognitive processing.

In contrast to the TD viewpoint, the aural speech signal, the building blocks or phonemes of speech, represent the foundation of the BU view. From this perspective, smaller units of meaning are combined and arranged to create the message. Field (2003) details the upward meaning-construction from the BU view: "perceiving and parsing the speech stream at increasingly larger levels beginning with auditory-phonetic, phonemic, syllabic, lexical, syntactic, semantic, propositional, pragmatic and interpretive" (p. 326). From a BU standpoint, listeners need to be able to identify the beginnings and endings of words, recognize intonation and stress patterns, and appropriately separate the speech stream into meaningful chunks. Without these abilities, learners may indeed feel overwhelmed, as they struggle to parse rapid speech into its constituent parts. Listeners need these BU abilities in order to, for instance, pick out key content words, infer speaker attitude, and understand thought groups.

While these may seem like competing or distinct viewpoints, most researchers agree that the two types of processing interact and are mutually beneficial (e.g., Lynch, 2009; Vandergrift, 2004). Personal preferences, learning styles, contexts, and/or listening objectives may affect the extent to which TD and BU processing are used in any single listening instance.

Influential models of listening (Anderson, 2005; Clark and Clark, 1977) and Siegel's (2015) more recent proposition have attempted to explain how these elements are sequenced, although there is no consensus. While these models of listening vary to a degree, they all recognize that listeners must attend to numerous linguistic and nonlinguistic sources almost simultaneously. Essentially, learners need the abilities to both decode linguistic input and use that information, along with the surrounding context, to build a (tentative) representation of meaning that must be constantly adjusted as new input is received (e.g., Field, 2008).

When it comes to coverage of TD and BU processing in L2 listening materials and classroom pedagogy, a noticeable imbalance toward TD approaches has been present. From the 1990s, many educators promoted the idea that contextual guesswork, listener background knowledge, and prediction could compensate for any misunderstandings when listening. Thus, typical classroom practice encouraged learners to make guesses and fill in for anything that was not understood. Listening activities in textbooks also encouraged this approach by dedicating significant time and page space for pre-listening schema activating stages, and left minimal time for actual listening. While listeners clearly draw on TD processes, more recent calls in the pedagogical literature have emphasized the need for a (re)introduction of BU listening practice. Several researchers (e.g., Field, 2008; Siegel and Siegel, 2015; Vandergrift and Baker, 2015) have made specific calls for more explicit BU attention for listening practice, which can benefit lower proficiency learners in particular. Thus, language classrooms that aim for a balance of both TD and BU development would devote equal awareness to these fundamental aspects of listening.

Many listeners also employ listening strategies, depending on situation and individual factors. Three types of listening strategies are commonly discussed in listening research and pedagogic literature: metacognitive, cognitive, and affective (e.g., O'Malley and Chamot, 1990; Oxford, 2011; see also Chapter 9). Metacognitive strategies include planning, monitoring, and evaluating listening and are integral parts of the metacognitive listening cycle (Vandergrift and Goh, 2012). Cognitive strategies are thought to be orchestrated by metacognitive strategies, and are those that listeners apply directly to incoming content; for example, listening for key words, attending to intonation, and predicting upcoming input are cognitive strategies. A number of pedagogic works have described how such strategies can be incorporated, either implicitly or explicitly, in the listening classroom (e.g., Mendelsohn, 1994, 2006; Siegel, 2013, 2015; Vandergrift and Goh, 2012).

Unlike metacognitive and cognitive listening strategies, which occur only in the listener's mind, affective strategies involve listeners' emotions and interactional competence (e.g., O'Malley and Chamot, 1990; Oxford, 2011; Rost, 2014b). Listeners often make efforts to relax, stay focused, and maintain confidence, which are all examples of affective strategies. Other recent ideas about strategic listening recognize the social and interactional nature of the skill (e.g., Lynch, 2009; Oxford, 2011). Strategies for interactional listening can include indicating non-comprehension or asking questions of conversation partners (e.g., for clarification or rephrasing). While L2 English learners may employ all types of listening strategy unconsciously in their L1, they need to learn to do the same in their L2. Listening strategy instruction (e.g., Mendelsohn, 1994, 2006; Siegel, 2015) has been promoted in the literature to help learners develop in these areas, both by transferring strategies they may already use in L1 listening to English and by developing strategies specifically necessary for deciphering the L2.

Some of these abilities can be transferred from the L1 to L2 English (e.g., making predictions, activating background knowledge, recognizing formal compared to informal situations). In such cases, learners may need only awareness raising of how they can apply processes similar to those in their L1 to their L2. Other elements may be specific to the L2, such as: understanding common chunks; blended speech; recognizing word beginnings and endings; developing the L2 aural vocabulary size; and understanding structural and generic patterns common to the L2. For these L2-specific skills, learners need to be exposed to explicit, scaffolded practice early on, where the scaffolding is slowly and subtly retracted so that more of the listening onus is on the learner.

While this description of L2 English listening may seem straightforward, making progress in aural comprehension of one's L2 can be a daunting, time consuming task. Often there is little evidence that progress is being made, which can lead to learner frustration and confusion. By understanding the various elements that contribute to listening competency, and considering how they can be developed, learners can progress from beginner to intermediate and eventually to advanced status. This evolution can take place through learner self-study, in the EFL classroom or, more likely, a combination of the two, and only through extensive contact with the aural L2 will learners gradually become accustomed to creating meaning from incoming sounds.

KEY LEARNING ISSUES

Several factors may influence the development of L2 English listening, the most important of which is contact time with the aural English. For learners in ESL contexts, taking advantage of the numerous opportunities for English is important. EFL learners may have access to successful English users in classes, business, or as acquaintances. With the range of internet sites catering to those who want more English input (e.g., www.elllo.org; www.englishcentral.com), opportunities to listen have become more accessible. Selecting listening materials at an appropriate level is also important. Learners and their teachers may wish to use the concept of 'i + 1' (i.e., input that is one step beyond the learner's current level) (Krashen, 1985) to provide a challenge, or choose materials that are easily understandable, in correspondence with principles of extensive reading and extensive listening (Renandya and Farrell, 2011; Waring, 2014). Choosing manageable listening tasks can also influence development, as they can lead to improved motivation and confidence. Listening materials that are well beyond current listening ability can lead to frustration.

Learning to listen can take place in several distinct contexts, and often a combination of these is most effective and motivating. In the L2 classroom, many learners and their teachers undergo a sequence of listening, answering questions, and checking those answers. While this may be the norm in many classrooms, the argument for more progressive and scaffolded listening pedagogy has been put forth (e.g., Field, 2008; Richards and Burns, 2012; Siegel, 2013, 2015; Vandergrift and Goh, 2012). Several of the activities suggested by these authors target the various elements of listening discussed earlier (i.e., TD and BU processing; a range of listening strategies). By incorporating practices like these, and others, teachers can become more active participants in *teaching* listening than they have been in the past. Beyond the classroom (see Chapter 13), learners' listening can improve through individual extensive listening (e.g., Renandya and Farrell, 2011), in which they listen to texts of their own choosing and at an appropriate level. Listening can also develop through spontaneous contact with the L2 in the real world; for example, through socializing or online media. Ideally, L2 learners will get a balance of structured and scaffolded classroom instruction that they can then activate and practice when listening to materials of interest and when interacting in the L2, either with non-native or native users.

ONE- AND TWO-WAY LISTENING

During their interaction with aural input, L2 learners need to become familiar with two types of encounters with spoken language: one- and two-way listening. One-way listening involves a single speaker or group of speakers who are separated from the listener in some way (such as a radio or TV program, internet video, traditional teacher-fronted monologue lectures, most standardized tests of listening), in which the listener does not have interactive access or options. The listener's role is restricted to recognition and interpretation of incoming sounds (Lynch, 2009); in other words, the purpose is "simply to listen for meaning" (Richards and Burns, 2012: x). A more relaxed version of one-way listening could be listening to a story or speech, where interruption or listener participation are possible but would go against social or pragmatic norms. The listener has to deal with, and have the cognitive capacity and endurance to make sense of, longer stretches. What can make one-way listening challenging is that listeners cannot ask for clarification or restatement, or even non-verbally demonstrate their lack of understanding.

In two-way listening, multiple parties are expected to interact and have certain mutually-agreed upon rights, such as asking for clarification. These are dialogic exchanges, in which two or more individuals work together to negotiate meaning. Such situations can include conversations, group discussions, and interactive lectures. Two-way listening allows participants to exercise social and interactive strategies in ways that are not (always) possible in one-way listening. Thus, two-way listening encourages listener participation and reaction, thereby more closely replicating real-life, back-and-forth flow of oral and aural communication (Lynch, 2009; Richards and Burns, 2012). While two-way listening is representative of real world interaction, many tests of listening ability (e.g., TOEFL, IELTS, etc.) rely on one-way listening; thus, depending on their context and objectives, learners may need to acquire proficiency in one- or two-way listening, or both.

DEFINING LISTENING ABILITY

A number of labels have been used to describe learners at different stages of listening development. These include novice, beginner, and low ability listeners, who can progress through the intermediate level towards being a competent, skilled, or proficient listener. An expert or native level of competency includes the ability not only to draw on linguistic input but also to recognize inferences, subtleties and humor, and to respond within an acceptable time. The expert listener can be viewed as a standard against which L2 learners can be measured (Field, 2008).

While designations such as those mentioned above are necessary for logistic and administrative purposes, it can be difficult for learners to understand and precisely define their listening ability. Measurements for other language skills are typically more straightforward and tangible. Reading speed can be calculated in words per minute, and the visual recognition of orthographic symbols signifies reading ability. When reading, learners typically have the opportunity to go back and reread, a luxury not usually associated with listening. Speaking can be measured by sustained conversation, acknowledged through verbal and non-verbal feedback from partners, and/or can be video recorded and watched. Writing, another productive skill, provides visual evidence of output in increasing larger amounts, ranging from single words to sentences and paragraphs, through to multi-page works. Since listening occurs within the mind, and besides note-taking or physical acknowledgements such as nodding, it can be confusing for learners to understand their current listening abilities and to know what their next objectives or progressive stages for this skill should be.

A further complication to understanding listening development is the fact that many tests of listening proficiency struggle to isolate aural comprehension from the other language skills. Tests that involve multiple choice or gap-fill questions inevitably involve reading and writing, respectively, and thus it becomes problematic to determine whether a learner answered incorrectly due to deficiencies related to listening or to other skills. Moreover, listening proficiency tests tend to assess listening in a broad sense, and may neglect to assess important components of listening (i.e., BU and TD processing, listening strategies) directly. Tests attempt to measure the sum of these components, making it difficult for learners and their teachers to know where they should focus their attention with regard to improving listening competency.

MEASURES OF LISTENING ABILITY

In order to help learners, teachers, and researchers distinguish levels of L2 listening ability, internationally recognized standards, such as those set by the Council of Europe's Common European Framework of Languages (CEFR), the Centre for Canadian Benchmarks, and the Cambridge IELTS test, provide descriptions of beginning, intermediate and advanced listeners. These three frameworks tend to focus on similar abilities at each level. To summarize, listeners at the novice level (CEFR A1/A2; IELTS Bands 3-4) can typically understand basic words and utterances on common topics (e.g., family, local environment) and in familiar situations (e.g., introductions, shopping) spoken clearly at a slow pace. In other words, understanding is limited to the immediate and concrete level.

Listening at the intermediate level entails understanding main ideas on an expanding array of topics, including school, work, and leisure. Mid-range listeners are developing the ability to follow more complex language in familiar areas, and are beginning to understand main ideas on not only concrete, but also abstract topics. As they progress to the advanced levels, listeners are able to handle longer aural output in a variety of genres, including unstructured speech, although some misunderstandings may occur. Advanced listeners are able to attune to a variety of accents after a brief familiarization period. At the expert level, rapid speech on any topic can be understood completely and with little effort. Learners may benefit from identifying which level they are currently at according to one of these benchmark systems, and focus on the skills needed to progress to the next level. In doing so, they can make improving their listening ability more manageable and tangible, although accurately measuring listening ability may always be somewhat arbitrary, due to its internal nature.

IMPLICATIONS FOR TEACHING AND ASSESSMENT

The previous discussion of L2 English listening leads to implications for the teaching and assessing of aural abilities in the ELT classroom. In order to develop well-rounded and holistic listening abilities, learners and their teachers should strive to target these specific aspects, although course objectives and learner needs may help guide pedagogic choices. It is clear that L2 listening consists of much more than answering comprehension questions. In fact, the traditional "comprehension approach" (Field, 2008: 5) focuses on the product of listening, rather than the processes that lead to understanding. The L2 listening classroom, therefore, should devote time to developing learners' BU and TD processing, as well as incorporating metacognitive, cognitive, and affective/interactional listening strategies; that is, the processes that eventually lead to comprehension.

Teachers may decide to place different priorities on these areas, based on learner proficiency levels, needs and objectives. Courses targeting lecture listening, general communication, and test preparation will ideally involve some universal and some distinctive features, in order to acknowledge specific listening purposes. For example, learners preparing specifically for listening examinations may wish to focus on one-way listening and utilizing BU processing and cognitive strategies to help them locate and select correct answers to multiple choice items. Test-taking strategies would also be advantageous for this group. On the other hand, learners preparing to study overseas on a foreign campus may need to prioritize a TD perspective and social or interactional strategies, to help with generic aural text structure and face-to-face communication (see also Chapter 11). More recent thinking with regard to L2 listening suggests that learners and teachers may wish to allocate time and resources to exercising working memory and expanding aural vocabulary in the L2 (e.g, Stæhr, 2009; Vandergrift and Baker, 2015).

Since most listening courses require aural texts for use both in and outside of class, teachers, and learners perhaps, may wish to consider the following points when selecting listening materials. In general, learners should be exposed to both one-way and two-way texts, to ensure that they are prepared for both types of listening situation. The rate of speech in materials is another important consideration. For the most part, it should be at an achievable yet challenging rate, which increases as learners' processes become more automatized. Introducing a range of accents and varieties of English will help learners prepare for encounters outside of their immediate sphere of communication, and acknowledges the World Englishes perspective. Content, of course, also plays a role, and situations and topics that are concrete and familiar to learners will likely be easier to comprehend. As their confidence increases, listening ability needs to be stretched with increasingly unfamiliar and/or abstract topics. All of these points relate to what is broadly termed as the 'level' of the materials. Teachers and learners should keep in mind that some materials should be achievable and that others should be challenging.

CONCLUSION

The purpose of this chapter has been to describe what L2 English learners and their teachers need to know about L2 listening development. It began by outlining general differences between L1 and L2 English listening, and then moved on to specify obstacles which L2 English users often face with regard to their listening ability. Several aspects of listening, including TD and BU processing as well as listening strategies, were suggested as explicit areas that listeners can develop to help their L2 listening ability progress. L2 listening was also discussed in terms of definitions, characteristics, and in relation to proficiency frameworks and tests. Suggestions for learning and teaching listening have included both in- and outside-of-class activities, and ideas for materials selection. While language learners may have varying reasons for learning to listen in English, they should be aware of the elements and options that are often difficult to identify for an invisible skill like listening.

Discussion Questions

1. What options do learners and teachers have for measuring listening ability? What are the pros and cons of these options?

2. Generally speaking, what obstacles to listening success do L2 English users face? What learning and teaching strategies or techniques can address these hurdles?

3. Consider the listening practice that you do or facilitate as a learner and/or teacher. To what extent does that practice correspond to the top-down, bottom-up, and strategic views of listening discussed in this chapter? What adjustments can be made to accommodate areas that receive less attention?

Key Readings

Brown, S. (2011). *Listening Myths*. Ann Arbor, MI: The University of Michigan Press.

Buck, G. (2001). *Assessing Listening*. Cambridge: Cambridge University Press.

Cutler, A. (2012). *Native Listening*. Cambridge, MA: MIT Press.

Field, J. (2008). *Listening in the Language Classroom*. Cambridge: Cambridge University Press.

Flowerdew, J., & Miller, L. (2005) *Second Language Listening: Theory and Practice*. New York: Cambridge University Press.

Richards, J. C. (1983). Listening comprehension: Approach, design, procedure. *TESOL Quarterly*, 17(12), 219–40.

Richards, J. C. & Burns, A. (2012). *Tips for Teaching Listening: A Practical Approach*. White Plains, NY: Pearson.

Rost, M. (2002). *Teaching and Researching Listening*. Essex: Longman.

Siegel, J. (2015). *Exploring Listening Strategy Instruction Through Action Research*. Basingstoke, UK: Palgrave Macmillian.

References

Anderson, J. R. (2005). *Cognitive Psychology and its Implications* (6th ed.). New York: Worth.

Brunfaut, T., & Révész, A. (2015). The role of task and listener characteristics in second language listening. *TESOL Quarterly*, 49(1), 141–168.

Clark, H., & Clark, E. (1977). *Psychology and Language: An Introduction to Psycholinguistics*. Orlando: Harcourt Brace Jovanovich.

Field, J. (2003). Promoting perception: Lexical segmentation in L2 listening. *ELT Journal*, 57(4), 325–333.

Field, J. (2008). *Listening in the Language Classroom*. Cambridge: Cambridge University Press.

Flowerdew, J., & Miller, L. (2005). *Second Language Listening: Theory and Practice*. New York: Cambridge University Press.

Krashen, S. D. (1985). *The Input Hypothesis: Issues and Implications*. London: Addison Wesley Longman Ltd.

Lynch, T. (2009). *Teaching Second Language Listening*. Oxford: Oxford University Press.

Mendelsohn, D. (1994). *Learning to Listen: A Strategy-based Approach for the Second-language Learner*. Carlsbad: Dominie Press.

Mendelsohn, D. (2006). Learning how to listen using listening strategies. In E. Usó-Juan & A. Martínez-Flor (Eds.), *Current Trends in the Development and Teaching of the Four Language Skills* (pp. 75–89). Berlin: De Gruyter Mouton.

O'Malley, J. M., & Chamot, A. U. (1990). *Learning Strategies in Second Language Acquisition*. Cambridge: Cambridge University Press.

Oxford, R. L. (2011). *Teaching and Researching Language Learning Strategies*. Harlow: Longman.

Renandya, W. A., & Farrell, T. S. C. (2011). 'Teacher, the tape is too fast!' Extensive listening in ELT. *ELT Journal*, 65(1), 52–59.

Richards, J. C. & Burns, A. (2012). *Tips for Teaching Listening: A Practical Approach*. White Plains, NY: Pearson.

Rost, M. (2014a). Listening in a multilingual world: The challenges of second language (L2) listening. *International Journal of Listening*, 28(3), 131–148.

Rost, M. (2014b). Developing listening fluency in Asian EFL settings. In T. Muller, J. Adamson, P. S Brown, & S. Herder (Eds.), *Exploring EFL Fluency in Asia* (pp. 281–296). Basingstoke, UK: Palgrave Macmillian.

Siegel, J. (2013). Methodological ingenuity for second language listening. In J. Schweiter (Ed.), *Studies and Global Perspectives on Second Language Learning and Teaching* (pp. 113–140). Charlotte: Information Age.

Siegel, J. (2015). *Exploring Listening Strategy Instruction through Action Research*. Basingstoke, UK: Palgrave Macmillian.

Siegel, J., & Siegel, A. (2015). Getting to the bottom of L2 listening instruction: Making a case for bottom-up activities. *Studies in Second Language Learning and Teaching*, 5(4), 637–662.

Stæhr, L. S. (2009). Vocabulary knowledge and advanced listening comprehension in English as a foreign language. *Studies in Second Language Acquisition*, 31, 577-607.

Vandergrift, L. (2004). Listening to learn or learning to listen? *Annual Review of Applied Linguistics*, 24, 3–25.

Vandergrift, L., & Baker, S. (2015). Learner variables in second language listening comprehension: An exploratory path analysis. *Language Learning*, 65(2), 390–416.

Vandergrift, L., & Goh, C. C. M. (2012). *Teaching and Learning Second Language Listening*. New York: Routledge.

Waring, R. (2014). Building fluency with extensive reading. In T. Muller, A. Adamson, P. S. Brown, & S. Herder (Eds.), *Exploring EFL Fluency in Asia* (pp. 213–230). Basingstoke, UK: Palgrave Macmillian.

CHAPTER 22

Learning Speaking

Christine C. M. Goh

INTRODUCTION

We often see students in a speaking class talking in pairs or small groups on a topic given by the teacher. Sometimes they are asked to present to the rest of the class what they have discussed. Some common activities include information-gap and problem-solving tasks, simulations and role-plays. These activities require learners to use the spoken language jointly to complete content, solve a problem or achieve a required goal. Apart from these forms of classroom practice, teachers may also inject an element of authentic learning into the process by asking students to go into the community and interact with people there, by conducting simple interviews and surveys or identifying conversation partners. Younger learners may be taught spoken English through activities such as play and games. These activities for teaching speaking, while useful in their own ways, often do not focus sufficiently on the process of *learning* to speak in a second language (L2). Teachers' attention is usually focused on what students need to do to practise speaking rather than with how and what students need to *learn* in order to speak more effectively. More critically, teachers and even learners themselves may overlook issues with learning to speak an L2 that affect confidence, willingness and ability to speak. This chapter explains what L2 speaking entails, and provides suggestions for using interesting and effective activities to enhance oral communication, as well as addressing learners' cognitive and social-affective needs holistically.

OVERVIEW

It is useful to begin our discussion of speaking competence by asking the question, 'What makes a competent L2 speaker?' Bygate (2005) describes a highly competent or expert speaker as someone who has rich oral repertoires and is able to exploit them for communicative purposes. Oral repertoires are mental stores of discourse patterns or routines in specific communicative events. For example, there are routines for telling a story, giving a lecture and participating in an interview. These routines consist of macro ways or moves for structuring spoken texts, as well as micro ways of exploiting grammar, vocabulary, and pronunciation and prosody to convey meaning. Bygate further posits that in order to develop competence in L2 speaking, learners need to acquire mastery of high-level oral processes, (i.e., conceptualising content, planning discourse moves and knowing when to use these moves), as well as low-level oral processes, (i.e., applying linguistic knowledge of grammar, vocabulary and phonology to formulate and articulate utterances).

During this process of 'parallel learning', as Bygate calls it, learners may also develop the ability to monitor and modify what they plan and say. The description of cognitive processes in parallel learning, which is based on a model of first language (L1) speech processing by Levelt (1989, cited in Bygate, 2005), alerts us to the challenges that L2 learners face at the respective levels of conceptualization (planning), formulation (structuring utterances) and articulation (voicing utterances). This model further gives us insights as to why learners may appear fluent and accurate in one situation (they are familiar with the topic, the context and routines, and are familiar with the grammar and vocabulary needed to express meaning), but are halting and unclear in another (they lack knowledge in one or more of these aforementioned features).

At the dawn of the Communicative Language Teaching era, Johnson (1981) put forward a description of a competent speaker that is still relevant today. He highlighted the importance of producing utterances that are not only grammatical but also appropriate on many levels, conforming to the speaker's aim, understanding of role relationships and the linguistic context: "The rapid formulation of utterances which are simultaneously 'right' on several levels is central to the communicative skill" (p. 11). Informed by Johnson's description of a proficient and effective L2 speaker, Goh and Burns (2012) proposed a model of speaking competence that consists of three interrelated components: knowledge of language and discourse, core speaking skills, and communication strategies (Figure 22.1).

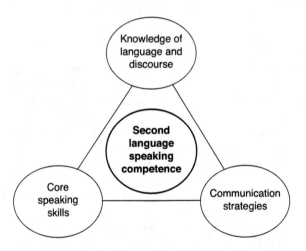

Figure 22.1   Aspects of Second Language Speaking Competence (Source: Goh & Burns, 2012: 53)

This conception of speaking competence emphasises both fluency and accuracy in oral language use, and affirms the importance of appropriateness through an understanding of how texts are organised. It points to the importance of L2 learners developing knowledge of language and discourse that supports them to express meaning, the oral repertoires and discourse routines that Bygate (2005) identified. As they acquire a wider range of grammatical forms for different genres of speech, learners will also develop further in the variety of structures of their utterances. This model also underscores the importance for learners to develop a range of skills to communicate for different purposes through short exchanges and extended discourse. Broadly, speaking skills may be categorised as: pronunciation (producing sounds and sound patterns); speech function (performing a precise communicative function or speech act); interaction management (regulating conversations and discussions); and discourse organisation (creating and structuring discourses in various spoken genres). Many of these skills are already familiar to adult learners, who express essential functions in human communication in their L1 (e.g., request, apologise, disagree, compliment), as well as skills for managing interactions and discourse. What they would need to learn is the language to express their intentions in L2 intelligibly, and in culturally and socially appropriate ways. Younger learners, on the other hand, would in fact be learning both language and pragmatics, or acceptable conventions for engaging with others orally, simultaneously. The inclusion of communication strategies recognises learners' limitations when expressing their ideas, or comprehending what others are saying in face-to-face interactions. Broadly, these are cognitive strategies for compensating vocabulary problems, metacognitive strategies for monitoring and evaluating what is being said, and interaction strategies for eliciting help during an interaction. Learners who are aware of how to use L2 communication strategies stand a better chance of being understood. Furthermore, by maintaining interaction with their interlocutors, they have more opportunities to produce comprehensible output which can enhance their L2 acquisition (Swain, 1995).

KEY LEARNING ISSUES

The process of learning to speak in an L2 is influenced by a number of external and internal factors. An awareness of these issues will enable teachers not just to plan interesting activities for practising speaking, but also to offer timely instructional support to help learners in their speaking development.

TEACHERS AND TEACHING MATERIALS

The way teachers teach L2 speaking is influenced by their beliefs about how speaking is developed and their knowledge of how it should be taught (Chen and Goh, 2014). Awareness about students' learning needs and problems will further influence their decisions. Teachers, therefore, should understand what L2 speaking competence comprises, and examine their assumptions when making instructional decisions. For example, if their view of speaking privileges grammatical accuracy or fluency in a narrow way, they may overlook the importance of developing learner knowledge about genres and discourse routines.

Teachers' ability to develop and adapt teaching materials will also have an impact on the quality of their students' learning experiences. They need a repertoire of teaching techniques and an understanding of the pedagogical principles that underpin effective techniques. In addition, teachers should know when and how to intervene in their students' learning process. Instead of leaving learners to practise speaking on their own, teachers can consider how to scaffold learners and give them feedback on their performance, so that they can eventually perform similar speaking tasks without their teachers' help. This can be done through materials (speaking activities and resources) that support and strengthen learning in explicit ways.

Most teachers use commercially produced coursebooks to teach speaking, and these are often influenced by one of two teaching approaches, namely direct/controlled approach and indirect/transfer approaches (Burns, 1998). The direct/controlled approach mainly focuses on developing accuracy in language forms through controlled language use and practice, in order to help learners produce grammatical utterances and accurate pronunciation. Techniques include drills, pattern practice, structure manipulation and consciousness-raising. The indirect/transfer approach promotes fluency through functional language use during communicative tasks such as simulations and information gaps. The aim is to develop learners' communicative competence, and their ability to transfer communication skills developed in the classroom to everyday communication outside it. This emphasis on communicative competence is also found in many curricula for teaching English to young learners (Garton, Copland, and Burns, 2011; see also Chapter 1).

Materials that are communication-oriented allow learners to develop greater fluency through speaking in pairs or groups, but they seldom promote attention to accuracy. Furthermore, once a speaking activity is completed, learners are deemed to have practised or even developed their speaking abilities. Students are hardly, if ever, asked to repeat a task, a practice that can have learning benefits (Bygate, 2001). Some may not have opportunities to do any pre-task planning that can support their speaking (Skehan and Foster, 2005). In addition, the activities provided in coursebooks seldom get students to examine the language that is used. The books may pre-teach a list of expressions and phrases to use, but do not offer learners a chance to analyse the language that they or expert speakers use, or the discourse strategies for structuring what is said. There are few opportunities for students to learn various discourse routines or genres of speaking explicitly (Burns, 1998; see also Chapter 25), in order to expand and enhance their oral repertoires.

Fluency tasks alone do not promote explicit learning of skills, language and strategies that are important to the overall development of speaking competence. Many coursebooks also do not provide information about the genres of speaking that students are required to learn. Typically, these are implied and learners are merely asked to speak to a certain situation and topic. The result of this approach is that students do not explicitly learn how certain types of spoken texts (e.g., narratives, recounts and expositions) are structured or understand how the different stages of the discourse move from one to the next in ways that are socially and culturally acceptable (Pryde, 2015). Students also seldom have the opportunity to become aware of spoken grammar and its relevance to learning to speak, particularly in ways that can help them differentiate between the nature of written and spoken language (Goh, 2009). In addition, most materials do not include metacognitive activities where students learn how to plan, monitor and evaluate their immediate speaking performance and overall speaking development over a period of time (Goh and Burns, 2012). With little attention given to explicit teaching of language and discourse, skills and communication strategies, we may be leaving students' speaking development too much to chance.

LEARNERS

Speaking is a cognitively demanding task, and L2 learners face pressure to think and speak at the same time. They tend to focus more on conveying the meaning of what they want to say with whatever linguistic resources are immediately available, and have little cognitive space to formulate their utterances in grammatically correct ways (Skehan, 1998). In other words, they do not have the luxury of time and processing capacity to monitor and evaluate what they say. To buy time for gathering their thoughts, strategic L2 speakers can learn space-holding strategies, such as by saying "I think that's a really interesting point and …". Learners are also often hindered by feelings of anxiety because their performance is open to immediate evaluation by others, and this can affect their self-image (Ohata, 2005; see also Chapter 8). To avoid looking ill-prepared or incompetent, learners may adopt the avoidance strategy of not speaking. Anxiety and negative self-perceptions of language competence can therefore affect learners' willingness to communicate (MacIntyre, 2007). All these are issues that teachers need to address.

L2 speaking is also challenging because learners have very little documentation of their performance once a task is completed. Unlike writing, speaking does not leave evidence of language use (unless speech is recorded), and learners are therefore unable to know where they have expressed themselves clearly or unclearly, analyse their mistakes in the formulation of utterances or assess the accuracy of their pronunciation. The transient nature of spoken language would therefore require learners' speech to be captured permanently for self-assessment and monitoring of progress. Learners who receive feedback on their performance and become more aware of their weaknesses have been shown to improve in their L2 speaking (Tan and Tan, 2010).

One aspect of L2 speaking competence that teachers and learners may overlook is that to be a good L2 speaker, learners need to be effective listeners as well (see Chapter 21). They need to pay attention to how other speakers speak and manage an interaction. By noticing how more competent speakers achieve this through language, gestures and collaborating with other participants in an interaction, learners can learn these abilities themselves. Speaking and listening are also strongly intertwined, particularly in contexts of face-to-face interaction, where the learners switch roles between speaker and listener. In order to ensure that a conversation can proceed and not flag, learners also need to seek clarification and other forms of assistance from their interlocutors.

Apart from using meaning-focused activities that emphasise fluency practice, teachers should help older and adult learners take greater responsibility for their own development. Firstly, they can increase learners' self-awareness as L2 speakers by considering their challenges, strengths and motivation. Secondly, they can deepen their understanding of the nature of L2 speaking processes, and the demands of the speaking tasks and routines that they engage in. This would include noticing features of spoken language such as pronunciation, grammar and discourse structures. Thirdly, they can examine their use of communication strategies and learn to use new ones effectively. All these actions are aimed at strengthening their metacognition, which is the human capacity for knowing about one's cognitive or mental processes and active regulation of these processes towards learning goals (Flavell, 1979). Teachers of children can model the metacognitive process by making explicit these thoughts and processes, so that children can learn to be reflective and strategic in their L2 oracy learning (Jones, 2008).

IMPLICATIONS FOR TEACHING AND ASSESSMENT

L2 speaking requires language learners to manage mental and articulatory processes simultaneously. In addition, it is influenced by affective factors such as confidence and anxiety. Learners therefore need a great deal of support from teachers, as well as peers, to develop in their speaking abilities. The more resourceful adult learners may increase their opportunities to use the language by seeking out conversation partners, using resources such as videos of speakers as their models, and memorising phrases and expressions to give the impression of fluency or enhance the clarity of their speech. Young learners, who are dependent on their teachers and less self-directed, can be supported with more age-appropriate learning tasks.

Activities for teaching speaking may be classified as meaning-focused output as well as language-focused learning activities (Nation and Newton, 2009). Meaning-focused speaking activities include a number of practice activities involving different genres of speech, such as narratives, speeches and conversations, as well as information/communication-gap tasks. Language-focused activities involve learners in focusing on language items such as pronunciation, vocabulary and grammar.

We can add to these two types of activities, a third category: metacognitive activities that develop learners' ability to be reflective and strategic in their learning of L2 speaking. Metacognition is a person's capability to think about their own thinking and learning, as well as orchestrating and managing their thinking and learning processes (Flavell, 1979). Two important components of learners' metacognition that directly impact their L2 learning are metacognitive knowledge and strategy. Examples of metacognitive knowledge for L2 speaking include knowledge of personal factors that influence speaking (person knowledge), demands and skills for L2 speaking (task knowledge), and strategies for improving speaking performance and communication (strategy knowledge).

Strategies are deliberate efforts that learners make to manage and direct cognitive or mental processes in language learning and communication, for the purpose of achieving learning and communication goals (see Chapter 9). They facilitate learning and use, and help learners cope with difficulties or compensate for a lack of linguistic knowledge. In face-to-face interactions, for example, learners may use several words to substitute an idea for which they do not have word in L2, or they may ask the person they are speaking with to slow down or repeat something – these are examples of communication strategies. In addition, learners need to employ learning strategies, particularly metacognitive strategies which enable them to plan, monitor and evaluate their overall L2 speaking endeavours (Table 22.1).

OVERALL SPEAKING DEVELOPMENT	
Planning	• Set short-term and long-term speaking goals. • Identify strengths that can be further developed. • Identify specific areas of weakness, where improvement is needed. • Establish some personal measures of improvement. • Identify strategies for achieving speaking goals.
Monitoring	• Consider progress against speaking goals. • Determine how close one is to achieving short-term and/or long-term speaking goals. • Review speaking goals. • Check whether mistakes are still being repeated in other speaking situations.
Evaluation	• Assess overall speaking achievement against established measures. • Assess the effectiveness of learning strategies. • Assess and review the appropriateness of learning goals.

Table 22.1   Metacognitive Strategies for Managing L2 Speaking Development

One way in which learner metacognition for L2 speaking can be enhanced is through introspection or reflection activities. Such activities can help learners become more aware of their own speaking abilities and achievements, but they need guidance on how to reflect and examine their own development. This is when some help from checklists or descriptions of learning objectives can be useful. With the help of these tools, learners can describe their abilities more precisely, self-assess their progress more confidently and improve their learning of L2 speaking in the process (Glover, 2011).

Based on the discussion of learning speaking in this chapter, the following suggestions for teaching and assessment are proposed:

1. Speaking lessons should include a combination of meaning-focused and language-focused activities. Meaning-focused activities encourage learners to practise their fluency, and provide the context for examining language subsequently.

2. The scope of meaning-focused activities can be broadened to include peer dialogues about learning needs and challenges. Learners can seek their teacher's and peers' advice on how to cope with these issues. Seeing that they are not alone can be reassuring and make the overall learning process more pleasant.

3. Speaking lessons should be viewed as structured learning experiences that enable learners to develop their competence in small manageable parts, so that their speech processes can develop over time.

4. Speaking lessons should allow learners to practise speaking about a topic or work on a task more than once so that they will have the benefit of 'rehearsals' or repetition, which is an important process in skill-learning.

5. Noticing the way specific speaking skills are demonstrated through the use of appropriate and accurate language is important. Lessons should therefore promote the habit of noticing the language that competent speakers produce (i.e., grammar, discourse structure, vocabulary and pronunciation) to achieve communicative goals.

6. Encourage learners to let their teachers know about their communicative needs and learning issues. Keeping a journal and sharing it with their teachers may help learners monitor their progress. Effective prompts focus on eliciting reflections from all dimensions of metacognitive thinking: personal (about themselves), task (about the type and demands of speaking tasks) and strategy (about the strategies they know and use).

7. Integrate metacognitive awareness activities with speaking activities where learners not only evaluate how they have performed, but also plan ways in which they can improve their speaking, manage any negative emotions, and set learning goals. This enables learners to exercise control over their own speaking development.

8. Identify clear criteria for assessment, and identify different points in a course where assessment can be conducted.

9. Assess students formatively by identifying the extent they have developed the skills, knowledge and strategies learnt.

10. Modify some speaking tasks in class into assessment tasks by limiting the usual kinds of support in learning to speak.

11. Encourage peer and self-assessment of speaking by creating opportunities for monitoring and evaluation of selected speaking tasks. Provide learners with tools such as checklists or means of recording themselves when speaking individually or in pairs/groups.

CONCLUSION

Speaking lessons should be powerful opportunities for students to *learn* speaking. Apart from the often-used communication practice activities that promote fluency, L2 learners need to develop knowledge, skills and strategies that can increase their speaking competence. As with other kinds of successful learning, there must be adequate time spent on tasks, avenues to examine one's own performance, seek corrections and improvement, and opportunities to repeat tasks with better skills, knowledge and insights. Learners also need support to develop metacognitive habits of mind with respect to L2 speaking, so that they can exercise control and develop motivation and engagement in the whole endeavour of learning to speak an L2.

Discussion Questions

1. From what you know or have experienced, how do teachers make decisions about the type of speaking activities to use in class?

2. Why do you think that learners' affective needs, such as overcoming anxiety, may sometimes be overlooked in the classroom? What can you do to find out about your students' perspectives?

3. Review the ideas in this chapter and discuss the main considerations when planning a speaking lesson or a speaking course. Are there other considerations that you think are important?

Key Readings

Bygate, M. (2005). Oral second language abilities as expertise. In K. Johnson (Ed.), *Expertise in Second Language Learning and Teaching* (pp. 104–127). Basingstoke, UK: Palgrave Macmillan.

Goh, C. C. M., & Burns, A. (2012). *Teaching Speaking: A Holistic Approach*. New York: Cambridge University Press.

MacIntyre, P. D. (2007). Willingness to communicate in the second language: Understanding the decision to speak as a volitional process. *The Modern Language Journal*, 91(4), 564–576.

Nation, I. S. P., & Newton, J. (2009). *Teaching ESL/EFL Listening and Speaking*. New York: Routledge.

References

Burns, A. (1998). Teaching speaking. *Annual Review of Applied Linguistics*, 18, 102–123.

Bygate, M. (2001). Effects of task repetition on the structure and control of oral language. In M. Bygate, P. Skehan, & M. Swain (Eds.), *Researching Pedagogic Tasks: Second Language Learning, Teaching and Testing* (pp. 23–48). Harlow: Pearson Education.

Bygate, M. (2005). Oral second language abilities as expertise. In K. Johnson (Ed.), *Expertise in Second Language Learning and Teaching* (pp. 104–127). Basingstoke, UK: Palgrave Macmillan.

Chen, Z., & Goh, C. C. M. (2014). Teacher knowledge about oral English instruction and teacher profiles: An EFL perspective. *Teacher Development: An International Journal of Teachers' Professional Development*, 18(1), 81–99.

Flavell, J. H. (1979). Metacognition and cognitive monitoring: A new area of cognitive-developmental inquiry. *American Psychologist*, 34(10), 906–911.

Foster, P., & Ohta, A. S. (2005). Negotiation for meaning and peer assistance in classroom language tasks. *Applied Linguistics*. 26(3), 402–430.

Garton, S., Copland, F., & Burns, A. (2011). Investigating global practices in teaching English to young learners. London: British Council.

Glover, P. (2011). Using CEFR level descriptors to raise university students' awareness of their speaking skills. *Language Awareness*, 20(2), 121–133.

Goh, C. (2009). Perspectives on spoken grammar. *ELT Journal*, 63(4), 303–312.

Goh, C. C. M., & Burns, A. (2012). *Teaching Speaking: A Holistic Approach*. New York: Cambridge University Press.

Johnson, K. (1981). Introduction. In K. Johnson & K. Morrow (Eds.), *Communication in the Classroom* (pp. 1–12). Harlow, UK: Longman.

Jones, D. (2008). Speaking, listening, planning and assessing: The teacher's role in developing metacognitive awareness. In R. Evans & D. Jones (Eds.), *Metacognitive Approaches to Developing Oracy: Developing Speaking and Listening with Young Children* (pp. 1–11). New York: Routledge.

MacIntyre, P. D. (2007). Willingness to communicate in the second language: Understanding the decision to speak as a volitional process. *The Modern Language Journal*, 91(4), 564–576.

Nation, I. S. P., & Newton, J. (2009). *Teaching ESL/EFL listening and speaking*. New York: Routledge.

Ohata, K. (2005). Potential sources of anxiety for Japanese learners of English: Preliminary case interviews with five Japanese college students in the US. *TESL-EJ*, 9(3), 1–21.

Pryde, M. (2015). Teaching language learners to elaborate on their responses: A structured, genre-based approach. *Foreign Language Annals*, 48(2), 168–183.

Skehan, P. (1998). *A Cognitive Approach to Language Learning*. Oxford: Oxford University Press.

Skehan, P., & P. Foster (2005). Strategic and on-line planning: The influence of surprise information and task time on second language performance. In R. Ellis (Ed.), *Planning and Task Performance in A Second Language* (pp. 193–216). Philadelphia: John Benjamins.

Swain, M. (1995). Three functions of output in second language acquisition. In G. Cook & B. Seidlhofer (Eds.), *Principle and Practice in Applied Linguistics* (pp. 125–144). Oxford: Oxford University Press.

Tan, Y. H., & Tan, S. C. (2010). A metacognitive approach to enhancing Chinese language speaking skills with audioblogs. *Australasian Journal of Educational Technology*, 26(7), 1075–1089.

CHAPTER 23

Learning Reading

Lawrence Jun Zhang

INTRODUCTION

Reading is as important a skill for first language (L1) users as it is for second language (L2) learners, particularly in this internet era, where texts are widely available in both print and digital forms. As a result, it is possible for learners of L2 English to learn how to read by different means and in different ways. However, in contexts where access to English is limited, or teachers' spoken language proficiency does not guarantee their successful execution of communicative-oriented teaching activities in the classroom or beyond, learning an L2 often starts with teachers using a short written text, which used to be mainly in print form and is increasingly in digital forms in hypermedia environments. In other contexts where the internet and other resources are available, the learning of L2 reading is proven to be easier when texts are provided with soundtracks, as is the case of audiobooks. Whichever is the case, either print or digital texts are used for teaching students general L2 proficiency in phonetics, phonology, listening, grammar, vocabulary, reading, and basic writing. Although reading is the means by which an L2 is supposed to be learned in some of those contexts, many learners still face challenges in learning L2 reading. Such challenges are evident at the beginning stages and perpetuate in learners' development towards advanced L2 reading skills.

Learning L2 reading is compounded by different ways in which an L2 curriculum is designed and implemented. The complexity increases as regards whether L2 learning takes place inside or outside the classroom, or if necessary resources are available (see Nunan and Richards, 2015). In light of these considerations, this chapter outlines the nature of reading; explains briefly how L2 reading works; highlights factors influencing L2 reading development; addresses the relationships among reading-fluency, reading-rate, and comprehension; shows differences between expert and novice L2 readers; and offers some practical strategies for learning L2 reading.

OVERVIEW

Reading development in L1 speakers and L2 learners shows some parallels. However, the major difference between the two groups lies in the oral/written vocabulary that determines learners' success in learning to read. Evidently, L1 speakers have already developed a large oral lexical base before embarking on learning to read in print or in multimedia environments in their L1. In contrast, L2 learners suffer severe constraints because the L2 they are learning to read is new to them, despite some of them having already developed advanced L1 literacy skills. This is particularly true of adults. Such novelty is a hurdle, which is greater for L2 learners whose L1 writing systems differ from that of the L2 they learn to read. For example, Chinese students who learn to read in English find it much easier than learning to read in Russian as an L2. This is because in their L1 literacy learning, they have already learned how to write Chinese characters with correct strokes in logographic form as well as in Romanised spelling, *pinyin*, so the English alphabet is no stranger for them to begin their L2 English reading with. For those L2 readers whose L1 shares the same alphabet, the degree of challenge is tremendously reduced. In addition to this obvious difference, we need to examine how our understanding of reading determines the way students learn L2 reading.

Reading is a complex process. The complexity becomes acute when contentions on how reading is defined are brought into the debate (see e.g., Adams, 1994). There are at least two opposing views on what reading should entail. Some argue that reading aloud is legitimate L2 reading; others disagree. The disagreement might be based on how the different stages of L2 learners' language development are understood. For the majority of L2 learners, reading aloud is necessary in learning L2 reading, because it helps them to develop the oral reading fluency that is a prerequisite for reaching text-reading fluency (Grabe, 2009). More significantly, reading aloud also gives L2 learners opportunities for practising grapheme-phoneme correspondences, in order to acquire high levels of automatic decoding skills. It also acquaints L2 learners with phonological awareness of how letters and letter combinations are pronounced and articulated to form a word, usually a necessary step for successful lexical access in order to read, regardless of whether the reading materials are in print or digital form (Koda, 2005).

L2 learners' successful and automatic decoding contributes to text-reading fluency, which in turn leads to reading comprehension. As learners' general L2 proficiency increases, their decoding skills help them to make smooth transitions from word-reading to text-reading and consequently reading comprehension. Given that texts are chunks of language that express semantic and pragmatic meanings, text-reading fluency is usually built upon learners' well-developed decoding skills. The National Institute of Child Health and Development (NICHD) defines reading fluency as "the ability to read a text quickly, accurately, and with proper expression" (NICHD, 2008: 3–5), and this ability is a prerequisite for subsequent reading comprehension. What needs to be made clearer is that the accuracy and rate at which learners read words in isolation and in context are crucial, but that learners need to move beyond that confinement so that they can develop text-reading fluency when they read words in passages, where these words are connected in meaningful ways, in specific contexts with complete and complex sentence structures (Kim, 2015: 459).

As learners' L2 proficiency increases, the primary focus in the reading process should be on how much comprehension readers achieve; hence meaning making is paramount, no matter whether the reading act takes place vis-à-vis a printed or a digital text. Obviously, the reading act itself for meaning making is determined and affected by at least three important variables: (1) reader; (2) text; and (3) reader-text interaction (Rumelhart, 1977; Zhang, 2010), which are discussed in some detail next.

The reader: It must be understood that L2 readers are not just members of a homogeneous group (Bernhardt, 1991). They are different in at least four respects:

1. different L1 literacy levels;
2. different L1 acquisition experience;
3. different L1 and L2 linguistic relationships; and
4. different degrees of shared cultural knowledge.

These factors need to be considered, because they might either facilitate or hinder the learning of L2 reading.

The text: Written texts are not always reader-friendly to L2 learners. They often have difficult vocabulary and organisational/discourse structures that are different from what L2 learners know about their L1 texts. Cohesive devices for building text cohesion are also different. Cohesion usually indicates how a text is organised and what purpose it is intended to achieve. Halliday and Hasan (1976), for example, list a number of devices that writers usually use to build text cohesion. These devices include synonymy, antonymy, repetition, paraphrase, substitution, transition markers, ellipsis, and parallelism, as well as other types of devices for linking the elements in a text. These, in turn, contribute to text coherence (see also Grabe, 2009).

Reader-text interaction: Different text types or genres serve different purposes (see Chapter 25). For this reason, a narrative text is different from an expository one, not only in the choice of lexical items, discourse structure and other linguistic choices, but also in their intended purposes. For example, a narrative text is to tell a story, or a series of stories, for entertaining the audience. An expository text usually discusses an issue, or argues for or against a particular position. Evidently, no texts are exactly of only one type or genre, but L2 readers might not be familiar with the ways in which these text types represent the information in them. This is really the time when readers have to interact with the text, using all their linguistic knowledge, schemata, and their L1 discourse knowledge, among other things, to approach the L2 text for ultimate comprehension.

Various 'models' have been proposed to show theorists' views on, or conceptualisations of, cognitive processes that are supposed to be involved in L1 reading. These are complex models. L2 reading, like L1 reading, is also regarded significantly as a mental activity. Given that all the L2 reading 'models' are based on L1 research-driven models, and no unique model specific to L2 reading is independent of L1 research (Ehrich, Zhang, Mu, and Ehrich, 2013), I briefly review three hypothetical models: 'Top-Down', 'Bottom-Up', and 'Interactive' models (Anderson, 2016). These models are useful in helping us understand how L2 readers might approach texts in different ways.

As discussed above, scholars view reading differently. For some, reading is a process where meaning takes central stage (e.g., Goodman, 1996); for others, decoding is of primary importance (Adams, 1994; Birch, 2015). The former is known as a 'top-down' approach, where the meaning-driven or reader-driven nature is explicit. As Goodman (1996:126) states, reading is "a psycholinguistic guessing game", where much of the meaning resides in the reader, who needs to interpret the text to derive it. Readers' top-down processing is essential to successful reading, and in many instances, reading involves readers' existing schematic knowledge (Goodman, 1996). Such a view is also widely shared among L2 researchers about readers who are already literate in their L1, because there are non-decoding factors contributing to reading success (Koda, 2005). In this internet age, the 'top-down' models probably become even more value-laden when L2 readers surf various websites for information, using many of their L1 strategies and experiences.

Advocates for 'bottom-up' models view reading as a process, where readers have to go through the text in a more linear fashion, starting from the smallest unit in print, or in digital, forms. Frequently, such a process is mainly text-bound. Word recognition is a highly regarded skill because of the emphasis on lexical reading. Readers are not expected to engage in actively interpreting the text meaning; in this view, meaning is self-evident as soon as you are able to decode all the words.

Recent understanding about L2 reading has been quite controversial, with some promoting the idea of developing learners' higher-level processes, such as metacognition and reading strategies (Zhang, 2008, 2010), with others calling for returning to the basics (Birch, 2015). The basics upon which L2 readers always depend are essential decoding skills for lexical access, in order to read and achieve comprehension successfully (Bernhardt, 1991; Birch, 2015).

As a synthesis of the above two polarised views on reading, several 'interactive' models have been proposed. For the sake of space, I focus on Stanovich's (2000) 'interactive-compensatory model', because other models are too technical and psycholinguistic in orientation. Stanovich has argued that in L1 reading, especially for beginning readers, top-down processes and bottom-up processes complement each other. He posits that poor L1 readers do not guess as accurately as their skilled peers, because skilled readers have such accurate and automatic perceptual abilities in word recognition that they do not usually need to guess; whereas poor readers have no way but to guess, often with limited success, due to their lack of linguistic proficiency.

Following this line of explication, we can see clearly that learning to read becomes a matter of developing highly accurate decoding skills. This means, too, that there is a 'short-circuit' effect for L2 learners whose linguistic proficiency is too low to make efficient reading possible (Alderson, 1984). Interactive models of reading in their broad sense have also been successfully advocated for L2 reading instruction, despite controversies over their practicality (see e.g., Bernhardt, 1991). Bottom-up and top-down models of reading are two polarities of the reading models mentioned above. Each has its own ways of helping teachers understand how learners learn L2 reading. But in reality, scholars comment that no exclusive 'bottom-up' reading processes take place in any individual (e.g., Hedgcock and Ferris, 2009).

Key Learning Issues

In learning L2 reading, a myriad of factors influences L2 readers' progress towards success. These factors are closely related to the three variables that determine and affect meaning making in L2 reading, which were discussed earlier in this chapter: (1) reader, (2) text, and (3) reader-text interaction. Specifically, seven key aspects relating to learning L2 reading are discussed in detail below (see also Bernhardt, 1991; Hedgcock and Ferris, 2009), which are manifested in learner individual differences (LIDs). In effect, these LIDs make L2 readers a dynamically diverse group along a continuum.

For a clearer understanding, these LIDs are categorised in broad terms into:

1. cognitive development and style preferences;
2. working memory;
3. reading performance and competence in the L1 and their relationship with the L2;
4. metalinguistic knowledge;
5. metacognitive knowledge;
6. different cultural traditions and practices that shape and define L2 reading; and
7. motivation for L2 reading success (see also Aebersold and Field, 1997).

In order to help L2 learners learn L2 reading successfully, teachers need to consider these differences carefully. For example, not all L2 readers have the same level of motivation for learning L2 reading. Nor do they have the same schema knowledge about the same text that they read or use the same strategies for learning L2 reading either in a traditional mode or multimedia or hypermedia environments (Nielsen, 1990). I explain these in detail below.

Cognitive development and style preferences: Learners' cognitive development and style preferences are significant in influencing L2 reading development. In fact, the degree of cognitive maturity impacts young language learners in learning L2 reading. As regards young adult or mature L2 learners, such a debate is less relevant, as these learners have different levels of proficiency in their L1, different L1 reading strategies, varying levels of motivations for learning L2 reading, and fairly personal decisions on their identity choices.

L2 learners, like any other human population, are born with different personalities, too. Some are more extrovert and others more introvert and reticent. Some L2 learners are inclined to learn L2 reading faster when the words and text are presented alongside with visuals and sound (for example on the internet), whereas others prefer hands-on activities that engage them proactively (Reid, 1995). Such learning style differences contribute to varying degrees of success in learning L2 reading.

Working memory: Also worth noting are various other factors relating to LIDs, which play a significant role equally for young adult or mature learners in an L2-rich environment in learning L2 reading. For example, all individuals are different in working memory capacity, some having more powerful working memory than others. Scientific evidence shows that working memory is directly related to language learning success (Wen, 2016). Although training can improve one's working memory, it is basically a trait that a person is born with (see e.g., Grabe, 2009; Koda, 2005).

Reading performance and competence in the L1 and their relationship with the L2: As mentioned above, L2 learners of English who come from an L1 whose writing system is drastically different from English (e.g., Russian, Japanese, or Chinese) will encounter difficulty in learning to read in L2 English. Such difficulty may be reflected in word recognition and the process of reading. In addition to the orthographic differences that may lead to difficulty in learning L2 reading, L2 learners' L1 performance and competence have been found to be closely related to their L2 reading (Alderson, 1984; Koda, 2005). L2 readers whose L1 reading proficiency and skills are stronger can learn L2 reading more effectively than their weaker counterparts. There is a possibility of skill transfer when reading in an L2. However, illiterate L1 speakers find it hard to learn to read in an L2, as compared with those who are already literate in their L1 (see e.g., Birch 2015; Koda, 2005).

A classic question that Alderson (1984) raised, about whether L2 reading is a language problem or a reading problem, has been successfully addressed in research over the past three decades. Various studies have now concluded that successful L2 reading requires both language ability and reading skills (see Grabe, 2009). There is a threshold that L2 learners need to achieve before they can employ any of the relatively higher-level processes such as reading strategies for meaning making. High L2 proficiency facilitates successful learning of L2 reading.

Metalinguistic knowledge: Learners' metalinguistic knowledge consists of their ability to describe and discuss aspects relating to the language by using specific grammatical concepts. Young adult and mature readers are different from children in the degree of explicitness in the knowledge they have about the language, with the former having stronger metalinguistic knowledge (see Chapters 1–3). Different cultures place different values on such knowledge in learning L2 reading and it is particularly the case in L2 programmes for adults.

Metacognitive knowledge: Flavell (1979) thinks that students' metacognitive knowledge comprises their understanding about themselves (person knowledge), learning strategies (strategy knowledge), and learning tasks (task knowledge). L2 learners' metacognitive knowledge has been found to be an important factor affecting their L2 reading success (Zhang, 2010). Anderson (2016) summarises that students' metacognitive knowledge guides and determines their success in self-assessment, understanding learning tasks for taking appropriate action, and use of strategies for effective L2 reading (Zhang, 2016).

Different cultural traditions and practices: Different cultural traditions and practices define and shape L2 reading in different ways. Therefore, L2 students of different L1 cultural backgrounds approach L2 reading differently, due to their previous learning experiences and values-laden practices in understanding and learning L1 literacy. Some cultures value oracy more than literacy, and other cultures do just the opposite. So, readers of different L1 backgrounds might highly regard reading aloud, recitation, and reading for comprehension in different ways. Because of varied L1 reading practices, the kind of reader schemas they bring to bear on their L2 reading interact necessarily with their reading process and comprehension.

Motivation for L2 reading success: To adapt from the inventor Thomas Edison, "Success is 1% inspiration and 99% perspiration". Success in L2 reading is very much analogous to the process of scientific discovery, that is, a highly motivated enterprise. Research shows that much of L2 reading success depends on the level of motivation and effort that learners invest in learning L2 reading. How students attribute value, show their attitude to, and enjoy L2 reading are some typical aspects relating to L2 readers' motivation (Unrau and Quirk, 2014). High levels of motivation and consistent effort contribute to L2 reading success, because motivated and hard-working L2 learners take stock of opportunities for learning and developing their L2 reading skills (see Chapter 6).

IMPLICATIONS FOR TEACHING AND ASSESSMENT

The seven areas of significance presented above have implications for how to develop L2 reading skills. For successful L2 reading to happen, L2 learners really need to take them into serious consideration. Since successful L2 reading is determined by learners' L2 language proficiency and effective ways or strategies for approaching L2 reading, the learning of L2 reading should involve both lower-level processes, such as decoding for word-reading, and higher-level processes that focus on comprehension. If we take L2 reading as a reader-centred activity, with due consideration of the individual/cognitive factors mentioned above, we have to see how novices distinguish themselves from expert L2 readers in the way they learn L2 reading. Many studies have shown the role of reading strategies in learning L2 reading successfully (Hedgcock and Ferris, 2009). Through awareness-raising activities, many L2 readers will find that their L1 reading strategies are naturally brought into their L2 reading to facilitate their reading comprehension.

Understandably, learners of different abilities and individual/cognitive differences need to learn how to monitor their progress, especially the effectiveness of strategies they use in developing their L2 reading ability. Assessment *of* learning is important, but assessment *for* learning (AfL) should be the guiding principle, if assessment is to be implemented at all. AfL should be a joint effort by teachers and students. Teachers and students work together in realising the learning goals, by changing the role of students from passive recipients to that of active decision-makers (Black, Harrison, Lee, Marshall, and Wiliam, 2004). The desire to learn decides to what extent students are willing to get involved in AfL, especially in activities such as self-assessment, self-monitoring and peer assessment (Carless, 2012).

To learn L2 reading successfully from the start, learners need to practise word-reading, or decoding skills, to get acquainted with grapheme-phoneme (form-sound) correspondences. These activities or strategies can be regarded as part of the metalinguistic awareness enterprise. Word-recognition fluency, once achieved, paves the way for passage/text-reading fluency. Practising reading rate and text-reading fluency, and reading for improving local and global comprehension of texts, all contribute to developing lower-level and higher-level processing skills. Building large sight/recognition vocabulary is a continuing process for improving L2 reading. Extensive reading of short texts suitable to the learners' L2 proficiency and age, either in print or on the internet, can be provided to serve these purposes.

Reading strategies are readers' deliberate and effortful mental or physical problem-solving moves in approaching a text for comprehension (Hudson, 2007). Therefore, student engagement in strategic reading in a dialogic learning environment should be advocated, so that strategies are incorporated into the reading programme for developing students into strategic readers, alongside the development of linguistic proficiency. Once the reading strategies become automatically available in the reading process, L2 readers, like their L1 counterparts, are said to have already acquired the reading skills for efficient reading comprehension. As Grabe (2009) comments, there are various possibilities for cultivating reading strategies that benefit L2 students' reading comprehension. Following Grabe's (2009: 332) synthesis of research findings, I would like to provide the following, non-exhaustive list of what researchers have found to be useful for developing students' L2 reading skills:

- Making predictions of upcoming text by reading the title.
- Becoming aware of discourse structure using genre knowledge (main ideas, main organizational patterns, clear signals of text structure, cohesive devices/markers in text).
- Being alert to the purpose of text.
- Skimming for a gist of the text.
- Scanning for main ideas.
- Activating schema knowledge to facilitate comprehension.
- Making inferences for drawing conclusions.
- Promoting extensive reading for continuous growth in vocabulary and reading ability.

Although the learning of L2 reading should be a joint effort by students and the teacher, AfL as teacher-initiated practice is important for evaluating students' learning outcomes for the purposes of supporting or improving their reading abilities. Such assessment usually gauges L2 students' knowledge, and skills that are learnt over time. Quite a number of AfL techniques are available and serve two main purposes: assessing reading abilities and assessing reading skills. These techniques range from teachers waiting 3–4 minutes for students' answers, teachers discussing the answers with students, and students engaged in group work for solving L2 reading problems, to students reviewing their own learning effectiveness. Teachers are not so quick in giving grades; instead, comments are offered for highlighting areas for improvement (see Grabe, 2009). Grabe (ibid.) points out that a number of strategy tasks are usually assessment practices. These strategies include, e.g.: categorising statements into different kinds (explicitly mentioned, inferable, or not invoked in the text); using the right schema knowledge; making a decision on the most suitable summary; identifying the organisational structure of a text; and classifying main ideas and supporting details, among many other strategies.

Given the significant role of motivation, teachers and students might need to work together in building up a strong relationship for developing the reading skills that these students aspire to possess (Unrau and Quirk, 2014). A wide array of practical strategies for motivating L2 learners in and outside the classroom includes: L2 peers reading together; performing the reading text; making full use of multimedia resources for reading; seeking and offering peer-feedback on reading comprehension; and engaging in discussions about the text, among many others.

Conclusion

This chapter discusses issues related to L2 reading, which range from how reading is understood, what is involved in learning L2 reading, and how to develop L2 reading proficiency and L2 reading skills. Such discussion is not only relevant to learning L2 reading through printed texts but also materials available in various forms, notably those hypertexts in hypermedia on the internet or other learning platforms. The ultimate aim of such discussion is to better understand L2 learners, so that assistance and instruction can be offered for them to become independent L2 readers.

Discussion Questions

1. In what ways is learning L2 reading, in either print or digital form, both a language problem and a reading problem?

2. In what ways can you monitor the reading strategies for reading print or online materials for the assessment of learning L2 reading?

Key Readings

Alderson, J. C. (2000). *Assessing Reading*. Cambridge: Cambridge University Press.

Anderson, N. J. (2016). *Exploring Second Language Reading: Issues and Strategies* (2nd ed.). Boston: Heinle/Thomson.

Grabe, W. (2009). *Reading in a Second Language: Moving from Theory to Practice*. Cambridge: Cambridge University Press.

Hedgcock, J. S., & Ferris, D. R. (2009). *Teaching Readers of English: Students, Texts, and Contexts*. New York: Routledge.

National Institute of Child Health and Human Development (NICHD) (2008). *Report of the National Reading Panel: Teaching Children to Read*. Washington, D.C.: U.S. Government Printing.

References

Adams, M. J. (1994). *Beginning to Read: Thinking and Learning about Print*. Cambridge, MA: MIT Press.

Aebersold, J. A., & Field, M. L. (1997). *From Reader to Reading Teacher*. Cambridge: Cambridge University Press.

Alderson, J. C. (1984). Reading in a foreign language: A reading problem or a language problem? In J.C. Alderson & A. H. Urquhart (Eds.), *Reading in a Foreign Language* (pp. 1–27). London: Longman.

Anderson, N. J. (2016). *Exploring Second Language Reading: Issues and Strategies* (2nd ed.). Boston: Heinle/Thomson.

Bernhardt, E. B. (1991). *Reading Development in a Second Language: Theoretical, Empirical, and Classroom Perspectives*. Norwood, NJ: Ablex.

Birch, B. M. (2015). *English L2 Reading: Getting to the Bottom*. New York: Routledge.

Black, P., Harrison, C., Lee, C., Marshall, B., & Wiliam, D. (2004). Working inside the black box: Assessment for learning in the classroom. *Phi Delta Kappan*, 86(1), 8–21.

Carless, D. (2012). *From Testing to Productive Student Learning: Implementing Formative Assessment in Confucian-heritage Settings*. New York: Routledge.

Ehrich, J., Zhang, L. J., Mu, J. C., & Ehrich, L. (2013). Are alphabetic-language derived models of L2 reading relevant to L1 logographic background readers? *Language Awareness*, 22(1), 39–55.

Flavell, J. H. (1979). Metacognition and cognitive monitoring: A new area of cognitive–developmental inquiry. *American Psychologist*, 34(10), 906–911.

Goodman, K. (1996). *On Reading*. Portsmouth, NH: Heinemann.

Grabe, W. (2009). *Reading in a Second Language: Moving from Theory to Practice*. Cambridge: Cambridge University Press.

Halliday, M. A. K., & Hasan, R. (1976). *Cohesion in English*. London: Longman.

Hedgcock, J. S., & Ferris, D. R. (2009). *Teaching Readers of English: Students, Texts, and Contexts*. New York: Routledge.

Hudson, T. (2007). *Teaching Second Language Reading*. Oxford: Oxford University Press.

Kim, Y. G. (2015). Developmental, component-based model of reading fluency: An investigation of predictors of word-reading fluency, text-reading fluency, and reading comprehension. *Reading Research Quarterly*, 50(4), 459–481.

Koda, K. (2005). *Insights into Second Language Reading*. New York: Cambridge University Press.

National Institute of Child Health and Human Development (NICHD) (2008). *Report of the National Reading Panel: Teaching Children to Read*. Washington, D.C.: U.S. Government Printing.

Nielsen, J. (1990). *Hypertext and Hypermedia*. New York: Academic Press.

Nunan, D., & Richards, J. C. (2015). *Language Learning Beyond the Classroom*. New York: Routledge.

Reid, J. (1995). *Learning Styles in the ESL/EFL Classroom*. Boston, MA: Heinle & Heinle.

Rumelhart, D. E. (1977). Toward an interactive model of reading. In S. Dornič (Ed.), *Attention and Performance VI* (pp. 575–603). Hillsdale, NJ: Lawrence Erlbaum.

Stanovich, K. E. (2000). *Progress in Understanding Reading: Scientific Foundations and New Frontiers*. New York: Guilford Press.

Unrau, N. J., & Quirk, M. (2014). Reading motivation and reading engagement: Clarifying commingled conceptions. *Reading Psychology*, 35(3), 260–284.

Wen, Z. (2016). *Working Memory and Second Language Learning*. Bristol, UK: Multilingual Matters.

Zhang, L. J. (2008). Constructivist pedagogy in strategic reading instruction: Exploring pathways to learner development in the English as a second language (ESL) classroom. *Instructional Science*, 36(2), 89–116.

Zhang, L. J. (2010). A dynamic metacognitive systems account of Chinese university students' knowledge about EFL reading. *TESOL Quarterly*, 44(2), 320–353.

Zhang, L. J. (2016). A dynamic metacognitive systems perspective on language learner autonomy. In R. Barnard & J. Li (Eds.), *Language Learner Autonomy: Teachers' Beliefs and Practices in East Asian Contexts* (pp. 150–166). Phnom Penh: IDP Education.

CHAPTER 24

Learning Writing

Neomy Storch

INTRODUCTION

In recent decades, we have witnessed extraordinary growth in educational programmes, research, and publications on second language (L2) writing[1], predominantly in English as a second or foreign language. Much of this interest can be attributed to changes in technology and the forces of globalization. Advances in technology have led to changes in the ways we communicate: more and more of our professional and social communicative acts are carried out in written form (e.g., emails, texts). Globalisation in our educational sector and workplaces has also meant that for many students and professionals, these communicative acts are being carried out in their L2. Thus there has been a growing need to learn to write competently in the L2. Another reason for this burgeoning research on L2 writing is the recognition that L2 writing facilitates L2 learning, because when learners write they focus on how best to express their ideas (see Manchón, 2011 on the notion of 'writing to learn' a second language).

This chapter begins by describing the processes and knowledge sources involved in producing a text, and what distinguishes writing in the L2 from writing in the first language (L1). It then proceeds to discuss some of the learning issues that have been identified and debated in research on L2 writing. Although some of these issues are of relevance to all L2 learners, this chapter focuses on issues that are of particular relevance to adult L2 learners learning to write for academic and professional purposes (see Chapters 1 and 2, which discuss learning issues faced by younger learners). The final section discusses the implications these learning issues have for L2 writing instruction and assessment.

OVERVIEW

Our understanding of what it means to be able to write in the L2 was initially informed by models of L1 composing processes. The most often cited models of writing (e.g., Hayes, 1996) present writing as a complex, recursive and generative process. It involves a number of phases, such as planning, drafting and redrafting, during which the writer draws on a range of information sources, including knowledge of language, text structure, and topic.

Various published syntheses of research (e.g., Silva, 1993) have shown that the composing processes in the L1 and the L2 are similar. However, L2 writers do seem to devote more attention to vocabulary searches and deliberations about grammar, often employing their L1 as a resource. Furthermore, at lower levels of L2 proficiency, retrieval of linguistic information is slower (Shoonen, Snellings, Stevenson, and van Geldern, 2009), and revisions tend to be at the word level. More proficient learners tend to revise larger chunks. Shoonen et al. (2009) propose that allocating scarce attentional resources to accuracy means less attention being available to content elaboration and higher order revision, resulting in lower quality texts.

However, as Candlin and Hyland (1999: 2) point out, writing "is much more than the generation of text-linguistic products." Writing, and particularly writing for academic and professional purposes, is now perceived as a situated social activity. What and how we write are influenced by a host of factors, including the specific context in which we write, institutional and cultural conventions in the broader context, and the tools used. Writing is also perceived as dialogic: when composing, the writer interacts with the text and with people – the intended reader, members of the disciplinary or professional community to which the writer belongs or wishes to belong, and the voices of other authors who have written about the topic. When writing, we communicate not only meaning but also our identity. Decisions, whether conscious or not, about the choice of words and structures, what content to include, and how to structure the text reflect our voice. For L2 writers, it is these broader dimensions of writing that often seem to pose the greatest challenges.

KEY LEARNING ISSUES

A considerable and growing body of research has investigated the differences in texts produced by L1 and L2 writers, as well as the salient features of texts produced by L2 writers at various levels of proficiency. This body of research highlights the difficulties that L2 writers face, particularly when writing for academic or professional purposes. It also alludes to the nature of L2 writing instruction needed in order to address these difficulties.

LINGUISTIC AND GRAMMATICAL QUALITY OF TEXTS

Despite the attention L2 writers pay to choice of vocabulary and grammatical accuracy when composing, research findings show that academic texts written by L2 writers show evidence of a limited lexical and syntactic repertoire. For example, Hinkel's (2003) large-scale empirical analysis of compositions written by first year university students showed that even relatively proficient L2 learners produced texts that differed significantly to texts produced by L1 writers. The texts produced by L2 writers were marked by the use of relatively simple syntactic and lexical features, features that are prevalent in conversational discourse rather than formal written discourse. Storch (2009), who compared the writing of international ESL students at the beginning and end of their first academic semester in an English medium university, found that although the students' vocabulary became more formal, their writing showed no progress in terms of lexical and syntactic sophistication, nor in grammatical accuracy. These findings suggest that immersion in an L2 context may not be sufficient to attain the high levels of linguistic proficiency required in writing for academic purposes.

TEXT STRUCTURE: RHETORICAL ORGANISATION, GENRES

An issue that has aroused much debate in the field of L2 writing is the influence of the L1 on L2 writing. The issue was originally raised by Kaplan (1966) in his work on contrastive rhetoric. Kaplan suggested that the preferred textual rhetorical organisation of certain language groups is unique, and therefore, if there are differences between learners' L1 and L2 preferred rhetorical patterns, such differences will result in a negative transfer. Texts written by L2 writers will show evidence of their L1 rhetorical organisation and affect comprehensibility.

Although the notion of a culturally unique rhetorical pattern has been criticised (e.g., Kubota and Lehner, 2004), research has shown that interlinguistic influences do exist, but that they are mediated by factors such as learners' previous writing instruction, writing experiences, and L2 proficiency. For example, a series of studies by Rinnert and Kobayashi (2009) found that previous L1 writing instruction shapes learners' L2 texts, particularly novice L2 writers. The researchers found that Japanese L2 learners of English who received intensive L1 writing instruction tended to rely heavily on the use of personal reflections in their L2 writing, a feature associated with Japanese texts. A subsequent case study (Kobayashi and Rinnert, 2013) of a multilingual writer (Japanese, English and Chinese) confirmed that the learning experiences, and proficiency in any languages learnt, influence the structure and the kind of information included in an L2 text.

The extensive literature on genres (see Chapter 25) has extended our understanding of text structure. Genres refer to "abstract, socially recognised ways of using language" (Hyland, 2002: 114). We tend to associate genres with text types, ranging from personal (e.g., invitations) and school-based genres (e.g., essays) to more professional genres (e.g., medical case reports). Genres show distinct organisational and linguistic features that are the product of social processes related to specific discourse communities. These distinct features are easily recognised and reproduced by members of the discourse communities.

In the field of academic writing, the work of Swales (1990, 2004) has been particularly influential. Swales produced a framework of information included in sections of research articles in English. The framework is organised into moves and steps: the purposes the moves serve, and the linguistic features associated with each step. The framework has been deployed in a large number of studies analysing academic genres in different disciplines and professions. However, researchers have also raised concerns about the dangers of treating genres as stable and devoid of personal intentions (e.g., Prior and Bilbro, 2012).

Genre scholars (e.g., Hyland, 2007) claim that all writers (L1 and L2) need to become aware of the expected rhetorical and linguistic features of certain 'valued genres' in order to be accepted as legitimate members of their discourse (academic or professional) community (see Chapters 14 and 15). However, for L2 writers, the challenge of mastering these genres may be compounded by cross-cultural differences. Studies comparing research articles produced in the same disciplinary area but in different languages (e.g., Loi, 2010; Sheldon, 2009) identified some cross-cultural differences. For example, Loi (2010) found differences in the number of moves and steps in articles written in the field of educational psychology by Chinese scholars in Chinese and in English.

However, cross-cultural differences do not necessarily mean negative transfer. Interviews with L2 learners (e.g., Leki, 2011; Morton, Storch, and Thompson, 2015) show that when confronted with new literacy demands, L2 writers draw not only on their knowledge of L1 genres but also on knowledge gained in their previous training in the L1 and the L2. Furthermore, the impact of previously acquired genre knowledge is complex and varies across individuals. Leki's findings (2011), for example, highlight the role played by learners' perceptions. Learners are unlikely to transfer and adapt previously acquired genre knowledge to new contexts if these new learning contexts are perceived as dissimilar to their previous contexts.

USE AND INCORPORATION OF SOURCES

Academic writing usually requires students to write research-based papers in which the students engage with, and incorporate, various source materials. One of the issues that has received much research attention is that of plagiarism. The term plagiarism is used to describe the act of copying unacceptable amounts of texts from source material, or the unattributed use of the work of others (Pecorari, 2008). The problem seems to be amplified by the availability of electronic sources of information, which makes 'cutting and pasting' so much easier than previously. Although the issue of plagiarism is not confined to L2 writers, there are indications that it is found more often in texts produced by L2 writers (Keck, 2006).

A range of reasons have been offered in the literature to explain this behaviour. Some, such as Pecorari (2008), suggest that this behaviour is not deliberate but due to difficulties L2 learners have in the correct incorporation of source material (e.g., paraphrasing and summarising) particularly if they are novice L2 writers with limited linguistic resources. However, even relatively advanced L2 learners have admitted their lack of confidence in this aspect of academic writing and a tendency to over-rely on the language and ideas of source texts (Pecorari, 2008; Thompson, Morton, and Storch, 2013). Others suggest that plagiarism may be due to cultural differences in how writers treat source material and notions of authorship and intellectual property (Pennycook, 1996). For example, Rinnert and Kobayashi (2005) reported that their Japanese students did not perceive borrowing without acknowledgement of the words of others as an act of transgression.

EXPRESSING AUTHORIAL IDENTITY

Research-based writing, particularly at graduate level, requires writers not only to incorporate and display a familiarity with the source materials, but also to express a stance about the material (Paltridge and Starfield, 2007). Writers are expected to position themselves in relation to the texts incorporated, and to express their distinctive authorial voice to their anticipated reader (Thompson, 2012). For students originating from linguistic and educational backgrounds that have different epistemological traditions to the L2 traditions, the notion and the construction of authorial identity in their L2 writing may present a significant challenge. For example, cross-linguistic research has shown that the construction of self-representation in academic texts is not the same across cultures (e.g., Sheldon, 2009).

L2 writers may also not be aware of how to construct an authorial identity in the L2. For example, Luzón's (2009) corpus analysis, which compared the use of the first person plural pronoun in English engineering reports produced by L2 learners of English and by expert L1 writers, showed that the L2 learners were not aware of how such pronoun constructions could be used strategically to construct their authorial identities as confident members of this discourse community.

IMPLICATIONS FOR TEACHING AND ASSESSMENT

Writing, whether in the L1 or the L2, is a recursive, socially situated, and dialogic process in which the writer communicates an intended meaning to a reader who expects the text to conform to particular rhetorical and linguistic conventions. This conceptualisation of writing supports a hybrid process/genre approach to writing instruction (Badger and White, 2000). This approach entails exposing learners to model genres, raising their awareness of rhetorical and linguistic features of these genres, engaging them in producing multiple drafts of the targeted genres, and providing them with feedback on these drafts. The genres selected for classroom activities and for assessment should be 'valued' genres: the type that students need to master if preparing for further study and professional pursuits which require them to write in the L2.

The approach to instruction also needs to take into account the issues that L2 writers face. Despite the merits of a genre approach to L2 instruction (Hyland, 2011), research on the differences in the linguistic quality of texts produced by L1 and L2 writers, even relatively proficient L2 writers, suggests a need for explicit (reactive or pre-emptive) teaching of formal academic or professional vocabulary and sophisticated grammatical structures. L2 writers who receive such explicit instruction, and targeted corrective feedback on their drafts, show noticeable improvements in their writing (see Storch and Tapper, 2009).

A genre approach to L2 writing instruction may assume that learners are 'clean slates'; that is, that they have no knowledge of the taught genre. Leki (2011) suggests that a more productive approach with such learners begins by tapping into learners' existing genre knowledge and building on that knowledge. Discussions with learners could reveal perceived cross-cultural similarities and differences, or perceptions arising from previous instruction. Others (e.g., Benesch, 2001) suggest a more critical approach, where L2 learners are encouraged to question rather than accept and reproduce the textual features embodied in valued genres. Hyland (2007, 2011), however, queries L2 writers' ability and willingness to question model genres. Harwood and Hadley (2004) suggest a compromise position, where L2 writers are taught the dominant features of disciplinary discourses, sourced from examples identified in discipline-specific corpora relevant to students' fields of study, whilst simultaneously recognising and respecting the need to explore cultural and rhetorical differences.

L2 writing classes for academic purposes also need to go beyond teaching learners how to use sources (paraphrasing, referencing conventions), to also include a discussion of why scholars incorporate and acknowledge the writing of others. Similarly, developing L2 writers' voice or authorial identity needs to go beyond a textual analysis of the linguistic means that experts use to reflect their voice. Wette (2014) recommends modelling the cognitive processes involved in the incorporation of source materials. Such modelling may also raise learners' awareness of how an authorial position takes shape. Canagarajah (2015) describes the kind of activities he implemented in his L2 writing class, which treat the resources that L2 (multilingual) writers have at their disposal as affordances to be drawn on. The activities included online discussions, peer feedback and textual analysis, as well as reflective online journals. In the journals, the students were asked to reflect on their evolving texts and on their trajectory as L2 writers. Canagarajah then presents a case study account of a learner's growing awareness of her multiple identities and her struggles with developing a voice. These struggles, however, ultimately lead to greater understanding of her literacy trajectory and the development of a more informed, multi-layered voice; merging sources from the past (previous training) and present (norms of academic writing in USA universities). At the same time, the journal entries provided the instructor with an opportunity to reflect and evaluate his own position on various key constructs in authorial voice construction.

Canagarajah's (2015) case study and other case study research (e.g., Morton et al, 2015) question traditional classroom assessment practices with a sole focus on the final product, and research on L2 writing development with a tendency to deploy only text-based measures (e.g., measures of linguistic accuracy, complexity and fluency). These practices and measures may not capture learners' evolving trajectories as L2 writers. For L2 writers, and particularly L2 writers learning to write for academic and professional purposes, writing development involves not only producing well written texts but also a growing understanding of the social and situated nature of writing and a greater awareness of themselves as writers. One assessment strategy is to engage students in peer response activities and assess the comments they provide on their peers' writing, in order to measure over time whether the learners develop greater insights into what constitutes successful texts. Another strategy is to include a reflective journal as an assessment task (e.g., online blogs) as illustrated in Canagarajah's (2015) study. Such journals may encourage learners to reflect on their writing trajectory, and at the same time enable teachers (and researchers) to assess whether learners are developing a deeper understanding of the complex nature of academic writing and of themselves as L2 writers.

CONCLUSION

The main purpose of this chapter was to consider what it means to learn to write in an L2, particularly at advanced levels. The chapter began broadly by describing the kind of cognitive processes and knowledge sources that learners draw on when producing a written text (in any language). It then focused more narrowly on the challenges of writing in the L2 for academic and professional purposes. The challenges discussed included mastery of advanced linguistic resources, an awareness of the distinguishing traits of valued genres in particular disciplines or professions, and the ability to incorporate source material appropriately and at the same time position oneself in relation to these materials. In order to address these often inter-related challenges, some pedagogical and assessment related suggestions were discussed, such as the use of reflective diaries (e.g., blogs). The development of innovative teaching and assessment practices is clearly an area requiring further investigation.

Discussion Questions

1. If the writing processes for L1 and L2 writers are similar, should L1 and L2 novice writers be allocated to different writing classes?

2. Has writing in the L2 or instruction in L2 writing affected your writing in your L1? If so, how?

3. Can you think of examples of genres that have changed over time? Which features changed? How can these changes be explained?

Key Readings

Belcher, D. (2012). Considering what we know and what we need to know about second language writing. *Applied Linguistics Review*, 3, 131–150.

Casanave, C. (2004). *Controversies in Second Language Writing: Dilemmas and Decisions in Research and Instruction*. Ann Arbor, MI: The University of Michigan Press.

Le Ha, P. (2009). Strategic, passionate but academic: Am I allowed in my writing? *Journal of English for Academic Purposes*, 8, 134–146.

Leki, I. (2007), *Undergraduates in a Second Language: Challenges and Complexities of Academic Literacy Development*. New York: Routledge.

Tardy, C. (2006). Researching first and second language genre learning: A comparative review and a look ahead. *Journal of Second Language Writing*, 15, 79–101.

References

Badger, R., & White, G. (2000). A process genre approach to teaching writing. *ELT Journal*, 54, 153–160.

Benesch, S. (2001). *Critical English for Academic Purposes: Theory, Politics and Practice*. Mahwah, NJ: Lawrence Erlbaum.

Canagarajah, A. S. (2011). Writing to learn and learning to write by shuttling between languages. In R. M. Manchón (Ed.), *Learning-to-Write and Writing-to-Learn in an Additional Language* (pp. 111–132). Amsterdam/Philadelphia: John Benjamins.

Canagarajah, A. S. (2015). "Blessed in my own way": Pedagogical affordances for dialogic voice construction in multilingual student writing. *Journal of Second Language Writing*, 27, 122–139.

Candlin, C. N., & Hyland, K. (1999). Introduction: Integrating approaches to the study of writing. In C. N. Candlin & K. Hyland (Eds.), *Writing: Texts, Processes and Practices* (pp. 1–18). London: Longman.

Harwood, N., & Hadley, G. (2004). Demystifying institutional practices: critical pragmatism and the teaching of academic writing. *English for Specific Purposes*, 23, 355–377.

Hayes, J. R. (1996). A new framework for understanding cognition and effect in writing. In C. M. Levy & S. Ransdell (Eds.), *The Science of Writing: Theories, Methods, and Individual Differences and Applications* (pp. 1–27). Mahwah, NJ: Lawrence Erlbaum.

Hinkel, E. (2003). Simplicity without elegance: Features of sentences in L1 and L2 academic texts. *TESOL Quarterly*, 37, 275–301.

Hyland, K. (2002), 'Genre: language, context, and literacy', *Annual Review of Applied Linguistics*, 22, 113–135.

Hyland, K. (2007). Genre pedagogy: Language, literacy and L2 writing instruction. *Journal of Second Language Writing*. 16, 148–164.

Hyland, K. (2011). Learning to write: Issues in theory, research and pedagogy. In R. M. Manchón (Ed.), *Learning-to Write and Writing- to-Learn in an Additional Language* (pp. 17–36). Amsterdam/Philadelphia: John Benjamins.

Kaplan, R. (1966). Cultural thought-patterns in intercultural education. *Language Learning*, 16, 1–20.

Keck, C. (2006). The use of paraphrase in summary writing: A comparison of L1 and L2 writers. *Journal of Second Language Writing*, 15, 261–278.

Kobayashi, H., & Rinnert, C. (2013). L1/L2/L3 writing development: Longitudinal case study of a Japanese multicompetent writer. *Journal of Second Language Writing*, 22, 4–33.

Kubota, R., & Lehner, A. (2004). Toward critical contrastive rhetoric. *Journal of Second Language Writing*, 13, 7–27.

Leki, I. (2011). Learning to write in a second language: Multilingual graduates and undergraduates expanding genre repertories. In R. M. Manchón (Ed.), *Learning-to-Write and Writing-to-Learn in an Additional Language* (pp. 85–110). Amsterdam/Philadelphia: John Benjamins.

Loi, C. (2010). Research article introductions in Chinese and English: A comparative genre-based study. *Journal of English for Academic Purposes*, 9, 267–279.

Luzón, M. (2009). The use of *we* in a learner corpus of reports written by EFL Engineering students. *Journal of English for Academic Purposes*, 8, 192–206.

Manchón, R. M. (2011). Situating the learning-to-write and writing-to-learn dimensions of L2 writing. In R. M. Manchón (Ed.), *Learning-to Write and Writing- to-Learn in an Additional Language* (pp. 3–16). Amsterdam/Philadelphia: John Benjamins.

Morton, J., Storch, N., & Thompson, C. (2015). What our students tell use: Perceptions of three multilingual students on their academic writing in first year. *Journal of Second Language Writing*, 30, 1–13.

Paltridge, B., & Starfield, S. (2007), *Thesis and Dissertation Writing in a Second Language: A Handbook for Supervisors*. Oxford: Routledge.

Pecorari, D. (2008). *Academic Writing and Plagiarism: A Linguistic Analysis*. London / New York: Continuum.

Pennycook, A. (1996). Borrowing others' words: Text, ownership, memory and plagiarism. *TESOL Quarterly*, 30, 201–230.

Prior, P., & Bilbro, R. (2012). Academic enculturation: Developing literate practices and disciplinary identities. In M. Castelló & C. Donahue (Eds.), *University Writing: Selves and Texts in Academic Societies* (pp. 19–31). Bingley, UK: Emerald.

Rinnert, C., & Kobayashi, H. (2005). Borrowing words and ideas: Insights from Japanese L1 writers. *Journal of Asian Pacific Communications*, 15, 31–56.

Rinnert, C., & Kobayashi, H. (2009). Situated writing practices in foreign language settings: The role of previous experience and instruction. In R. M. Manchón (Ed.), *Writing in Foreign Language Contexts: Learning, Teaching and Research* (pp. 23–48). Bristol, UK: Multilingual Matters.

Sheldon, E. (2009). From one *I* to another: Discursive construction of self-representation in English and Castilian Spanish research articles. *English for Specific Purposes*, 28, 251–265.

Shoonen, R., Snellings, P., Stevenson, M., & van Geldern, A. (2009). Towards a blueprint of the foreign language writer: The linguistic and cognitive demands of foreign language writing. In R. M. Manchón (Ed.), *Writing in Foreign Language Contexts. Learning, Teaching, and Research* (pp. 49–76). Bristol, UK: Multilingual Matters.

Silva, T. (1993). Towards an understanding of the distinct nature of L2 writing: The ESL research and its implications. *TESOL Quarterly*, 27, 657–677.

Storch, N. (2009). The impact of studying in a second language (L2) medium university on the development of L2 writing. *Journal of Second Language Writing*, 18(2), 103–118.

Storch, N., & Tapper, J. (2009). The impact of an EAP course on postgraduate writing. *Journal of English for Academic Purposes*, 8(3), 207–223.

Swales, J. (1990). *Genre Analysis*. Cambridge: Cambridge University Press.

Swales, J. (2004). *Research Genres: Explorations and Applications*. Cambridge: Cambridge University Press.

Thompson, C., Morton, J. & Storch, N. (2013). Where from, who, why and how? A study of the use of sources by first year L2 university students. *Journal of English for Academic Purposes*, 12(2), 99–109.

Thompson, P. (2012). Achieving a voice of authority in PhD theses. In K. Hyland & C. S. Guinda (Eds.), *Stance and Voice in Written Academic Genres* (pp. 117–133). New York: Palgrave Macmillan.

Wette, R. (2014). Teachers' practices in EAP writing instruction: Use of models and modelling. *System*, 42, 60–69.

Note

1 I use the term second language (L2) writing here to refer to writing in an additional language; that is, additional to the learner's first or native language. Although I acknowledge the problematic nature of the term L2 (see Canagarajah, 2011), in this chapter I use the term L2 writing for the sake of expediency. L2 writing is used as an umbrella term to cover second and foreign language writing.

SECTION 7

LEARNING THE SOCIAL USES OF ENGLISH

Chapters in this section focus broadly on the acquisition of different dimensions of second language (L2) communicative competence, and discuss how learners acquire the ability to use language for effective communicative purposes. They highlight the important role of cultural, social, community and personal practices in acquiring knowledge of how language is used appropriately and effectively.

In the first chapter, **Susan Feez** and **Zuocheng Zhang** discuss the nature of genres in L2 learning, and show how genres are characterized in different theoretical traditions. Learning genres involves mastering a repertoire of texts, as they are used for different communicative purposes. The notion of text connects linguistic choices to the social contexts and discourse communities in which texts are used. They describe how genre-based pedagogies for English learners are based on explicit teaching of the nature and use of genres, and move from guided to independent practice.

Next, **Marie Stevenson** addresses the area of literacy as a feature of L2 learning and development. She points out that an understanding of literacy has moved beyond a textual paradigm (literacy viewed as embodied in language), to a process paradigm (literacy viewed in terms of the strategies that learners employ and the processes they engage in when comprehending or producing texts), and to a social paradigm (literacy seen as situated in social practices, and embedded in contexts of use). She takes a sociocultural perspective on English literacy development, comparing in-class versus out-of-class literacy practices. For many learners, these may involve two or more languages, and differences in literary practices may reflect the learners' cultural background. She points out that there is often a disjuncture between in-class and out-of-class literacy practices.

In her chapter, **Naoko Taguchi** examines how social and interpersonal contexts shape L2 pragmatic competence in English, both as a receptive skill (understanding the speaker's intentions that may not be reflected in the surface level of utterances) and as a productive skill (expression of self and identity). She sees the development of pragmatic competence as linked to participation in social practices that draw on different kinds of pragmatic resources.

In the final chapter in this section, **Farzad Sharifian** extends the notion of pragmatics to the nature of intercultural communication. He observes that interaction between language users from multiple cultural backgrounds is increasingly a normal aspect of communication worldwide, making the development of intercultural competence an essential aspect of L2 learning. This involves the ability to adjust social interaction to accommodate different cultural expectations and norms. He introduces the notion of 'metacultural competence' to describe the knowledge and skills interlocutors draw on in the process of intercultural communication.

The chapters in this section stress, in their various ways, the importance of meaning as the primary driver of language learning. They emphasize that the way language learning takes place is through interaction with others in the many intercultural and social situations of daily life. In this process, learners acquire the ability to be communicative participants, and to understand and use language in ways that are shaped by, and also shape, their multiple contexts of use. Learners of both first and other languages must learn to recognize, analyze, compose and respond to interactions that are meaningful and relevant in their lives. The authors argue that learning development processes that are important to learners will take account of language appropriate for participation in a range of cultural and social practices.

CHAPTER 25

Learning Genres

Susan Feez and Zuocheng Zhang

INTRODUCTION

Learning to use a second language includes learning how to comprehend and compose texts in order to participate in the community in which the language is used. While each text is a unique expression of its immediate social context, it would be "impossible to communicate … if each time we constructed a text we had to start from scratch" (Butt, Fahey, Feez, and Spinks, 2012: 251). For this reason, over time, in each discourse community, recognisable and expected ways of exchanging meanings, or genres, "have become conventionalized through repeated use" (Tardy, 2013: 2278). For second language learners, learning genres means building a repertoire of these text patterns to guide their language use in ways that are recognised as effective for achieving their goals in the target language.

The ways genres are deployed in texts that respond to the demands of specific social contexts are complex and varied. This has led to the emergence of different approaches to conceptualising genre and teaching and learning about genres. These differing orientations reflect "the range of traditions and intellectual resources" informing the study of genre over several decades, and "the pedagogical goals and conditions from which it has emerged and to which it has responded" (Bawarshi and Reiff, 2010: 209).

OVERVIEW

In second language education, understandings about genre have been shaped by a variety of intellectual traditions, including literary, linguistic, rhetorical, ethnographic, critical and intercultural traditions (Bawarshi and Reiff, 2010). These intellectual traditions converge in the three genre traditions that have had the most impact on second language education: genre in the Systemic Functional Linguistics (SFL) tradition; genre in the English for Specific Purposes (ESP) tradition; and Rhetorical Genre Studies (RGS) (Gebhard and Harman, 2011; Hood, 2013; Hyon, 1996; Johns, 2002; Johns, Bawarshi, Coe, Hyland, Paltridge, Reiff, and

Tardy, 2006; Rose and Martin, 2012). In all these three traditions, genre is considered from the perspective of text in social context. The relations between generic conventions and individual adoptions or adaptations of these conventions constitute the nature of genre, but in each tradition these relations are modelled differently, generating distinctive *approaches* to learning genres.

KEY LEARNING ISSUES

In reviewing some of the key learning issues, we highlight below two areas in particular: understanding genres and learning genres in a second language. Understanding genres relates to the notion of knowledge about whole texts and their use in social contexts and related textual conventions, while learning genres is concerned with building and consolidating this knowledge.

UNDERSTANDING GENRES

TEXTS IN SOCIAL CONTEXTS

The SFL genre tradition is integrated into a broader social semiotic theory for studying meaning and the way it varies from one social context to the next. SFL has developed an extravagant analytical architecture that relates the context of language use and the meanings in texts systematically (Halliday and Matthiessen, 2014; Kress and van Leeuwen, 2006; Rose and Martin, 2012). In this tradition, text and social context are unified. The immediate social context is found in the patterned choices from the language system that weaves meanings into texts and governs the variety of language, or *register*, which characterises each text. The meanings in a text are made real in words and grammar and are made accessible through sounds or script. The way meanings are distributed across a text also structures the text in accord, more or less, with an overall structural pattern recognisable to those who share the same cultural context, giving the text a unity and rhetorical direction through which the purpose of the text is achieved. Texts which share the same relatively stable structural patterns for achieving the same purpose are said, in the SFL tradition, to belong to the same genre. Genres in this tradition are defined as "recurrent configurations of meaning [that] enact the social practices of a given culture" (Martin and Rose, 2008: 6).

In the ESP tradition (see Chapter 15), genres are understood as communicative events characterised by conventional text structures used consistently for communication in specific discourse communities (Bhatia, 2004; Swales, 1990). In an academic community, for example, genre is 'a socially approved way in which students show what they know, what they can do, and what they have learned in a course of study' (Johns et al., 2006: 235; see also Chapter 14). Context in this tradition is theorised in terms of discourse communities, which, with their community-specific communicative purposes, embody the contexts that shape, influence and constrain the textual features of texts. Genres are, therefore, constituted by a discourse community's expectations, conventions and options, all of which are discoverable through corpus linguistic analysis (Hyland, 2015) and ethnographic approaches (Johns et al., 2006).

The tradition of RGS is based on an understanding of genre as typified rhetorical responses to recurring social situations, a type of dynamic and strategic rhetorical social action, framed by the sociocultural context (Artemeva, 2009; Miller, 1984). By responding and contributing to social contexts, individuals build knowledge about their world, and are socialised into the contexts in which they live, work and study. The RGS perspective draws on traditional rhetoric to analyse the way texts of particular genres make appeals to facts and logic (*logos*), emotions and feelings (*pathos*), and truth and credibility (*ethos*) (Bawarshi and Reiff, 2010). In this tradition, genres are also analysed using ethnographic and Critical Discourse Analysis (CDA) approaches, in order to investigate the power structures they enact. Viewing genre through a critical lens is an approach the RGS tradition shares with New Literacy Studies (NLS) of school education (Gebhard and Harman, 2011). In NLS, the contribution of genre to multimodal meaning making is also explored (Kalantzis, Cope, Chan, and Dalley-Trim, 2016).

TEXTUAL CONVENTIONS AND INDIVIDUAL TEXTS

All genre traditions draw attention to recurring textual conventions used to classify texts, as well as the ways these conventions are customised to generate texts tailored to meet the demands of individual contexts. The differing theoretical and analytical orientations that underpin these traditions, however, have led to different ways of identifying and labelling the conventions used to classify texts belonging to the same genre. Moreover, these different orientations result in distinctive ways of thinking about how genres can be adapted to generate individual texts composed to achieve particular goals in specific contexts.

The SFL analytical architecture makes it possible to describe a text in terms of both convention (genre) and variation (register), either in the detailed analysis of generic structure, patterned meanings and probable vocabulary and grammar choices proposed by Hasan (see Butt et al., 2012), or by using the SFL genre model designed for educational contexts (Martin and Rose, 2008; Rose and Martin, 2012; Rothery, 1996). In this model, genres have been characterised as "staged, goal-oriented social processes" (Martin and Rose, 2008: 6) to draw attention to the recurring conventional stages used in texts of the same genre to achieve similar social goals. How these stages are variously enacted in specific texts is explained in terms of meanings shaped by variables in the immediate situation (register), and given substance in the discourse features, words and grammar of the text. The situational variables that account for the language variety, or register, of a text are *field* (what is going on), *tenor* (who is taking part), and *mode* (how the text is communicated). While the meanings in a text reflect the immediate situation, shifts in the expression of these meanings as the text unfolds signal each successive stage of the genre enacted in the text.

In the ESP tradition, genres are types of communicative events used in academic or professional contexts, including, for example, an essay, research article, speech or annual report. A text is recognised as enacting a certain genre on the basis of a sequence of moves, and steps within moves, that make up the text (Paltridge, 2007; Swales, 1990). Well-known studies of moves common to texts of the same genre include the study of the four parts of introductions to academic journal articles (Swales, 1990), and the seven-move structure used in promotional literature (Bhatia, 2004). Genres are also viewed as "community processes" in which genre users engage with the resources and practices of the community to construct membership and individuality (Hyland, 2015: 24).

In contrast, the RGS tradition does not focus on typical stages or moves that identify genres, but instead on the way knowledge about genre can be used to understand social contexts and social participation. Dynamic and critical orientations to the study of genre in the RGS tradition draw attention to the variability of genres over time, the impact of the use of genres in social settings on the identity of users, and the capacity of genres to entrench power and effect change in these settings (Freedman and Medway, 1994; Miller, 1984).

LEARNING GENRES IN A SECOND LANGUAGE

Learning genres provides a framework for learning how to piece together at the level of whole texts what can otherwise be quite fragmented knowledge about the target language. Learning genres also means learning how to use these texts in real contexts, in ways that resonate with audience expectations and achieve social purposes of value and interest to the learner.

Genre learning based on the SFL approach has been applied to first and second language education in both school and post-school settings. Beginning adult learners of English as an additional language might build a repertoire of spoken genres to meet their immediate needs, while primary school students might learn elementary genres to meet the language demands of the curriculum. These foundational repertoires can be later expanded to include discipline-specific genres, and genre combinations used for specialised and longer spoken, written and multimodal texts in the secondary school, workplace and higher education (Christie and Derewianka, 2008; Derewianka and Jones, 2016; Feez, 2002; Hood, 2010; Rothery, 1996; Rose and Martin, 2012; Schleppegrell, 2004). SFL genre analysis has mapped the main genres learners need to control to be successful in English-medium educational contexts in terms of three main genre families, namely, story genres, information genres, and genres that evaluate and persuade. SFL genre analysis also reveals how these families of genres evolve in response to social and technological change and increasing levels of specialisation in language use (Rose and Martin, 2012).

The focus of ESP genre learning, in contrast, is concentrated specifically on helping second language learners participate effectively in tertiary education or professional workplaces. Learners build knowledge of genres that characterise specific settings and discourse communities. This includes knowledge about relations between genres, and the move structure and lexicogrammatical features of texts used for the communicative purposes underlying the genres (Hyland, 2004).

Like ESP genre learning, RGS genre learning also has a more specific focus. RGS emerged from rhetorical and composition studies in first language higher education in North America. It offers students studying in this context a critical orientation to participation in university writing. While genre knowledge in the SFL and ESP traditions is understood to be transportable from the classroom to real life, many in the RGS tradition consider that genre is too complex to be explicitly taught in educational settings and transferred beyond the classroom (Freedman, 1993). Nevertheless, some in the RGS tradition argue that the complexity of genre may be taught explicitly to university students through strategies such as creating "a temporary analytical space" in which genre learners are guided to move between the analysis of the rhetorical situation and the genre required by the situation (Bawarshi and Reiff, 2010: 195). A further strategy is to teach students to be ethnographic researchers (Johns et al., 2006), so they can appreciate the interaction between text and social context in genre production and consumption.

Teaching and learning about genres emerged as part of the 'social turn' in second language education of the 1980s and 1990s, a change in direction from purely behavioural and cognitive approaches. The more recent 'multilingual turn' has led to recognition of second language learners as *emergent bilinguals* who continue to function in their first language as they learn one or more additional languages (García, 2014; Ortega, 2013). Learning genres has been identified as a means for second language learners to understand how dominant language varieties and cultures work, and to build a repertoire of powerful genres in the target language while maintaining the first language and culture (Gebhard and Harman, 2011). Moreover, the demands placed on second language learners in educational and professional contexts are now compared with the language demands these contexts also place on speakers of non-standard language varieties. In learning contexts comprising users of multiple languages and dialects, learning genres can contribute to building knowledge of intercultural rhetoric, that is, socially recognised ways of using language across multiple languages, dialects, cultures, and sub-cultures (Connor, 2011).

Increased awareness of multimodal meaning making, especially in the context of digital technology use, means that learning genres now necessarily involves learning about multimodal genres. This includes learning to recognise that meanings made by one semiotic mode may differ from those made by another in complementary, or contradictory, ways. When, for example, the spoken language in a plenary address constructs the speaker's identity as innovative researcher, the speaker's facial expressions may be performing the identity of friendly colleague (Zhang, 2015). Newer communication media, such as Twitter, blogging and instant messaging, also open up new rhetorical possibilities and variations. One example is the company blog allowing customers to appropriate corporate texts for their own communicative ends (Creelman, 2015).

IMPLICATIONS FOR TEACHING AND ASSESSMENT

A genre-based orientation to second language education has led to a re-evaluation of learner-centred pedagogies popular in the 1970s and 1980s, and an emphasis on achieving equitable outcomes for students (Gebhard and Harman, 2011; Rose and Martin, 2012). Because the conventionalised textual features of genres are shaped by both social context and user agency, the teaching and assessment of genre learning needs to be organised with both context and agency in mind. Many language educators use genre as a starting point for designing pedagogies based on contextualised language use in ways that address the needs of learners. To this end, genre pedagogies often feature clear language learning goals, explicit instruction on how to use target genres, a metalanguage for talking about texts, collaborative and independent practice, a critical orientation to genre conventions, and possibilities for text innovation in the target context, alongside principled assessment criteria.

Knowledge about genre has many dimensions, including knowledge about social purpose, subject matter and audience, as well as knowledge about language functions and forms. This complexity is accounted for in the detail of the SFL model of language, but for teaching purposes it has been recast to support strategic decisions about what to teach and how to teach it (Derewianka and Jones, 2016; de Silva Joyce and Feez, 2012). In a parallel approach to teaching English for academic purposes, Tardy (2009) identifies four dimensions of knowledge that overlap to build genre expertise: formal (for example, generic structure, words, grammar); process (producing, distributing, and consuming texts); rhetorical (for example, purpose, users, expectations, conventions); and subject matter (for example, disciplinary knowledge).

The evolution of genre-based pedagogies over recent decades has been fuelled by dynamic exchanges between different genre traditions, as well as by insights gathered from a range of disciplines and research approaches. The origin of the SFL genre tradition lies in the analysis of literary genres and everyday spoken genres (for example, Hasan, 1996a). When this analysis was applied to writing pedagogy in Sydney primary schools, an educational linguistics known as the Sydney School emerged, and with it a genre-based pedagogy tailored to support the learning needs of students from non-dominant language backgrounds (Rose and Martin, 2012). This pedagogy is designed as a three-stage teaching and learning cycle, each stage comprising a distinct type of interaction, an approach that has also become a resource for those working within the ESP tradition (Hyland, 2004; Paltridge, 2007).

In the first modelling stage of Sydney-school genre pedagogy, through teacher-directed activities, students are introduced explicitly to knowledge about the target genre in its cultural setting, as well as language and image conventions typical of the genre and of the language variety used to enact the genre in the immediate context. Language learning goals and assessment criteria are shared with students. One or more model texts are used to draw students' attention to, and build a metalanguage for talking about, the expected staging and language features of the genre, as well as how these are enacted in the immediate context in order to build the field, establish the tenor and communicate effectively in the relevant mode. Activities are adjusted in response to on-going diagnostic assessment of the students' needs against the assessment criteria.

In the second stage, teacher and students work together in order to apply knowledge about the target genre and language variety to the collaborative construction of texts. Activities might include group work to build field knowledge of a related topic and to generate spoken rehearsals of texts belonging to the target genre (Gibbons, 2015), followed by the whole class contributing to a joint construction of a text scribed by the teacher, who models the drafting process by thinking out loud using the shared metalanguage. The teacher uses formative assessment to monitor the students' developing knowledge, skill and confidence, intervening and providing feedback as needed, and gradually withdrawing support, until by the third stage students are engaged independently in activities in which they build subject-specific topic knowledge, and comprehend and construct texts in the target genre. These independent activities are used for summative assessment of students' achievement against the shared criteria. Students are also encouraged to consider how to transfer and extend their knowledge and skill into related contexts.

The extensive repertoire of activities and teaching strategies familiar to second language teachers is a valuable resource for teachers designing genre-based teaching. Drill and practice exercises, skills-based instruction, communicative activities and process-oriented strategies can all be matched to specific stages of the pedagogy, as can strategies for analysing need, monitoring progress and assessing achievement. To contribute to the cumulative building of knowledge and skill that is a feature of genre pedagogy, Rose and Martin (2012) propose the addition of a preparation phase at the beginning of each task to build on earlier learning, and an elaboration phase at the end to extend learning in preparation for the next task.

Genre pedagogy provides the ideal context for the integration of all four language skills, listening, speaking, reading and writing, in ways that echo their use in authentic contexts. While pedagogy derived from all three genre traditions was originally developed largely to teach writing, it has also been adapted to the teaching of listening and speaking (Burns, 2001) and reading (Adoniou and Macken-Horarik, 2007; Rose and Martin, 2012).

It is in the application of genre to pedagogy that the strengths of all three genre traditions have begun to coalesce, while at the same time highlighting some key distinctions and concerns. For example, the design of SFL genre pedagogy incorporates two principles that resonate with other genre traditions: if learners, especially those from non-dominant language backgrounds, are to gain access to academic knowledge, dispositions and identities, these need to be made visible (Bernstein, 2000), and learning about them is a function of collaborative social interaction with more capable others (Vygotsky, 1978). Nevertheless, some enactments of SFL genre pedagogy have been criticised for teaching the stages of genres as if they were rules to be copied, rather than adaptable and contestable conventions, and without attending to register variation, or to discourse or grammar features. Learning genres in this way encourages mere reproduction, rather than enabling students to analyse, reflect on and question dominant genre conventions and discourse strategies as a pathway towards the students becoming producers of knowledge themselves (Hasan, 1996b). In response to such criticism, subsequent accounts of SFL genre pedagogy have highlighted how mastery of educational genres not only gives students access to powerful discourses, but also builds the capacity to critique and contest these discourses.

CONCLUSION

Concerns about pedagogies that risk perpetrating reductive, prescriptive and accommodationist orientations to genre, and thereby restricting the agency of learners as well as their capacity to express their identity and individuality, have emerged not only from the SFL tradition, but also from the ESP tradition (Dudley-Evans and St John, 1998) and the RGS tradition (Freedman and Medway, 1994), alongside strategies for addressing this risk.

Ethnographic strategies, in particular, have been proposed as a means of enhancing learner agency in the context of learning genres. By becoming a participant in a target context, learners build knowledge of the context, and focus conscious attention on genre conventions (Cheng, 2011). They are also able to link what has been learned about one genre to other genres and contexts (Johns et al., 2006) and experience firsthand how the genre in focus is one action in a chain of activities enacted in genre sets (Devitt, 2004) and genre chains (Swales, 2004), for example, the job application genre chain.

When explicit teaching is enriched with purposeful problem-solving activities, learners develop deep insights into a genre, including the choices that are possible, as well as constraints placed on use of the genre within disciplinary and professional practices. In this way, the genres experienced in the classroom foreshadow future novel contexts. When related texts are themselves innovative uses of the genre potential, learners come to appreciate that genre learning does not necessarily mean abandoning flexibility or critical thinking, and a balance is achieved between disciplinary and professional conventions and personal agency.

Discussion Questions

1. Reflect on your own use of your first language in everyday and professional contexts. What kinds of spoken, written or multimodal texts do you use in these contexts? For which of them do you apply your knowledge of genre in relatively unconscious and uncritical ways? For which of them do you apply your knowledge more consciously and critically, and why?

2. Is your experience the same when using genres in your second or additional language? In what ways is this experience different? How would you account for these differences?

3. How might you use knowledge about genre to design second language teaching and learning, for example, resources and lessons that prepare learners to participate in target social contexts?

Key Readings

Bawarshi, A. S., & Reiff, M. J. (2010). *Genre: An Introduction to History, Theory, Research, and Pedagogy*. West Lafayette, IN: Parlor Press.

Hyland, K. (2004). *Genre and Second Language Learning*. Ann Arbor, MI: The University of Michigan Press.

Johns, A. M. (Ed.) (2002). *Genre in the Classroom: Multiple Perspectives*. London and New York: Routledge.

Paltridge, B. (2007). Approaches to genre in ELT. In J. Cummins & C. Davison (Eds.), *International Handbook of English Language Teaching, Part 1* (pp. 931–943). New York: Springer.

Rose, D., & Martin, J. R. (2012). *Learning to Write, Reading to Learn: Genre, Knowledge and Pedagogy in the Sydney School*. London: Equinox.

References

Adoniou, M., & Macken-Horarik, M. (2007). Scaffolding literacy meets ESL: Some insights from ACT classrooms. *TESOL in Context*, 17(1), 5–14.

Artemeva, N. (2009). Stories of becoming: A study of novice engineers learning genres of their profession. In C. Bazerman, A. Bonini, & D. Figueiredo (Eds.), *Genre in a Changing World* (pp. 158–178). West Lafayette, IN: Parlor Press.

Bawarshi, A. S., & Reiff, M. J. (2010). *Genre: An Introduction to History, Theory, Research, and Pedagogy*. West Lafayette, IN: Parlor Press.

Bernstein, B. (2000). *Pedagogy, Symbolic Control and Identity: Theory, Research, Critique* (Revised ed.). Lanham, MD: Rowman and Littlefield Publishers.

Bhatia, V. K. (2004). *Worlds of Written Discourse: A Genre-based View*. London / New York: Continuum.

Burns, A. (2001). Analysing spoken discourse: Implications for TESOL. In A. Burns & C. Coffin (Eds.), *Analysing English in a Global Context: A Reader* (pp. 123–148). London and New York: Routledge.

Butt, D., Fahey, R., Feez, S., & Spinks, S. (2012). *Using Functional Grammar: An Explorer's Guide* (3rd ed.). South Yarra, VIC: Macmillan Education Australia.

Cheng, A. (2011). ESP classroom research: Basic considerations and future research questions. In D. Belcher, A. M. Johns, & B. Paltridge (Eds.), *New Directions in English for Specific Purposes* (pp. 44–72). Ann Arbor, MI: The University of Michigan Press.

Christie, F., & Derewianka, B. (2008). *School Discourse: Learning to Write Across the Years of Schooling*. London / New York: Continuum.

Connor, U. (2011). *Intercultural Rhetoric in the Writing Classroom*. Ann Arbor, MI: The University of Michigan Press.

Creelman, V. (2015). Sheer outrage: Negotiating customer dissatisfaction and interaction in the blogosphere. In E. Darics (Ed.), *Digital Business Discourse* (pp. 160–185). New York: Palgrave Macmillan.

Devitt, A. J. (2004). *Writing Genres*. Carbondale: Southern Illinois University Press.

Derewianka, B., & Jones, P. (2016). *Teaching Language in Context* (2nd ed.). Melbourne: Oxford University Press.

de Silva Joyce, H., & Feez, S. (2012). *Text-based Language and Literacy Education: Programming and Methodology*. Sydney: Phoenix Education.

Dudley-Evans, T., & St John, M. J. (1998). *Developments in English for Specific Purposes: A Multi-disciplinary Approach*. Cambridge: Cambridge University Press.

Feez, S. (2002). Heritage and innovation in second language education. In A. Johns (Ed.), *Genres in the Classroom* (pp. 43–69). Mahwah, NJ: Lawrence Erlbaum.

Freedman, A. (1993). Show and tell? The role of explicit teaching in the learning of new genres. *Research in the Teaching of English, 27*(3), 222–51.

Freedman, A., & Medway, P. (Eds.) (1994). *Genre and the New Rhetoric*. London: Taylor & Francis.

García, O. (2014). Multilingualism and language education. In C. Leung, & B. V. Street (Eds.), *The Routledge Companion to English Studies* (pp. 222–254). New York: Routledge.

Gebhard, M., & Harman, R. (2011). Reconsidering genre theory in K-12 schools: A response to school reforms in the United States. *Journal of Second Language Writing, 20*, 45–55.

Gibbons, P. (2015). *Scaffolding Language, Scaffolding Learning: Teaching Second Language Learners in the Mainstream Classroom* (2nd ed.). Portsmouth, NH: Heinemann.

Halliday, M. A. K., & Matthiessen, C. M. M. (2014). *An Introduction to Functional Grammar* (4th ed.). London and New York: Routledge.

Hasan, R. (1996a). The nursery tale as genre. In C. Cloran, D. Butt, & G. Williams (Eds.), *Ways of Saying, Ways of Meaning: Selected Papers of Ruqaiya Hasan* (pp. 51–72). London: Cassell.

Hasan, R. (1996b). Literacy, everyday talk and society. In R. Hasan, & G. Williams (Eds.), *Literacy in Society* (pp. 377–424). London and New York: Longman.

Hood, S. (2010). *Appraising Research: Evaluation in Academic Writing.* London: Palgrave Macmillan.

Hood, S. (June 2013). Systemic functional linguistics [article]. Retrieved from http://genreacrossborders.org/research/systemic-functional-linguistics

Hyland, K. (2004). *Genre and Second Language Learning.* Ann Arbor, MI: The University of Michigan Press.

Hyland, K. (2015). Genre, discipline and identity. *Journal of English for Academic Purposes, 19,* 32–43.

Hyon, S. (1996). Genre in three traditions: Implications for ESL. *TESOL Quarterly, 30*(4), 693–722.

Johns, A. M. (2002). Introduction. In A. M. Johns (Ed.), *Genre in the Classroom: Multiple Perspectives* (pp. 3–13). London and New York: Routledge.

Johns, A. M., Bawarshi, A., Coe, R. M., Hyland, K., Paltridge, B., Reiff, M. J., & Tardy, C. (2006). Crossing the boundaries of genre studies: Commentaries by experts. *Journal of Second Language Writing, 15,* 234–249.

Kalantzis, M., Cope, W., Chan, E., & Dalley-Trim, L. (2016). *Literacies* (2nd ed.). Cambridge: Cambridge University Press.

Kress, G., & van Leeuwen, T. (2006). *Reading Images: The Grammar of Visual Design* (2nd ed.). London and New York: Routledge.

Martin, J. R., & Rose, D. (2008). *Genre Relations: Mapping Culture.* London: Equinox.

Miller, C. R. (1984). Genre as social action. *Quarterly Journal of Speech, 70,* 151–67.

Ortega, L. (2013). SLA for the 21st century: Disciplinary progress, transdisciplinary relevance and the bi/multilingual turn. *Language Learning, 63,* 1–24.

Paltridge, B. (2007). Approaches to genre in ELT. In J. Cummins & C. Davison (Eds.), *International Handbook of English Language Teaching, Part 1* (pp. 931–943). New York: Springer.

Rose, D., & Martin, J. R. (2012). *Learning to Write, Reading to Learn: Genre, Knowledge and Pedagogy in the Sydney School.* London: Equinox.

Rothery, J. (1996). Making changes: Developing an educational linguistics. In R. Hasan & G. Williams (Eds.), *Literacy in Society* (pp. 86–123). London: Longman.

Schleppegrell, M. J. (2004). *The Language of Schooling: A Functional Linguistics Perspective.* Mahwah, NJ: Lawrence Erlbaum.

Swales, J. M. (1990). *Genre Analysis: English in Academic and Research Settings.* Cambridge: Cambridge University Press.

Swales, J. M. (2004). *Research Genres: Explorations and Applications.* Cambridge: Cambridge University Press.

Tardy, C. M. (2009). *Building Genre Knowledge.* West Lafayette, IN: Parlor Press.

Tardy, C. (2013). Genre-based language teaching. In C. A. Chapelle (Ed.), *The Encyclopedia of Applied Linguistics* (pp. 2278–2281). West Sussex: Blackwell Publishing.

Vygotsky, L. S. (1978). *Mind in Society: The Development of Higher Psychological Processes.* Cambridge, MA: Harvard University Press.

Zhang, Z. C. (2015). Disagreements in plenary addresses as multimodal action. In B. C. Camiciottoli & I. Fortanet-Gómez (Eds.), *Multimodal Analysis in Academic Settings: From Research to Teaching* (pp. 17–38). London: Routledge.

CHAPTER 26

Learning Literacy

Marie Stevenson

INTRODUCTION

Conceptualizations of literacy have changed dramatically over the past decades, from predominantly referring to the ability to read and write via the medium of traditional print to encompassing an increasingly diverse range of media and modalities. Inextricably intertwined with changing conceptualizations have been technological developments that have created new means of representing meaning, interacting, and accessing information. However, in relation to second or foreign language learning, the term 'literacy' is a relative newcomer, with reading and writing traditionally being viewed as two of the four 'skills', and as discrete rather than interconnected entities.

Broadly speaking, there are three theoretical paradigms through which literacy can be viewed (Kern, 2000). Firstly, there is the textual paradigm, in which literacy is viewed as embodied in language: in grammar and lexis, but also in genres, rhetorical and discourse features, and in interpersonal features that express the attitudes, opinions, and voices of the writer and others. Seen from this perspective, learning to read and write in English as a second language is about understanding different genres and the textual features associated with these genres, about mastering these textual features, both within and beyond the level of the sentence as well as, in the case of writing, being about the expression of identity and voice. Secondly, there is the process paradigm, in which literacy is viewed in terms of the strategies that learners employ, and the processes they engage in when comprehending or producing texts. Seen from this perspective, learning to read and write in English as a second language is about the development of an individual repertoire of skills and strategies that the reader or writer applies to the act of reading or writing, whether online or offline. Reading strategies such as skimming, scanning, summarizing and paraphrasing are often emphasized as being important for English learners, as are writing processes such as planning, organizing, drafting, and revising. Thirdly, there is the social paradigm, in which literacy is seen as situated in social practices, and embedded in contexts of use. Seen from this perspective, learning to read and write in English as a second language is about understanding the expectations and mastering the practices of these particular social or cultural contexts in which learning takes place.

As Kern (2000) has pointed out, for second language reading and writing, the textual and cognitive paradigms have tended to predominate. However, in recent years there has been a growing interest in the social contexts surrounding second language reading and writing, and a concomitant greater use of the term 'literacy'. Because of this ongoing shift in emphasis, the current chapter focuses on sociocultural perspectives on literacy learning in English, and issues relating to these perspectives that are of relevance for English language learning in both second language and foreign language settings.

OVERVIEW

The notion of literacy as situated within social and cultural practices underpins sociocultural perspectives on literacy (e.g., Gee, 1996; Street, 1993). According to Barton and Hamilton (2000: 22), "Literacy practices are the general cultural ways of utilizing written language which people draw upon in their lives." Thus the things we do in our everyday lives, such as writing a shopping list, texting a friend that we are running late for an appointment, or reading advertising billboards while sitting on the bus, as well as the things we do in our academic or professional lives, such as emailing a colleague, writing a report, or looking for literature in an online library catalogue, are also literacy practices. Literacy practices draw on the conventions, resources, beliefs and values of the discourse community in which they are situated, and so may vary across discourse communities and cultures (Street, 2005). Discourse communities are groups in society that share common goals and that engage in communication to achieve those goals (Swales, 1990).

Some sociocultural perspectives on literacy place particular emphasis on the rapidly changing nature of discourse communities, and the literacy practices associated with these changes. For example, the multiliteracies perspective put forward by the New London Group (1996) focuses in particular on two kinds of changes: the growing cultural and linguistic diversity emerging in the process of globalization, and the growing multiplicity of communications channels and media (Cope and Kalantzis, 2000). In the multiliteracies approach, meaning making occurs through a variety of communicative channels in which both written-linguistic modes of meaning and audio-visual modes of meaning are involved.

Critical literacy, which aims to raise awareness that texts are shaped by the social, cultural and political contexts within which they are created, and to equip readers to use this awareness to interpret texts critically (Fajardo, 2015), is emphasized by some sociocultural perspectives (Perry, 2012). Critical literacy has its roots in the work of Freire (1972), who saw the process of learning to read as one of engaging with oppressive political realities, and critically reflecting on how disadvantaged people could free themselves from this oppression and transform their worlds. Thus, in its most radical forms, critical literacy is viewed as being a tool for political and social liberation. However, more moderate forms focus primarily on uncovering the multiple meanings contained in texts, on discerning values and assumptions underlying texts (Unsworth, 2001), on examining how writers position themselves and their readers, and on examining how multimodality is used to express meanings in texts.

Much of the theorization of sociocultural perspectives on literacy has arisen from the consideration of first language literacy. Within the field of second language literacy, scholarship has primarily been directed towards second language immigrant contexts and second language academic literacy contexts. However, it is increasingly recognized that a social view of literacy is also of relevance in foreign language learning contexts. Below, issues are discussed that are of relevance to learning English literacy in both immigrant and foreign language (FL) settings.

KEY LEARNING ISSUES

IN-CLASS VERSUS OUT-OF-CLASS LITERACY PRACTICES

An important learning issue for second language reading and writing is the disjunct between in-class and out-of-class literacy practices. Out-of-class literacy practices are known to be rich and diverse (e.g., Barton and Hamilton, 2000; Skilton-Sylvester, 2002), from the kinds of functional writing adults do as part of everyday life, to literacies related to youth culture, such as graffiti and social media, to community-based practices associated with religious, social or leisure affiliations. Adding to this richness and diversity is the multilingual nature of English learners' communicative repertoires, with two or more languages involved that may have intricate patterns of usage, and that may be combined in complex or unexpected ways. With the advent of the digital age and increasing globalization, readers and writers of English in both immigrant and FL settings may engage in a rich variety of online multilingual and multimodal practices that enable them to communicate globally and to build a digital identity in English.

In contrast, in-class practices for developing learners' English literacy may not display the same richness and diversity, and are sometimes narrowly language-based, with a focus on using texts as vehicles to teach or practice grammar and vocabulary, and little opportunity for meaningful engagement or ownership of English literacy practices. Moreover, in some contexts – particularly FL contexts – literacy practices may be strongly assessment-driven, with passing a written examination being the main purpose for learning to read and write in English. This may result in a set of literacy practices that have little currency outside the language classroom, and which may limit learners in seeing English literacy as connecting meaningfully to their lives outside the classroom.

The disjunct between out-of-class and school literacy practices may mean that learners' literacy practices outside the classroom, in either the first or the second language, may not be valued in classroom settings. For example, Norton (2010) points out that parents and teachers may be dismissive of children's English literacy practices outside the classroom, such as reading comic books or chatting online, and that as a consequence children may also make a distinction between 'real reading' as prescribed by the teacher, and the 'fun reading' they engage in outside the classroom. Moreover, in immigrant settings, lack of recognition of home and community literacy practices may lead to disempowerment. For example, Rubinstein-Avila (2007) found that the out-of-class first-language Spanish performative literacy practices of an eighth-grade girl who had immigrated to the USA from the Dominican Republic, such as reciting passages from the Bible, were not valued in the USA school setting, leading to frustration and loss of confidence. Even when out-of-class literacy practices take place in English, they may not be valued in school settings. Skilton-Sylvester (2002) describes Nan, a Cambodian immigrant girl in the USA learning in an elementary classroom, who was a prolific writer and performer of stories in English at home, but who at school was struggling to comprehend the textbooks she was expected to read, and was positioned in the classroom as deficient in terms of English literacy.

However, the literacy practices engaged in by English learners outside the classroom may also be empowering. Learners use literacy outside the classroom strategically and agentively to express their personal feelings and opinions, seek and exchange information, maintain and develop social relations, construct desirable identities for themselves, and to assist others (Haneda, 2006). For example, the phenomenon of 'literacy brokering', which involves seeking and/or providing informal assistance about some aspect of a text or literacy practice (Perry, 2009), has been shown to be an empowering literacy practice in immigrant settings. Orellana, Reynolds, Dorner, and Meza (2003) documented how immigrant children took on brokering roles in which they assisted adult family members with understanding difficult texts, such as letters from school or a jury summons. Engagement in these practices gave these immigrant children the opportunity to take action in the social world, and gave them a status in their families and in the community that they would not otherwise have had. Empowerment in both immigrant and FL settings can also occur through learners' engagement in out-of-class, multilingual, transnational, digital literacy practices that allow learners to construct relationships with people and communities that span geographical distances. According to scholars and educationalists, it is highly desirable for learners to be able to build on empowering out-of-class literacy practices inside the classroom.

CULTURAL VARIATION IN LITERACY PRACTICES

A second issue is the difficulties that learners from different cultural backgrounds may experience in mastering literacy practices in settings in which English is used as the language of communication. This issue is of crucial importance in immigrant settings, where learners may struggle to engage in the functional literacy practices associated with daily life, such as applying for a bank loan or completing a tax form, which may be carried out quite differently in learners' cultures of origin, creating barriers to participation in society. In immigrant settings, differences between the dominant culture and the culture of origin in home literacy practices, and in beliefs and values concerning the family's role in developing a child's literacy, may impede the development of school literacy in English (Hammer and Miccio, 2004). The home literacy practices of middle class families in English-speaking settings may be more similar to school literacy practices than are the practices of some minority communities (e.g., Perry, 2009). To give an example, reading aloud, which is known to be of benefit to children's literacy development (Reese and Gallimore, 2000), may be less common in families of some minority communities.

Cross-cultural differences associated with academic literacy practices are important for learners in a wide variety of learning contexts. In many foreign language classes around the world, at both secondary and tertiary level, learners are taught to write essays in English, sometimes simply because this is part of the curriculum, but sometimes as preparation for exams such as IELTS or TOEFL, which need to be passed in order to gain admission to university degree courses for which English will be the medium of instruction. These degrees are often completed in English-speaking countries but, with the growing internationalization of education, it is also becoming more common for English to be the medium of instruction in university programs in non-English-speaking countries. Thus, an understanding of the expectations and conventions surrounding English academic literacy practices can be important for learners. For example, it has been claimed that learners from non-western cultural backgrounds find textual practices, including citation practices, surrounding the expression of academic voice particularly challenging (e.g., Pecorari, 2003; Ramanathan and Atkinson, 1999). When confronted with unfamiliar literacy practices, learners may feel loss of identity and lack of validation of their previous learning experiences (Li, 2004), and failure to understand or conform to conventions may, in some cases, even lead to accusations of academic dishonesty, with serious academic consequences.

However, care needs to be taken in making generalizations about cultural differences (Cheng, 2006), and the notion of 'culture' in fact transcends the notion of ethnic and national differences. Holliday (1999) made a distinction between large cultures, based on ethnic or national distinctions and small cultures, which are defined in terms of smaller social groupings bound together by specific practices and discourse, such as legal culture, business culture or classroom culture. In this vision of culture, the classroom can be said to have its own culture. From this perspective, both first language and second language students can be viewed as novices who are struggling to understand the discourse practices and expectations in their current educational or classroom context.

CRITICAL LITERACY

A third issue is the question of whether second language learners need to develop critical literacy in reading and writing in English. Although, as mentioned, there are both radical and moderate conceptions of critical literacy, the various forms share a common value that the goal of literacy education is to empower students to become questioning and analytical.

Although over the past decades, versions of critical literacy have been adopted in second language classrooms (Luke and Dooley, 2011), Fajardo (2015) points out that critical literacy still remains marginalized in second language classrooms, particularly FL classrooms. Fajardo (2015) notes that a "discourse of neutrality" (Pennycook, 1997: 256) predominates in language teaching, and many language teachers see themselves as contributing to learners' welfare by teaching them to communicate, rather than by encouraging them to question values, assumptions and power relations. Moreover, in some settings, the questioning of accepted norms may be considered to be culturally inappropriate, and in some contexts may even be a potentially dangerous practice for both teachers and learners. Alford (2001) makes the point that learners are sometimes resistant to critical literacy: they may already be socialized in their expectations concerning language learning, or in culturally specific interaction patterns that determine who can say what and to whom, and hence may find it uncomfortable or distasteful to be expected to adopt a style of critique that is not generally practiced, valued or sanctioned in their particular educational and cultural contexts.

However, proponents of critical literacy in the language classroom argue that social, cultural and political meanings are inherent in texts, and so simply cannot be separated from them (Alford, 2001). They also point to the need for learners to be able to negotiate the ever burgeoning and diversifying number of texts written in English they are confronted with in the modern digitalized and globalized world (e.g., Wilson, 2014; see also Chapters 34–36). In many settings around the world, readers are exposed to a diverse range of texts in English via the internet, some of which may be topical, controversial or even radicalized, and readers may need to be able to evaluate the veracity of the information presented and the authority of the sources. Another argument given for English learners' need of critical literacy is that understanding positions, values, perspectives and contexts inherent in texts from other cultures can be considered to be a crucial aspect of intercultural competence, which is currently recognized to be an integral part of language learning (see Chapter 28). Alford (2001) points out that bicultural multilingual students have more ways of reading texts than monolingual students. According to Zhang (2015) and Cope (2015), developing critical literacy allows learners to better understand the cultures of the English-speaking countries in which they are living or with which they are communicating – or will communicate with – from afar, and ultimately enables them to participate more fully in discourse communities that are relevant to them.

IMPLICATIONS FOR TEACHING AND ASSESSMENT

IN-CLASS AND OUT-OF-CLASS LITERACY PRACTICES

Where possible, teachers need to engage in "bridging practices" (Marissa, 2013: 230) to lessen the divide between in-class and out-of-class literacy practices. Marissa (2013) distinguishes three disconnects that need to be bridged:

1. the semiotic disconnect;

2. the identity disconnect; and

3. the life skill disconnect.

The semiotic disconnect is that literacy outside the classroom typically has a meaningful social purpose, whereas schools often frame literacy as an end in itself. Where possible, teachers can create social purposes for classroom literacy activities. The identity disconnect is that online literacy practices create opportunities for learners to construct more desirable identities and to try on new selves, and develop a confident voice, whereas in-class literacy practices sometimes restrict learners' identities, by getting them to take on academic identities that they do not feel confident or comfortable with. The life skills disconnect is that learners may not perceive the skills in the classroom as being valuable skills for life. If English academic literacy skills are being taught, teachers need to find ways of getting students to see that the practices they are learning are – or will be – of benefit to them in the real world. If general English is being taught, teachers need, where possible, to develop tasks that meet learners' current or perceived future out-of-class needs. Lam (2013) stresses that we need to consider how educational practices may call on learners' out-of-class literacy repertoires as resources for classroom literacy learning. In particular, teachers need to think of ways to promote multilingual literacy practices. However, teachers need to be aware that learners sometimes take strong ownership of their out-of-class literacy practices and do not like teachers encroaching on these. In some EFL settings, teachers may need to actively encourage students to engage in out-of-class literacy practices. Olsson (2011) found that Swedish learners with more out-of-class literacy practices in English had better English writing proficiency than students with little exposure to English literacy practices outside the classroom. Burns (2003) suggests getting learners to reflect on their out-of-class literacy practices in both the first and the second language by keeping a journal.

CULTURAL VARIATION IN LITERACY PRACTICES

It is important for teachers to be aware that literacy practices may vary across cultures, and that this variation may influence learners' familiarity with English literacy practices and their proficiency in these practices. However, as mentioned previously, it is suggested that taking a small-c approach to culture (Holliday, 1999), in which learners' previous literacy experiences are investigated more generally, in terms of prior learning experiences, assumptions and expectations rather than in terms of their specific cultural backgrounds, may be preferable. Gutiérrez and Rogoff (2003) stress that it is important to respect the literacy practices that learners already possess in their first language.

An ethnographic perspective can be taken with learners being positioned as researchers of their own literacy practices (Rogers and Street, 2011). A learner-as-researcher perspective is more commonly associated with the development of academic literacy in tertiary settings, but in a general English classroom, for example, in immigrant settings, it would also be feasible to apply such an approach to the development of functional literacy.

CRITICAL LITERACY

In deciding whether to teach critical literacy, teachers need to reflect on their beliefs concerning their role as teachers of English literacy: do they see their role as using texts primarily as a medium through which to teach grammar and vocabulary, or also to encourage students to think deeply about texts, and hence about the world, or even to use texts to take social action in the world outside the classroom?

English teachers who decide to teach critical literacy – particularly those teaching in cultural settings other than their own – need to display sensitivity towards the cultural, social and political contexts in which they are teaching, and to know when to push boundaries and when to respect them. However, critical literacy does not need to equate with examining controversial social or political issues, and it does not need to be synonymous with uncovering ideologies in texts. Critical literacy can be applied to a wide range of texts, from children's picture books to advertisements to song lyrics. In its most moderate forms, it might go no further than encouraging learners to think deeply about possible interpretations of a text, about the author's intentions in writing the text, and about the effects of the text on the reader. Critical literacy does not have a distinctive instructional methodology, but can be applied in a variety of ways (see Behrman, 2006; Luke and Dooley, 2011).

CONCLUSION

There are three main paradigms through which literacy can be viewed: a textual paradigm, a cognitive paradigm and a sociocultural paradigm. This chapter has examined second language literacy from sociocultural perspectives, because these perspectives are gaining increasing emphasis in English teaching, and because aspects of the other two perspectives are covered elsewhere (see Chapters 23 and 24). The chapter has provided an overview of issues relating to sociocultural perspectives on literacy that are of relevance for learning English in both immigrant and foreign language settings. Three issues that may impact on the manner in which learners' English literacy develops are: possible gaps between in-class and out-of-class literacy practices; possible cultural differences between English literacy practices and learners' first language literacy practices; and learners' ability to engage in critical literacy, that is, to think critically about texts. In order to weigh up the relevance of these issues to particular learning contexts, teachers need to carefully consider their learners' needs, as well as the constraints of the teaching context. Foreign language teachers are particularly encouraged to reflect on these issues, as they are ones that have traditionally been neglected in developing English literacy in foreign language settings.

Discussion Questions

1. To what extent do you think that literacy practices in the English language classroom should mirror out-of-class literacy practices? To what extent is it acceptable to have literacy practices that do not exist outside the language classroom, and which serve no social purpose beyond demonstrating some aspect of learners' proficiency to teachers?

2. Is it of value for teachers to consider cultural differences in literacy practices between the first language and English, or does this only lead to stereotyping learners in terms of their cultural backgrounds?

3. To what extent do you think it is the role of English language teachers to develop students' critical literacy?

Key Readings

Barton, D., & Hamilton, M. (2000). Literacy practices. In D. Barton, M. Hamilton, & R. Ivanič (Eds.), *Situated Literacies: Reading and Writing in Context* (pp. 7–15) London: Routledge.

Haneda, M. (2006). Becoming literate in a second language: Connecting home, community, and school literacy practices. *Theory Into Practice*, 45(4), 337–345.

Kern, R. (2000). *Literacy and Language Teaching*. Oxford: Oxford University Press.

Luke A., & Dooley, K. (2011). Critical literacy and second language learning. In E. Hinkel (Ed.), *Handbook of Research in Second Language Teaching and Learning, Volume II* (pp. 856–867). New York: Routledge.

Rogers, A., & Street, B. (2011). Using ethnographic approaches to understanding and teaching literacy: Perspectives from both developing and western contexts. Viden om Læsning (Knowledge About Reading) special issue, World Literacy Day, 8 Sept 2011: 'Jorden læser (Literacy Around the World)'.

References

Alford, J. (2001). Critical literacy and second language learning in the mainstream classroom: An elusive nexus? In P. Singh & E. McWilliam (Eds.), *Designing Education Research: Theories, Method and Practices* (pp. 127–139). Flaxton, Australia: Post Pressed.

Barton, D., & Hamilton, M. (2000). Literacy practices. In D. Barton, M. Hamilton, and R. Ivanič (Eds.), *Situated Literacies: Reading and Writing in Context* (pp. 7–15). London: Routledge.

Behrman, E.H. (2006). Teaching about language, power and text: A review of classroom practices that support critical literacy. *Journal of Adolescent & Adult Literacy*, 49(6), 490–498.

Burns, A. (2003). Reading practices: From outside to inside the classroom. *TESOL Journal*, 12(3), 18–23.

Cheng, A. (2006). Analyzing and enacting academic criticism: The case of an L2 graduate learner of academic writing. *Journal of Second Language Writing*, 15, 279–306.

Cope, B., & Kalantzis, M. (Eds.) (2000). *Multiliteracies: Literacy Learning and the Design of Social Futures*. London: Routledge.

Cope, J. (2015). Empowering English language learners: The importance of developing critical literacy skills. *The IAFOR Academic Review*, 1(7), 23–26.

Fajardo, M. (2015). A review of critical literacy beliefs and practices of English language learners and teachers. *University of Sydney Papers in TESOL*, 10, 29–56.

Freire, P. (1972). *Pedagogy of the Oppressed*. Harmondsworth, UK: Penguin Books.

Gee, J. P. (1996). *Sociolinguistics and Literacies: Ideology in Discourses* (2nd ed.). London: Taylor & Francis.

Gutiérrez, K. D., & Rogoff, B. (2003). Cultural ways of learning: Individual traits or repertoires of practice. *Educational Researcher*, 32(5), 19–25.

Hammer, C. S., & Miccio, A. W. (2004). Home literacy experiences of Latino families. In B. H. Wasik (Ed.), *Handbook of Family Literacy* (pp. 305–328). Mahwah, NJ: Lawrence Erlbaum.

Haneda, M. (2006). Becoming literate in a second language: Connecting home, community, and school literacy practices. *Theory into Practice*, 45(4), 337–345.

Holliday, A. (1999). Small cultures. *Applied Linguistics*, 20(2), 237–264.

Kern, R. (2000). *Literacy and Language Teaching*. Oxford: Oxford University Press.

Lam, W. S. E., (2013). Multilingual practices in transnational digital contexts. *TESOL Quarterly*, 47(4), 820–825.

Li, Y. (2004). Learning to live and study in Canada: Stories of four EFL learners from China. *TESL Canada Journal / Revue TESL du Canada*, 22(2), 25–43.

Luke A., & Dooley, K. (2011). Critical literacy and second language learning. In E. Hinkel (Ed.), *Handbook of Research in Second Language Teaching and Learning, Volume II* (pp. 856–867). New York: Routledge.

Marissa, D. N. (2013). *Intertextuality, Identity Works, and Second Language Literacy Development in the Digital Media: An Ethnographic Case Study of two Indonesian College Students' Literacy Practice on Twitter.* Doctoral dissertation, University of Maryland.

New London Group (1996). A pedagogy of multiliteracies: Designing social futures. *Harvard Educational Review*, 66(1), 1–31.

Norton, B. (2010). Identity, literacy and English-language teaching. *TESL Canada Journal / Revue TESL du Canada*, 28(1), 1–13.

Olsson, E. (2011). *"Everything I read on the Internet is in English": On the Impact of Extramural English on Swedish 16-year-old Pupils' Writing Proficiency.* Doctoral thesis, University of Gothenburg, Sweden.

Orellana, M. F., Reynolds, J., Dorner, L., & Meza, M. (2003). In other words: Translating or "para-phrasing" as a family literacy practice in immigrant households. *The Reading Research Quarterly*, 38 (1): 12–34.

Pecorari, D. (2003). Good and original: Plagiarism and patchwriting in academic second-language writing. *Journal of Second Language Writing*, 12, 317–345.

Pennycook, A. (1997). Vulgar pragmatism, critical pragmatism, and EAP. *English for Specific Purposes*, 16(4), 253–269.

Perry, K. H. (2009). Genres, contexts and literacy practices: Literacy brokering among Sudanese refugee families. *Reading Research Quarterly*, 44(3), 256–276.

Perry, K. H. (2012). What is literacy? A critical overview of sociocultural perspectives. *Journal of Language & Literacy Education*, 8(1), 50–71.

Ramanathan, V. & Atkinson, D. (1999). Individualism, academic writing, and ESL writers. *Journal of Second Language Writing*, 8, 45–75.

Reese, L. J. & Gallimore, R. (2000). Immigrant Latinos' cultural model of literacy development: An evolving perspective on home-school discontinuities. *American Journal of Education*, 108(2), 103–134.

Rogers, A., & Street, B. (2011). Using ethnographic approaches to understanding and teaching literacy: Perspectives from both developing and western contexts. Viden om Læsning (Knowledge About Reading) special issue, World Literacy Day 8 Sept 2011: 'Jorden læser (Literacy Around the World)'.

Rubinstein-Avila, E. (2007). From the Dominican Republic to Drew High: What counts as literacy for Yanira Lara?' *Reading Research Quarterly*, 42(4), 568–589.

Skilton-Sylvester, E. (2002). Literate at home but not at school: A Cambodian girl's journey from playwright to struggling writer. In G. Hull & K. Schultz (Eds.), *School's Out: Bridging Out-of-School Literacies with Classroom Practice* (pp. 61–95). New York: Teachers College Press.

Street, B. V. (1993). *Cross-cultural Approaches to Literacy*. Cambridge: Cambridge University Press.

Street, B. V. (2005). At last: Recent applications of new literacy studies in educational contexts. *Research in the Teaching of English*, 39 (4), 417–423.

Swales, J. (1990). *Genre Analysis: English in Academic and Research Settings*. Cambridge: Cambridge University Press.

Unsworth, L. (2001). *Teaching Multiliteracies across the Curriculum: Changing Contexts of Text and Image in Classroom Practice.* Buckingham, UK: Open University.

Wilson, B. (2014). Teach the how: Critical lenses and critical literacy. *English Journal*, 103(4), 68–75.

Zhang, G. (2015). Learning critical literacy in ESL classrooms. *Creative Education*, 6, 1316–1321.

CHAPTER 27

Learning Pragmatics

Naoko Taguchi

INTRODUCTION

Both expert and common-sense knowledge tell us that learning a language involves more than learning grammar and vocabulary. Linguistic forms certainly provide us with functional abilities to perform a variety of communicative tasks (e.g., greeting, small talk). However, linguistic knowledge alone does not guarantee successful communication, because communication is typically situated in the extra-linguistic domain – social contexts and uses of a language. For instance, in real-life situations, people often convey meaning in an indirect manner. Comprehending indirect meaning requires us to draw on our inferential skills, as well as our knowledge of contexts, social conventions, and semiotic resources, to assist with comprehension. Similarly, when producing meaning, the social context mediates our linguistic choice. Our understanding of context (e.g., settings, participant roles, and norms of interaction), communicative goals, and the type of 'self' that we want to project (formal or informal) affects our way of speaking. Hence, forms, meaning, and context of use are closely intertwined. Pragmatic competence – ability to understand the speaker's intention or to convey one's intention appropriately in a situation – is a critical aspect of our communicative competence.

This chapter discusses learning processes in second language (L2) pragmatics. I will first describe the construct of pragmatic competence by surveying the treatment of that construct in various frameworks of communicative competence and interactional competence (Bachman and Palmer, 1996, 2010; Canale and Swain, 1980; Celce-Murcia, 2007; Young, 2008). I will then discuss two major contexts where pragmatics learning has typically been examined:

1. naturalistic contexts that support incidental learning of pragmatics (e.g., study-abroad settings); and

2. instructional contexts where select pragmatic features are directly taught.

I will conclude the chapter with implications for pragmatics teaching and assessment.

OVERVIEW

PRAGMATIC COMPETENCE AS A COMPONENT OF COMMUNICATIVE COMPETENCE

Building on Hymes' (1972) model of communicative competence, which emphasizes forms and their use in social contexts, researchers in L2 pedagogy and assessment have developed theoretical models of communicative competence specific to L2 learners (Bachman and Palmer, 1996, 2010; Canale, 1983; Canale and Swain, 1980). These models specify constituents of L2 proficiency. Notable in these models is the explicit recognition of pragmatic competence as a critical constituent of L2 ability.

Canale and Swain's (1980) model conceptualizes communicative competence as consisting of four sub-components: grammatical, sociolinguistic, strategic, and discourse competence (added in Canale, 1983). Sociolinguistic competence refers to the ability to interpret and produce an utterance appropriately in context, which fulfils the pragmatics concern. The sociolinguistic component works together with other components – knowledge of grammar, discourse-level coherence, and compensatory strategies – to enable learners to perform communicative acts.

A successor of this model is Bachman and Palmer's (1996, 2010) model. This model includes three components: organizational knowledge, pragmatic knowledge, and strategic competence. The organizational knowledge is Canale and Swain's grammatical and discourse competencies. The pragmatic knowledge corresponds to Canale and Swain's sociolinguistic competence, but it is more explicitly articulated. Bachman and Palmer's pragmatic knowledge involves two sub-components:

1. functional knowledge, which enables us to interpret relationships between utterances and communicative goals (e.g., knowledge of how to perform a speech act of apology); and
2. sociolinguistic knowledge, which enables us to create utterances that are appropriate in context (e.g., knowledge of whether or not an apology is needed in a certain situation, or which form to use to apologize in a situation).

Unlike Canale and Swain's model, strategic knowledge in Bachman and Palmer's model goes beyond compensatory strategies and includes metacognitive strategies (e.g., planning).

PRAGMATIC COMPETENCE IN INTERACTION

Although early models of communicative competence clarified pragmatic competence as a critical component of L2 ability, these models treated pragmatic competence as an ability that exists within individual cognition as a stable trait, independent from social interaction. In more recent years, pragmatic competence has been incorporated into a broader conceptual framework that focuses on the dialogic, interactive nature of communication. Celce-Murcia (2007) has proposed a model that involves interactional competence with two sub-components: *action competence* and *conversation competence.* Action competence involves functional knowledge of how to perform speech acts, while conversational competence refers to knowledge of conversation mechanisms (e.g., turn-taking, back-channeling). These two components together explain how communicative functions are achieved in interaction.

Although the componential view is still prominent in Celce-Murcia's model, another model focusing on interaction – interactional competence (Young, 2008) – presents a discursive-oriented view of meaning emerging from a socio-semiotic system. Interactional competence views language ability as jointly constructed by participants in discourse. Learners bring a variety of resources to an interaction, including: knowledge of participants and linguistic forms specific to register; knowledge of speech acts, turn-taking, and repair; and recognition and production of discourse boundaries (Young, 2008). These resources are not totally in contrast with early models of communicative competence. Knowledge of register, speech acts, and use of boundary-signalling devices reflect pragmatic considerations. However, the difference is that interactional competence rejects the view that these components reside within individuals. Instead, this model views these components working in unison and shared among participants in interaction.

To illustrate, early models of communicative competence considered speech acts as representing the one-to-one correspondence between an utterance and function. For instance, a speech act of invitation is often associated with conventional forms of '*Would you like to* + verb' or '*How about* + verb.' Pragmatic competence involves understanding the form-function connection and contextual specifics that determine the connection. But in reality, a speech act is not a pre-planned action. It arises in the course of conversation through participants' reactions to each other's contribution to the on-going discourse. The conventional forms of invitation may or may not appear, depending on how a conversation unfolds. Unlike traditional models that disregard this interactive nature of speech acts, interactional competence views pragmatic acts as mutually constructed in interaction through a variety of resources that participants bring to interaction.

In summary, the last four decades has illustrated an increasingly fine-tuned conceptualization of pragmatic competence. The literature demonstrates that pragmatic competence involves at least four dimensions:

1. linguistic knowledge;

2. functional knowledge;

3. sociolinguistic knowledge; and

4. ability to use these knowledge bases to co-construct a communicative act in interaction.

The next section discusses how pragmatic competence develops, focusing on two areas in which pragmatic development is typically examined: learning contexts and instructional interventions. Due to the paucity of existing research on children or young adult learners (see Chapters 1 and 2), my discussion inevitably focuses on adult L2 learners (see Chapter 3).

KEY LEARNING ISSUES

LEARNING PRAGMATICS IN CONTEXT: FOCUS ON THE STUDY-ABROAD CONTEXT

Pragmatic development has been examined in diverse contexts, including study-abroad settings, formal classrooms, immersion contexts, immigrant situations, heritage learner environments, and technology-enhanced learning contexts (see Taguchi, 2015a, for a review; Taguchi and Roever, 2017). Although the centrality of context in pragmatics learning has been well established, more recent questions involve what resources and elements in context facilitate pragmatic development. Recent studies have revealed an intricate association between opportunities for pragmatic practice available in context, and individuals' investment in those opportunities. This trend is most visible in the line of study-abroad research, which is the focus of this section.

The study-abroad context is considered beneficial for pragmatics learning for several reasons. First, it provides learners with opportunities to participate in sociocultural activities. These social practices, aided by feedback and modeling from local members, can assist learners' socialization into appropriate pragmatic behaviors. A second benefit is the diversity of communicative situations available in that context; by interacting with locals from different backgrounds in different social situations, learners understand that their linguistic choices are closely related to the characteristics of the situation. They also come to understand that their choices have a real-life consequence on the outcome of the interaction.

Existing findings support these benefits of studying abroad. For example, Nguyen (2011) documented developing interactional resources of an ESL learner as she participated in conversations with her ESL teacher. Analysis of interactional moves between the learner and her ESL teacher revealed that at the beginning of the semester the learner's responses to the instructor-initiated topics were brief, containing simple turn construction units and non-verbal signals (e.g., nodding). In the later period, the learner started to produce multi-unit responses in longer turn construction units. This change was interpreted from a perspective of learning-as-participation. Opportunities for learning were provided by the teacher's topic offerings, which allowed the learner to respond to the topic with expanded answers. Taguchi (2015b), on the other hand, described a case of one learner of Japanese in Japan who showed a dramatic improvement with the use of different speech forms. The interview data revealed this learner's involvement in different communities (i.e., a university club, a peer discussion group, and a part time job). By participating in these communities, composed of distinct settings, goals, and memberships, this learner gained access to context-rich practice of different speech forms.

Although these studies documented pragmatics learning occurring through participation in social practices, the study-abroad context does not always bring about a desired outcome. A line of research on identity and subjectivity (see Chapter 10) has shown that learners are not always willing to participate in pragmatic practices in the local community. They sometimes reject adopting the normative use of honorifics or gendered speech when these norms do not align with their L1-based cultural values or their sense of self. For instance, in Iwasaki's (2011) study, identity affected L2 Japanese learners' choice of speech forms while abroad. The learners knew which speech form (polite or plain) to use in situation, but they did not conform to the norm: some learners wanted to project the image of a formal self and resorted to using the polite form, while others wanted to sound casual and opted for the plain form to express solidarity.

These cases of restricted social participation reinforce the complexity of the study-abroad context for pragmatics learning. Although this context can serve as a site for learning pragmatics, which often goes beyond what students learn in textbooks or classroom instruction, the context alone is not sufficient to understand what actually leads to pragmatics learning. It is the product of contextual affordances and learners' positioning that determines whether learners can take advantage of the context to grow pragmatically while abroad.

The relationship between contextual affordances, individual characteristics, and pragmatics learning is also seen in formal classrooms and technology-supported environments. In content-based classes (see Chapter 30), the instructor and students use target language as a shared language to present their views, to give feedback, and to display support for each other, which serve as opportunities for pragmatics learning. Kääntä's (2014) study in an English immersion context revealed that students often disagree with each other or correct each other's mistakes. Through routine participation in these 'risky' interactions, L2 English learners gradually develop politeness strategies to cope with interpersonal communication in a classroom.

Similarly, technology-enhanced contexts have recently expanded the options of pragmatics learning (see Taguchi and Sykes, 2013, for a review). Typical tools for computer-mediated communication (CMC), such as email, chat, blogs, social networking sites, and videoconferencing programs (e.g., Skype and Google hangouts), allow learners to interact with other users of the language and develop a sense of community through shared activities. Tsai and Kinginger (2015) analyzed advice giving and receiving between L2 English learners in CMC-based peer review sessions. They showed that the asymmetrical relationship between the advice giver and receiver was compromised through the use of various face-saving strategies, which emerged from the speakers' concerns toward maintaining interpersonal relationships.

In summary, the context for pragmatics learning involves a number of different domains of communication that supply pragmatics-focused input. These domains differ by participant frameworks, settings, and goals of interaction; as a result, they involve different types of pragmatic forms and functions to learn and internalize. Qualitative studies, such as those summarized above, provide an account of the intricate relationship between pragmatics learning and contextual specifics.

LEARNING PRAGMATICS THROUGH EXPLICIT AND IMPLICIT INSTRUCTION

The previous section discussed how pragmatics learning occurs incidentally through direct participations in context-specific activities. Another approach to learning, albeit a more common inquiry than naturalistic exposure, is direct instruction. Researchers and teachers have explored ways to incorporate pragmatics in teaching, as seen in a range of teachers' guides and resource books in TESOL (e.g., Houck and Tatsuki, 2011). These resources show how we can incorporate the key elements of pragmatics – social context, functional language use, and norms of interaction – into pedagogical activities and tasks. Some teaching tips emerging from these resources involve: raising learners' awareness of pragmatic features and sociocultural norms of interaction; engaging learners in pragmatically-focused practice; and guiding learners' discovery of pragmatic rules (Cohen and Ishihara 2013).

Parallel to this pedagogical effort, a number of empirical studies have emerged to assess effectiveness of instruction in pragmatics learning. Studies during the 1990s revealed that most pragmatic features are teachable, leading to a generalization that instruction can facilitate pragmatics learning. More recent research has concentrated on the methods debate addressing the single question: which instructional method is most effective for pragmatics learning? The result of this research on practice is about 30 existing intervention studies to date, which have compared different teaching methods by measuring the degree of learning from pre- to post-instruction. Previous studies mainly compared explicit and implicit teaching method by adopting Schmidt's (2001) noticing hypothesis that focuses on attention in learning (Taguchi, 2015c). The explicit method involves direct explanations of pragmatic features, whereas the implicit method holds back explanations and instead aims to develop learners' understandings of the target features by using input flood, input enhancement, consciousness-raising tasks, and indirect feedback (Kasper, 2001).

Existing findings have generated several observations. First, explicit teaching is generally more advantageous than implicit teaching on two specific pedagogical features: overt pragmatic explanation and production-based practice of the target pragmatic features. This is shown in Fordyce's (2014) study, which compared the effect of explicit and implicit treatment on L2 English learners' use of epistemic stance markers. In the explicit teaching condition, students received explanations about epistemic markers, along with exposure to the markers and feedback on their epistemic forms in writing. By contrast, in the implicit condition students were just exposed to texts that contained epistemic forms. Significant gains after the instruction were found in both groups, but the explicit group outperformed the implicit group on the frequency and range of the epistemic forms they used in the post-test writing samples.

The second observation is that the implicit teaching condition can be as effective as the explicit condition when it taps on two learning mechanisms: noticing and processing (Taguchi, 2015c). Common characteristics of effective implicit activities involve having learners attend to input and derive pragmatic forms and functions, along with their contextual features, and then reinforcing the noticing by having them process the form-function-context associations. For instance, consciousness-raising activities that push learners to compare and analyze different pragmatic forms and social factors were found to be as effective as their explicit counterpart in teaching English requests (Takimoto, 2009). Collaborative dialogues that engage learners in discussing pragmatics were also found to be effective in Taguchi and Kim's (2015) study involving junior high school students learning English as a foreign language.

These findings indicate that learning issues in pragmatics are closely related to the quantity and quality of processing depth (Taguchi, 2015c). Learners who learn pragmatic features from direct explanation combined with production practice, or learners who are guided to discover pragmatic rules, may process pragmatic features at a deeper level than those who just receive input. As a result, the former group can develop a higher level of awareness of target pragmatic rules, which essentially reinforces their knowledge of the rules.

IMPLICATIONS FOR TEACHING AND ASSESSMENT

So far, this chapter has presented an evolving definition of pragmatic competence over the last four decades, as well as the current literature on how this competence can be learned and developed. Critically, what learners acquire (the construct and its key dimensions) informs what resources and materials are necessary to develop the competence. Pragmatic competence involves several specific elements: linguistic knowledge; sociocultural knowledge of how forms work to produce social meanings; and ability to interact with others to co-construct social acts. These knowledge and interactional abilities develop through recurring opportunities to observe sociocultural norms of interaction, and variations in the norms. It is also critical for learners to experience consequences of their pragmatic behaviors through participation and feedback. Learning contexts that afford these elements – be it study-abroad, classroom, or technology-based contexts – are likely to promote pragmatics learning. These elements can also be furnished via instruction, particularly through well-designed materials and tasks that promote learners' noticing of target pragmatic features and processing of the features.

In concluding this chapter, I will present several implications for teaching and assessment of L2 pragmatics. First, benefits of the naturalistic and instructional environments examined in this chapter tell us that these two environments are complementary to each other in promoting pragmatic development. Hence, researchers and practitioners can seek ways to bridge these two contexts to maximize students' learning. Knowledge of pragmatic features learned via direct instruction should transfer to real-world situations, because the outside (naturalistic) context is the place where learners' pragmatic competence is actually tested. Whether or not learners are able to utilize their learned pragmatic knowledge in real-life situations is a form of assessment, because it can reveal the robustness of their knowledge. At the same time, it is a form of teaching. In promoting the 'after effect' of instruction, teachers can encourage learners to observe and practice target pragmatic behaviors outside the classroom, so that their pragmatic knowledge continues to develop. If learners are in a non-target-language-context, authentic materials and medias (e.g., films, TV dramas) could serve as useful resources to apply learned pragmatic knowledge. Social networking sites can also provide a context-rich, high-stakes environment where learners can practice pragmatics with target language speakers (see Chapter 36).

Another implication relates to pragmatic assessment. As illustrated in the changing definition of pragmatic competence in this chapter, there is a real interest in pragmatics-in-interaction in the current literature, which focuses on how a pragmatic act is jointly constructed among participants in conversation over turns. Kasper's (2006) call for discursive pragmatics is the initiative of this trend (see also Ross and Kasper, 2013; Taguchi and Roever, 2017). Recent studies in this paradigm have applied Conversational Analysis (CA) to study action, meaning, and context in pragmatic acts (Sacks, Schegloff, and Jefferson, 1974). A future assessment of pragmatics can take up on these recent trends. When assessing pragmatics in interaction, we can adopt the performance-based approach that examines wide-ranging interactional features beyond linguistic elements. Fluency and conversation management, ability to accomplish mutual understanding, and ability to repair communication breakdowns are some of those interactional features. Yoon's (2015) study can serve as a model in such practice. She adapted features of conversation (e.g., turn-taking, response tokens, question-answer sequences) to develop rating protocols of role-play performance of speech acts in L2 English. These features can be traced over time through recurring speech events with the same participant(s), so their ability to participate in interaction successfully could serve as an indicator of pragmatics learning and development.

CONCLUSION

This chapter discussed the construct of pragmatic competence and key issues for learning pragmatics. Pragmatic competence is understood as a multi-facet construct of several distinct dimensions, including linguistic knowledge, sociocultural knowledge, and ability to interact. Because pragmatics involves a socially-situated practice, learning contexts that offer opportunities to observe and practice local norms of interaction are critical for pragmatic development. However, because local conventions of interaction are not salient, it is often difficult for learners to recognize how people convey appropriate levels of politeness or directness. Hence, explicit and implicit instructions that make learners become aware of those social conventions of speaking are equally important. Future research can further investigate optimal conditions for learning pragmatics in both naturalistic and instructed settings so that classroom instructors can be informed about how to use available teaching materials and resources to maximize pragmatics learning in a classroom.

Discussion Questions

1. Have you ever taught pragmatics in a language classroom? What methods and tasks do you think are effective in teaching and assessing pragmatic competence?

2. When immigrants move to an English-speaking country (e.g., the USA, Britain) for a job opportunity, what kind of pragmatic knowledge and skills do you think they need, as opposed to those of study-abroad students or sojourners (e.g., how to make small talk)? What instructional approach or materials are appropriate to serve their needs? Create a hypothetical situation to address this question.

3. Besides contexts and instruction, individual learner characteristics can also greatly influence pragmatics learning. What characteristics can affect pragmatics development and why? For example, do you think learner characteristics such as age, motivation, and personality influence pragmatics learning? Can you think of any examples?

Key Readings

Bardovi-Harlig, K. (2013). Developing L2 pragmatics. *Language Learning*, 63, 68–86.

Ishihara, N., & Cohen, A. (2010). *Teaching and Learning Pragmatics: Where Language and Culture Meet*. Harlow, UK: Pearson Longman.

Ross, S., & Kasper, G. (2013). *Assessing Second Language Pragmatics*. New York: Palgrave Macmillan.

Taguchi, N. (2017). Interlanguage pragmatics. In A. Barron, Y. Gu, & G. Steen (Eds.), *The Routledge Handbook of Pragmatics*. Abingdon / New York: Routledge.

Taguchi, N., & Roever, C. (2017). *Second Language Pragmatics*. Oxford: Oxford University Press.

References

Bachman, L. F., & Palmer, A. S. (1996). *Language Testing in Practice: Designing and Developing Useful Language Tests*. Oxford: Oxford University Press.

Bachman, L. F., & Palmer, A. S. (2010). *Language Testing in Practice*. Oxford: Oxford University Press.

Canale, M., & Swain, M. (1980). Theoretical aspects of communicative approaches to second language teaching and testing. *Applied Linguistics*, 1, 1–47.

Canale, M. (1983). From communicative competence to communicative language pedagogy. In J. C. Richards & R. W. Schmidt (Eds.), *Language and Communication* (pp. 2–27). London: Longman.

Celce-Murcia, M. (2007). Rethinking the role of communicative competence in language teaching. In E. Alcón Soler & M. P. Safont Jordà (Eds.), *Intercultural Language Use and Language Learning* (pp. 41–57). Dordrecht, The Netherlands: Springer.

Cohen, A. D., & N. Ishihara (2013). Pragmatics. In B. Tomlinson (Ed.), *Applied Linguistics and Materials Development* (pp. 113–126). London / New York: Bloomsbury.

Fordyce, K. (2014). The differential effects of explicit and implicit instruction on EFL learners' use of epistemic stance. *Applied Linguistics*, 35, 6–28.

Houck, N., & Tatsuki, D. (2011). *Pragmatics from Research to Practice: New Directions*. Alexandria, VA: TESOL.

Hymes, D. H. (1972). On communicative competence. In J. B. Pride & J. Holmes (Eds.), *Sociolinguistics* (pp. 269–293). Baltimore, USA: Penguin Books Ltd.

Iwasaki, N. (2011). Learning L2 Japanese "politeness" and "impoliteness": Young American men's dilemmas during study abroad. *Japanese Language and Literature*, 45, 67–106.

Kääntä, L. (2014). From noticing to initiating correction: Students' epistemic displays in instructional interaction. *Journal of Pragmatics*, 66, 86–105.

Kasper, G. (2001). Classroom research on interlanguage pragmatics. In K. Rose & G. Kasper (Eds.), *Pragmatics in Language Teaching* (pp. 33–62). Cambridge: Cambridge University Press.

Kasper, G. (2006). Introduction. *Multilingua – Journal of Cross-Cultural and Interlanguage Communication*, 25(3), 243–248.

Nguyen, H. T. (2011). A longitudinal microanalysis of a second language learner's participation. In G. Pallotti & J. Wagner (Eds.), *L2 Learning as Social Practice: Conversation-Analytic Perspectives* (pp. 17–44) Honolulu: University of Hawai'i, National Foreign Language Resource Center.

Ross, S., & Kasper, G. (2013). *Assessing Second Language Pragmatics*. New York: Palgrave Macmillan.

Sacks, H., Schegloff, E. A., & Jefferson, G. (1974). A simplest systematics for the organization of turn-taking for conversation. *Language*, 50, 696–735.

Schmidt, R. (2001). Attention. In P. Robinson (Ed.), *Cognition and Second Language Instruction* (pp. 3–32). Cambridge: Cambridge University Press.

Taguchi, N. (2015a). Contextually speaking: A survey of pragmatics learning abroad, in class and online. *System*, 48, 2–30.

Taguchi, N. (2015b). *Developing Interactional Competence in a Japanese Study Abroad Context*. Bristol, UK: Multilingual Matters.

Taguchi, N. (2015c). Instructed pragmatics at a glance: Where instructional studies were, are, and should be going. *Language Teaching*, 48, 1–50.

Taguchi, N., & Kim, Y. (2015). Collaborative dialogue in learning pragmatics: Pragmatic-related episodes as an opportunity for learning request-making. *Applied Linguistics*.

Taguchi, N., & Roever, C. (2017). *Second Language Pragmatics*. Oxford: Oxford University Press.

Taguchi, N., & Sykes, J. M. (2013). *Technology in Interlanguage Pragmatics Research and Teaching*. Amsterdam/Philadelphia: John Benjamins.

Takimoto, M. (2009). The effects of input-based tasks on the development of learners' pragmatic proficiency. *Applied Linguistics*, 30, 1–25.

Tsai, M.-H. and Kinginger, C. (2015). Giving and receiving advice in computer-mediated peer response activities. *CALICO*, 32, 82–112.

Yoon, S.-J. (2015). Validity argument for assessing L2 pragmatics in interaction using mixed methods. *Language Testing*, 32, 199–225.

Young, R. (2008). *Discursive Practices in Language Learning and Teaching*. Malden, MA and Oxford: Wiley-Blackwell.

CHAPTER 28

Learning Intercultural Competence

Farzad Sharifian

INTRODUCTION

Marked by an increase in the speed of globalisation, the twenty-first century has witnessed a revolution in the contexts and contents of intercultural communication. Technological advances such as chat rooms, email, personal weblogs, Facebook, Twitter, and mobile text messaging on the one hand, and the accelerated pace of people's international mobility on the other, have given a new meaning to the term 'intercultural communication' (e.g., Sharifian and Jamarani, 2013). It is now the default context of communication in everyday life. This makes the development of intercultural competence essential for many individuals worldwide. This chapter presents a review of theories and models of intercultural competence, followed by a discussion of approaches to learning and developing intercultural competence. The last section explores the implications of the discussion for teaching and assessment.

OVERVIEW

Generally, intercultural competence is defined as knowledge and skills that enable speakers to communicate effectively and appropriately with speakers of other cultural backgrounds (e.g., Byram, 2012). Hammer (2015: 483) defines intercultural competence as "the capability to shift one's cultural perspective and appropriately adapt one's behaviour to cultural differences and commonalities." From the outset, it must be clear that intercultural competence does not necessarily involve communicating with speakers of other languages; it is not uncommon to communicate with people who share our language but not our culture. English is used by many speech communities that do not necessarily share the original cultural systems associated with those languages – hence the concept of World Englishes (Sharifian, 2015b). Many other languages, such as Arabic, Mandarin, French, Spanish, and German, are also spoken in more than one country and territory, and each variety of these languages is associated with cultural systems that are partly unique to particular speech communities.

Since the inception of the notion of 'intercultural competence', dozens of models and frameworks of intercultural competence, or terms with a similar focus, have been proposed by scholars across various disciplines. Spitzberg and Changnon (2009) review 20 of these models and divide them into the following categories:

- Compositional models
- Co-orientational models
- Developmental models
- Adaptational models

Compositional models outline the components of intercultural competence without elaborating on the relationship between the elements. Spitzberg and Changnon (2009) refer to Howard-Hamilton, Richardson, and Shuford (1998) as an example of a compositional model, in that case composed of three main components: attitudes, knowledge, and skills. Under 'attitudes', the authors state that interculturally competent interactants need to value their own group, appreciate risk taking, and devalue discrimination. Under 'knowledge', they list 'knowledge of self as it relates to cultural identity', awareness of similarities and differences across cultures, and understanding of intersecting oppressions (e.g., race and religion). The list of skills in this model includes elements such as the 'ability to identify and articulate cultural similarities and differences' and the 'ability to communicate cross-culturally'. Spitzberg and Changnon note that such models often define and label some elements too broadly (e.g., engaging in self-reflection) while proposing others that reflect a much narrower range of action (e.g., challenging discriminatory acts).

Co-orientational models focus on understanding as an outcome of interaction between speakers from different cultural backgrounds. As an example, Spitzberg and Changnon refer to Fantini's (1995) model, where the focus is on elements closely associated with linguistic processes, and on the convergence in the worldviews of speakers: both are necessary for co-orientation. Spitzberg and Changnon maintain that the influential model developed by Byram and colleagues (e.g., Byram, 2008) shares features with co-orientational models. For Byram, intercultural competence involves five elements:

- **Attitudes:** Curiosity and openness, readiness to suspend disbelief about other cultures, and belief about one's own culture.
- **Knowledge:** Of social groups and their products and practices in one's own and in one's interlocutor's country, and of the general processes of societal and individual interaction.
- **Skills of interpreting and relating:** Ability to interpret a document or event from another culture, explain it, and relate it to documents from one's own culture.
- **Skills of discovery and interaction:** Ability to acquire new knowledge of a culture and cultural practices, and ability to operate knowledge, attitudes, and skills under the constraints of real-time communication and interaction.
- **Critical cultural awareness / Political education:** Ability to evaluate critically and on the basis of explicit criteria perspectives, practices, and products in one's own and other cultures and countries.

Spitzberg and Changnon (2009) note that the important factor of time is missing in both compositional and co-orientational models. Time is a factor in a given interaction and in longer-term intercultural relationship building, and lies at the heart of developmental models. King and Baxter Magolda (2005) represent such models as being built on the premise that "over time, interactants progress from relatively *ethnocentric* understandings of other cultures to a more *ethnorelative* comprehension and appreciation [original emphases]" (Spitzberg & Changnon, 2009: 21). According to developmental models, individuals progress from a monocultural mindset and worldview to more pluralistic and multicultural perspectives and worldviews. Spitzberg and Changnon (2009: 24) note the importance of developmental models in "drawing attention to the evolutionary nature of interaction and relationships", but also highlight that such models neglect to identify the traits that compose interpersonal and intercultural competence.

Adaptational models, according to Spitzberg and Changnon, emphasise the process of adaptation as an element and a criterion of intercultural competence. For example, 'communication accommodation theory' (Giles and Ogay, 2007) shows how interactants adapt and adjust their communicative styles, including vocal patterns and gestures, to accommodate others. Since this adaptation aims to minimise the social differences between the interactants, an interactant from the non-dominant group is likely to make a greater effort to accommodate an interactant from the dominant group. This theory acknowledges the role of mediating factors such as context and identity.

Spitzberg and Changnon (2009) observe the wide range of useful models of intercultural competence and evaluate the considerable similarities, as well as the extensive diversity, in the scope and elements of these models. Liu (2012: 271) observes that "by and large, three common themes emerge from various definitions of intercultural competence: the practice of empathy, perspective taking, and adaptability, all of which implies awareness of the 'self' and positive orientations to the 'other' in achieving intended intercultural communication outcomes." Spitzberg and Changnon (2009) note that all models and theories of intercultural competence include three basic components: motivation, knowledge, and skills.

Spitzberg and Changnon (2009) point out that existing models have put too much emphasis on the cognitive, rather than the emotional, aspects of intercultural encounters[1]. They also raise the important question of "*where competence is located* [original emphasis]" (Spitzberg and Changnon, 2009: 44). While most models largely view competence as residing in the mind of the individual, some consider it to be located in the interaction itself.

Another challenge for existing models of intercultural competence is their notion of 'culture'. Spitzberg and Changnon (2009: 6) define culture as "a primitive theoretical term, concerned with enduring yet evolving intergenerational attitudes, values, beliefs, rituals/customs, and behavioral patterns into which people are born but that is structurationally created and maintained by people's ongoing actions." Many scholars (e.g., Fuchs, 2005; Grillo, 2003) have found such definitions of culture too broad and abstract (see Kramsch, 2012), with a tendency towards essentialism. An alternative is the model of metacultural competence (Sharifian, 2013), which draws on the newly developed discipline of Cultural Linguistics (Sharifian, 2015a). Unlike very broad and binary notions of culture (source culture versus target culture), the concept of metacultural competence focuses on a dynamic and pluralistic view of cultural encounters and experiences.

The focus of metacultural competence is not on culture itself, but on cultural conceptualisations. Metacultural competence enables interlocutors to communicate and negotiate their cultural conceptualisations. These are conceptual structures such as 'cultural schema' (or 'cultural model'), 'cultural category' (including 'cultural prototype'), and 'cultural metaphor' (Sharifian, 2011). Cultural schemas are culturally constructed conceptual structures (or pools of knowledge *heterogeneously* shared by the members of a speech community). They enable us to interpret and communicate knowledge, which is often inescapably culturally mediated, as well as cultural experiences. Many lexical items of human languages index cultural schemas (see Chapters 18 and 19). Cultural schemas also provide a basis for the enactment and understanding of many speech acts.

Cultural categories are cognitive categories with a cultural basis. Categorisation is a basic human cognitive process, and plays an important role in our cognitive development from early childhood. The cultural milieu classifies objects, events, and experiences into categories based on similarities and differences, and we tend to take these categories for granted. Although categorisation in early life tends to be rather idiosyncratic – for example, anything round may be categorised as a ball – culture and language soon guide the categorisation processes. Not only does culture, through language, determine the categories at our disposal, it also presents us with certain prototypes for those categories. For example, different speech communities may have different prototypes for the cultural category of FOOD.

Cultural conceptual metaphors are conceptual metaphors rooted in cultural systems, such as ethnomedical traditions and religion (Sharifian, Dirven, Yu, and Neiemier, 2008). They are cognitive structures that allow us to understand one conceptual domain in terms of another. In American and British varieties of English, expressions such as 'saving time' and 'spending time' reflect conceptualisation of TIME AS COMMODITY. Recent research in cultural linguistics suggest that some conceptual metaphors that use the human body as the source domain, such as HEART AS THE SEAT OF EMOTIONS, have their origin in ethnomedical and other cultural traditions (e.g., Sharifian et al., 2008).

An important element of metacultural competence is conceptual variation awareness, or the awareness that different languages or language variants are used by different speech communities to encode their respective cultural conceptualisations. Metacultural competence also involves the ability to consciously employ strategies such as conceptual explication strategy, which clarifies, where needed, conceptualisations with which interlocutors may not be familiar.

Importantly, metacultural competence enables interlocutors to negotiate intercultural meanings through the use of conceptual negotiation strategies. This is reflected, for example, in seeking conceptual clarification when one feels that a certain expression may carry a hidden meaning. Active interest in learning about other interlocutors' cultural conceptualisations is important in the successful communication of cultural conceptualisations, and ultimately in developing metacultural competence.

KEY LEARNING ISSUES

LEARNING INTERCULTURAL COMPETENCE

In recent years, many scholars have emphasised the importance of intercultural education, and its goal of developing intercultural competence (e.g., Byram, 2008; Liddicoat and Scarino, 2013). In the field of foreign language education, the goal of communicative competence has been replaced by that of intercultural communicative competence ('intercultural competence' for short) (e.g., Byram, 1997). Beamer (1992) briefly reviews several models of learning intercultural competence, and offers a new one. She refers to the model developed by Bennett (1986), known as the Developmental Model of Intercultural Sensitivity, which identifies six stages in the development of intercultural sensitivity. The first three stages are 'ethnocentric': denial of difference; defence against difference (the learner perceives their own culture as better than the other); and minimisation of difference (the learner accepts some level of difference but focuses on universals). The next three stages are 'ethnorelative': acceptance of difference; adaptation to difference (the learner empathises with people from other cultures and adopts their behaviour when interacting with them); and integration of difference (the learner can integrate multiple sets of values into their identity). Beamer notes two valuable premises in the models that she reviews: (a) learning is incremental, and (b) "the individual's internal perceptions, challenged through personal experience, are the starting point for learning intercultural competence" (Beamer, 1992: 291).

Beamer's own model is built on several underlying principles:

- Cultures are learnable.
- All cultural perspectives are equally valid.
- Cultural bias always exists, and is acknowledged by the interculturally competent communicator.
- Culture governs communicative behaviour.

The model is composed of five elements: "a) acknowledging diversity, b) organizing information according to stereotypes, c) posing questions to challenge stereotypes, d) analysing communication episodes and, e) generating 'other cultures' messages" (Beamer, 1992: 291). The aim of the model is to effectively decode signs from other cultures and to convey the intended meaning to speakers from other cultures.

These models of learning intercultural competence, as with models of intercultural competence itself, rely on the broad notion of 'culture', and treat intercultural contexts as binary and fixed. In the twenty-first century, intercultural contexts are often much more complex, involving spaces where languages and culture intersect.

DEVELOPING INTERCULTURAL COMPETENCE

Some scholars have expressed concern about the term 'learning' in the context of intercultural competence, preferring the notion of 'developing' (e.g., Byram, Nichols, and Stevens, 2001). Comparing 'learning' and 'developing', Vande Berg maintains that:

> [w]hen a learner learns, the change occurs within an existing set of knowledge or skills, within the boundaries of an already existing framework or worldview that he or she has earlier (and unconsciously) constructed ... On the other hand, when a learner develops, this is change of a different order, one that entails the reordering or reconstructing of worldview, a transformation of basic assumptions and understandings about the world and the individual's place in it. (Vande Berg, 2015: 230–231)

Thus, reading or hearing about cultural differences may not lead to any change of behaviour or attitude, or to the development of intercultural competence. It is only when such learning (combined with interactions with members from other cultural backgrounds over time) has an impact on the learner's attitude toward cultural diversity, and consequently their behaviour, that intercultural (or metacultural) competence starts to emerge.

DEVELOPING INTERCULTURAL/METACULTURAL COMPETENCE THROUGH NEW TECHNOLOGY

In recent decades, scholars and practitioners have increasingly explored the potential for new technology to help learners develop intercultural competence. As Liaw (2006: 51) puts it, "computer networks are seen as a channel for interactivity and authenticity and for developing learners' intercultural competence." A key word in this context is 'telecollaboration' or 'online intercultural exchange', which refers to the use of CMC (Computer-Mediated Communication) to bring together learners from geographically distant locations to develop their intercultural/metacultural competence through collaborative tasks (e.g., Chun, 2015; O'Dowd, 2013). Telecollaboration can be set up in a variety of settings through the use of "web-based tools and resources, such as email, forums, blogs, wikis, text-chat, voice chat, videoconferencing, and social networking sites" (Chun, 2015: 5; see also Chapters 34–36).

Telecollaborations, both synchronous (e.g., text or video chat) and asynchronous (e.g., email), are becoming an integral part of learning additional languages (e.g., Pasfield-Neofitou, 2012). Chun (2015: 17) maintains that "telecollaboration can be instrumental in language and culture learning, awareness raising, highlighting rich points, and development of ICC [intercultural communicative competence] by providing learners with a variety of opportunities for both linguistic and cultural experiences." However, she warns us about certain constraints. For example, she observes that learners from different cultural backgrounds may prefer different technologies to be used for intercultural exchanges (Chun, 2015). These constraints may be partly alleviated if telecollaborations are combined with other intercultural activities, such as exchange programmes (e.g., Houghton, 2014).

Other activities for promoting intercultural competence, particularly in the foreign/second language classroom, include translation (see Chapter 31). Translation involves considering concepts that are not shared by both cultures, and as such could be used as 'cultural awareness raising tools' (Elorza, 2008). The usefulness of telecollaboration for developing intercultural competence equally applies to the notion of metacultural competence.

IMPLICATIONS FOR TEACHING AND ASSESSMENT

While intercultural competence was conceptualised in terms of *learning* in early models, more recent approaches have viewed it as a matter of *development*. In this respect, teaching intercultural competence means providing learners with opportunities to develop intercultural/metacultural competence. Clearly, a wealth of studies and publications have focused on how new technology allows teachers to connect their students with learners and speakers from various cultural backgrounds in geographically distant locations, allowing them to engage in intercultural interactions and, ultimately, develop intercultural/metacultural competence. It is widely recognised that reading and talking about cultural differences does not necessarily develop intercultural/metacultural competence (Vande Berg, 2015).

A context where the development of intercultural competence is essential is the foreign language class. Sercu et al. (2005: 1) argue that "foreign language education is, by definition, intercultural. Bringing a foreign language to the classroom means connecting learners to a world that is culturally different from their own. Therefore, many foreign language educators are now expected to exploit this potential and promote the acquisition of intercultural competence in their learners." Sercu (2006) observes that this focus on intercultural competence is associated with new professional demands on language teachers. They are now expected to be equipped with the knowledge, skills, and attitudes that underlie intercultural competence, and to help develop intercultural competence in their students.

In terms of assessment, Fantini (2009) argues that since intercultural competence contains many dimensions, assessing the inherent skills, attitudes, awareness, and knowledge poses a significant challenge. He rightly observes that traditional models of assessment have ignored attitudes and awareness. Fantini argues that a significant shortcoming of the assessment tools of many models of intercultural competence is that they ignore language proficiency. He observes, for example, that second language proficiency enhances all other dimensions of intercultural competence, both qualitatively and quantitatively. He maintains that grappling with a second language allows us to confront how we perceive, conceptualise, express, behave, and interact. It promotes alternative communication strategies on *someone else's terms*, helping expand and transform our habitual view of the world. Conversely, lack of second language proficiency constrains us to think and act entirely within our native system, a decidedly ethnocentric approach (Fantini, 2009).

Thus, assessing language proficiency in a second language is an important part of assessing intercultural competence in itself. Fantini adds two other important considerations about assessment: (a) which components of intercultural competence are being assessed, and (b) which test types (in terms of format, technique, and strategy) best suit the assessment of those components. Fantini presents a list, with brief descriptions, of a range of instruments available for assessing various components and dimensions of intercultural competence, such as the IDI (Intercultural Development Inventory).

CONCLUSION

Intercultural competence is an integral component of global citizenship in the twenty-first century. It is no longer merely a fashionable term, but a necessity for the daily interactions of many speakers worldwide. However, the very global processes that have brought people from different cultural backgrounds together have made 'culture' a complex and multidimensional concept. This requires us to move away from simplistic notions of culture, in favour of more nuanced and dynamic models that match the reality of today's world.

Developing intercultural/metacultural competence has, in some contexts, become an integral part of learning additional languages. Language teachers are now expected to be equipped with intercultural competence, and to provide opportunities for their learners to develop it too. In fact, the whole notion of language education needs to be reconceptualised as teaching/learning/assessing those languages *for intercultural communication*. This calls for serious reconsideration of all aspects of teaching and assessing additional languages, and of ongoing re-evaluation.

Discussion Questions

1. Do you think learning a second language contributes to the development of intercultural competence? If yes, how?

2. Do you consider yourself as 'coming from the cultural background of X'? If yes, what culture, and what does it mean in the context of intercultural competence?

3. To what extent do you think you are equipped with intercultural/metacultural competence? Do you think you need to make any further efforts in that direction?

Key Readings

Bennett, J. M. (Ed.) (2015). *The Sage Encyclopedia of Intercultural Competence*. London: Sage Publications.

Deardorff, D. K. (Ed.) (2009). *The Sage Handbook of Intercultural Competence*. Thousand Oaks, CA: Sage Publications.

Feng, A., Byram, M., & Fleming, M. (2009). *Becoming Interculturally Competent through Education and Training*. Bristol, UK: Multilingual Matters.

Liddicoat, A. J., & Scarino, A. (2013). *Intercultural Language Teaching and Learning*. Oxford: Wiley-Blackwell.

Sercu, L., et al. (2005). *Foreign Language Teachers and Intercultural Competence: An International Investigation*. Clevedon, UK: Multilingual Matters.

References

Asser, M., & Langbein-Park, A. (2015). Cultural intelligence. In J. M. Bennett (Ed.), *The Sage encyclopedia of Intercultural Competence* (pp. 164–169). London: Sage Publications.

Beamer, L. (1992). Learning intercultural competence. *Journal of Business Communication*, 29, 285–303.

Bennett, M. J. (1986). A developmental approach to training for intercultural sensitivity. *International Journal of Intercultural Relations*, 10(2), 179–196.

Byram, M. (1997). *Teaching and Assessing Intercultural Communicative Competence*. Clevedon, UK: Multilingual Matters.

Byram, M. (2008). *From Foreign Language Education to Education For Intercultural Citizenship: Essays and Reflection*. Clevedon, UK: Multilingual Matters.

Byram, M. (2012). Intercultural competence. In C. A. Chapelle (Ed.), *The Encyclopedia of Applied Linguistics* (pp. 2767–2770). Oxford: Wiley-Blackwell.

Byram, M., Nichols, A., & Stevens, D. (2001). *Developing Intercultural Competence in Practice*. Clevedon, UK: Multilingual Matters.

Chun, D. M. (2015). Language and culture learning in higher education via telecollaboration. *Pedagogies: An International Journal*, 10(1), 5–21.

Elorza, I. (2008). Promoting intercultural competence in the FL/SL classroom: Translations as sources of data. *International Journal of Bilingual Education and Bilingualism*, 8(4), 261–277.

Fantini, A. E. (1995). Language, culture, and world view: Exploring the nexus. *International Journal of Intercultural Relations*, 19, 143–153.

Fantini, A. E. (2009). Assessing intercultural competence: Issues and tools. In D. K. Deardorff (Ed.), *The Sage Handbook of Intercultural Competence* (pp. 456–476). Thousand Oaks, California: Sage.

Fuchs, S. (2005). *Against Essentialism: A Theory of Culture and Society*. Cambridge, MA: Harvard University Press.

Giles, H., & Ogay, T. (2007). Communication accommodation theory. In B. Whaley & W. Samter (Eds.), *Explaining Communication: Contemporary Theories and Exemplars* (pp. 293–310). Mahwah, NJ: Lawrence Erlbaum.

Grillo, R. D. (2003). Cultural essentialism and cultural anxiety. *Anthropological Theory*, 3(2), 157–173.

Hammer, M. R. (2015). Intercultural competence development. In J. M. Bennett (Ed.), *The Sage Encyclopedia of Intercultural Competence* (pp. 483–485). London: Sage Publications.

Houghton, S. A. (2014). Exploring manifestations of curiosity in study abroad as part of intercultural communicative competence. *System*, 42, 368–382.

Howard-Hamilton, M. F., Richardson, B. J., & Shuford, B. (1998). Promoting multicultural education: A holistic approach. *College Student Affairs Journal*, 18, 5–17.

King, P. M., & Baxter Magolda, M. B. (2005). A developmental model of intercultural maturity. *Journal of College Student Development*, 46, 571–592.

Kramsch, C. (2012). Teaching culture and intercultural competence. In C. Chapelle (Ed.), *The Encyclopedia of Applied Linguistics* (pp. 5555–5560). Oxford: Wiley-Blackwell.

Liaw, M. (2006). E-learning and the development of intercultural competence. *Language Learning and Technology*, 10(3), 49–64.

Liddicoat, A. J., & Scarino, A. (2013). *Intercultural Language Teaching and Learning*. Oxford: Wiley-Blackwell.

Liu, S. (2012). Rethinking intercultural competence: Global and local nexus. *Journal of Multicultural Discourses*, 7(3), 269–275.

O'Dowd, R. (2013). The competences of the telecollaborative teacher. *Language Learning Journal*, 43(2), 194–207.

Pasfield-Neofitou, S. E. (2012). *Online Communication in a Second Language: Social Interaction, Language Use, and Learning Japanese*. Bristol, UK: Multilingual Matters.

Sercu, L. (2006). The foreign language and intercultural competence teacher: The acquisition of a new professional identity. *Intercultural Education*, 17(1), 55–72.

Sercu, L., with Bandura, E., Castro, P., Davcheva, L., Laskaridou, C., Lundgren, U. et al. (2005). *Foreign Language Teachers and Intercultural Competence: An International Investigation*. Clevedon, UK: Multilingual Matters.

Sharifian, F. (2011). *Cultural Conceptualisations and Language: Theoretical Framework and Applications*. Amsterdam/Philadelphia: John Benjamins.

Sharifian, F. (2013). Globalisation and developing metacultural competence in learning English as an International Language. *Multilingual Education*, 3(7). Available at: http://www.multilingual-education.com/content/pdf/2191-5059-3-7.pdf

Sharifian, F. (2015a). Cultural linguistics. In F. Sharifian (Ed.), *The Routledge Handbook of Language and Culture* (pp. 473–492). Abingdon / New York: Routledge.

Sharifian, F. (2015b). World Englishes. In J. M. Bennett (Ed.), *The Sage Encyclopedia Of Intercultural Competence* (pp. 875–776). London: Sage Publications.

Sharifian, F., Dirven, R., Yu, N., & Neiemier, S. (Eds.) (2008). *Culture, Body, and Language: Conceptualizations of Internal Body Organs Across Cultures and Languages*. Berlin / New York: De Gruyter Mouton.

Sharifian, F., & Jamarani, M. (Eds.) (2013). *Language and Intercultural Communication in The New Era*. New York / Abingdon: Routledge.

Spitzberg, B. H., & Changnon, G. (2009). Conceptualizing intercultural competence. In D. K. Deardorff (Ed.), *The Sage Handbook of Intercultural Competence* (pp. 2–52). Thousand Oaks, CA: Sage Publications.

Vande Berg, M. (2015). Developmentally appropriate pedagogy. In J. M. Bennett (Ed.), *The Sage Encyclopedia of Intercultural Competence* (pp. 229–233). London: Sage Publications.

Note

[1] See the notion of 'cultural intelligence' (e.g., Asser and Langbein-Park, 2015), which includes 'emotional intelligence'.

SECTION 8

APPROACHES TO LEARNING ENGLISH

The primary focus in this section is on the diversity of means available to facilitate the learning of a second language (L2), those that are available in the classroom as well as those involving out-of-class learning. They consider different, new, and not so new, approaches and modes through which language can be productively learned.

In his chapter, **Ali Shehadeh** reviews the role of tasks in language learning, noting the various ways in which the notion of tasks has been understood by both researchers and teachers. While tasks were initially proposed as a way of developing grammatical resources in the L2, 'task' is now used more broadly to describe meaning-focused activities that are central to the teaching of all four skills. The assumptions behind claims for task-based teaching are clarified, and their role in developing fluency, accuracy and complexity of language as reflected in use of target-language grammar is discussed.

The next chapter, by **John Macalister**, takes up the issue of language learning and content. He first provides an overview of some of the theoretical advances underpinning the concept of the integration of language and content, and then points out the importance of developing robust curricular approaches to guide both learning input and learning output. He offers a model based on the development of meaning and fluency, but which also takes account of the need for a focus on form and accuracy.

Guy Cook re-examines the role of translation in language learning, a topic that has long been neglected in both research and practice. He considers the role of translation as a learning resource, highlighting the fact that learners inevitably use other languages they know as a reference point in learning, and that this bilingual knowledge base can be a productive learning resource. He notes that in a multilingual globalized world such practices are commonplace in daily life, but appear not to have been noticed by the applied linguistics research community. He examines both learning through translation and learning for translation, and provides examples of classroom activities that use translation as a source for both learning and communication.

Gregory Hadley considers the role of textbooks in promoting language learning – a resource that is sometimes viewed as detrimental rather than facilitative in providing opportunities for authentic language input and use. Objections to textbook use are both ideological and pedagogical. He considers the role of textbooks in the light of second language acquisition (SLA)-based learning claims, as well as those arising from task-based approaches. Arguing that textbooks can be seen as a potentially useful resource when used and adapted in the light of current SLA principles, he proposes a role for their effective use.

In the last chapter in this section, **Averil Coxhead** and **Oliver J. Ballance** review the use of English language corpora, the types of corpora that have been developed, and how corpora can be used to support data-driven teaching and learning, particularly in relation to lexical development. The extensive databases of both spoken and written language now available provide access to information on the nature of the lexical features of specific genres, domains and text types that may be crucial for learners in academic or specific purposes contexts, and are a resource that can be used by both teachers and learners. Ways of engaging learning with corpora are discussed, along with the issues that need to be considered when adopting a corpus-informed approach in teaching.

This set of chapters alerts us to recent developments in thinking about how the learning and teaching of an L2 can be approached. However, it also reminds us of approaches to and modes of learning that have been marginalized or taken for granted over the years. It draws our attention to the fact that ways of facilitating language learning are not, and never will be, monolithic, and that no one-size-fits-all methodological position will respond to English language learners' diverse needs and preferences.

CHAPTER 29

Learning Through Tasks

Ali Shehadeh

INTRODUCTION

The construct of 'task' has attracted both researchers and teachers worldwide in the last three decades. Researchers use tasks as a research tool to collect and analyze learner data and learner language so that they can make principled conclusions on how languages are learned, and teachers use tasks as a teaching tool so that they get learners to use the second/foreign language (L2) in a meaningful and purposeful way (see, for example, Samuda and Bygate, 2008). The main purpose of this chapter is to explore learning an L2 through tasks. The chapter will first define the notion of 'task' as an L2 learning tool. Next, it will illustrate the most common task-types and criteria for task selection and design in L2 research and pedagogy. After that, the chapter will provide an overview of the major perspectives on L2 learning through tasks. Finally, it will illustrate ways of utilizing tasks and implementing task-based learning for L2 teaching and assessment.

OVERVIEW

It is valuable to first consider what is meant by a task for second language learning. Here various definitions that have been proposed are reviewed.

'TASK' DEFINED

There is no uniform definition or description of the notion of 'task'; Ellis (2003: 2–9), for example, offers nine sample definitions of task. The study and description of task has been approached from different perspectives, and for different purposes. Second language acquisition (SLA) researchers describe tasks in terms of their usefulness for collecting data and eliciting samples of learners' language for research purposes. For example, Bialystok (1983: 103) suggests that a communication task must:

1. stimulate real communicative exchange;
2. provide incentive for the L2 speaker/learner to convey information;
3. provide control for the information items required for investigation; and
4. fulfill the needs to be used for the goals of the experiment.

Others look at tasks from a purely classroom interaction perspective. Some definitions of a classroom task are very specific. For instance, Willis (1996b: 53) defines a classroom task as "a goal-oriented activity in which learners use language to achieve a real outcome." Willis also suggests that language use in tasks is likely to reflect language use in the outside world. Other definitions are more general. Nunan (1989) proposes that a communication task "is a piece of classroom work which involves learners in comprehending, manipulating, producing, or interacting in the target language while their attention is principally focused on meaning rather than form" (Nunan, 1989: 10).

Skehan (1996: 20) views classroom and L2 research tasks as "activities which have meaning as their primary focus. Success in the task is evaluated in terms of achievement of an outcome, and tasks generally bear some resemblance to real-life language use." Ellis (2003: 9–10) lists six "criterial features of a task"; he mentions all the aspects listed by Skehan above, and also includes the concept of task as a "workplan for learner activity", which "requires learners to employ cognitive processes", and "can involve any of the four language skills." Shehadeh (2005: 18–19), summarizing the various definitions of the notion of 'task', defines a language learning task as:

- an activity
- that has a non-linguistic purpose or goal
- with a clear outcome
- and that uses any or all of the four language skills in its accomplishment
- by conveying meaning in a way that reflects real-world language use.

Key Learning Issues

Task-based language learning has taken into account different considerations: task-types and task selection, and the nature and purpose of task-based learning, which involves considering the discourse/interaction, cognitive, sociocultural and pedagogic bases of tasks.

TASK-TYPES AND TASK SELECTION

Criteria for task selection and design in L2 research and pedagogy have been approached from different perspectives. Some SLA researchers (e.g., Lynch, 1988: 127) have pointed out that in selecting communication tasks, it is important to make the linguistic features of the language (phonological, syntactic, pragmatic, etc.), the medium (phonic, graphic), the skills (listening, reading, writing, speaking) and the format of the tasks consistent with the objectives of the study and/or the use in the L2 classroom. Lynch argues that the selection of task-focused discourse, in which both the native speaker (NS) and the non-native speaker (NNS) are actively engaged in a real and concrete task, rather than merely listening to each other in a passive way, is essential for the purpose of collecting data and for use in the L2 classroom (Lynch, 1988: 322).

One of the early and most comprehensive classifications of communication tasks used in L2 research and pedagogy was proposed by Pica, Kanagy and Falodun (1993). Pica et al. identify the following five main types of communication tasks used in L2 research and pedagogy:

- **Jigsaw tasks:** Tasks that require speakers to exchange given information (e.g., completing a partially missing chart).

- **Information-gap tasks:** Tasks that involve organizing given information (e.g., arranging historical events in a chronological order, ordering pictures to make a story).

- **Problem-solving tasks:** Tasks that require the exchange of information to solve a problem (e.g., how to reduce the environmental pollution, predicting the final part of a story).

- **Decision-making tasks:** Tasks that require the exchange of opinions and making decisions or reaching unanimity (e.g., conducting a project, planning a party).

- **Opinion-exchange tasks:** Tasks that require the exchange of opinions. (e.g., mixed-sex education, students wearing uniforms at secondary or high school).

(For a fuller illustration and description of how these task-types promote L2 learning, see Pica et al., 1993.)

Other task-types commonly used in L2 research and pedagogy are dictogloss tasks and role-play tasks (see LaPierre, 1994; Swain and Lapkin, 1998):

- **Dictogloss task:** A task whereby learners are required to reconstruct a text read by the teacher as closely as possible to the original text (e.g., reconstructing a text about camping or desertification).

- **Role-play tasks:** Tasks that present students with two or more situations, for instance, and asking them to work in pairs or groups and play a specific role (e.g., a receptionist and a visitor, a manager and a clerk).

Research findings into the study of task and task-types (e.g., task variables, task difficulty, and task-sequencing) can provide teachers with "information about significant task variables acquired through research [and] assist teachers in deciding what tasks to use and when" (Ellis, 2000: 194).

The notion of 'task' constitutes the basis of the approach to L2 learning and teaching now known as task-based learning (TBL). In the following section, TBL will be briefly defined, and the various perspectives and approaches to it illustrated.

TASK-BASED LEARNING

Task-based learning (TBL) is an approach to L2 learning and teaching and a teaching methodology in which classroom tasks constitute the main focus of instruction. The syllabus in TBL is organized around tasks and activities, rather than in terms of grammar or vocabulary (Richards and Schmidt, 2010). There is a strong belief that TBL facilitates SLA and makes L2 learning and teaching more principled and more effective. This belief is supported by theoretical and pedagogical considerations. In this section, we will consider the various perspectives and bases that have aimed to date to account for how tasks and TBL can facilitate L2 learning. For each basis, I first present the perspective proposed, the theoretical conclusions based on that perspective, and the way in which tasks are seen to facilitate learning from that perspective.

THE DISCOURSE/INTERACTION BASIS

The discourse/interaction basis of TBL has been approached from two different perspectives: the input perspective and the output perspective.

According to the input perspective, interaction provides learners with an opportunity to receive feedback on the level of their comprehension in the L2, which results in negotiated modification of conversation with their speech partners that leads to comprehensible input, which, in turn, is necessary for SLA (Krashen, 1985; Long, 1996). Likewise, negotiation draws learners' attention to the formal properties of the target language (TL), i.e., to focus their attention on form, as they attempt to produce it. Learners' noticing of and paying attention to linguistic form is also necessary for SLA (Long, 1998; Schmidt, 1998). It is concluded that negotiation of meaning and modification of input are necessary for L2 learning. How do tasks facilitate L2 learning according to this perspective? Research has shown that tasks provide learners with excellent opportunities for negotiating meaning, modifying input, and focusing on the formal properties of the L2 (Ellis, Tanaka, and Yamazaki, 1994).

According to Swain (1995), learner output also plays an important role in the acquisition process because it:

- 'forces' learners to move from semantic to more syntactic analysis of the TL;
- enables them to test hypotheses about the TL; and
- helps them to consciously reflect on the language they are producing.

These all make it possible for learners to notice a gap between what they want to say in the L2 and what they can say, which prompts them to stretch their current interlanguage capacity in order to fill in the gap, and this enables learners "to control and internalise linguistic knowledge" (Swain, 1995: 126). In other words, output presents learners with unique opportunities for active deployment of their cognitive resources (Izumi, 2002). It is thus concluded that learner output is not just a sign of acquired knowledge, but also a sign of learning at work.

How do tasks facilitate L2 learning according to this perspective? Research has shown that tasks provide learners with excellent opportunities to modify their output towards comprehensibility and active deployment of their cognitive resources (Iwashita, 1999; Shehadeh, 2004; Swain and Lapkin, 1995, 1998), and that this represents "the internalization of new linguistic knowledge, or the consolidation of existing knowledge" (Swain and Lapkin, 1995: 374).

COGNITIVE BASIS

The cognitive perspective on L2 learning stipulates that learner performance has three basic aspects: fluency, accuracy, and complexity. *Fluency* refers to the learner's capacity to communicate in real time, accuracy to the learner's ability to use the TL according to its norms, and *complexity* to the learner's ability to use more elaborate and complex TL structures and forms (Skehan, 1998). These three aspects can be influenced by engaging learners in different types of production and communication. To do so, it is necessary to identify what task-types, variables, and dimensions promote fluency, accuracy, and/or complexity in L2 learners, and use them accordingly. These three aspects of learner performance are thus important for both effective communication, i.e., fluency and accuracy, and progress and development of the L2, i.e., complexity (Skehan, 1998).

How do tasks facilitate L2 learning according to this perspective? Research has shown that task-based instruction can promote fluency, accuracy, and complexity in learners (Ellis, 2005). For instance, if a teacher wants to promote fluency, he or she engages learners in meaning-oriented tasks; and if the goal is to promote accuracy or complexity, the teacher engages learners in more form-focused tasks.

SOCIOCULTURAL BASIS

According to Vygotsky (Rieber and Carton, 1987), external activities which learners participate in are the main source of mental and cognitive activities. When individuals interact, their cognitive processes awaken. These processes, which occur on the interpsychological (or social) plane, include both cognitive and language development. The language development moves from the intermental plane to the intramental plane, on the assumption that what originates in the interpsychological sphere will eventually be represented intrapsychologically, that is, within the individual. In other words, external activities are transformed into mental ones through the processes of approximation and internalization. With respect to L2 learning, this means that learners collaboratively construct knowledge as a joint activity. This co-construction of knowledge engages learners in cognitive processes that are implicated in L2 learning. Thus, social interaction mediates learning, as explained by Ellis (2000: 209): "Learners first succeed in performing a new function with the assistance of another person and then internalise this function so that they can perform it unassisted", a process often referred to as *scaffolding*. It follows that collaborative construction of knowledge in a joint activity is an important source of L2 learning.

How do tasks facilitate L2 learning according to this perspective? Research has shown that tasks are successfully accomplished by learners as a joint activity, and that this process of joint accomplishment indeed contributes to L2 learning (e.g., LaPierre, 1994). Also, studies have shown that jointly performed tasks enable students to solve linguistic problems that lie beyond their individual abilities (Swain and Lapkin, 1998).

PEDAGOGICAL BASIS

Finally, recent approaches to L2 teaching methodology, such as communicative language teaching and task-based language teaching, emphasize student autonomy and student-centered instruction as effective ways of learning. This is because in these approaches:

- students take much of the responsibility for their own learning;
- they are actively involved in shaping how they learn;
- there is ample teacher–student and student–student interaction;
- there is an abundance of brainstorming activities, pair work, and small-group work; and
- the teacher's role is more like a facilitator or advisor of learning than an instructor or lecturer who spoon-feeds learners with knowledge (Edwards and Willis, 2005; García Mayo, 2007).

It is concluded that internally driven devices (e.g., self-noticing), as opposed to external techniques and external feedback (e.g., clarification requests), must be encouraged in the L2 classroom, because there is strong empirical evidence to suggest that internal attention-drawing devices are more facilitative of L2 learning than external attention-drawing techniques (Izumi, 2002; Shehadeh, 2004).

How do tasks facilitate L2 learning according to this perspective? TBL is an ideal tool for utilizing these principles in the L2 classroom. For instance, research has shown that task-based pair and group activities that are generated by students, or are sensitive to students' preferences, ensure not only that students take responsibility for much of the work, but also that there is greater student involvement in the learning process (e.g., Edwards and Willis, 2005; Shehadeh, 2005).

Overall, and based on the various perspectives presented above, it is no wonder that tasks are now viewed by many scholars as "the devices that provide learners with the data they need for learning" (Ellis, 2000: 93). Similarly, Van den Branden, Bygate, and Norris state that:

> ... there is widespread agreement that tasks, potentially at least, offer a uniquely powerful resource both for teaching and testing of language. In particular, they provide a locus for bringing together the various dimensions of language, social context, and the mental processes of individual learners that are key to learning. There are theoretical grounds, and empirical evidence, for believing that tasks might be able to offer all the affordances needed for successful instructed language development, whoever the learners might be, and whatever the context. (Van den Branden, Bygate, and Norris, 2009: 11)

Van den Branden et al. base these statements on the extensive and varied literature on task-based learning, teaching and assessment that has appeared across many journals, edited volumes, monographs, and special issues in refereed journals, which speaks of the potential of TBL as an approach to L2 learning and teaching, and as a teaching methodology in which classroom tasks constitute the main focus of instruction and assessment (Van den Branden et al., 2009: 1).

IMPLICATIONS FOR TEACHING AND ASSESSMENT

Implementation research into utilizing task-based learning and teaching (TBLT) for L2 teaching and assessment has addressed several issues, including the following:

- How do we implement the principles underlying the various perspectives on task-based learning in a classroom context?
- How can TBLT be implemented in different learning and teaching contexts (e.g., ESL vs. EFL settings)?
- How can we use tasks with learners at all levels?
- How can task-based language learning and teaching be used with multilevel, mixed-ability students?
- How do we design task-based language courses?
- How can TBLT be used for specific classroom activities, for a whole semester, or for a full academic curriculum?
- How is the syllabus in task-based language teaching organized?
- What is the methodology of task-based language teaching?
- How are learners tested in a TBLT context?

Scholars have proposed different models and frameworks for task-based teaching and assessment to be employed by classroom teachers (e.g., Nunan, 1989; Skehan, 1998; Willis, 1996a, 1996b). Others devote whole volumes to addressing implementation issues (e.g., Byrnes and Manchón, 2014; Edwards and Willis, 2005; García Mayo, 2007; González-Lloret and Ortega, 2014; Long, 2015; Samuda and Bygate, 2008; Shehadeh and Coombe, 2010, 2012; Thomas and Reinders, 2015). It is beyond the scope of this chapter to illustrate these frameworks and implementation models. For convenience, I will provide only some illustrative examples of successful task-based language teaching and assessment.

Iwashita and Li (2012) investigated patterns of teacher–student and student–student interaction in a task-based oral EFL classroom in a university setting in China. The study was conducted against the backdrop of classroom-based TBLT research in Asian counties in general, and in China in particular, that has focused to date mainly on the factors that ostensibly hinder the implementation of communicative TBLT methodologies in these contexts. By contrast, these investigators found strong and active student participation in the classroom, and extensive teacher–student and student–student interaction, despite the large class size and the students' unfamiliarity with a teaching methodology that was very different from the traditional Chinese way of learning and teaching.

Utilizing technology in task-based instruction, Canto, de Graaff, and Jauregi (2014) illustrate the Networked Interaction in Foreign Language Acquisition and Research (NIFLAR)'s technology-mediated, task-based framework for the development of intercultural competence, and discuss its application to both video-web task-based communication and the virtual world *Second Life* by Dutch learners of Spanish communicating with native-speaker teachers of Spanish.

Focusing on assessment, finally, Winke (2010) explains how to use online tasks for formative language assessment, which is defined as assessment that is used in "evaluating students in the process of 'forming' their competencies and skills" (Brown, 2004: 6). She demonstrates how these tasks provide continuous feedback to the teacher and learners, and how this feedback can be used for making decisions about ongoing instructional procedures and classroom tasks.

CONCLUSION

In conclusion, there is now an enormous interest in the construct of task as a learning and teaching tool, and the task-based language learning, teaching and assessment approach that has stemmed from it, as evidenced by the numerous publications, symposiums, colloquiums, conference presentations, and indeed whole conferences that are specifically dedicated to TBLT (Van den Branden et al., 2009). The most notable of these is the formation of the International Consortium on Task-based Language Teaching (ICTBLT) in 2005, which holds a biennial international conference on the topic, now transformed into a professional association, the International Association for Task-Based Language Teaching (IATBLT).

In spite of all the potential value of TBLT noted above, traditional language-centered and teacher-centered instruction still persists in many EFL/ESL settings in the world. Adams and Newton (2009), for example, citing evidence from a large body of classroom-based research on current English teaching in Asia, state that "[r]esearch conducted across East Asian contexts has overwhelmingly suggested that … English language teaching … remains traditional with an explicit grammar-teaching focus" (p. 2). Some traditional language-centered and teacher-centered instruction can still be found in other parts of the world too, including Europe (Shehadeh, 2012). A number of factors have been identified as challenges for adopting TBLT in these ESL/EFL settings, including administrative constraints, exam pressures, cultural pressures and expectations, time pressures, and available materials (see Adams and Newton, 2009; Shehadeh, 2012, for overviews).

Nonetheless, many scholars, language professionals and practicing teachers, armed with insights from SLA research findings, empirical findings on effective instructional techniques, and cognitive psychology, strongly believe that task-based language learning, teaching and assessment facilitates SLA and makes L2 learning and teaching more successful and more effective. But these professionals also point to the need for further research into the notion of 'task' and the various aspects of, and perspectives on, the task-based language learning, teaching and assessment approach.

Discussion Questions

1. Do you think TBLT can be applied in your teaching context? Why / Why not?

2. What aspects of TBLT could you investigate in your own classroom?

3. What kind of data would you need to collect in order to investigate the difference in achievement between students in a student-centered TBLT class and students in a traditional language-centered, teacher-centered class?

Key Readings

Bygate, M. (Ed.) (2015). *Domains and Directions in the Development of TBLT: A Decade of Plenaries from the International Conference*. Amsterdam/Philadelphia: John Benjamins.

Byrnes, H., & Manchón, R. M. (Eds.) (2014). *Task-based Language Learning: Insights from and for L2 Writing*. Amsterdam/Philadelphia: John Benjamins.

Ellis, R. (2003). *Task-based Language Learning and Teaching*. Oxford: Oxford University Press.

Long, M. (2015). *Second Language Acquisition and Task-Based Language Teaching*. Oxford: Wiley-Blackwell.

Shehadeh, A., & Coombe, C. (Eds.) (2010). *Applications of Task-based Learning in TESOL*. Alexandria, VA: TESOL.

Shehadeh, A., & Coombe, C. (Eds.) (2012). *Task-based Language Teaching in Foreign Language Contexts: Research and Implementation*. Amsterdam/Philadelphia: John Benjamins.

Van den Branden, K., Bygate, M., & Norris, J. (Eds.) (2009). *Task-based Language Teaching: A Reader*. Amsterdam/Philadelphia: John Benjamins.

Willis, J. (1996). *A Framework for Task-based Learning*. Harlow, UK: Longman.

References

Adams, R., & Newton, J. (2009). TBLT in Asia: Constraints and opportunities. *Asian Journal of English Language Teaching*, 19, 1–17.

Bialystok, E. (1983). Some factors in selection and implementation of communication strategies. In C. Faerch & G. Kasper (Eds.), *Strategies in Interlanguage Communication* (pp. 100–118). London: Longman.

Brown, H.D. (2004). *Language Assessment: Principles and Classroom Practice*. White Plains, NY: Pearson ESL.

Byrnes, H., & Manchón, R. M. (Eds.) (2014). *Task-based Language Learning: Insights from and for L2 Writing*. Amsterdam/Philadelphia: John Benjamins.

Canto, S., de Graaff, R., & Jauregi, K. (2014). Collaborative tasks for negotiation of intercultural meaning in virtual worlds and video-web communication. In M. González-Lloret & L. Ortega (Eds.), *Technology-mediated TBLT: Researching Technology and Tasks* (pp. 183–212). Amsterdam/Philadelphia: John Benjamins.

Edwards, C., & Willis, J. (Eds.) (2005). *Teachers Exploring Tasks in English Language Teaching*. London: Palgrave Macmillan.

Ellis, R. (2000). Task-based research and language pedagogy. *Language Teaching Research*, 4, 193–220.

Ellis, R. (2003). *Task-based Language Learning and Teaching*. Oxford: Oxford University Press.

Ellis, R. (Ed.) (2005). *Planning and Task Performance in a Second Language*. Amsterdam/Philadelphia: John Benjamins.

Ellis, R., Tanaka, Y., & Yamazaki, A. (1994). Classroom interaction, comprehension, and the acquisition of L2 word meanings. *Language Learning*, 44, 449–491.

García Mayo, M. (Ed.) (2007). *Investigating Tasks in Formal Language Learning*. Clevedon, UK: Multilingual Matters.

González-Lloret, M., & Ortega, L. (Eds.) (2014). *Technology-mediated TBLT: Researching Technology and Tasks*. Amsterdam/Philadelphia: John Benjamins.

Iwashita, N. (1999). Tasks and learners' output in nonnative–nonnative interaction. In K. Kanno (Ed.), *Studies on the Acquisition of Japanese as a Second Language* (pp. 31–53). Amsterdam/Philadelphia: John Benjamins.

Iwashita, N., & Li, H. (2012). Patterns of corrective feedback in a task-based adult EFL classroom setting in China. In A. Shehadeh & C. Coombe (Eds.), *Task-based Language Teaching in Foreign Language Contexts: Research and Implementation* (pp. 137–162). Amsterdam/Philadelphia: John Benjamins.

Izumi, S. (2002). Output, input enhancement, and the noticing hypothesis: An experimental study on ESL relativization. *Studies in Second Language Acquisition*, 24, 541–577.

Krashen, S. D. (1985). *The Input Hypothesis: Issues and Implications*. London: Longman.

LaPierre, D. (1994). *Language Output in a Co-operative Learning Setting: Determining its Effects on Second Language Learning*. Unpublished master's thesis, University of Toronto.

Long, M. H. (1996). The role of the linguistic environment in second language acquisition. In W. C. Ritchie & T. K. Bhatia (Eds.), *Handbook of Second Language Acquisition* (pp. 413–468). San Diego: Academic Press.

Long, M. H. (1998). Focus on form in task-based language teaching. *Working Papers in ESL*, 16(2), 35–49.

Long, M. (2015). *Second Language Acquisition and Task-Based Language Teaching*. Oxford: Wiley-Blackwell.

Lynch, A. J. (1988). *Grading Foreign Language Listening Comprehension Materials: The Use of Naturally Modified Interaction*. Unpublished doctoral thesis, University of Edinburgh.

Nunan, D. (1989). *Designing Tasks for the Communicative Classroom*. Cambridge: Cambridge University Press.

Pica, T., Kanagy, R., & Falodun, J. (1993). Choosing and using communication tasks for second language research and instruction. In G. Crookes & S. Gass (Eds.), *Tasks and Language Learning: Integrating Theory and Practice* (pp. 9–34). Clevedon, UK: Multilingual Matters.

Richards, J. C., & Schmidt, R. (2010). *Longman Dictionary of Language Teaching and Applied Linguistics* (4th ed.). London: Longman.

Rieber, R. W., & Carton, A. S. (Eds.) (1987). *The Collected Works of L. S. Vygotsky, Volume 1: Thinking and Speech*. New York: Plenum Press.

Samuda, V., & Bygate, M. (2008). *Tasks in Second Language Learning*. Basingstoke, UK: Palgrave Macmillan.

Schmidt, R. (1998). The centrality of attention in SLA. *Working Papers in ESL*, 16(2), 1–34.

Shehadeh, A. (2004). Modified output during task-based pair interaction and group interaction. *Journal of Applied Linguistics*, 1, 351–382.

Shehadeh, A. (2005). Task-based language learning and teaching: Theories and application. In C. Edwards & J. Willis (Eds.), *Teachers Exploring Tasks in English Language Teaching* (pp. 13–30). London: Palgrave Macmillan.

Shehadeh. A. (2012). Broadening the perspective of task-based language teaching scholarship: The contribution of research in foreign language contexts. In A. Shehadeh & C. Coombe (Eds.), *Task-based Language Teaching in Foreign Language Contexts: Research and Implementation* (pp. 1–20). Amsterdam/Philadelphia: John Benjamins.

Shehadeh, A., & Coombe, C. (Eds.) (2010). *Applications of Task-based Learning in TESOL*. Alexandria, VA: TESOL.

Shehadeh, A., & Coombe, C. (Eds.) (2012). *Task-based Language Teaching in Foreign Language Contexts: Research and Implementation*. Amsterdam/Philadelphia: John Benjamins.

Skehan, P. (1996). A framework for the implementation of task-based instruction. *Applied Linguistics*, 17(1), 38–62.

Skehan, P. (1998). *A Cognitive Approach to Language Learning*. Oxford: Oxford University Press.

Swain, M. (1995). Three functions of output in second language learning. In G. Cook & B. Seidlhofer (Eds.), *Principle and Practice in Applied Linguistics: Studies in Honor of H. G. Widdowson* (pp. 125–144). Oxford: Oxford University Press.

Swain, M., & Lapkin, S. (1995). Problems in output and the cognitive processes they generate: A step towards second language learning. *Applied Linguistics*, 16, 371–391.

Swain, M., & Lapkin, S. (1998). Interaction and second language learning: Two adolescent French immersion students working together. *Modern Language Journal*, 82, 320–337.

Thomas, M., & Reinders, H. (Eds.) (2015). *Contemporary Task-based Language Teaching in Asia*. London: Bloomsbury.

Van den Branden, K., Bygate, M., & Norris, J. (Eds.) (2009). *Task-based Language Teaching: A Reader*. Amsterdam/Philadelphia: John Benjamins.

Willis, J. (1996a). *A Framework for Task-based Learning*. Harlow, UK: Longman Addison-Wesley.

Willis, J. (1996b). A flexible framework for task-based learning. In J. Willis & D. Willis (Eds.), *Challenge and Change in Language Teaching* (pp. 52–62). Oxford: Heinemann ELT.

Winke, P. (2010). Using online tasks for formative language assessment. In A. Shehadeh & C. Coombe (Eds.), *Applications of Task-based Learning in TESOL* (pp. 173–185). Alexandria, VA: TESOL.

CHAPTER 30

Learning Through Content

John Macalister

INTRODUCTION

Readers of a certain age and educational background may remember the Duponts. They were the family whose unexceptional lives introduced each unit of our French language textbook. Unit by unit we learned what Monsieur and Madame Dupont – they were never gifted given names – and their two children, probably called Jean and Marie, did at home, at school, in each of the four seasons and so on. Not, of course, that any of us really cared. Their lives unfolded on the pages of our textbook simply as a means of teaching French grammar.

This fragment of memory serves to illustrate the state of much language learning in the time before communicative language teaching was introduced to, and began to influence, the language teaching profession. While descendants of the Duponts still inhabit the pages of at least some language learning materials, their presence has become a thing of the past in many learning and teaching contexts around the world. Since the 1970s, there has been a steady shift away from a focus on learning *about* the language to learning how to *use* the language. In Johns and Davies (1983)'s memorable if under-appreciated terms, it has been a shift from treating text as a linguistic object to viewing text as a vehicle for information. This is the shift from grammar-translation to pedagogical approaches that treat language as a means of making meaning. It is in this tradition that learning through content sits.

OVERVIEW

Learning through content is often captured under the term Content-Based Instruction (CBI), which can, in practice, take many forms, which in turn generates many names (Reynolds, 2015, evaluates eight forms of CBI, each with a different acronym, for example). At times CBI is contrasted with Content and Language Integrated Learning (CLIL), but, as Cenoz (2015) has recently demonstrated, it is in their accidental, not their essential, features that they differ. As an example, CBI tends to be seen as North American in origin, CLIL as European; this is an accidental feature. In both CBI and CLIL, however, language and content are integrated; this is an essential feature. In this chapter, then, the idea of learning through content is intended to include all programmes where content is learnt through the medium of a second language, wherever they may sit on the continuum from content-driven (as in immersion education) to language-driven (such as theme-based courses in university preparation programmes) (Met, 1998). In other words, and to underline the point, this chapter is concerned with learning through content; it is not a discussion of CBI and CLIL.

Interest in, and support for, learning through content is usually traced back to the success of French immersion programmes in Canada, the first of which was established in 1965. Today, there is considerable empirical evidence (see, for example, a recent review by Tedick and Wesely, 2015) of its positive benefits for language learning. It is the case, however, as Swain (1988) points out, that content teaching does not necessarily equate with effective language teaching. The following section considers issues in learning through content that require thought, because of the impact they can have on the effectiveness of language learning. In doing so, it draws on both second language acquisition theory and empirical research.

Key Learning Issues

LEARNING THROUGH INPUT

Recognition of the importance of input (e.g., Krashen, 1985) was a considerable influence on communicative language teaching and was, in turn, a catalyst for the attention given to content selection in the 1970s. Possibly the purest example of the Input Hypothesis is traditional extensive reading, where the reading is everything. More generally, there was a realisation in language teaching circles that content needed to be meaningful to learners, in order to engage and motivate them. In that regard, the lives of the Duponts certainly did not meet that benchmark.

Decisions about content are, then, one of the fundamental issues for consideration. Language teachers on language-driven courses arguably have more freedom to select content than those on content-driven courses, where the content may be drawn from specific curricula, such as history or science. Where there is some freedom to choose, decisions can be suitably informed by information about what may be engaging, motivating and meaningful to learners and can be drawn from environment analysis (for an overview of the factors involved in such analysis, see Nation and Macalister, 2010: 14–23).

However, content or topic is not sufficient in itself as a basis for selection. A key word associated with input is 'comprehensible'. It is not, in other words, sufficient for a text to match learners' interests; they also need to understand it. Because of its importance in determining comprehension, one aspect of language that has received a large amount of research attention is vocabulary (see Chapter 18). The ideal is for learners to be familiar with 95–98% of a text's vocabulary; less than that and the text is too hard. The proportion of a text's vocabulary that a learner will be familiar with is, of course, determined by that learner's vocabulary size. However, when we consider that a learner needs a vocabulary size of 8,000–9,000 word families to read text successfully, and 5,000–6,000 word families for successful listening (Nation, 2006), it is evident that authentic input is not usually suitable for language learners. This point has pedagogical implications that will be returned to later in this chapter.

Input theorists argue that language learning occurs incidentally through reading (see Chapter 23): as they read, learners become increasingly familiar with the words that form the 2–5% of unknown vocabulary. Much of the research looking at language learning through extensive reading has focused on vocabulary, and one key finding is the importance of repeated exposure to new words for learning to occur. This is where commercially published graded readers can play a role, as they control and ensure repetition of new vocabulary. Lexical gains through extensive reading are known to be fragile (Waring and Takaki, 2003), and this fragility is heightened without repeated encounters. This is demonstrated in Waring and Takaki's study, where substitute words (e.g., *windle* for *house*) were used, and thus learners had no opportunity for meeting these words outside the graded reader they were placed in.

Extensive reading and graded readers are most likely to be found in language-driven programmes. In content-driven programmes, where content is drawn from a specific discipline, a number of specialised word lists exist, lists that identify high frequency vocabulary within that discipline. An example of such a list is the Technical Nursing Education Word List (Mukundan and Jin, 2012). Such lists can assist in reducing the lexical burden of input materials. Familiarity with a relatively small number of words can have high returns in terms of lexical coverage, and because the number of words is relatively small they can be taught directly, rather than relying upon incidental learning as described above.

While vocabulary plays an important role in comprehension, it is not the only aspect of language that needs attention. It is also the case that there are occasions when lexical adaptation measures are not appropriate, as students need to master discipline-specific language and discourse. In their report of an approach to professional development with history teachers, Schleppegrell, Achugar, and Oteíza (2004) use functional linguistic analysis to promote a focus on how language conveys meaning. In history texts, for instance, verbs rather than conjunctions are often used to express cause-effect relationships (e.g., *established* rather than *because*). Teachers were encouraged to develop metalinguistic awareness in their students, in order to better comprehend the input. This approach was a response to the fact that learners had identified linguistic causes for their finding the texts unengaging and challenging. The potential contribution of developing a learner's linguistic metalanguage to both language and content learning is an area of ongoing investigation (Schleppegrell, 2016).

LEARNING THROUGH OUTPUT

As mentioned earlier, a concern raised by Swain (1988) is that language learning does not automatically occur through content learning, which failure, she suggests, may result from a lack of sustained output opportunities. Indeed, one of the arresting findings of Tedick and Wesely's (2015) study was the lack of development of productive skills among one group at least of learners in content-based classrooms, majority-language learners in immersion programmes. This finding would suggest that for language learning to occur through content, input alone is not enough. It also suggests that teachers may attend more to content learning than to language learning.

When learners are provided with output opportunities, they need to recall the language required to convey their intended meaning. In doing so, they have the chance to form and test hypotheses about language, and to have their hypotheses confirmed or challenged by the feedback they receive. Such feedback does not, of course, have to come from the teacher; it may also come from peers, or from the learner him- or herself. There is no doubt that learners are able to self-correct. This can be seen in the use of the 4/3/2 technique, in which students talk for reducing amounts of time (typically four minutes, then three minutes, then two minutes) on the same topic to a different partner each time; however, as they do not receive error correction feedback, changes in accuracy may be erratic. In one small-scale study, for instance, a learner corrected *the Buddhism religion* to *the Buddhist religion* from one turn to the next, but at the same time introduced an error by producing *believe to the Buddhist religion*, rather than repeating the earlier, and correct, *believe in* (Macalister, 2014).

LEARNING THROUGH INTERACTION

While output can be an individual activity, such as writing an essay or delivering a monologue, often it involves working with others. Another insight into how learning occurs through output is provided by Swain and Lapkin (1998), who examined the language-related episodes, for both form and lexis, that occurred in interaction between two French immersion students when carrying out a jigsaw task. Through the students' dialogue, they argued, language learning happens. While this early study has been criticised, and alternative explanations for the learning considered (Thwaites, 2014, provides a succinct discussion of this literature), the central point remains well-accepted – through producing output, learners are noticing gaps in their own language when, for example, they find they lack the linguistic resources to convey the intended meaning; when working with others, they may also notice gaps in each other's language which, working together, they can resolve.

One of the functions of output, Swain argues (see e.g., Kowal and Swain, 1997: 292–293), is that it can compel learners to shift from semantic to syntactic processing, or provide an awareness of the relationship of words to each other. This function can be seen in the use of two interactive group tasks – a dictogloss (Wajnryb, 1990) and a cloze task – in another French immersion classroom (Kowal and Swain, 1997). The purpose was to focus learners' attention on the form-meaning relationship of language, and while both were found to work, the dictogloss allowed the learners to notice their own linguistic gaps (e.g., realising the information carried by verb tense endings) rather than being constrained by the narrower, teacher-selected focus of the cloze.

Along with the Input and the Output Hypotheses, then, the Interaction Hypothesis (Long, 1996) contributes to language learning success when learning through content. The three are complementary, in that learners need comprehensible input in order to re-use it in productive output (clearly, if the input is not comprehensible, the quality of the output will be severely compromised), and when the output is produced in interaction with others, learning can occur through the occurrence of language-related episodes.

LEARNING THROUGH FACILITATION

In her 1988 article, Swain imagines the type of teaching that might have occurred when language learning did not accompany learning through content – teacher-fronted question-and-answer along the lines of teacher initiation–student response–teacher evaluation (Cazden, 1988). Schleppegrell et al. (2004) also describe typical teacher behaviour – the use of graphic organisers, visual aids, and pre-teaching vocabulary. What these two depictions share is an emphasis on comprehension of the content, and a lack of attention by the teacher to morphological and syntactic carriers of meaning.

For learning to occur, the role of teachers in facilitating language learning needs to be considered. This can be done by employing the range of types of corrective feedback: explicit correction, recasts, clarification requests, metalinguistic clues, elicitation, and repetition (these are handily discussed by Tedick and de Gortari, 1998, in an article intended for teachers in content-based situations; they also suggest elicitation as the most effective form of corrective feedback).

A further point to make is that, in order to facilitate learning, teachers need to be proficient in the target language. Teachers' proficiency – or lack of it – is one of the reasons given for the failure of the Malaysian experiment of teaching Mathematics and Science in English in secondary schools (Lee, 2014). Introduced in 2003, a decision to discontinue it was taken in 2009, and it ended in 2012. It is, then, not just the *learners'* language proficiency that needs to be considered in learning through content situations.

IMPLICATIONS FOR TEACHING AND ASSESSMENT

To repeat a point made earlier, learning through content does not in itself guarantee language learning; decisions about content determine *what* is taught, not *how* it is taught.

Consideration of how language is learned through content has implications for teaching, with properly informed language curriculum design being one way of addressing many of the issues discussed above. One curricular approach that has great potential for learning through content is that of the four strands (Nation, 2007; Lightbown, 2014: 65–70, also proposes the four strands as a pedagogical framework). In this approach, which draws on language acquisition research and theory such as that discussed in the previous section, roughly equal time is dedicated to each of four strands of language learning:

1. Meaning-focused input, which occurs through reading and listening.
2. Language-focused learning.
3. Meaning-focused output, which occurs through speaking and writing.
4. Fluency development, which should occur with all four skills.

In this approach, it is not enough to equate, for example, a reading activity with meaning-focused input. For that strand of language learning to exist, it needs to meet certain conditions. An illustration of how these conditions can be achieved in terms of reading can be found in Macalister (2011), who also shows how attention to the use of pronouns – the language-focused learning strand – can result from a meaning focus. The same caveat about needing to meet certain conditions is true of each of the four strands, and any teacher or curriculum designer or materials writer interested in applying this approach needs to develop an understanding of those conditions.

Another implication, particularly for teachers working at the content-led end of the continuum, is to give thought to where language support is going to be provided, and by whom. In at least some immersion programmes, content classes are supplemented by language (or language arts) classes, with the ideal situation being that these classes are taught by different people.

Consideration of comprehensible input has a further implication for teaching, in that teachers need to some extent to be needs analysts (for an overview of needs analysis, see Nation and Macalister, 2010: 24–36). In effect, this means that teachers need two pieces of information: they need to know the language demands of the text, and they also need to know the language level of the learners. Because of its importance in determining comprehension, vocabulary measures are a useful tool in providing this information. Two tests of learners' vocabulary that are widely available and practical to use are the Vocabulary Levels Test (Nation, 2001) and the Vocabulary Size Test (Nation and Beglar, 2007); both provide measures of receptive vocabulary, with the former providing information for vocabulary frequency level as well as for the Academic Word List (Coxhead, 2000). Information about learners' vocabulary size can then be compared with information about the lexical demands of a text, which can easily be discovered by using the VocabProfile tool on Tom Cobb's website (www.lextutor.ca). The results of such analysis can then prompt further action. If the text is too hard, for instance, then teachers need to adapt the text, which may include replacing lower frequency words with higher frequency synonyms, such as *cook* for *chef,* or omitting (perhaps replacing) the text altogether. Such efforts are necessary if students are to have successful learning experiences.

A final implication relates to assessment. There is a great deal that could be said about assessment when learning through content (Coyle, Hood, and Marsh, 2010, for instance, devote a chapter to assessment in CLIL), but for current purposes a single point needs to be made. Because both content and language are being taught, there needs to be clarity about what is being assessed (cf., Stoller, 2008: 66). This can be more complicated than it appears at first glance; if, for instance, learners write about a topic they have been studying, are they being rewarded for understanding of the topic or for linguistic accuracy and complexity? Teachers, therefore, need to be clear about their learning objectives and communicate these, and the criteria for assessment, to their learners.

CONCLUSION

As noted at the outset, learning through content can take many forms and appear under many names. But whether occurring in immersion education or in a university preparation course, whether context-driven or language-driven, it has been found to be effective for second language learning. To be effective, however, it needs to be done well. If it is to be more than just content learning, its implementation needs to be informed by, and respond to, second language acquisition theory and research. Influential hypotheses, including those about input, output, and interaction, need to be incorporated into the selection of content, and into the format and presentation of lessons. By giving attention to the learning issues raised in this chapter, and considering the consequent implications for professional development, learning through content can deliver language learning rewards to the learners.

Discussion Questions

1. This chapter has focused on issues that should be considered when implementing a content-based approach, but there are other issues that could have been discussed. One such issue is the roles and responsibilities of the language teacher in CBI/CLIL. How well prepared are you, as a language teacher, for dealing with unfamiliar content? If teaching unfamiliar content makes you anxious, what steps can you take to improve your confidence?

2. If you had to develop an in-service course for language teachers unfamiliar with learning through content, what one main idea would you make the focus of the training? Why would you concentrate on that idea?

3. Examine your own recent teaching. Thinking of the four strands approach, are there sufficient opportunities for learners to engage in meaningful, productive language use? If there are not, what changes could you introduce to your teaching?

Key Readings

Brinton, D. M., & Snow, M. A. (Eds.) (2017). *The Content-based Second Language Classroom* (2nd ed.). Ann Arbor, MI: The University of Michigan Press.

Coyle, D., Hood, P., & Marsh, D. (2010). *Content and Language Integrated Learning*. Cambridge: Cambridge University Press.

Lightbown, P. M. (2014). *Focus on Content-based Language Teaching*. Oxford: Oxford University Press.

Macalister, J. (2011). Today's teaching, tomorrow's text: exploring the teaching of reading. *ELT Journal*, 65(2), 161–169. https://doi.org/10.1093/elt/ccq023

Nation, P. (2007). The Four Strands. *Innovation in Language Learning and Teaching*, 1(1), 1–12.

Swain, M. (1988). Manipulating and complementing content teaching to maximize second language learning. *TESL Canada Journal*, 6(1), 68–83.

References

Cazden, C. B. (1988). *Classroom Discourse: The Language of Teaching and Learning*. Portsmouth, NH: Heinemann.

Cenoz, J. (2015). Content-based instruction and content and language integrated learning: The same or different? *Language, Culture and Curriculum*, 28(1), 8–24. https://doi.org/10.1080/07908318.2014.1000922

Coxhead, A. (2000). A new academic word list. *TESOL Quarterly*, 34(2), 213–238.

Coyle, D., Hood, P., & Marsh, D. (2010). *Content and Language Integrated Learning.* Cambridge: Cambridge University Press.

Johns, T., & Davies, F. (1983). Text as a vehicle for information: the classroom use of written texts in teaching reading as a foreign language. *Reading in a Foreign Language,* 1(1), 1–19.

Kowal, M., & Swain, M. (1997). From semantic to syntactic processing: How can we promote it in the immersion classroom? In R. K. Johnson & M. Swain (Eds.), *Immersion Education: International Perspectives.* Cambridge: Cambridge University Press.

Krashen, S. D. (1985). *The Input Hypothesis: Issues and Implications.* London: Longman.

Lee, S. C. (2014). A post-mortem on the Malaysian content-based instruction initiative. *Journal of Asian Pacific Communication,* 24(1), 41–59. https://doi.org/10.1075/japc.24.1.03lee

Lightbown, P. M. (2014). *Focus on Content-based Language Teaching.* Oxford: Oxford University Press.

Long, M. H. (1996). The role of the linguistic environment in second language acquisition. In W. C. Ritchie & T. K. Bhatia (Eds.), *Handbook of Second Language Acquisition* (pp. 413–468). San Diego: Academic Press.

Macalister, J. (2011). Today's teaching, tomorrow's text: exploring the teaching of reading. *ELT Journal,* 65(2), 161–169. https://doi.org/10.1093/elt/ccq023

Macalister, J. (2014). Developing speaking fluency with the 4/3/2 technique: An exploratory study. *The TESOLANZ Journal,* 22, 28–42.

Met, M. (1998). Curriculum decision-making in content-based language teaching. In J. Cenoz & F. Genesee (Eds.), *Beyond Bilingualism: Multilingualism and Multilingual Education* (pp. 35–63). Clevedon, UK: Multilingual Matters.

Mukundan, J., & Jin, N. Y. (2012). Development of a technical Nursing Education Word List (NEWL) *International Journal of Innovation in English Language Teaching and Research* 1(2), 105–124.

Nation, I. S. P. (2001). *Learning Vocabulary in Another Language.* Cambridge: Cambridge University Press.

Nation, I. S. P. (2006). How large a vocabulary is needed for reading and listening? *The Canadian Modern Language Review,* 63(1), 59–82.

Nation, I. S. P., & Macalister, J. (2010). *Language Curriculum Design.* New York and London: Routledge / Taylor & Francis.

Nation, P. (2007). The four strands. *Innovation in Language Learning and Teaching,* 1(1), 1–12.

Nation, P., & Beglar, D. (2007). A vocabulary size test. *The Language Teacher,* 31(7), 9–13.

Reynolds, K. M. (2015). *Approaches to Inclusive English Classrooms: A Teacher's Handbook For Content-based Instruction.* Bristol, UK: Multilingual Matters.

Schleppegrell, M. J. (2016). Content-based language teaching with functional grammar in the elementary school. *Language Teaching,* 49(1), 116–128. https://doi.org/10.1017/S0261444814000093

Schleppegrell, M. J., Achugar, M., & Oteíza, T. (2004). The grammar of history: Enhancing content-based instruction through a functional focus on language. *TESOL Quarterly,* 38(1), 67–93. https://doi.org/10.2307/3588259

Stoller, F. L. (2008). Content-based instruction. In N. Van Deusen-Scholl & N. H. Hornberger (Eds.), *Encyclopedia of Language and Education* (2nd ed.), *Volume 4: Second and Foreign Language Education* (pp. 59–70). New York: Springer.

Swain, M. (1988). Manipulating and complementing content teaching to maximize second language learning. *TESL Canada Journal*, 6(1), 68–83.

Swain, M., & Lapkin, S. (1998). Interaction and second language learning: Two adolescent French immersion students working together. *The Modern Language Journal*, 82(3), 320–337. https://doi.org/10.2307/329959

Tedick, D. J., & de Gortari, B. (1998). Research on error correction and implications for classroom teaching. *ACIE Newsletter*, 1(3).

Tedick, D. J., & Wesely, P. M. (2015). A review of research on content-based foreign/second language education in US K-12 contexts. *Language, Culture and Curriculum*, 28(1), 25–40. https://doi.org/10.1080/07908318.2014.1000923

Thwaites, P. (2014). Maximizing learning from written output. *ELT Journal*, 68(2), 135–144. https://doi.org/10.1093/elt/cct098

Wajnryb, R. (1990). *Grammar Dictation*. Oxford: Oxford University Press.

Waring, R., & Takaki, M. (2003). At what rate do learners learn and retain new vocabulary from reading a graded reader? *Reading in a Foreign Language*, 15(2), 130–163.

CHAPTER 31

Learning Through Translation

Guy Cook

INTRODUCTION

The title of this chapter begs the question of what a language student is learning, and why. These questions need to be considered before we can consider how learning might or might not be enhanced 'through translation'. Answers will vary from place to place and student to student, according to age, stage, needs, preferences and traditions. Answers are also often implicit rather than explicit. Thus, very often (in answer to the question *what?*) it has been implicitly assumed that a new language is best approached in isolation from all other languages learners already know (see Chapter 5). Where this is the case, it is also often assumed that what is being studied is the new language as it is used by native speakers in monolingual communication. Next (in answer to the question *why?*) it is assumed that students are learning this isolated native-like language in order to use it on its own, in the same way as its monolingual speakers do, to become a sort of surrogate native speaker. Neither of these assumptions, however, is necessarily or even usually the case, especially in the contemporary world, for a number of reasons.

For one thing, despite the determined efforts of many theorists, syllabus designers and teachers, we cannot keep the language we are learning separate from one(s) we know already, even if we want to. Connecting new to existing knowledge, and using the latter to make sense of the former, is a universal and productive human learning strategy, so learners make connections, even if they are forbidden to do so. As Henry Widdowson remarks in an argument for the bilingualization of learning:

> [W]hile in the classroom the teachers try to keep the two languages separate, the learners in their own minds keep the two in contact. (Widdowson, 2003: 150)

Additionally, students might actively need to learn about the relationship between the two (or more) languages concerned, and how to use them together rather than apart. They might find it helpful, interesting, reassuring and useful to be able to relate the two. Attitudes to learning through translation have suffered greatly from an ascendant assumption that these two facts are not the case: that learners can keep the new language apart from ones they already know, and that they will need to use it in isolation from them. It has also often been assumed that making connections between the two (or more) languages is not what they want, that explanations and translations are somehow less enjoyable and rewarding than monolingual learning. In reality, however, many people, though not all, find translation an enjoyable, challenging, and intellectually satisfying activity.

Translation is one of a number of ways of using the students' own language(s) to aid learning. Others include own-language explanation and discussion, the use of bilingual resources, and the use of the own language for planning and managing learning. Conventional objections to such own-language activities, usually based on assertion rather than evidence, include the beliefs that they slow down acquisition and impede fluency, that they do not reflect students' needs, and that they are unpopular. All of these objections are highly questionable, especially in the contemporary, globalised world. In a world of mass migration, multilingual societies, online interaction, and international communication, there are many common situations where languages are used together, and there is constant to and fro movement between them. In mixed language partnerships, immigrant and migrant families, multicultural and multilingual schools, mixed nationality workforces, international businesses, multilingual announcements (e.g., in airports, road signs, and food labels), in films, news, and on social media, translation and negotiation between languages is widespread and commonplace.

Additionally, the purposes of language learning – especially of the ascendant international language of English – are generally instrumental. People learn English in order to study, work, travel, migrate, and for none of these purposes are they likely to leave their own language(s) behind. A person who is employed on the basis of their knowledge of English is likely to be required to mediate between people whose English is weaker than their own, and people who speak English but not the language of their workplace. For example, someone who gets a job in Brazil, Russia or China involving international communication will be mediating, and very often translating, in person or online, between speakers of Portuguese, Russian or Chinese, and speakers of English as a lingua franca. As Edward Said put it some time ago, in an analysis of the relation between English language learning and neo-imperialism:

> The reason for the large numbers of students taking English was given frankly by a somewhat disaffected instructor: many of the students proposed to end up working for airlines, or banks, in which English was the worldwide lingua franca … You learned English to use computers, respond to orders, transmit telexes, decipher manifests, and so forth. (Said, 1994: 369)

This widespread communicative need for translation and multiple language use has immediate implications for a discussion of learning through translation.

OVERVIEW

WHAT IS MEANT BY 'TRANSLATION' IN THE CONTEXT OF LANGUAGE TEACHING?

Translation, by definition, involves at least two languages. As such, it was ruthlessly and rigorously derogated throughout the last century, and even earlier, by language learning theorists who dogmatically believed that a language was most successfully learned monolingually, without any reference to students' own language(s) (Cook, 2010). Consequently, it was outlawed in much language teaching and learning practice.

Translation is not, however, the only way in which students' own language(s) can be used in teaching and learning. In the classroom, teachers might also use the students' own language(s) for explanation, discussion, direction, discipline, or to establish and maintain good student-teacher relationships (Hall and Cook, 2012). Students, for their part, might use it to ask questions, express their opinions, or request help (none of which are easy to do in a language you are learning, especially in the early stages). In addition, both in the classroom and outside it, students might make use of bilingual resources, such as dictionaries, grammar books, and online translation programmes. The line between translation and other bilingual activities is therefore difficult to draw; they merge into each other, and many own-language activities involve snippets of translation. Thus, when we talk about translation in language learning, we may mean something broader than the traditional activity of producing an other-language equivalent of a whole sentence or text; it may be a brief interjection by a teacher, or the swift retrieval of a single word from a bilingual dictionary, for example. In addition, as no translation is exact, it is also hard to draw a line between attempts to produce as accurate an equivalent as possible, and rough explanations or commentary on what has been said. The limited characterisation of translation in language learning by its opponents, as the production of extended equivalents of sentences or texts which are then assessed for formal accuracy, has constrained ideas about its role in learning.

KEY LEARNING ISSUES

LEARNING THROUGH AND/OR FOR TRANSLATION

We need to distinguish between:

1. learning *through* translation (i.e., deploying translation as a means of developing knowledge of, and ability to use, a new language system); and

2. learning *for* translation (i.e., seeing an ability to translate as an aim, perhaps a major aim, of learning).

Indeed, translation can be seen as a fifth skill to add to the traditional four (Naimushin, 2002; see also Chapters 21–24). When considering any learning activity, despite some considerable overlaps, it is always useful to consider which of these two is most important, as in each case the strategies and content we adopt will be different. We should bear in mind, however, that although one or other may be dominant, the two can never be completely isolated from each other.

It has often been assumed that (2) has a very limited applicability, and is relevant only to those going on to become professional translators and interpreters. This however, as indicated in the preceding discussion, is a weak assumption; translation, far from being a specialised skill confined only to professionals, is a widespread communicative use of language, likely to be needed by most language learners. (Imagine claiming that you speak the language, then going to the doctor with a relative, to a restaurant with friends, or being asked by your boss to explain an email, but not being able to translate for them.) The weak assumption that bilingual skills like translation are specialised, and not of general use, has been implicit in a good deal of second language acquisition (SLA) and English language teaching research. As Sridhar and Sridhar (1986: 5) neatly put it, "SLA researchers seem to have neglected the fact that the goal of SLA is bilingualism."

The contemporary language learner, in other words, needs much more than to enter a monolingual situation and try to pass off as being as close as possible to native speakers, as was often assumed in communicative language teaching materials. They need an ability to move, mediate, and translate between languages, metalinguistic knowledge and awareness of differences between languages and cultures, and international comprehensibility (i.e., the ability to use a language with other non-native speakers). Though all of these have always been important aspects of learning a language, they have become even more crucial with rapid changes in communication and international contact, and, in the case of English, its growth as the major language of international communication.

In addition, a learner's own language(s) is a crucial part of their individual and cultural identity (see Chapter 10), fulfilling social and creative as well as transactional functions; learning a new language should not mean that they must put that identity aside. Again, this is particularly relevant to the learning of English. The international ascendancy of English poses a potential threat to other languages and cultures. It should be possible for the contemporary English language learner whose reasons for learning English are instrumental rather than integrative, to maintain an own-language and new-language identity simultaneously, rather than substituting the latter for the former. Translation has an important role to play in making this possible.

GRAMMAR TRANSLATION

One of the reasons for negative attitudes to translation in language learning has been its association with Grammar Translation, a way of learning originating in the nineteenth century. Each unit of a Grammar Translation course, or chapter of a textbook – the two are significantly often the same – presents new vocabulary by means of translation equivalents; this is followed by explicit explanation of grammar rules in the student's own language; the unit/chapter then concludes with written translation exercises, which are assessed only for formal accuracy. Each unit deploys only vocabulary and grammar which has already been encountered in the current or earlier units/chapters. Learning is thus accumulative, and the learner never encounters linguistic items which they have not been taught. It is the synthetic syllabus *par excellence*, "one in which the different parts of a language are taught separately and step by step so that acquisition is a process of a gradual accumulation of parts" (Wilkins, 1976: 2). The reaction against Grammar Translation was certainly understandable, as its neglect of spoken language, fluency and communication meant that it only directly developed a limited range of language skills. Nevertheless, the obvious weaknesses of Grammar Translation, which are easily and frequently mocked, do not mean that it has no role to play in language learning, if appropriately supplemented with other approaches, or treated as a component, rather than an entire means of learning.

As a component of learning, it has a number of distinct advantages. It can develop a learner's explicit knowledge of the structure of the new language, and indeed of their own language too, giving a sense of confidence and organisation. The fact that there are no linguistic surprises or unknowns can imbue a sense of security which may be helpful to learning. It can also achieve certain kinds of knowledge and understanding which are often less easily available in monolingual and communicative courses. For example, it can prevent a learner from avoiding, and thus never learning, difficult forms. A speaker/learner whose goal is only communicative success will often avoid areas of the language with which they know they have problems. A learner of French, for example, might choose an expression which achieves their communicative aim but does not involve a subjunctive; or they might avoid a gap in their vocabulary by simply avoiding a topic or expression. In Grammar Translation this is much less likely to happen, as the learner is constrained by the sentence or text to be translated; weaknesses and gaps are exposed, both for the learner and their teacher, and can then be addressed and remedied. One particular benefit is the exposure of *faux amis*, or 'false friends', (words which appear to be equivalent but are not). For example, the Italian word *simpatico* does not mean 'sympathetic', as an English-speaking learner of Italian might easily suppose, but 'likeable'. Thus, whereas this misconception by a student in a monolingual communicative course might pass unnoticed – as an utterance such as *quest'uomo è molto simpatico* is both grammatically correct and meaningful, even though it is intended to mean 'This man is very sympathetic' – a student asked to translate it would immediately have their error brought to their attention by their teacher.

FORM-FOCUSED TRANSLATION ACTIVITIES

One of the criticisms of Grammar Translation has often also been that it encourages a translation which is too literal, and too word for word. (Defining the notions of literal translation is of course a perennial issue in translation theory and translation studies but one which we cannot deal with fully here.) Butzkamm (2001) has argued that extremely literal, morpheme-by-morpheme translation, which he calls mirror translation – to the point where the result is weird, incorrect or even meaningless – can be very helpful by giving the learner a capacity to generate original utterances in a way which more free and communicative translation does not. Thus, if one takes (my example, not Butzkamm's) the French phrase *s'il vous plaît*, which is conventionally and functionally equivalent to the English 'please', and translates it morpheme by morpheme as 'if it you pleases', this is clearly not only an inappropriate translation, but also incorrect English. Nevertheless, by understanding how it breaks down, and moving through stages towards a more appropriate translation –

if it you pleases
if it pleases you.
if you please
please

– the learner gains the power to generate new French sentences on the same pattern, for example: *si le vin vous plaît* ('if you like the wine'); *si le jardin vous plaît* ('if you like the garden'). They will also gain insight into the difference between this polite *vous* form, *s'il vous plaît*, and the more familiar *tu* form, *s'il te plaît*. None of this would be available in an immediate move from the original French *s'il vous plaît* to the conventional English 'please'. It is important to emphasise, however, that mirror translation is a learning device; no-one is advocating such hyper-literal equivalents as communicatively successful translation.

COMMUNICATIVE TRANSLATION ACTIVITIES

Nevertheless, despite some advantages, neither Grammar Translation nor mirror translation would be successful as a learning tool, nor particularly enjoyable if used too extensively. There are, however, translation activities which can be all the things which Grammar Translation was not: ones which focus upon fluency and communication, which include spoken as well as written translation. There are now a number of available textbooks packed with imaginative and entertaining activities (Deller and Rinvolucri, 2002; Duff, 1989; González Davies, 2004; Kerr, 2013). Thus, translation may be incorporated into tasks, as it often is in authentic communication. One student might be given instructions in one language and have to translate it for another student, who performs the task. There could be role plays in which one student plays a person who only speaks language A, another student a person who only speaks language B, and a third student a person who speaks both. Students might be asked to provide or comment upon film subtitles; to play with and criticise the output of online translation programmes or compare one with another (e.g., Google Translate and

BabelFish); to try their hand at spoken interpretation; to play 'broken telephone' (a game in which a message is whispered by one student to the next, with the result that the final version is often radically changed from the original) around the class with alternations between languages. All such activities, and many more available in the books cited above, can be enjoyable, mimic authentic situations, and develop fluency and language awareness.

PEDAGOGIC ADVANTAGES OF LEARNING THROUGH TRANSLATION

In addition to functioning as a direct aid to learning, translation and other own-language use can also aid learning indirectly, by enhancing the learning environment. As Canagarajah (1999: 132) observes, activities involving students' own languages can have the effect of "putting students at ease, conveying teacher's empathy and, in general, creating a less threatening atmosphere." They can also help to consolidate teacher–student relationships, as there are other things going on in a language classroom than language learning. As Edstrom (2006: 290) concludes, on her reasons for speaking to her students in their own language: "The point is that my concern about my students as individuals, as human beings, at times transcends my concern for their L2 acquisition process."

While this observation applies more to general conversation in the own language, translation is nevertheless part of a general bilingual atmosphere in the classroom, one which many students find more friendly and less threatening than enforced monolingualism (Hall and Cook, 2013). Brooks-Lewis advances this feeling eloquently when she writes about trying to learn Spanish in a monolingual classroom:

> I felt I had walked into the second act of a three act play, or that I had gotten into the wrong classroom. I had enrolled in a beginning class because I wanted to learn the language, so of course I could not understand anything the teacher was saying, and wondering why she acted as if I should was worrisome, making an already stressful situation even more so. (Brooks-Lewis, 2009: 217)

In addition, in situations where the teacher knows the students' own language less well than they do, all bilingual activities, and especially translation, use a resource with which the student has expertise, and this can also enhance their feeling of status and mutual respect, in a way which contrasts positively with those situations in which they are forbidden to draw upon that resource and therefore feel infantilised.

IMPLICATIONS FOR TEACHING AND ASSESSMENT

MIXED LANGUAGE AND SHARED LANGUAGE CLASSES

The last point above raises an important caveat about the successful use of translation. It is clearly going to be different in classes where:

- a single language is shared by all students and their teacher (e.g., a secondary or university class in Brazil taught by a native Portuguese speaker);
- a single language is shared by all students, but not by the teacher (e.g., a secondary school English class in Japan taught by a native-English speaker teacher who does not speak Japanese); or
- students speak a variety of languages (e.g., a private language school in London).

In the first case – perhaps the commonest throughout the world – the use of translation is fairly straightforward. The teacher knows both languages better than the students, and is familiar with translation problems between them; students can therefore work on the same activities together under her guidance and she will be able to assess problems and achievements. Here, activities can be both form-focused and communicative. In the second case, although the whole class can work on the same activities, the teacher will not be able to provide guidance or assess results so well; on the other hand, translation in such classes may have a truly authentic quality, as students may be providing the teacher with new information through translation. In the third case, however, the use of translation is more problematic, though also authentic and feasible. Recent books on translation activities, such as Kerr (2013), provide numerous examples of possible activities. To give just one: students may be asked to provide subtitles for a short piece of film in their own language and discuss some of the problems with the class. In these last two cases, however, where the teacher is not herself proficient in translation from the language involved, activities will of necessity be communicative rather than form-focused. A greater range of activities is thus available to a bilingual teacher in a class with a shared language. Typically (though not necessarily), this teacher will be a non-native speaker teacher of the language being taught, and, where translation is concerned, as in many other aspects of language teaching, she will be at an advantage over the native-speaker teacher who does not know the students' language(s).

ACHIEVING A BALANCE BETWEEN BILINGUAL AND MONOLINGUAL ACTIVITIES

As many writers have observed, the outlawing of translation did not result in its elimination, but rather in its continued use, though in a rather haphazard, guilt-ridden, and unprincipled manner. In the absence of clear research findings and guidance, teachers may change languages in an arbitrary manner (Hall and Cook, 2013; Turnbull and Dailey-O'Cain, 2009), or resort to own-language use simply because they are tired and short of time. Now that translation is beginning to be rehabilitated as a valuable learning tool and a needed skill, the issue of how and when it should be used, and in what quantity can at last be discussed.

No-one, however, as far as I am aware, is advocating a return to an exclusive use of translation as a means of learning. The issue, as with other own-language activities, is to achieve a 'judicious' or 'optimal' use of the learners' own language with an 'appropriate' combination of intra- and cross-lingual activities (Stern, 1992). Butzkamm and Caldwell (2009) argue that a structured and principled deployment of the own language, rather than its unplanned incidental occurrence in notionally monolingual teaching, can increase rather than decrease the use of the new language for communication. (They give the example of the 'sandwich technique', in which a teacher deliberately inserts an oral translation before an unknown phrase, in order to convey meaning as rapidly and completely as possible.) Forman (2010) formulates ten principles for its judicious use, based on observation and teacher interviews in a Thai university. Macaro (1997) identifies an 'optimal position' in which a strategic use of the own-language is seen as enhancing learning, and Macaro (2009: 39) suggests that this involves teachers making a judgment about "the possible detrimental effects of not drawing the learners' attention to aspects of their first language, or not making comparisons between the first and second languages." The notion of allowing teachers and students to move between one language and another fits well with the empowering notion of 'translanguaging', which regards the language produced by bilinguals "not as two autonomous language systems as has traditionally been the case, but as one linguistic repertoire" (García and Wei, 2014: 2).

CONCLUSION

Teachers should therefore make principled choices, depending on the nature of their classes and the needs of their students, on how best to use translation as an aid to learning. Not long ago, there was virtually no support or guidance in the literature on how to do this, but mercifully this is no longer the case, and there are now a growing number of theoretical, descriptive and practical sources of guidance (see Key Readings).

Where it is possible within syllabus constraints, translation can also be an invaluable tool in diagnosis and assessment. In addition to providing insight into a student's ability to translate as a necessary skill in itself, a variety of translation tasks, given as part of a test, can give a clear indication of every aspect of language proficiency, from pronunciation, lexis, and grammar through to fluency and communication.

Discussion Questions

1. How might the use and usefulness of translation vary with the stage and age of the learner?

2. In what ways might the use and usefulness of translation vary with the language being learned?

Key Readings

Butzkamm, W., & Caldwell, J. A. W. (2009). *The Bilingual Reform: A Paradigm Shift in Foreign Language Teaching*. Tübingen: Narr Studienbücher.

Cook, G. (2010). *Translation in Language Teaching: An Argument for Reassessment*. Oxford: Oxford University Press.

Hall, G., & Cook, G. (2012). Own language use in language teaching and learning: The state of the art. *Language Teaching*, 45(3), 271–308.

Kerr, P. (2013). *Translation and Own-language Activities*. Cambridge: Cambridge University Press.

Laviosa, S. (2014), *Translation and Language Education: Pedagogic Approaches Explored*. London: Routledge.

Widdowson, H. G. (2003). *Defining Issues in English Language Teaching* (pp. 149–165). Oxford: Oxford University Press.

References

Brooks-Lewis, K. A. (2009). Adult learners' perceptions of the incorporation of their L1 in foreign language teaching and learning. *Applied Linguistics*, 30(2), 216–235.

Butzkamm, W. (2001). Learning the language of loved ones: On the generative principle and the technique of mirroring. *English Language Teaching Journal*, 55(2), 149–154.

Butzkamm, W., & Caldwell, J. A. W. (2009). *The Bilingual Reform: A Paradigm Shift in Foreign Language Teaching*. Tübingen: Narr Studienbücher.

Canagarajah, A. S. (1999). *Resisting Linguistic Imperialism in English Teaching*. Oxford: Oxford University Press.

Cook, G. (2010). *Translation in Language Teaching: An Argument for Reassessment*. Oxford: Oxford University Press.

Deller, S., & Rinvolucri, M. (2002). *Using the Mother Tongue*. London: English Teaching Professional / Delta.

Duff, A. (1989). *Translation* (Resource Books for Teachers). Oxford: Oxford University Press.

Edstrom, A. (2006). L1 use in the L2 classroom: One teacher's self-evaluation. *The Canadian Modern Language Review*, 63(2), 275–292.

Forman, R. (2010). Ten principles of bilingual pedagogy in EFL. In A. Mahboob (Ed.), *The NNEST lens: Non-native English speakers in TESOL*. Newcastle, UK: Cambridge Scholars Publishing.

García, O., & Wei, L. (2014). *Translanguaging: Language, Bilingualism and Education*. London: Palgrave Macmillan.

González Davies, M. (2004). *Multiple Voices in the Translation Classroom: Activities, Tasks and Projects*. Amsterdam/Philadelphia: Benjamins.

Hall, G., & Cook, G. (2012). Own language use in language teaching and learning: The state of the art. *Language Teaching*, 45(3), 271–308.

Hall, G., & Cook, G. (2013). The use of learners' own languages in ELT: Exploring global practices and attitudes. The British Council. Available at: https://www.teachingenglish.org.uk/article/own-language-use-elt-exploring-global-practices-attitudes [Accessed 10 August 2015].

Kerr, P. (2013). *Translation and Own-language Activities*. Cambridge: Cambridge University Press.

Macaro, E. (1997). *Target Language, Collaborative Learning and Autonomy*. Bristol, UK: Multilingual Matters.

Macaro, E. (2009). Teacher use of codeswitching in the second language classroom: Exploring 'optimal' use. In M. Turnbull & J. Dailey-O'Cain (Eds.), *First Language Use in Second and Foreign Language Learning* (pp. 35–49). Bristol, UK: Multilingual Matters.

Naimushin, B. (2002). Translation in foreign language teaching: The fifth skill. *Modern English Teacher*, 11 (4), pp. 46–49.

Said, E. (1994). *Culture and Imperialism*. London: Vintage.

Sridhar, K, & Sridhar, S. (1986). Bridging the paradigm gap: Second language acquisition theory and indigenized varieties of English. *World Englishes*, 5(1), 3–14.

Stern, H. (1992). *Issues and Options in Language Teaching*. Oxford: Oxford University Press.

Turnbull, M., & Dailey-O'Cain, J. (2009). Concluding reflections: Moving forward. In M. Turnbull & J. Dailey-O'Cain (Eds.), *First Language Use in Second and Foreign Language Learning* (pp. 182–207). Bristol, UK: Multilingual Matters.

Widdowson, H. G. (2003). *Defining Issues in English Language Teaching* (pp. 149–165). Oxford: Oxford University Press.

Wilkins, D. (1976). *Notional Syllabuses*. Oxford: Oxford University Press.

CHAPTER 32

Learning Through Textbooks

Gregory Hadley

INTRODUCTION

In the wide world of English language education, few issues have been as divisive as that of language learning through textbooks. Opinions vary, ranging from those who see language textbooks as "an authoritative and accessible tool which can both facilitate learning and make it more enjoyable" (Richards, 1993: 6), to those who treat textbooks with quiet insouciance, describing them as "necessary evils" (Sheldon, 1988: 237), to those at the far end of the spectrum who declare not only that language textbooks "currently make a significant contribution to the failure of many learners of English" (Tomlinson, 2008: 3), but also approve of those who have consigned their textbooks to the flames in an effort to prevent their use in the language classroom (Meddings and Thornbury, 2011: 11–12). The polarized nature of this scholarly debate has so exacerbated the unease felt by educators about the role of textbooks in second language classrooms, that before one can consider how language textbooks (LTs) contribute to second language learning, it is first necessary to address the question of whether or not they aid in learning at all.

The question at the forefront of this chapter is: Does learning take place through textbooks, and if so, how? The concerns it raises will be examined from the viewpoint of students, teachers, and the institution, and I will close with some implications for pedagogy and assessment.

OVERVIEW

In their most basic form, language textbooks (LTs) are defined as print or electronic collections of pedagogic materials that seek both to stimulate language learning and to support language instruction. In prototypical terms, this definition encompasses all LTs, regardless of where they sit along the cline between *Global LTs*, which are intended for an international 'market' (Gray, 2002), and *Locally Produced LTs*, which are designed to satisfy specific national, cultural, and tightly-focused learning outcomes (Frank, 2005; Masuhara, 2011).

Not all LTs are created equal, and a further distinction needs to be made between effective and ineffective LTs. Physical and theoretical differences aside, effective LTs have certain qualities, and interact with a number of known quantities. Some of the common qualities of effective LTs are their provision of productive and receptive language tasks (speaking, pronunciation, listening, reading, and writing), the logical sequencing of communicative activities, the focus on form, and the presentation of lexicogrammatical items that will support tasks and activities, as well as anticipate communication breakdowns (Baralt, Gilabert, and Robinson, 2014; Ellis, 2001; Loewen, 2003; Long, 2000; Nunan, 2004; Robinson, 2001; Schmitt, 2008). Richards (2015: 602–603, 605) identifies further qualities, describing effective LTs as interesting to learners, organized in terms of content, consistent in style, clear in providing goals and strategies, and stimulating meaningful interaction and instructive feedback. Features such as these are not context dependent, and can be found in the wide variety of LTs available to students and teachers today. Effective LTs are also inextricably linked to the known quantities of the students, teachers, and the institution. This "interconnected dynamic relationship" (McGrath, 2013: xi) means that the relative effectiveness of an LT can shift, depending upon the experience and attitudes of the teachers, the nature of the institution, and whether the LT satisfies learner and institutional needs.

The point here is that when responding to the doubts raised about LT effectiveness, answers should be found through investigations of LTs that have effective qualities, and which have been used by experienced teachers who, after making informed choices about the needs of their learners and the concerns of their specific pedagogical context, are actively engaging students in the task of learning. Surprisingly, however, much of the research on learning through textbooks not only overlooks these important conditions, but characterizes LT research as "something of a 'black art'" (Low, 1989: 153), and "fundamentally a subjective, rule-of-thumb activity" (Sheldon, 1988: 245), one that "can do no more than reflect our own personal views of what facilitates language acquisition" (Masuhara and Tomlinson, 2008: 23).

While work of this type has certainly yielded valuable insights, more objective cases of empirical research are needed. Along these lines, one recent study (Hadley, 2013) reported on a six-year investigation, in which a global LT, *Interchange Third Edition: Full Contact* (Richards, Hull, Proctor, and Shields, 2005), was used with nearly 700 Japanese university students. During a 30-week academic year, students attended 4 language classes a week for 45 minutes, and one class a week for 90 minutes. Experienced classroom language teachers holding graduate degrees in Teaching English to Speakers of Other Languages (TESOL) staffed the program, and the presentation of the LT material was consistently maintained in a uniformly systematic manner. Two-tail t-tests of the paired means of the learners' pre-test and post-test scores were conducted every year for six years. At both 95% and 99% levels of statistical probability, the means of the post-tests were significantly higher than those of the pre-test at the beginning of each year, with large to medium effect sizes.

LT critics have been unmoved by these findings. Thornbury (2015: 101) describes the findings as "a riposte to the anti-coursebook lobby, but it is not the *coup de grâce*", while Tomlinson writes:

> I am not convinced that this proves that the coursebook facilitated language learning and I have seen no convincing evidence that a global coursebook has facilitated durable language acquisition. But to be fair, I have seen no convincing evidence that a global coursebook has ever not facilitated durable language acquisition" (Tomlinson, 2016: 4).

But until compelling empirical evidence is brought to bear to support the narrative of LT ineffectiveness, these and other expressions of incredulity must remain solidly within the realm of rhetoric. Admittedly, one study alone is insufficient for making bold assertions, but other objective LT investigations (e.g., Guilloteaux, 2013; Nitta and Gardner, 2005) are also beginning to find that, when used in a consistent, pedagogically-informed manner by competent teachers, second language learning through textbooks does take place.

KEY LEARNING ISSUES

Having now dispensed with the question of *if*, let us turn our attention to *how* LTs can effectively contribute as tool for language learning. We will study this question from the student, teacher, and institutional perspective.

THE STUDENT PERSPECTIVE

While second language learners will vary in the levels of motivation they bring to their studies, most students tend to view their language textbook as an important resource for supporting their study of the target language. In part, it is the physicality of the LT which reassures students engaged in the often-abstract experience of learning a language. Students also appreciate the clearly delineated and incremental framework found in effective LTs, because this helps them to recognize what they must learn both in the short and long term (Richards, 2015: 618). Student views such as these are supported by second language acquisition research, which finds that learners experience greater success in the target language when guided incrementally. This process entails starting from basic, almost mechanical tasks, and moving onwards toward increasingly complex levels of language reformulation (Robinson, 2001). An effective LT is organized so that tasks are steadily graded from the functionally simple to the cognitively complex, and will have communication rather than grammatical drilling as its aim. Communicative interaction is enhanced through the LT's bank of graded tasks, which will range from individual assignments that can be completed either before or after class, to collaborative pair and group work tasks during class. Classroom-based activities contain knowledge gaps that act as catalysts for meaningful output and reformulation. The lexical items presented in the LT provide material support for learners when communication breakdowns take place during classroom tasks, and resource material for later task recycling (Baralt et al., 2014; Kim, 2009).

Practice opportunities found in effective LTs facilitate authentic interaction, both with the teacher and with other students. Authentic interaction does not always imply or necessitate authentic language, however. Shortall's (2007) corpus study of beginning and low-intermediate LTs found textbook language to be almost always contrived, but concludes that it is more important to highlight aspects of the target language so that learners can begin noticing and then learning them. Essentially, until the upper-intermediate and advanced levels, pedagogy trumps authenticity. Schmidt (1990), concurs, arguing that only after becoming conscious of certain grammatical structures, lexical items, and other features of the language, can learners then start to incorporate new language into their existing knowledge base. Authentic interaction emerges by practicing a variety of tasks, through which students begin to notice new aspects of the language as important to their progress. LTs not only support students in the classroom; outside of class, they are a resource for autonomous learning. Without a textbook, students are far more dependent upon the teacher, and with the exception of those highly-motivated learners who will search out answers to questions on the internet or from other resources, most will have to wait until their next class to ask questions or to further their opportunities for expansion. Effective LTs, especially those that make use of modern technology, set learners free: they help them to continue learning on their own through expansion assignments, listening tasks, and supplemental online materials. Therefore, from the student perspective, LTs help to create a pedagogic 'third space' – a place where they receive the tools necessary for collaborating with teachers as they work towards building up their knowledge of the target language.

THE TEACHER PERSPECTIVE

McGrath (2002: 8) lists several metaphors used by language teachers to describe their views of LTs in the classroom: *Straitjacket*, *Crutch*, *Holy Book*, *Survival Kit*, *Compass*, *Springboard*, *Supermarket*, and *Recipe*. These are helpful in appreciating the dynamic interaction between the role of LTs in language learning, teacher experience, and teacher attitudes towards textbooks in general (Figure 32.1).

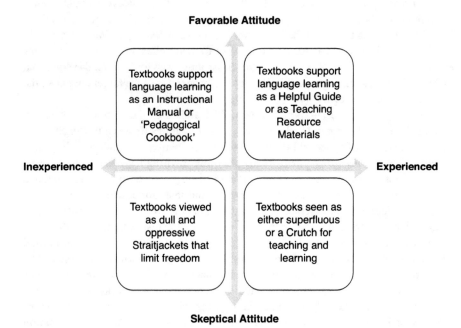

Figure 32.1 Interaction Between Teachers, Teacher Experience and Attitudes Towards Textbooks

Inexperienced language teachers are still expected to deliver effective lessons, and the metaphors of recipe and supermarket suggest how, if viewed favorably by the teacher, a well-designed LT can provide the basic pedagogic materials and step-by-step instructions for how to 'cook up', as it were, a lesson suitable for classroom consumption. In such situations, both students and teachers are learning through textbooks: the students are learning the language, and the inexperienced teacher is learning how to teach the language. Teachers with more experience, if unopposed to LTs, use them as a compass or springboard, in that the textbooks are there to suggest other directions or as a potential starting point for a particular lesson. Ideas for enhancing content interest for their learners, how much emphasis one might want to place on one skill over another, or what types of activities might fit with the dynamics of the teaching environment, are just some of the other ways that LTs support teachers as they help students make progress in the language. For both experienced and inexperienced teachers, having an organized, portable, and pre-packaged set of colorful, aesthetically-pleasing materials is not only superior to the clutter and shuffle of handmade teacher materials, they are economical, both in terms of money and in the time spent for lesson preparation.

Teachers who dislike LTs can equally affect its impact in the classroom. More qualitative studies are needed to investigate why some teachers with little language teaching experience eschew textbooks but, from my past work as a teacher trainer, common reasons that I have encountered have been the influence of a former teacher they wished to emulate in the classroom, a desire for close friendships with the learners, or a feeling of intimidation with the technical aspects of the teacher's manual. Some teachers excel in questioning authority, and not using (or misusing) the LT represents an attempt to escape from a managerial straitjacket. Other language teachers, especially those with decades of classroom experience, may approach the topic of using LTs in a manner similar to that of a gourmet chef, who has been asked to follow a cookbook made for young people just starting out on their own. Such accomplished educators can maintain an anti-textbook stance because they have internalized so many pedagogic 'recipes' that they can adjust to whatever people, conditions, or 'ingredients' they happen to encounter. Getting to this level of expertise takes time, however, and by opposing the use of the LT in the classroom, or characterizing it as a crutch, they implicitly posit themselves as somehow superior to their colleagues and deny students the opportunity to benefit from its presence in the classroom. Crawford (2002: 84) notes that when teachers take on the mantle of sole authority and progenitor of the target language, the class takes on imperial overtones.

While the graphical representation in Figure 32.1 addresses the interaction between teachers and LTs at the classroom level, there are other dynamics between the teacher and the institutional level that further add to the complexities involved in understanding how learning through textbooks takes place. Many teaching environments are supportive of the learning process; however, as a result of the spread of globalization, where language learners may be viewed as resources which 'flow' to the institution, and where teachers must 'service' the learners, experience and attitudes become irrelevant. My own experience within such environments is that there is little time or interest in teacher opinions, so long as they teach according to the prescribed processes designed to ensure educational quality. The textbook here is part of the mechanization of the educational experience. The transformation of many educational institutions into places where language teachers labor under crushing workloads, while being subjected to the remorseless panopticon of constant managerial assessment, is steadily spreading around the world. Combined with the overwhelming flow of learners in the classrooms, language teachers are placed in a situation where, metaphorically speaking, they look for the sign stating, 'In Case of Emergency, Break Glass' and use their LTs as survival kits. Even here, in spite of the unpleasant circumstances, learning through textbooks is possible. Such were the conditions of my earlier study (Hadley, 2013), and the LT not only saved teachers from burnout, they were also consoled in knowing that the students did improve, and with significant impact. When the LT becomes a survival kit, it is often only a matter of time before one notes its shift to becoming a holy book. This does not imply that language learning still cannot take place, but what it does mean is that certain methods, skills, and types of practice become a constant throughout the institution, to which we will now turn our attention.

THE INSTITUTIONAL PERSPECTIVE

The educational institution may not immediately come to mind when discussing the topic of learning through LTs. However, the actions and decisions of the institution both create and maintain the invisible structures and processes within which education takes place. Institutions vary, and while not all treat the LT as a holy book, most will still give it a central role in their efforts to support successful language learning. This role is played as part of the cyclical process of demonstrating accountability, establishing coherence, maintaining uniformity, and standardizing assessment.

Institutions are often exposed to the concerns of outside stakeholders, such as education ministries, accreditation bodies, and parents. LTs help institutions to demonstrate their accountability to stakeholder concerns, by acting as physical proof that a coherent curriculum has been established and is being regularly implemented in the class. The LT is justifiable in the minds of many administrators and stakeholders, because it is seen as representing the result of years of classroom testing and research, and as a resource which has been derived from the expertise of some of the best thinkers in the field of second language learning. For institutional decision-makers, LTs produced by a major publisher will have, if not an air of authority, then at least a stamp of approval. There is comfort in knowing that it is in the classroom as a source of reliable support to teachers and students engaged in the task of second language learning. Reliability leads to uniformity, which is another important concern of most educational institutions – especially for those using the LT as the template for the language curriculum. The textbook acts as a constant standard that will counteract chaos arising from differences in the level of training, attitudes, and goals among students and teachers. Learning through textbooks is accomplished by maintaining uniformity around what is to be studied, when it is studied, and sometimes even how the language should be studied. While this position will be seen as anathema to some teachers and learners, from the perspective of the institution, the uniform standards represented within the textbook create the possibility for standardized testing, which allows institutions to assess empirically whether learning has taken place, how much learning has occurred, and whether the LT still fits with the goals of the learners, teachers, and the overall curriculum. Collecting and then acting upon this objective evidence not only leads to the discovery of new strategies for language learning; assessment based on the LT feeds back into accountability, which in turn begins the cyclical process all over again.

IMPLICATIONS FOR TEACHING AND ASSESSMENT

In considering the question of how learning through textbooks takes place from the perspective of students, teachers, and the institution, one key implication of this discussion has been the relationship between the LT and the teacher. As much as some today might wish to remove language teachers from the equation and automate language learning through digital means, teachers are necessary for students to learn through textbooks. To borrow a metaphor from Graves (2000: 175), who likens the LT to a musical instrument, just as a piano cannot play itself, neither can a textbook teach by itself, and even when a textbook is less than effective, it can still sing in the hands of a skilled language teacher. This is not to discount the necessary interaction among the students, the institution and the LT, but when seeking to stimulate successful learning through textbooks, the focus should be upon what is pragmatically within the teacher's locus of control. To this end, Richards states:

> Teachers in training can benefit ... from learning how to analyze and review textbooks as well as finding effective ways of using them, including localising them for their specific teaching contexts. (Richards, 2015: 626)

This notion of localization is an important part of teaching. Students and teachers are likely to want to extend, and contextualize, the content of the LT according to their interests and needs. However, localization should not be used as a pretext for jumping into the vast unknown: one must learn how to bend the LT without breaking it. Otherwise, assessment becomes increasingly difficult. With regard to assessment, judging textbooks based upon subjective feelings, aesthetic preferences, and political ideologies may be satisfying at one level, but more emphasis needs to be placed on objective study of what students have learned. Localization notwithstanding, teachers need to understand the underlying design of the textbook and work to its strengths, and then to evaluate the degree to which the LT has enabled language learning. In this way, textbook assessment can shift away from that of a 'black art', towards more objectively informed pedagogy that is state-of-the-art.

Conclusion

Language learning is certainly possible without textbooks, but in most situations around the world, effective textbooks provide an important source of support for both students and teachers. This chapter has argued, from an empirical perspective, that language students do learn through textbooks, so long as the textbooks have effective qualities, such as including sufficient practices in productive and receptive tasks, clear goals, and engaging content, as well as providing sufficient lexical and grammatical support for in-class reference and out-of-class study. Learning through textbooks happens when teachers are experienced, and when they do not view the LT as a threat to second language acquisition. Learning through textbooks is fostered by teachers who treat them as a resource, used to help learners achieve greater development in their language. If the LT is used judiciously by the institution to help maintain accountability, coherence, and uniformity, then the quality of learning can be better standardized and assessed for future improvement. In these and many other ways, effective LTs are a vital resource in the second language classroom, and in the hands of well-trained teachers, will continue to contribute to language learning for many years to come.

Discussion Questions

1. Examine a textbook that you currently use to assess its potential effectiveness for your learners. To what extent does it meet the needs of your learners? Could you make the lessons more salient to the needs of your learners and goals of your educational institution?

2. This chapter has employed various metaphors to describe the contribution of textbooks to second language learning. Think of other metaphors that might describe how LTs operate in the classroom. What do these metaphors suggest with regard to how you view textbooks?

Key Readings

Garton, S., & Graves, K. (Eds.) (2014). *International Perspectives on Materials in ELT*. Basingstoke, UK: Palgrave Macmillan.

Harwood, N. (Ed.) (2013). *English Language Teaching Textbooks: Content, Consumption, Production*. Basingstoke, UK: Palgrave Macmillian.

McGrath, I. (2016). *Materials Evaluation and Design for Language Teaching* (2nd ed.). Edinburgh: Edinburgh University Press.

Richards, J. C., & Renandya, W. A. (Eds.) (2002). *Methodology in Language Teaching: An Anthology of Current Practice*. Cambridge: Cambridge University Press.

Tomlinson, B. (Ed.) (2013). *Developing Materials in Language Teaching*. London and New York: Bloomsbury.

References

Baralt, M., Gilabert, R., & Robinson, P. (2014). An introduction to theory and research in task sequencing and instructed second language learning. In M. Baralt, R. Gilabert, & P. Robinson (Eds.), *Task Sequencing and Instructed Second Language Learning*. London and New York: Bloomsbury.

Crawford, J. (2002). The role of materials in the language classroom: Finding the right balance. In J. C. Richards & W. A. Renandya (Eds.), *Methodology in Language Teaching: An Anthology of Current Practice* (pp. 80–92). Cambridge: Cambridge University Press.

Ellis, R. (2001). Investigating Form-Focused Instruction. *Language Learning*, 51(Supplement 1), 1–46.

Frank, M. (2005). The Shibata project: A Freirean approach to community-based research in the EFL classroom. *Keiwa College Research Journal*, 14, 275–287. Retrieved from www.keiwa-c.ac.jp/wp-content/uploads/2012/12/kiyo14-15.pdf

Graves, K. (2000). *Designing Language Courses: A Guide for Teachers*. Boston: Heinle & Heinle Thompson Learning.

Gray, J. (2002). The global coursebook in English language teaching. In D. Block & D. Cameron (Eds.), *Globalization and Language Teaching* (pp. 151–167). London and New York: Routledge.

Guilloteaux, M. (2013). Language textbook selection: Using materials analysis from the perspective of SLA principles. *The Asia-Pacific Education Researcher*, 22(3), 231–239.

Hadley, G. (2013). Global textbooks in local contexts: An empirical investigation of effectiveness. In N. Harwood (Ed.), *English Language Teaching Textbooks: Content, Consumption, Production* (pp. 205–238). Basingstoke, UK: Palgrave Macmillian.

Kim, Y. J. (2009). The effects of task complexity on learner–learner interaction. *System*, 37(2), 254–268.

Loewen, S. (2003). Variation in the frequency and characteristics of incidental focus on form. *Language Teaching Research*, 7, (315–345).

Long, M. H. (2000). Focus on form in task-based language teaching. In R. Lambert & E. Shohamy (Eds.), *Language Policy and Pedagogy: Essays in Honor of A. Ronald Walton* (pp. 179–192). Amsterdam/Philadelphia: John Benjamins.

Low, G. (1989). Appropriate design: The internal organisation of course units. In R. K. Johnson (Ed.), *The Second Language Curriculum* (pp. 136–154). Cambridge: Cambridge University Press.

Masuhara, H. (2011). What do teachers really want from coursebooks? In B. Tomlinson (Ed.), *Materials Development in Language Teaching* (2nd ed., pp. 236–266). Cambridge: Cambridge University Press.

Masuhara, H., & Tomlinson, B. (2008). Materials for general English. In B. Tomlinson (Ed.), *English Language Learning Materials: A Critical Review* (pp. 17–37). London / New York: Continuum.

McGrath, I. (2002). *Materials Evaluation and Design for Language Teaching* (1st ed.). Edinburgh: Edinburgh University Press.

McGrath, I. (2013). *Teaching Materials and the Roles of EFL/ESL Teachers: Practice and Theory*. London and New York: Bloomsbury.

Meddings, L., & Thornbury, S. (2011). *Teaching Unplugged: Dogme in English Language Teaching*. Peaslake and New Delhi: Delta / Viva Books.

Nitta, R., & Gardner, S. (2005). Consciousness-raising and practice in ELT coursebooks. *ELT Journal*, 59(1), 3–13.

Nunan, D. (2004). *Task-Based Language Teaching*. Cambridge: Cambridge University Press.

Richards, J. C. (1993). Beyond the text book: The role of commercial materials in language teaching. *RELC Journal*, 24(1), 1–14.

Richards, J. C. (2015). *Key Issues in Language Teaching*. Cambridge: Cambridge University Press.

Richards, J. C., Hull, J., Proctor, S., & Shields, C. (2005). *Interchange Third Edition: Full Contact. Student's Book 1, 2 & 3*. New York: Cambridge University Press.

Robinson, P. (2001). Task complexity, task difficulty, and task production: Exploring interaction in a conceptual framework. *Applied Linguistics*, 22, 22–57.

Schmidt, R. (1990). The Role of consciousness in second language learning. *Applied Linguistics*, 11(2), 129–158.

Schmitt, N. (2008). Review article: Instructed second language vocabulary learning. *Language Teaching Research*, 12(3), 329–363.

Sheldon, L. (1988). Evaluating ELT textbooks and materials. *ELT Journal*, 42(4), 237–246.

Shortall, T. (2007). The L2 syllabus: corpus or contrivance? *Corpora*, 2(2), 157–185. https://doi.org/10.3366/cor.2007.2.2.157

Thornbury, S. (2015). English language teaching textbooks: content, consumption, production. *ELT Journal*, 69(1), 100–102. https://doi.org/10.1093/elt/ccu066

Tomlinson, B. (2008). *English Language Learning Materials: A Critical Review*. London / New York: Continuum.

Tomlinson, B. (2016). Achieving a match between SLA theory and materials development. In B. Tomlinson (Ed.), *SLA Research and Materials Development for Language Learning* (pp. 3–22). New York: Routledge.

CHAPTER 33

Learning Through a Corpus

Averil Coxhead and Oliver J. Ballance

INTRODUCTION

This chapter focuses on what corpus-based learning can offer language teachers and learners. Corpora can provide large quantities of language data from a wide range of contexts and registers, which enables language learners and teachers to investigate patterns in vocabulary and grammar in written and spoken corpora in relation to their language learning goals. The chapter begins with an overview of the nature of learning through a corpus, followed by a discussion of the indirect and direct use of corpora, for classroom-based or self-access use of corpora by learners themselves. The chapter ends with a discussion of possible implications for teaching and assessment when learning through a corpus.

OVERVIEW

A corpus is, at a minimum, a language database. Strictly, a corpus is a language database that has been designed to be representative of a language, or a subset of a language. For example, the British National Corpus consists of texts that were intended to represent "the full range of British English language production, both spoken and written" (Burnard, 2002: 53). More loosely, learning through a corpus means learning through language data, whether or not a corpus was compiled with the intention of representing a broader language population. As a substantial collection of language data, a corpus can be used to find out more about various aspects of language, such as the frequency and range of grammatical and lexical patterns of use. However, exactly what can be found out will be determined by the contents of the corpus consulted.

There are many types of corpora available, including monolingual corpora and bilingual corpora. Many written and spoken corpora from different contexts are available online for searching, browsing and analysing in relation to vocabulary, grammar and discourse. Some examples are the British Academic Written English (BAWE) corpus (Nesi and

Gardner, 2012), the British Academic Spoken English (BASE) corpus (Thompson and Nesi, 2001), the Michigan Corpus of Academic Spoken English (MICASE) (University of Michigan, n.d.) and the RCPCE Profession-specific Corpora (Hong Kong Polytechnic University, n.d.). The extraordinary website for the Corpus of Contemporary American English (Davies, n.d. a) allows users to search a corpus of over 440 million words for words and phrases. Tom Cobb's (n.d.) Compleat Lexical Tutor website allows users to search a wide variety of corpora. There are also corpora which contain samples of language learners' output or production, such as writing or speaking. A good example of such a corpus is the International Corpus of Learner English (ICLE) (see Granger, n.d., for more).

As well as distinguishing between the types of corpora available, it is useful to distinguish between direct and indirect exploitation of corpora for language learning (Römer, 2011). Learning though a corpus directly is often referred to as *data-driven learning* (DDL). In DDL, learners access either a corpus or extracts from a corpus, which function as input materials for language learning. Learning through a corpus indirectly refers to the exploitation of corpus artefacts, such as word lists and other outputs of corpus analysis. Such artefacts can be generated in relation to published materials or student-generated texts, and then used by teachers and materials writers to produce or evaluate language learning materials, to set appropriate goals for learners, or to assess learners' performance. This distinction between direct and indirect use can also be interpreted in relation to what it is that a corpus provides: used directly by learners, a corpus can provide extensive exemplification; used indirectly, a corpus can facilitate evidence-based descriptions of language.

KEY LEARNING ISSUES

LEARNING INDIRECTLY THROUGH A CORPUS

In vocabulary studies, two uses of corpora that influence second language learning have been word list development and the selection of items for language tests. In word list research, corpora have become a favoured methodology, because gathering data about the frequency and range of grammatical and lexical patterns in written and spoken texts is much more easily managed using computer-based counting. Word lists now regularly inform the development of language learning dictionaries and textbooks. They can also be used to help learners set goals for vocabulary learning, by identifying which words are most worth learning first. Word lists developed from specialised corpora can help learners with specialised language learning goals in the same way. For example, Coxhead's Academic Word List (AWL) (2000) and Gardner and Davies' (2014) Academic Vocabulary List (AVL) were developed for pre-university students in English for Academic Purposes courses. Greene and Coxhead (2015) report on academic vocabulary in middle school texts in the USA.

Word lists can be used to find out more about the vocabulary burden of a given variety of spoken or written texts in English (Nation, 2013, 2016). Using Paul Nation's British National Corpus (BNC) lists (Nation, 2006), we can find out how many words in a text are from the first 1,000 most frequently used words, the second most frequently used 1,000 words, and so on. This means we can find out how many and what kinds of words occur in a variety of texts. This kind of information is helpful for determining whether materials suit learners' needs or are appropriate to their proficiency level. For example, reading novels, newspapers, and academic texts requires knowledge of around 8,000–9,000 of the most common word families, plus proper nouns (Nation, 2006). Tom Cobb's (n.d.) VocabProfile tool on the Compleat Lexical Tutor website is useful for analysing texts in this way. It should be noted that these kinds of counts do not take into account aspects of a text which can help with learning vocabulary or understanding the text, such as definitions or explanations.

Word lists made up of multi-word units or formulaic sequences are also becoming available. Such research tells us more about the patterns of words when they occur together, and this kind of information is vital for language teaching and learning. See, for example, Simpson-Vlach and Ellis's (2010) list of Academic Formulas, Shin and Nation's (2008) list of high frequency collocations, and Garnier and Schmitt's (2015) list of phrasal verbs and their most frequent meanings for pedagogical purposes.

Corpora have also been used in the development of some language tests. An example of such a test is Nation's Vocabulary Size Test (see Nation and Coxhead, 2014), which was developed by drawing on Nation's BNC-COCA lists. Other examples of corpus-based research in test development that make use of frequency-based word lists are the Vocabulary Levels Test (Schmitt, Schmitt, and Clapham, 2001) and the New Vocabulary Levels Test (Webb, Sasao, and Ballance, 2017). These tools are helpful for finding out more about the number and type of words learners know in English.

As well as the widespread use of word lists in a wide variety of ESL materials writing and testing contexts, corpora are also being used to inform textbooks and grammars more generally: see, for example, Conrad and Biber's (2009) *Real Grammar: A Corpus-Based Approach to English*.

LEARNING DIRECTLY THROUGH A CORPUS

With access to corpora that represent relevant genres, domains or text types (see Chapter 25), large numbers of examples of a linguistic phenomenon can be compiled quickly and easily. While it has always been possible to search individual texts for instances of a word or phrase, searching a corpus using appropriate tools will identify every instance of that word or phrase in millions of words of text. Corpora provide teachers and learners with access to an incredibly rich source of exemplification. This is important in second or foreign language learning, because a large number of examples can facilitate noticing, and provide repeated encounters and a basis for making generalisations. Furthermore, the ability to access a wide variety of examples, in conjunction with the ability to delimit the source of the examples, allows teachers and learners to investigate questions they have about language. They can find examples of language use that may not be covered by reference works, or investigate language use that appears to contradict reference works. For example, a corpus of academic English can be used to find examples of when academic writers *do* use personal pronouns. Basically, corpora can help learners find examples of linguistic phenomenon that may not be readily available in textbooks or other learning or teaching materials.

An interesting study by Csomay and Petrović (2012) provides an example of corpus-based materials being used for language learning. The researchers were interested in opportunities for learning presented in the movies and TV programmes. They used a mini-corpus of television shows and movies to look at legal terminology in context. They focused on legal terms such as *bar*, *constitute*, *warrant*, and *excuse*, and found these legal terms were unevenly dispersed in the movies and TV corpus (depending on episodes and scenes), and that this vocabulary accounted for more than 5% of the corpus. The researchers drew on their corpus to develop concordances for analysis of the target vocabulary in context.

In addition to the number and variety of examples corpora can provide, corpora can also provide access to examples of attested usage from contexts and registers that may be otherwise inaccessible. For instance, the ICE-NZ Corpus (School of Linguistics and Applied Language Studies, Victoria University of Wellington, n.d.) can be used to exemplify features of New Zealand English without travelling to New Zealand. The RCPCE Profession-specific Corpora (Hong Kong Polytechnic University, n.d.) can be used to exemplify actual business communications in an international context. Access to relatively inaccessible language varieties makes corpora a particularly useful resource for teaching and learning English for specific purposes (see Chapter 15).

Although learner use of corpora is still predominantly focused on learner use of concordances, it is also important to consider the potential for using other types of corpus-tools with learners. While concordances support both qualitative and quantitative interrogation of language data, learners may also be able to benefit from using quantitative summaries of corpus data such as the word lists discussed above, or even collocation lists, key-word lists, distribution profiles or word sketches. In fact, such quantitative summaries of corpus data may actually be easier for learners to use than concordances.

Nevertheless, however useful corpora may be as a source of exemplification, there are important factors to consider in relation to how learners access these examples. A teacher who intends to use corpus data with learners directly needs to decide whether or not the learners will be involved in managing the data. This distinction is usually made in terms of *hands-on* and *hands-off* use, but is also sometimes discussed in terms of *paper-based* exercises (Boulton, 2010). Although this may at first sight appear to be a resourcing issue (whether or not there are sufficient computers available), the most important aspect of this decision is probably the degree of control the teacher has over the data and its effect on the complexity of the language learning task. If learners are presented with a fixed selection of corpus data, exercises can be relatively circumscribed. If learners are using corpus tools to search the data for themselves, not only is the exercise potentially more complicated, but the learning outcomes from the exercise can be expected to be more open-ended, and may sometimes require the teacher to adjust their own understanding of the phenomenon being investigated (Johns, 1991).

Exploring these issues a little more deeply, early interest in learning through a corpus explored hands-off learning through paper-based materials based on concordance lines taken from a corpus (Thurston and Candlin, 1997, 1998). Commonly, such DDL materials present concordance data as an input-text, alongside a series of questions that can be answered by consulting the data. Other common exercises are gap-fill exercises based on concordance lines, error correction and translations. These materials are typically used for learning about the different senses or uses of a word, learning about sets of synonyms, or learning about the lexical and grammatical patterns a word commonly appears in. Johns (2002) provides an excellent overview of approaches to this kind of teacher-mediated, hands-off, learner use of corpus data, recommending that concordance lines are carefully selected and arranged to facilitate hypothesis formation and testing on the part of the learner. Exercises can also be designed around presenting language learners with other types of corpus data, such as word lists, keyword lists, word sketches and collocation lists.

Much of the early enthusiasm for presenting learners with materials derived from corpus data was the view that commercially produced language learning materials were based on invented examples that did not reflect authentic language use (Johns, 1991, 2002). Now that corpus data is commonly used to inform the content of commercially produced language learning materials (Flowerdew, 2012), teachers should carefully consider whether the time it takes to produce well-designed corpus-based materials is justified in their circumstances. Boulton (2010) suggests at least one reason for exploring hands-off DDL is its potential to provide a relatively unthreatening introduction to using corpus data directly, thereby preparing them for hands-on use in the future. In hands-off use, the learner does not have to learn how to use any software, and the teacher can mediate between the learner and data by selecting both the quantity and quality of data to present.

Learning through a corpus hands-on not only involves the learner engaging with corpus data, but also getting to grips with some form of corpus technology. Some examples of advanced software packages include *WordSmith Tools* (Scott, 2012) and *AntConc* (Anthony, 2014). There are freely accessible online platforms that allow users to perform a wide range of corpus searches, as well as an increasing number of pedagogically orientated websites that provide greatly simplified interfaces (see a sample list of useful websites at the end of this chapter). Teachers who are considering introducing their students to hands-on learning through corpora have a range of options in terms of just *how* hands-on the usage they envisage for their students will be, and how much or how little learning about corpora and the corpus interface will be required.

Hands-off concordancing and relatively simple, user-friendly hands-on concordancing have both tended to focus on learning about particular words through a corpus. Learning about writing through a corpus has been dominated by strongly hands-on approaches. Using a corpus as a writing aid often seeks examples that are relevant to a learner's particular context of writing (see Flowerdew, 2017). That is, it often requires corpus searches to be tailored to each individual writer's specific needs. Typically, this involves an extensive period of training for learners while they learn how to conduct corpus searches for themselves, some basic corpus linguistic principles, how to use a wide range of corpus search technologies to an advanced level, and sometimes even how to construct a corpus of their own. Yoon (2011) provides a very accessible overview of studies that report on learners using corpora as writing aids.

IMPLICATIONS FOR TEACHING AND ASSESSMENT

Learning through a corpus presents at least three main challenges for second language learning and assessment. First, interrogating and interpreting corpus data can be challenging. Some studies have reported learners struggling to form corpus searches that were appropriate to their needs (Pérez-Paredes, Sánchez-Tornel, and Alcaraz Calero, 2012; Pérez-Paredes, Sánchez-Tornel, Alcaraz Calero, and Jiménez, 2011). Other researchers have found that learners are prone to over-generalising, under-generalising or otherwise misconstruing corpus data (Kennedy and Miceli, 2001). In other words, it is not only possible to learn through a corpus, but also to mislearn.

Second, many language learners conceptualise language as a set of rules to be learnt, but corpus data has been instrumental in changing our theoretical understanding of language. Corpus data can conflict with a rule-based view of language, because what is and what is not found in a corpus will be determined by the type and quantity of its texts. Raw corpus data will typically include many exceptions, ambiguities, and sometimes even typos or performance errors. It is important to realise when working with corpus data that something being absent from a corpus does not necessarily indicate that it is not permissible in a language. Equally, the presence of a counter-example does not necessarily indicate that a generalisation is not an otherwise useful one.

Consulting corpus data does not always lead to the identification of clear-cut linguistic rules. Rather, one can expect a proportion of the data extracted to contradict traditional linguistic descriptions, but to support formation of other, perhaps even original, generalisations. This view of language, in which context is fundamental to interpretation and creativity and change are normal aspects of language use, can blur the boundaries between what is usual, what is exceptional, and what is erroneous. A very clear yet concise introduction to these issues is provided by the classic *Corpus, Concordance, Collocation* (Sinclair, 1991). As Hanks (2013) points out, working with corpus data has prompted many linguists to become less interested in asking what is *possible* in a language, and increasingly interested in the question of what is *probable*. As such, in its strongest form, learning through a corpus hands-on requires a degree of intellectual sophistication and tolerance of ambiguity.

The third potential challenge to teaching and learning with corpora arises from the cognitive demands of learning through a corpus, in relation to both the linguistic difficulty of the data presented and the conceptual complexity of the language learning task.

Language learning is itself already a very cognitively demanding task. Using language as data or learning how to use new technologies can both be considered cognitively complex tasks in their own right. Therefore, some learners may find balancing the demands of language learning against those of other cognitively complex tasks very challenging indeed.

While the technical and conceptual complexity of corpus use is not a problem for learners in indirect learning through a corpus, Byrd and Coxhead (2010) point out some challenges associated with using corpus artefacts in classrooms, including a lack of information about the context of items from word lists. Few existing word lists have distinguished between commonly recognised homonyms such as *bank* (the bank of a river or a financial institution), and evidence from lexicography suggests that the exact sense of a word is inseparable from its context of use (Hanks, 2013). Thus, reliable interpretation of a word list depends on sufficient knowledge of the context of the items on a word list. Byrd and Coxhead (2010) also point out that that repetitions of multi-word units (see Chapter 19) may not be particularly frequent. This is important to bear in mind when thinking about the pedagogical applications of multi-word unit lists, because high frequency items give better return for learning than low frequency items (see Nation, 2013). The most frequent multi-word units on a list may still be rather infrequent in texts in general. For example, Byrd and Coxhead (2010) point out that in a corpus of 3.5 million words, *on the basis of* occurs only once per ~7,500 words. These points also relate to the assessment of language learning through a corpus, as teachers consider what aspects of language are the focus of assessment, including the form, meaning or use of vocabulary items, grammatical features of texts, or patterns of vocabulary in texts.

CONCLUSION

This chapter has looked at various kinds of learning through a corpus, from the use of artefacts developed for teaching and learning such as word lists and tests, through to learning directly or indirectly using a corpus. We have suggested a range of resources and considered some implications of learning through a corpus. While we have focused mostly on written corpora, there are many kinds of corpora available, including spoken and multimedia. The powerful opportunities for learning provided by corpora are well worth investigating further for learners, teachers, and researchers.

Discussion Questions

1. Investigate at least one of the websites for corpora mentioned in this chapter. Select three or four words or multi-word units to search for in a corpus. Compare their use in different kinds of corpora (spoken versus written; learner language versus professional writers; or English for Academic Purposes or general purposes, for example). What patterns of use surprised or interested you? How could you use this information with your language learners, and why?

2. In what ways have you used corpus work in your language teaching? Have you used artefacts of corpus research? If so, what have you used, when, why and how? What kinds of hands-on or hands-off activities have you used?

Key Readings

Flowerdew, L. (2012). *Corpora and Language Education*. Basingstoke, UK: Palgrave Macmillan.

McEnery, T., Xiao, R. & Tono, Y. (2006). *Corpus-Based Language Studies: An Advanced Resource Book*. London: Routledge.

O'Keeffe, A., & McCarthy, M. (Eds.) (2010). *The Routledge Handbook of Corpus Linguistics*. Abingdon: Routledge.

O'Keeffe, A., McCarthy, M. & Carter, R. (2007). *From Corpus to Classroom: Language Use and Language Teaching*. New York: Cambridge University Press.

Reppen, R. (2010). *Using Corpora in the Language Classroom*. New York: Cambridge University Press.

Sinclair, J. (Ed.) (2004). *How to Use Corpora in Language Teaching*. Amsterdam/Philadelphia: John Benjamins.

Useful Websites

Anthony, L. (2014). *AntConc (Version 3.4.3)*. Tokyo, Japan: Waseda University.

Cobb, T. (n.d.). *Compleat Lexical Tutor v.8*. Available at: www.lextutor.ca

Davies, M. (n.d. a). *Corpus of Contemporary American English*. Available at: http://corpus.byu.edu/coca/

Davies, M. (n.d. b). *Corpus.byu.edu*. Available at: http://corpus.byu.edu/coca/

Granger, S. (n.d.). *International Corpus of Learner English (ICLE)*. Available at: https://uclouvain.be/en/research-institutes/ilc/cecl/icle.html

Hong Kong Polytechnic University (n.d.). *RCPCE Profession-specific Corpora*. Available at: http://rcpce.engl.polyu.edu.hk/index.html

Just the word (n.d.). Available at: www.just-the-word.com

Kilgarriff, A. (n.d.). *Sketch Engine for Language Learning (SkELL)*. Available at: https://www.sketchengine.co.uk/skell/

School of Linguistics and Applied Language Studies (n.d.). *ICE-NZ Corpus*. Available at: http://www.victoria.ac.nz/lals/resources/corpora-default

Schoppmann, C. & Lipski, S. (n.d.). *Linguee*. Available at: www.linguee.com/

Scott, M. (2012). *WordSmith Tools Version 6*. Stroud, UK: Lexical Analysis Software.

University of Michigan (n.d.). *Michigan Corpus of Academic Spoken English (MICASE)*. Available at: http://quod.lib.umich.edu/cgi/c/corpus/corpus?c=micase;page=simple.

Witten, I. (n.d.). *Flexible Language Acquisition (FLAX)*. Available at http://flax.nzdl.org/greenstone3/flax

References

Boulton, A. (2010). Data-driven learning: Taking the computer out of the equation. *Language Learning*, 60(3), 534–572.

Burnard, L. (2002). The BNC: Where did we go wrong? In B. Kettemann & G. Marko (Eds.), *Teaching and Learning by Doing Corpus Analysis* (pp. 51–70). Amsterdam / New York: Rodopi.

Byrd, P., & Coxhead, A. (2010). On the other hand: Lexical bundles in academic writing and in the teaching of EAP. *University of Sydney Papers in TESOL*, 5, 31–64.

Conrad, S., & Biber, D. (2009). *Real Grammar: A Corpus-Based Approach to English*. New York: Pearson Education ESL.

Coxhead, A. (2000). A new academic word list. *TESOL Quarterly*, 34(2), 213–238.

Csomay, E., & Petrović, M. (2012). "Yes, your honor!": A corpus-based study of technical vocabulary in discipline-related movies and TV shows. *System*, 40, 305–315.

Flowerdew, J. (2017). Corpus-based approaches to language description for specialized academic writing. *Language Teaching*, 50(1), 90–106.

Flowerdew, L. (2012). *Corpora and Language Education*. Basingstoke, UK: Palgrave Macmillan.

Gardner, D., & Davies, M. (2014). A new academic vocabulary list. *Applied Linguistics*, 35(3), 305–327.

Garnier, M., & Schmitt, N. (2015). 'The PHaVE List: A pedagogical list of phrasal verbs and their most frequent meaning senses. *Language Teaching Research*, 19(6), 645–666. https://doi.org/10.1177/1362168814559798

Greene, J. W., & Coxhead, A. (2015). *Academic Vocabulary for Middle School Students: Research-Based Lists and Strategies for Key Content Areas*. Baltimore, MD: Brookes Publishing Co.

Hanks, P. (2013). *Lexical Analysis: Norms and Exploitations*. Cambridge, MA: MIT Press.

Johns, T. (1991). From printout to handout: grammar and vocabulary teaching in the context of data-driven learning. In T. Johns & P. King (Eds.), *Classroom Concordancing* (pp. 27–45). Birmingham, UK: University of Birmingham.

Johns, T. (2002). Data-driven learning: The perpetual challenge. In B. Kettemann & G. Marko (Eds.), *Teaching and Learning by Doing Corpus Analysis* (pp. 107–117). Amsterdam / New York: Rodopi.

Kennedy, C., & Miceli, T. (2001). An evaluation of intermediate students' approaches to corpus investigation. *Language, Learning & Technology*, 5(3), 77–90.

Nation, I. S. P. (2006). How large a vocabulary is needed for reading and listening? *Canadian Modern Language Review*, 63(1), 59–82.

Nation, I. S. P. (2013). *Learning Vocabulary in Another Language* (2nd ed.). Cambridge: Cambridge University Press.

Nation, I. S. P. (2016). *Making and Using Word Lists for Language Learning and Testing*. Amsterdam: John Benjamins.

Nation, P., & Coxhead, A. (2014). Vocabulary size research at Victoria University of Wellington, New Zealand. *Language Teaching*, 47(3), 398–403.

Nesi, H., & Gardner, S (2012). *Genres Across the Disciplines: Student Writing in Higher Education*. Cambridge: Cambridge University Press.

Pérez-Paredes, P., Sánchez-Tornel, M., & Alcaraz Calero, J. M. (2012). Learners' search patterns during corpus-based focus-on-form activities: A study on hands-on concordancing. *International Journal of Corpus Linguistics*, 4, 482–515.

Pérez-Paredes, P., Sánchez-Tornel, M., Alcaraz Calero, J. M., & Jiménez, P. (2011). Tracking learners' actual uses of corpora: guided vs non-guided corpus consultation. *Computer Assisted Language Learning*, 3, 233–253.

Römer, U. (2011). Corpus research applications in second language teaching. *Annual Review of Applied Linguistics*, 31, 205–225.

Schmitt, N., Schmitt, D., & Clapham, C. (2001). Developing and exploring the behaviour of two new versions of the Vocabulary Level Test. *Language Testing*, 18, 55–88.

Shin, D., & Nation, I.S.P. (2008). Beyond single words: the most frequent collocations in spoken English. *ELT Journal*, 62(4), 339–348.

Simpson-Vlach, R., & Ellis, N. (2010). An academic formulas list: New methods in phraseology research. *Applied Linguistics*, 31(4), 487–512.

Sinclair, J. M. (1991). *Corpus, Concordance, Collocation*. Oxford: Oxford University Press.

Thompson, P., & Nesi, H. (2001). The British Academic Spoken English (BASE) corpus project. *Language Teaching Research* 5(3), 263–264.

Thurston, J., & Candlin, C. N. (1997). *Exploring Academic English: A Workbook for Student Essay Writing*. Sydney, Australia: NCELTR.

Thurston, J., & Candlin, C. N. (1998). Concordancing and the teaching of the vocabulary of academic English. *English for Specific Purposes*, 17(3), 267–280.

Webb, S., Sasao, Y., & Ballance, O. (2017). The updated Vocabulary Levels Test: Developing and validating two new forms of the VLT. *ITL – International Journal of Applied Linguistics*, 168(1), forthcoming.

Yoon, C. (2011). Concordancing in L2 writing class: An overview of research and issues. *Journal of English for Academic Purposes*, 10(3), 130–139.

SECTION 9

TECHNOLOGY AND LEARNING ENGLISH

Today's learners are not simply consumers of media, but assume new roles as creators of media, using technology accessible through smartphones and mobile devices. This new world requires teachers to make a shift from a focus on developing linguistic competence to developing language as a component of social practice – a switch in focus from teaching language to designing language-learning projects that engage learners in multimodal media practices. The chapters in this section consider these factors.

Rodney H. Jones provides a broad view of the role of technology in second language (L2) learning, pointing out that all learning is mediated through tools of different kinds, current forms of technology being one part of a broader range of potential resources. In considering the role of technology in language learning, he identifies the need to focus on the affordances, as well as the constraints, technology offers. Rather than adding to the extensive documentation of the kinds of technologies available, he shows how technologies shape the way meaning is made and expressed through language, the forms in which both input and output are recorded and transmitted, and the kinds of interactions possible among learners, as well as how they help learners develop autonomous learning. He points out, as do several other contributors to this book, how the advent of the internet and digital technology has changed the way many people learn and use an L2.

Nicky Hockly and **Gavin Dudeney** examine some of the many affordances for learning provided by out-of-class online learning through the use of the internet and mobile technologies, in both formal and informal language learning contexts. They describe the specific features of online learning that provide successful learning opportunities, particularly those in which the language is used for collaborative interaction. Learning that results from such processes may be intentional or incidental to other activities – for example, gaming. Factors that can influence the effectiveness of online learning are reviewed, including course design, task design and teacher training.

In the final chapter, **Christopher Jenks** describes how social media have helped reshape the nature of social interaction, and the types and forms of communication that they mediate, as well as the opportunities for language learning that they make possible. He describes how the networking nature of social media not only shapes both what and how content is shared and exchanged, but also creates new forms of opportunities for learners to engage with multimodal forms of language. Asynchronous and synchronous communication result in different types of interaction, some supporting the development of fluency and others providing more opportunity for accuracy. Issues of voice and identity emerge, as learners participate in online communities that require the development of skills of intercultural competence. Jenks suggests that language now becomes a means of developing a network of family, friends or colleagues, through social activities that can drive L2 learning.

The chapters in this section touch in different ways on the notion of what affordances are available and exploitable for language learning, be they different approaches taken to learning inside and outside the classroom, or types of environments (actual and virtual) and media that make a difference to how learners can choose to learn. The wide range of learning opportunities available encompasses communicating through language tasks, integrating language and content, and deriving insights about language from corpora. In addition, the advent of multimedia technologies has greatly expanded opportunities for networking, collaboration and community-building which can shape and extend both the learning and teaching of languages.

CHAPTER 34

Learning Through Technology

Rodney H. Jones

INTRODUCTION

With the rise of digital media and their increasingly pervasive use in educational settings, more and more attention is being paid to the ways technology can facilitate language learning. Most discussions about the effects of technology on language learning, however, have focused rather narrowly on 'new media' (computers, the internet, and mobile devices), ignoring the fact that *technological mediation* has been a central component of language learning ever since the invention of the printing press. While understanding the effects of digital technologies on language learning is of primary importance, especially as such technologies are becoming so much part of the fabric of our everyday communicative practices, doing so requires a more general understanding of *technological mediation* itself (see Norris and Jones, 2005), and the ways it influences both cognitive and social processes.

OVERVIEW

The most important thing to remember when trying to make sense of the impact of technological mediation on language learning is that *all* learning is mediated through tools which act both to support users' cognitive development and to connect them to the social contexts in which learning takes place. Vygotsky (1962) divided these tools into *psychological tools* (such as languages and counting systems), and *technological tools* (such as printed texts and other media). "An essential key to understanding human social and psychological processes", according to Vygotsky, "is the tools … used to mediate them" (Wertsch, 1990: 113). More recent scholars have taken this idea even further, arguing, as does Clark (2003), that the advance of human culture (including the development of language) has always depended on our ability to use technologies to mediate our interaction with the environment. Humans are, Clark insists, 'natural born cyborgs.'

Another important thing to remember, when considering the effect of technology on language learning, is that all technologies are biased (Innes, 1951). All tools bring with them different affordances and constraints when it comes to the psychological and social actions (including actions associated with learning and communicating) that we can perform with them. Writing, for example, allows us to record language in a form that is more permanent than spoken language and to transport it over space and time, affordances which, according to the literacy scholar Walter Ong (1988), facilitated the development of modern 'rational' thought and cultural memory. A constraint of writing is that it is less efficient at transmitting the phonological and non-verbal aspects of spoken language, affordances that are more associated with electronic media (television, radio, and audio and video recording devices). As a result of their inherent biases, technologies do not just affect how we learn language, but also how we use it in our everyday lives. In some respects, learning a language is as much a matter of learning how to use the technologies through which language is recorded and transmitted, as it is learning a set of grammatical or phonological conventions.

Finally, technologies do not just affect how we learn and use language, but also the *ideologies* that we adopt regarding what we consider to be 'correct' or 'standard' language, or the 'best way' to learn language. The invention of the printing press, for example, played a big role in the development of standard grammars and lexicons, giving rise to a bias in both linguistics and language teaching towards written language over spoken language (Linell, 2011). Advances in audio recording, especially as they were implemented in the context of language laboratories, played an important role in ensuring the prominence of the audiolingual approach that dominated language learning in the mid-twentieth century.

My goal in this chapter is not to present an account of the various methods and techniques associated with different language learning technologies, nor to review the considerable literature on the effectiveness of different technologies used in different ways to learn language (for such reviews see Kenning, 2007; Salaberry, 2001). Rather, I will attempt to lay out the key aspects of *technological mediation* which impact on the way people learn language, providing for learners (and teachers) a framework with which to understand and evaluate their own use of technology in language learning.

Key Learning Issues

Technologies influence language learning in at least four ways. First, they influence the kinds of meanings that can be made with language, and thus, the kinds of meaning-making processes that learners are given the opportunity to practice. Second, they determine the ways we can record, preserve and transmit language, affecting the type and quality of input learners are exposed to and what they are able to do with that input, as well as how they are able to reflect on their output. Third, they affect the kinds of interactions learners are able to have with the language, the kinds of people they are able to interact with, and the roles they are able to play in these interactions. Finally, technologies play a role in learners' ability to develop autonomy in their learning, to determine their own learning trajectories, and to apply what they have learned to authentic situations.

MEANING MAKING

As I mentioned above, perhaps the most important effect technology has on language learning is on the types of language it allows us to produce – or, more accurately, the types of 'meaning making' it allows us to engage in. Different technologies channel their users into particular kinds of meaning making: written texts, for example, channel them into forms of asynchronous, decontextualized meaning making, whereas spoken language channels them into more multimodal, context dependent forms of communication, in which meaning can depend as much on resources like prosody and gesture as it does on words and grammar. New forms of communication, made possible by digital technologies, are introducing new forms of meaning making which depend on the rich combination of words and images arranged in hypertextual rather than linear patterns (Jones and Hafner, 2012; Kress, 2003).

Using different material resources for making meaning requires different kinds of skills. Learners who spend the bulk of their time studying and producing written texts are sometimes less able to engage effectively in conversations, not because they are deficient in lexical or grammatical knowledge, but because they lack ability to apply that knowledge to conventions of meaning making in spoken language (see also Chapter 22). Similarly, those who spend most of their time practicing speaking are likely to have more difficulty producing effective written texts. Most considerations of the relationship between channel and meaning making have not gone much beyond this spoken/written binary. Many technologies used for language learning, however, have the effect of disturbing that binary. Audio recording technologies, for example, put students in situations in which they need to produce and interpret spoken language without many of the resources (such as gesture and facial expression) normally associated with speech, and technologies like SMS and instant messaging, although regarded as forms of writing, employ many of the discourse conventions of spoken language. The main point is that whenever people communicate through technologies, they are not just using 'language' – they are using particular combinations of communicative resources, each with their own particular potentials for meaning making. Much of what it means to be a competent user of language is understanding how to effectively exploit the different modes and media we have available to us, in order to make the kinds of meanings we want to make.

ENTEXTUALIZATION

Related to the fact that different technologies make possible different forms of meaning making is the fact that they also make possible different means of *entextualizing* language (Jones, 2009) – that is, of creating artefacts that can be transported from place to place, reviewed and analyzed, and manipulated in various ways. Entextualization – what Bauman and Briggs (1990: 73) define as "the process of rendering discourse extractable, of making a stretch of linguistic production into a unit – a *text* – that can be lifted out of its interactional setting" – has an enormous impact on language learning, dramatically increasing both the learner's ability to be exposed to comprehensible input and to engage with that input in meaningful ways. The technology of writing, for example, gives learners access to a range of linguistic artefacts which they can read and review multiple times, and the technology of audio recording not only gives them the chance to listen to a variety of speakers and accents, and to replay stretches of talk over and over again, but also gives them the opportunity to 'entextualize' (record) their own voices and reflect on their own linguistic performance.

Entextualization acts as an important cognitive support for language learning in several ways. First, it serves as an aid to memory, rendering linguistic behavior more durable so that learners can return to it and revise or review it when necessary. Second, texts serve as instruments through which input can be made more comprehensible and salient (Warschauer and Meskill, 2000). Texts do not just preserve language; they also give us the opportunity to manipulate it, annotate it, edit it, recontextualize it, and divide it up into more manageable units. Finally, technologies of entextualzation encourage reflexivity. The most obvious example of this is when learners engage in their own acts of entextualization, and so are able to read, listen to, or watch representations of their own linguistic performance. But even engaging with texts made by others provides useful opportunities for learners to monitor and reflect upon their linguistic performance.

The feature of digital technologies that is sometimes overlooked in discussions about their potential to aid language learning is the range of new ways they facilitate entextualization. Not only do computers allow us to store a staggering number of texts, and to access millions more through the internet, but they also allow us to search through these texts in sophisticated ways, and to create concordances that can reveal patterns of language use. Many learners nowadays carry around with them (in the form of smartphones) devices which allow them to record written texts, voice, images and videos in nearly any situation in which they find themselves, and most interactions that they engage in using these devices – from SMS chats to comment threads on social networking sites – are preserved in the form of 'persistent conversations' (Erickson, 1999) that come to constitute an archive of their past language use and a record of their progress (see also Chapter 36).

INTERACTION

The third important dimension of technological mediation for language learning is the way in which technologies either amplify or constrain opportunities for social interaction, and the kinds of patterns of participation within these interactions that they make possible. There is, among many researchers in language acquisition, a longstanding conviction that effective learning requires more than just comprehensible input and reflexivity, but also requires opportunities for learners to engage in authentic, spontaneous and purposive communication with others (see, for example, Long, 1981; see also Chapter 11). Interaction, however, is not a simple or unitary thing – people use language to interact for a variety of different purposes, through a variety of different channels, with a variety of different opportunities for participation. As Goffman (1981) points out, our conventional concept of communication involving simple roles of 'speaker' and 'listener' does not accurately convey the patterns of participation in most real-life communication. There are many different kinds of speakers and listeners – from performers and audiences to partners in conversation, from addressees to overhearers – who have very different kinds of rights and roles in interaction. Different technologies help to create the conditions for these different patterns of participation, or as Goffman (1981) calls them, 'participation frameworks'.

Printed materials, for example, enable a kind of asynchronous, one-way interaction in which readers generally cannot 'talk back' to writers, whereas new forms of reading, made possible by hypertext and Web 2.0, allow readers to formulate their own pathways through texts and to interact with the writer and other readers through comments (Jones and Hafner, 2012). Language laboratories and computer labs in which learners sit in separate cubicles, often wearing earphones, can severely constrain opportunities for interaction, and when interaction is part of activities involving these technologies, as when students are asked to have conversations with 'partners' in language labs, these conversations are usually highly controlled, contrived, and limited to dyadic interactions. Networked computers and the internet have revolutionized the opportunities for participation and interaction open to language learners. Not only are learners able to take the roles of 'authors' or 'broadcasters', engaging in the kind of one-to-many communication that heretofore was only the province of the few, but they can also engage in complex multiparty interactions in chatrooms and on social networking sites.

Multiparty interactions in digital networks are very different from group discussions in classrooms. First of all, such networks give students a chance to seek out and interact with people who have similar interests within what linguist James Gee (Gee, 2004; Gee and Hayes, 2011) calls 'affinity spaces', in which motivation for communication is generally much higher than it is in the artificially formed groups characteristic of language classrooms. Second, networked communication provides a greater variety of participant roles than does group discussion. Participants in networked interaction can address large groups of people, break off for discussions in small groups or pairs, 'lurk' or 'listen in' to other people's conversations, or engage in a variety of 'low cost' forms of interaction such as 'liking' (Jones and Hafner, 2012). The value of this interaction for language learners is that it gives them a wide range of opportunities to engage in what Lave and Wenger (1991) call 'legitimate peripheral participation', allowing them to gradually build up the skills and confidence that they will need to participate more fully both socially and linguistically in these communities.

AUTONOMY

Finally, technologies have a potential impact on learners' capacity to develop autonomy in their language learning: that is, their capacity to take control of their own learning trajectories and develop strategies for learning independent of teachers and of staged materials written for language learning. Technology, of course, has been a central feature of self-access centres, which have typically made available to students things like audio recordings, video tapes, and more recently, computer programs to assist them in learning independently (Gardner and Miller, 1999).

Recently, however, more attention has been paid to the opportunities learners have to build autonomy outside of controlled spaces like self-access centres. In this respect, the internet has made the self-access centre obsolete. It has given learners access wherever they are to nearly all of the multimedia resources they used to have to go to self-access centres to use, as well as many of the support services normally associated with self-access centres, such as vocabulary glosses, graded exercises, language learning games and other activities, and interaction with online teachers and other learners.

The shift that digital technology has brought about in the way we understand autonomy in language learning, however, goes far beyond the expansion of self-access opportunities into cyberspace. The capacities introduced by digital media and the internet for accessing information and initiating interaction do not just facilitate the development of conditions more traditionally associated with autonomy (such as the chance to plan and monitor one's own learning), but also create new conditions, such as possibilities to initiate relationships with all sorts of people, and to explore and create new kinds of learning opportunities according to one's own interests and abilities (Ito et al., 2008). As Benson observes:

> Early work on autonomy... placed a high priority on the collection and provision of resources through self-access and on programmes to train learners in their use for self-directed learning. Learner control was, in effect, both institutionalized and other-initiated. The advent of digital literacies, however, means that autonomous language learning is more likely to be self-initiated and carried out without the intervention, or even knowledge, of language teachers. (Benson, 2013: 840)

This shift in focus has led to a greater appreciation for learners' everyday literacy practices such as blogging, social networking, and online gaming (Chik, 2013; see also Chapter 13), and how these practices can create unique and powerful opportunities for language learning, even when language and learning are not necessarily foregrounded or explicitly attended to.

Another important, though still nascent, capacity of digital technologies to enhance autonomy lies in the capacity of digital texts to 'read their readers' (Jones, 2015), and to adapt themselves to individual users' needs or interests. Adaptive systems are a central component in most everyday internet experiences, such as online shopping sites that make recommendations to customers, and search engines which filter content based on users' past behavior. Now such technologies are finding their way into language learning programs that use algorithms to analyze the way learners interact with them and provide recommendations and feedback based on this analysis (Kerr, 2015).

IMPLICATIONS FOR TEACHING AND ASSESSMENT

In this chapter I have suggested a framework for analyzing the effects of technology on language learning, which can be expressed in a series of questions which learners and teachers can consider when introducing different forms of technological mediation into the learning process:

1. What kind of meanings does this technology allow users to make that might be different from those that can be made with other technologies? How might this meaning-making potential affect the forms of language and communicative skills that can be practiced?

2. How does this technology allow users to create, store, and transmit texts, and to review and reflect on them? What effect might this capacity have on users' ability to be exposed to useful input?

3. What sorts of social interactions does this technology make possible? What sorts of participant roles are made available to them, and what kinds of opportunities might these interactions provide for meaningful language practice?

4. What opportunities does this technology provide for learners to plan and monitor their own learning, and to create new learning opportunities for themselves?

Asking these questions will not just sensitize teachers to the inherent 'biases' built into the technologies they use in their classrooms, but also to the affordances for learning that students might exploit in their use of technology outside the classroom, including affordances for self-monitoring and self-assessment.

CONCLUSION

The most important insight we can take away from an analysis of technological mediation and language learning is that technologies – from the printed word to digital video – do not just change the way we can learn language, but also change the way people *use* language. New technologies give rise to new social practices, involving new linguistic forms, new forms of interaction, and new communicative roles and social identities for people. When looked at from this perspective, the focus of our inquiry into the relationship between language learning and technology shifts from questions about how technology is changing the way language can be learned, to questions about how technology is changing the kind of language we must learn, and the kinds of things we must learn to do with language.

Discussion Questions

1. Choose a technology that you have used to learn or teach language and analyze it based on the four dimensions of technological mediation introduced in this chapter: meaning making, entextualization, interaction, and autonomy. What does your analysis tell you about how the technology might affect how people learn language and the kind of language they might learn?

2. We often think of the ways technologies aid language learning, but technologies can also constrain opportunities for learning. Can you think of any examples of this constraint?

3. Different technologies seem to fit better with different theories of how languages are learned. What theories of language acquisition are supported by the following technologies: print media; audio recordings; the internet; and Web 2.0?

4. Technology does not just change the way we learn language, but also the way we use language in our everyday lives. Choose a technology and consider how it has altered the kinds of language and communicative practices language learners need to master.

Key Readings

Blake, R. J. (2008). *Brave New Digital Classroom: Technology and Foreign Language Learning.* Washington, D.C.: Georgetown University Press.

Jones, R. H., & Hafner, C. A. (2012). *Understanding Digital Literacies: A Practical Introduction.* London: Routledge.

Kenning, M.-M. (2007). *ICT and Language Learning: From Print to the Mobile Phone.* Basingstoke, UK: Palgrave Macmillan.

Nunan, D., & Richards, J. C. (Eds.) (2015). *Language Learning Beyond the Classroom.* London / New York: Routledge.

Stanley, G. (2013). *Language Learning with Technology: Ideas for Integrating Technology in the Classroom.* Cambridge: Cambridge University Press.

References

Bauman, R., & Briggs, C. L. (1990). Poetics and performance as critical perspectives on language and social life. *Annual Review of Anthropology*, 19, 59–88.

Benson, P. (2013). Learner autonomy. *TESOL Quarterly*, 47(4), 839–843. http://doi.org/10.1002/tesq.134

Chik, A. (2013). Naturalistic CALL and digital gaming. *TESOL Quarterly*, 47(4), 834–839. http://doi.org/10.1002/tesq.133

Clark, A. (2003). *Natural-Born Cyborgs: Minds, Technologies, and the Future of Human Intelligence.* Oxford: Oxford University Press.

Erickson, T. (1999). Persistant conversation: An introduction. *Journal of Computer-Mediated Communication*, 4(4), 0–0. http://doi.org/10.1111/j.1083-6101.1999.tb00105.x

Gardner, D., & Miller, L. (1999). *Establishing Self-access: From Theory to Practice.* Cambridge: Cambridge University Press.

Gee, J. P. (2004). *Situated Language and Learning: A Critique of Traditional Schooling.* New York: Routledge.

Gee, J. P., & Hayes, E. R. (2011). *Language and Learning in the Digital Age.* New York: Routledge.

Goffman, E. (1981). *Forms of Talk.* Oxford: Blackwell.

Innes, H. (1951). *The Bias of Communication.* Toronto: University of Tornoto Press.

Ito, M., Horst, H., Bittanti, M., Boyd, D., Herr-Stephenson, B., Lange, P., Pascoe, C. J., & Robinson, L. (2008). Living and learning with new media: Summary of findings from the Digital Youth Project. Chicago, IL: The John D. & Catherine T. MacArthur Foundation.

Jones, R. H. (2009). Dancing, skating and sex: Action and text in the digital age. *Journal of Applied Linguistics*, 6(3), 283–302.

Jones, R. H. (2015). Discourse, cybernetics, and the entextualization of the self. In R. H. Jones, A. Chik, & C. A. Hafner (Eds.), *Discourse and Digital Practices: Doing Discourse Analysis in the Digital Age* (pp. 28–47). London: Routledge.

Jones, R. H., & Hafner, C. A. (2012). *Understanding Digital Literacies: A Practical Introduction*. London: Routledge.

Kenning, M.-M. (2007). *ICT and Language Learning: From Print to the Mobile Phone*. Basingstoke, UK: Palgrave Macmillan.

Kerr, P. (2015). Adaptive learning. *ELT Journal*, 70(1), 88–93. https://doi.org/10.1093/elt/ccv055

Kress, G. (2003). *Literacy in the New Media Age*. London; New York: Routledge.

Lave, J., & Wenger, E. (1991). *Situated Learning: Legitimate Peripheral Participation*. Cambridge: Cambridge University Press.

Linell, P. (2011). *The Written Language Bias in Linguistics: Its Nature, Origins and Transformations*. London: Routledge.

Long, M. H. (1981). Input, interaction and second language acquisition. In H. Winitz (Ed.), *Native Language and Foreign Language Acquisition: Annals of the New York Academy of Sciences*, 379, 259–278. New York: New York Academy of Sciences.

Norris, S., & Jones, R. H. (2005). *Discourse in Action: Introducing Mediated Discourse Analysis*. London: Routledge.

Ong, W. J. (1988). *Orality and Literacy: The Technologizing of the Word*. New York: Methuen.

Salaberry, M. R. (2001). The use of technology for second language learning and teaching: A retrospective. *The Modern Language Journal*, 85(1), 39–56. http://doi.org/10.1111/0026-7902.00096

Vygotsky, L. S. (1962). *Thought and Language*. Cambridge, MA: MIT Press.

Wertsch, J. V. (1990). The voice of rationality in a sociocultural approach to mind. In L. C. Moll (Ed.), *Vygotsky and Education: Instructional Implications and Applications of Sociohistorical Psychology* (pp. 111–126). Cambridge: Cambridge University Press.

Warschauer, M., & Meskill, C. (2000). Technology and second language learning. In J. Rosenthal (Ed.), *Handbook of Undergraduate Second Language Education* (pp. 303–318). Mahwah, NJ: Lawrence Erlbaum.

CHAPTER 35

Online Language Learning

Nicky Hockly and Gavin Dudeney

INTRODUCTION

Since the 1980s, computers have become increasingly widespread in language teaching (see Chapter 34). Initially expensive and limited to institutional deployment (for example, in the shape of computer labs in universities), computers these days – especially in the form of mobile devices – enable users to easily access learning materials outside of formal learning environments. Language learners can not only access a wealth of online learning materials and authentic content, but can also interact with others in real time (synchronously) via text chat or videoconferencing, or not in real time (asynchronously) via online forums or blogs, and all in the target language. These new contexts for language learning, made possible by the affordances of new technologies and the increasing shift from desktop to mobile technologies, has necessitated a new descriptive vocabulary.

OVERVIEW

The landscape of online language learning is replete with terminology; the plethora of terms used to describe it can frequently obstruct the view. For example, terms like *e-learning, web-enhanced learning*, and *distance learning*, as well as *blended learning, hybrid learning*, and *mixed learning*, are often used interchangeably to refer to learning which is supported by technology, both in and outside the classroom. The first three terms frequently imply fully online learning, while the latter three terms most often refer to a combination of face-to-face (that is, classroom-based) and online learning. In this chapter, we focus on *fully online* language learning – that is, learning that takes place outside of the classroom via internet-enabled technologies, with no face-to-face contact between teachers and students. Although we focus on fully online learning contexts and opportunities in this chapter, it goes without saying that these contexts will frequently form only one part of a learner's language learning endeavours, which may well include face-to-face learning. However, due to limitations of space, in this chapter we focus only on research and issues related to the *online* learning opportunities currently available for language learning. We start with a brief overview of the research that has been carried out into online language learning. We then examine online language learning within the context of formal language courses, and in increasingly informal learning scenarios. Finally, we discuss the implications for teaching and assessment. Our focus is mainly on post-secondary contexts – that is, on adults learning a second or foreign language – as this is where the great majority of research into online language learning has been carried out to date.

KEY LEARNING ISSUES

With the advent of networked computers and internet-based communication tools, learning a language fully online has been feasible from the early 1990s. The influence of sociolinguistics in second language acquisition research meant that online course designers were aware of the all-important communicative aspect of language learning, and efforts to include this dimension resulted in an increased attention to online community building, communication and learner characteristics (e.g., White, 2006). Early providers of online language courses included the OU (Open University) in the United Kingdom, which launched their first online language course in French in 1995, and provided a significant body of early research into online language learning. In this section, we review the key issues that have interested researchers, and examine the range of contexts in which it is now possible to learn a language online. The rise of mobile technologies and the greater availability of free digital learning materials have both impacted significantly on learning opportunities for English language learning, as we shall see in the sections below.

ONLINE LANGUAGE LEARNING RESEARCH

In a seminal article published in 2006, White reviewed ten years of online language learning research, and identified a shift in focus from structural and organisational issues to a greater emphasis on transactional issues, as more diverse opportunities for communication in online environments emerged. Research during this first decade included a focus on pedagogical themes such as online course development, course evaluation, teaching roles, and learner support. The technologies used to deliver online language learning were also an important research area, as were what White called "learner contributions" (2006: 247) – that is, the expectations and beliefs, metacognitive knowledge, strategy use, affective factors, and self-management that learners bring to the online learning experience. These are all issues that remain relevant to online language learning research today.

A significant question that has hung over online language learning since its inception is to what extent online courses are 'better' (or worse) than their face-to-face equivalents. Suspicions about the effectiveness of online language courses initially centred around their lack of opportunities for oral interaction between participants, as well as the high student attrition rates from which many university-level courses, in a range of disciplines, seemed to suffer. Nevertheless, a 2010 meta-study, reviewing over 1,000 empirical studies into online versus face-to-face learning carried out between 1996 and 2008, concluded that a blended approach provided the best learning outcomes (Means, Yoyama, Murphy, Bakia, and Jones, 2010). There has since been a move away from the direct comparison of face-to-face and online versions of a course – what Blake calls "the wrong research question" (2009: 823) – towards research into the specific features of online (and blended) learning in specific contexts. As the research issues described earlier amply illustrate, the quality and effectiveness of an online course depends on a wide range of factors, not simply on whether it is delivered online or face-to-face.

Building on her 2006 article, White more recently suggests that a robust online language learning research agenda might focus on "theory, pedagogy, technologies, learner contributions, innovation and less commonly taught languages", and within these includes "the distinctive features and practices of distance language teaching, task design for synchronous settings, mentoring, multimodal learning environments, the transfer speaking skills, and learners' affective experiences" (2014: 124). White's suggestions are particularly relevant to the formal online language courses that typically take place in universities.

Much of the online language learning research available to date has taken place in formal academic learning contexts with young adult university students; however, there is an increasing number of opportunities to learn a language online beyond the confines of schools and universities. We turn our attention to these below.

MASSIVE OPEN ONLINE COURSES

Although Massive Open Online Courses (MOOCs) have been on offer since the early twenty-first century, English language learning MOOCs are a relatively recent phenomenon. Of hundreds of MOOCs offered worldwide by 2014, only 26 were language learning MOOCs; these were offered by universities and educational institutions primarily in Spain and the United States of America, but also in Australia, the United Kingdom, and Mexico, with Spanish and English as the most popular languages (Bárcena and Martín-Monje, 2014). MOOCs tend to attract impressive numbers. For example, in 2014, the British Council's first iteration of an English language MOOC called 'Exploring English: Language and culture' attracted more than 122,000 enrolments from over 190 countries. Of these enrolled students, 60% actually started the course, and 19% of these starters fully participated by posting comments in online discussion forums regularly, while half of the starters posted at least one comment in the course forums. During the 6 weeks of the course there were over 350,000 comments posted; one discussion thread proved particularly popular ('How do you feel when you speak English?'), with a total of over 30,000 responses (Chris Cavey, Open Learning Manager, English and Exams, personal communication, 9 March 2015).

However, the extent to which participation in a MOOC leads to improved language learning outcomes is a moot point. Measuring language gains is challenging. With such large numbers of participants, MOOCs tend to rely on peer- or self-evaluation, which raises the issue of reliability. More recently, some university MOOCs have started to offer course certification for a fee, which may include some form of assessment (e.g., an assignment); however, these assessments can vary widely in format and validity. Attrition in MOOCs remains high; clearly, issues of learner self-motivation and learner autonomy are particularly pertinent. Although often free and voluntary, many MOOCs replicate traditional online course approaches based on multimedia input and comprehension questions, followed by forum discussions. These so-called 'xMOOCs' are essentially predicated on an input-response transmission model of learning. Potentially of more interest for language learning are the so-called 'cMOOCs', which foreground connections and interactions between participants (often via social networking tools) as the basis for the collaborative construction of knowledge. Nevertheless, at the time of writing, the authors were unable to find robust research into learners' language acquisition in a language MOOC, arguably because, as Sokolik points out, "if MOOCs are in their infancy, Language MOOCs are positively neonatal" (2014: 16).

VIRTUAL WORLDS

Virtual worlds (such as Second Life) and Massively Multiplayer Online Role-Playing Games (MMORPGs, such as World of Warcraft) provide 3D online spaces that can support language development, in both formal and informal ways. For example, English language learning classes (and teacher training) in Second Life were offered under the auspices of the European Union-funded Avalon project (see http://avalonlearning.eu), while virtual schools such as LanguageLab (now Immerse Learning) offered language classes to students in several languages. Not many virtual schools survived the initial hype and subsequent slump in enthusiasm for formal language learning in online worlds, however. What has proven more durable are 3D online games, which can provide opportunities for language learning in the form of unstructured interactions between players online; in these contexts, language learning is not the main aim, but is instead secondary to taking part as effectively as possible in gameplay via the second or foreign language. A Swedish study with secondary school learners found that those who regularly played MMORPGs in English outside of school improved their linguistic competence, and showed particular gains in vocabulary acquisition, in comparison to non-gamer students in the same class (Sundqvist and Sylvén, 2012). Other studies into the effects of MMORPGs on language acquisition with young adults also show overall positive findings, such as providing learners with enhanced target language output during gameplay, which can result in gains in vocabulary comprehension (e.g., Rankin, Gold, and Gooch, 2006) and vocabulary learning strategies (Bytheway, 2015), and development of discourse management strategies and enhanced learner motivation (e.g., Peterson, 2012), as well as overall linguistic gains (e.g., Suh, Kim, and Kim, 2010). For more on the potential of digital games to support English language learning, see Reinders (2012).

COMMERCIAL PROVIDERS

Some commercial providers of online language learning materials, such as Rosetta Stone, have been operating since the early days of language learning via CD-ROMs. Others are more recent arrivals whose offerings are tailored to the rapid growth in mobile computing; for example, providers such as busuu and Duolingo deliver language learning content via smartphones. Providers like Rosetta Stone offer students automated language learning activities online in the main, but also supplement these with (spoken and written) interaction with other students and online tutors, in an attempt to provide learners with opportunities to interact in the target language (for example, via their online learning company Livemocha, acquired in 2013). The mobile language learning apps of Duolingo and similar providers, on the other hand, currently provide content only, often in the form of multiple choice, dictation, and translation exercises.

Some of these commercial providers (e.g., busuu and Duolingo) use adaptive learning (see Kerr, 2014 for further discussion) to determine what pre-packaged language content to serve up to individual learners, and when. Adaptive learning uses computer-generated algorithms to identify gaps in a learner's linguistic knowledge, based on how successfully they complete activities; the learner is then served further content to provide practice in areas that are identified as weak. Adaptive learning models see language learning as a linear, incremental and steadily progressive process, and they are based primarily on behaviourist learning principles. Mobile learning apps such as Duolingo have proved to be extremely popular, despite the decontextualised sentences and often seemingly random selection of vocabulary items that can be found as part of their learning content. Providing examples from the platforms Duolingo, iKnow! and Voxy (including this one from iKnow!, 'She found a place in which to posit the flowerpot'), Kerr comments, "It is reasonable to conclude that course providers such as these have invested more time and money on the technology than educational expertise" (2014: 8). Research into the effectiveness of this approach to online learning is difficult to find. Despite positive gains in pre- and post-study (multiple choice) test scores for learners of Spanish using Duolingo over an eight-week period, noted in a study by Vesselinov and Grego (2012), rates of attrition in this study – and others – remain high. This situation has implications for assessment, as we will see below.

IMPLICATIONS FOR TEACHING AND ASSESSMENT

The implications for teachers of offering language courses online are many. The most likely scenario for language teachers is that of formal online language classes, either as part of a blended approach, or as a fully online language course. Mishra and Koehler (2006) suggest that teacher's content knowledge (what to teach) and pedagogical knowledge (how to teach it) need to be supplemented by robust technological knowledge (in this case, how to work effectively with – and within – the online medium). This is known as the TPACK model, and refers to a teacher's need for integrated Technological, Pedagogical and Content Knowledge; this model has potential in pre- and in-service teacher training, and although not designed only for online teaching contexts, it is clearly relevant to those, as well as to face-to-face teaching contexts. Either way, the TPACK model provides a useful reference point for teacher training programmes looking to enhance teachers' online teaching skills.

In addition, Selim (2007) identifies eight factors that tertiary institutions need to consider for the effective deployment of online learning in any discipline:

1. the instructor's attitude towards and control of the technology;
2. the instructor's teaching style;
3. student motivation and technical competency;
4. student interactive collaboration;
5. e-learning course content and structure;
6. ease of on-campus internet access;
7. effectiveness of information technology infrastructure; and
8. institutional support of e-learning.

Many online learning experts have pointed out that the design of an online course, coupled with effective teacher training, are fundamental. For example, as Palloff and Pratt have recently argued, "One of the main issues continues to be adequate faculty training to construct and deliver high-quality courses. Few campuses currently offer the type of training the faculty need to succeed online" (2013, Kindle Loc. 22).

The issue of assessment in online courses is a challenging one. Progress is frequently measured via internal achievement tests, while research into gains in language proficiency that are pegged to recognised standardised proficiency tests is less common (Tarone, 2015). Online and telephone-based standardised language proficiency tests can be administered online; well-known online tests currently include the American Council on the Teaching of Foreign Languages' (ACTFL) *Assessment of Performance towards Proficiency in Languages (AAPPL)*, Pearson's *Versant*, and Brigham Young University's *WebCape*, as well as the *EF Standard English Test*. Nevertheless, there is research that reports that in both achievement tests and proficiency tests, online language education is at least as effective as its offline equivalent (Blake, Wilson, Cetto, and Pardo-Bellester, 2008); in some cases, online students outperform offline students, particularly in written production (e.g., Chenoweth and Murday, 2003). Nevertheless, as Warschauer (2015) points out, most assessment of online language learning takes place with beginner and intermediate level learners; it is less clear to what extent the research holds true for advanced level online language courses, or for LCTL (Less Commonly Taught Languages) courses.

Assessment is more problematic when applied to mobile platform language learning apps. Duolingo, for example, has an initial online placement test to determine a user's level of proficiency; the app then recommends content for the user to study based on this test. However, discrete-item grammar/vocabulary online placement tests of this type are not designed to measure a learner's overall linguistic competence, so measuring learning outcomes directly in these platforms is of limited use. In addition, the extremely high levels of attrition mean that researchers who attempt to apply external measures of proficiency find it challenging to collect sufficient data. For example, Nielson (2011) investigated two commercial self-study online language programmes, Rosetta Stone, and Auralog's Tell Me More (ATMM), and attempted to assess learning outcomes via achievement and oral proficiency tests (using *Versant* and ACTFL's *Oral Proficiency Interview*). However, with Rosetta Stone, only 1 out of 150 participants completed the course, and with ATMM, only 4 out of 176 participants completed; this meant that the results from the study were severely limited, leading the researcher to conclude that "this method of language training yielded very limited proficiency gains in only a handful of learners" (2011: 125). Nielson suggested that these "commercial products might most effectively be used as *supplements* [original emphasis] to teacher-led language learning courses, rather than as stand-alone products" (ibid.).

CONCLUSION

In summary, developments in hardware and software have freed online language learning from the confines of the institutional virtual learning environment; the rise of MOOCs, game-based learning, and mobile-based language learning apps are ample testament to this trend. Nevertheless, caveats remain. To what extent teachers are prepared for online learning (among other factors), is essential to its success. Assessment of online language learning remains a challenging area, particularly in informal learning contexts. Much research to date has been carried out in structured online language learning environments. However, as online language learning opportunities have moved beyond the confines of the formal course, so too it falls to research agendas to do the same.

Discussion Questions

1. Based on your reading of this chapter, what issues do institutions need to address to ensure that they offer good quality online courses to language students? Make a list. How might each issue be addressed in practical terms?

2. Choose an online self-study mobile platform language provider (e.g., Duolingo, busuu, etc.). Keeping in mind the issues and caveats raised in this chapter about online language learning, assess the effectiveness of the programme. How might the programme supplement a more formal online language course?

3. How might a teacher training programme ensure that teachers are prepared to teach English online? What elements of technological, pedagogical and content knowledge (as per the TPACK model) need to be taken into account?

Key Readings

Hockly, N., & Clandfield, L. (2010). *Teaching Online*. Peaslake, Surrey: Delta Publishing.

Kerr, P. (2014). *Adaptive Learning*. The Round. Available at: http://the-round.com/resource/a-short-guide-to-adaptive-learning-in-english-language-teaching/ [Accessed 10 September 2015].

Palloff, R., & Pratt, K. (2013). *Lessons from the Virtual Classroom: The Realities of Online Teaching*. San Francisco, CA: Jossey Bass.

Reinders, H. (Ed.) (2012). *Digital Games in Language Learning and Teaching*. Basingstoke, UK: Palgrave Macmillan.

Tarone, E. (2015). Perspectives. *The Modern Language Journal,* 99(2), 392–393.

References

Bárcena, E., & Martín-Monje, E. (Eds.) (2014). *Language MOOCs: Providing Learning, Transcending Boundaries*. Berlin: De Gruyter Open.

Blake, R. J. (2009). The use of technology for second language distance learning. *The Modern Language Journal*, 93, 822–835.

Blake, R. J., Wilson, N. L., Cetto, M., & Pardo-Bellester, C. (2008). Measuring oral proficiency in distance, face-to-face, and blended classrooms. *Language Learning & Technology*, 12, 114–127.

Bytheway, J. (2015). A taxonomy of vocabulary learning strategies used in massively multiplayer online role-playing games. *CALICO Journal*, 32(3), 508–527. http://dx.doi.org/10.1558/cj.v32i3.26787

Chenoweth, N. A., & Murday, K. (2003). Measuring student learning in an online French course. *CALICO Journal*, 20, 284–314.

Kerr, P. (2014) *Adaptive Learning*. The Round. Available at: http://the-round.com/resource/a-short-guide-to-adaptive-learning-in-english-language-teaching/ [Accessed 10 September 2015].

Means, B., Yoyama, Y., Murphy, R., Bakia, M., & Jones, K. (2010). *Evaluation of Evidence-based Practices in Online Learning: A Meta-analysis and Review of Online Learning Studies*. Washington, D.C.: U.S. Department of Education.

Mishra, P., and Koehler, M. J. (2006). Technological pedagogical content knowledge: A framework for teacher knowledge. *Teachers College Record*, 108(6), 1017–1054.

Nielson, K. (2011). Self-study with language learning software in the workplace: What happens? *Language Learning & Technology*, 15, 110–129.

Palloff, R., & Pratt, K. (2013). *Lessons from the Virtual Classroom: The Realities of Online Teaching*. San Francisco, CA: Jossey Bass.

Peterson, M. (2012) Language learner interaction in a massively multiplayer online role-playing game. In H. Reinders (Ed.), *Digital Games in Language Learning and Teaching* (pp. 70–93). Basingstoke, UK: Palgrave Macmillan.

Rankin, Y., Gold, R., & Gooch, B. (2006). 3D role-playing games as language learning tools. In E. Gröller & L. Szirmay-Kalos (Eds.), *Proceedings of Eurographics 2006*, 25(3), 33–38. New York: ACM.

Reinders, H. (Ed.) (2012). *Digital Games in Language Learning and Teaching*. Basingstoke, UK: Palgrave Macmillan.

Selim, H. M. (2007). Critical success factors for e-learning acceptance: Confirmatory factor models. *Computers & Education*, 49(2), 396–413.

Sokolik, M. (2014). What constitutes an effective language MOOC? In E. Bárcena & E. Martín-Monje (Eds.), *Language MOOCs: Providing Learning, Transcending Boundaries*. Berlin: De Gruyter Open.

Suh, S., Kim, S. W., & Kim, N. J. (2010). Effectiveness of MMORPG-based instruction in elementary English education in Korea. *Journal of Computer Assisted Learning*, 26(5), 370–378.

Sundqvist, P., & Sylvén, L. K. (2012). World of VocCraft: Computer games and Swedish learners' L2 vocabulary. In H. Reinders (Ed.), *Digital Games in Language Learning and Teaching* (pp.189–208). Basingstoke, UK: Palgrave Macmillan.

Tarone, E. (2015). Perspectives. *The Modern Language Journal*, 99(2), 392–393.

Vesselinov, R., & Grego. J. (2012). *Duolingo Effectiveness Study.* Available at: http://static. duolingo.com/s3/DuolingoReport_Final.pdf [Accessed 10 September 2015].

Warschauer, M. (2015). Online foreign language education: What are the proficiency outcomes? *The Modern Language Journal*, 99(2), 394–397.

White, C. (2006). Distance learning of foreign languages. *Language Teaching* 39, 247–264.

White, C. (2014). The distance learning of foreign languages: A research agenda. *Language Teaching* 47, 538–553.

CHAPTER 36

Learning Through Social Media

Christopher Jenks

INTRODUCTION

Internet-based social platforms, such as Twitter and YouTube, are inextricably connected to how life is organized and conducted; they are, for example, used to report political events, carry out work-based tasks, organize social activities and events, and complete school-related projects. Despite their importance in society, it is often argued that such platforms disconnect the user from the 'real world', lead to fictitious or 'virtual' relationships, and are mere supplementary or secondary tools for the purpose of language learning. These observations and opinions belie a world where life is conducted in, and through, the intermeshing of technological tools and physical spaces, or what Augé (2009) refers to as 'supermodernity'. The blurring of temporal, spatial, technological, and physical boundaries that has occurred as a result of living in supermodern times has led many researchers to consider (or reconsider) how internet-based social platforms shape social structures (e.g., communicative expectations), phenomena (e.g., viral videos) and activities (e.g., language learning).

This chapter builds on this line of investigation by exploring how English language learning is achieved in, and through, internet-based social platforms (or what is commonly referred to as 'social media'). Although social media is a term that is widely used, few studies in fact define what it means. Social media is defined here as a set of online tools (e.g., websites and applications) that offers users the ability to create and consume information, share content, interact with each other, and jointly work on tasks. Social media examples include, but are not limited to: social networking (e.g., Facebook, Twitter, Bebo, and Myspace); discussion boards (e.g., Gaia, Online, 4chan, IGN, and City-Data.com); blogs (e.g., WordPress, Blogger, Tumblr, and Typepad); wikis (e.g., Wikispaces, TWiki, Wikia, and Wikipedia); social curation (e.g., Pinterest, Flipboard, Feedly, and Scoop.it!); and video sharing (e.g., YouTube, TED, Vine, and Vimeo). Given the number of platforms that exist (and quickly fall out of use), this chapter focuses on how the communicative and collaborative tools that are embedded in social media shape learning possibilities. Put differently, this chapter is not organized according to the different social media platforms that exist, as doing so would require an entire book devoted to the topic. More importantly, such an approach would overlook the many communicative similarities that exist across platforms, as well as their pedagogical consequences. Before discussing how online communicative and collaborative tools facilitate English language learning, it is important to explore the nature of social media.

OVERVIEW

Empirical studies and technical reports suggest that social media is changing the way people communicate and consume information (cf., Mitchell, 2012). Yet, communication and information are not only shaped by what platform is used (e.g., Twitter's 140-character limit) – what is commonly referred to as the mediating effects of technology (cf., Jenks, 2014) – more importantly, social media is transforming social practices, cultural norms, and discursive behaviors. For example, the popularity of social media has changed the way content providers allow users to consume information. Traditional paper-based news reporting outlets, for example, have been forced to alter content delivery methods to reflect how societies rely on mobile phones for media consumption. Mundane activities that are often done in solitude, like reading the news, are now connected to a larger network of users that have the ability to shape how information is interpreted (e.g., the comments section below news articles). The sharing and network nature of social media has not only changed how content is consumed, but has also provided more opportunities for users to create, and interact with, information. For English language learners, this has meant more exposure to, and encounters with users of, the target language.

TYPES AND PURPOSES OF SOCIAL MEDIA

Consuming, creating, and sharing information are activities that characterize most of what people do online. This observation represents a natural progression of online communication behavior: humans are inherently social, and internet-based applications and services represent this primordial characteristic (cf., Web 2.0). However, the rapid increase in social media use complicates attempts to identify what is unique about this "new" way of consuming information, as everything now is ostensibly 'social'. To further complicate the current discussion, seminal and ongoing work to identify different types of social media belie the overlapping and co-dependent nature of different platforms. For example, Facebook is often classified as a personal/sharing network, though this platform allows users to engage in other activities that fall under different social media types, such as video-sharing, collaboration, discussion, and online reviews, to name a few. Therefore, it is important to think of social media not as comprising different platforms (e.g., Facebook vs. YouTube), but rather as a collection of tools that are embedded and used within applications. This distinction is important, as any discussion of online language learning must be grounded in the ways in which technology mediates communication. That is to say, Facebook is not, in itself, a platform for language learning. Rather, the communication and sharing tools embedded within this platform, such as text-based comment threads, provide language learning opportunities. Moving the discussion of social media away from platforms requires an understanding of technological affordances.

TECHNOLOGICAL AFFORDANCES IN SOCIAL MEDIA

Social media does not necessarily offer new technological tools for communication and collaboration, but does allow users to use existing technology in unique ways. For example, the ability to send text-based messages has existed for many years, but social media provides a platform to reach a larger audience (e.g., sending a message to all of your Twitter followers). Using old online communication technology for new social tasks offers learning opportunities that transcend traditional forms of language learning (see next section). Before discussing these unique learning opportunities, it is important to establish how 'old' technology mediates online communication.

Social media, like all forms of computer-mediated interaction, can be thought of as offering two forms of communication: asynchronous and synchronous. The former type of communication occurs with some delay between, to use an outdated computational model, message transmission and reception (e.g., discussion boards); the latter is conducted in what is often referred to, albeit somewhat incorrectly, as 'real time' (e.g., chat rooms). The effects of synchronicity on language learning have been investigated extensively. Research has shown, for example, that synchronous communication offers more opportunities for students to participate and results in more overall language production than in face-to-face classrooms (Kern, 1995; see also Chapters 12 and 13). Asynchronous communication places less interactional stress on students, by offering more planning time than required in synchronous communication (Abrams, 2003); as a result, language production is often more complex in asynchronous interaction. However, because synchronous communication places interactional demands on the learner that are similar to face-to-face encounters, it is thought of as a better technology for developing fluency and turn-taking skills (cf., Negretti, 1999).

Social media content, like all information stored online, is packaged and delivered in three, often co-occurring, modes of communication: text, image (motion and still), and audio (see Kress and van Leeuwen, 2001). Although scholarship has done much to understand how students interact in a particular mode of online communication (for videoconferencing, see Wang, 2006; for audio-only communication, see Jenks, 2014; for text-based chat, see Herring, 1999), surprisingly few researchers have compared learning opportunities across text, image, and audio platforms. This gap in the literature is partly the result of scholarship being primarily concerned with understanding how learning opportunities in a particular mode of online communication compare with second language development in face-to-face classrooms. Despite the historical preference for using face-to-face classrooms as a baseline for comparison, some research has analyzed the interaction and learning opportunities in two modes of online communication. Jepson (2005), for instance, shows that repair moves, including the negotiation of meaning, are more abundant and successful in voice chat than text-based interactions. Yanguas (2012) examines learning in video and audio platforms, and discovers that the latter mode of communication leads to better listening scores.

The scholarship devoted to examining language learning in online environments, as outlined above, provides a great deal of understanding regarding how technology mediates English development. However, much of this research has examined online applications and platforms that, while they can be considered social media according to the definition provided above, are no longer widely used and/or are not available for public use. Although such research is still helpful in understanding how text-, image-, or audio-dependent communication tools shape particular aspects of linguistic development, such as listening, pronunciation, and vocabulary acquisition, the increasing popularity of online information consumption and collaboration forces researchers to rethink what is meant by, and the consequences of, language learning and use in social media contexts.

BEYOND THE FOUR SKILLS

Social media provides opportunities for students to develop skills that are traditionally viewed as foundational to linguistic development (see Chapters 21–24). Indeed, computer-mediated communication scholarship, which subsumes the body of work cited in the previous section, generally investigates some aspect of learning that can be categorized into at least one language skill: speaking, listening, writing, or reading. As a result, research has yet to fully understand how social media provides learning opportunities that transcend the four traditional language skills. For example, what are the pragmatic and interactional norms of a social media platform? How do users achieve membership in online communities? Does social media provide opportunities for users from geographically dispersed regions to achieve interculturality? How does the popularity of social media transform existing notions of language learning for users who grow up in a world that is dominated by online technology? In other words, social media platforms, in addition to providing opportunities to learn the four language skills, are spaces where learners can develop interactional competence, acquire the pragmatic skills necessary to be members of online communities, master the expertise to communicate in intercultural encounters, and become digitally literate. Some of these learning outcomes are the focus of discussion in the following section.

KEY LEARNING ISSUES

Language learning through social media does not happen in a vacuum. Put differently, integrating social media in classroom instruction does not, in itself, guarantee successful language learning outcomes. Yet, social media possesses a primordial quality that is unparalleled by other pedagogical tools. For example, Mitchell (2012) notes that the language learners in her study experienced ongoing linguistic and technological difficulties when using Facebook. Despite these challenges, Facebook was successfully used to learn and communicate in English. This demonstrates, as noted by Mitchell (ibid.), that the learners valued the idea of being on Facebook more than the ongoing linguistic and technological challenges of using this platform. Why are such platforms inherently captivating? As others have demonstrated, Mitchell's study (ibid.) establishes that humans are inherently social, language is a means to carry out, and is thus part and parcel of, this sociality, and platforms like Twitter and YouTube are mere microcosms of society at large.

Thus, when attempting to understand how social media mediates language learning, it is important to be cognizant of the larger societal issues that represent why learners use such platforms, such as the primal desire for belonging. It must also be stated that using social media to learn English requires knowing grammar, vocabulary, and the like, but possessing such linguistic competence does not in any way guarantee that learning will occur. For example, providing weekly updates on Facebook requires language production, but the more important social action that takes place in so doing is community participation. English language learning through social media can only occur when a user invests the time in using a platform to develop a network of family, friends, or colleagues.

BEING A COMMUNITY MEMBER

The core activity of social media is participating in a network of users with similar interactive goals. Users of social media, however, possess not only common objectives, but also shared practices that represent their unique ways of communicating and collaborating online. These shared practices create distinct communities and cultural norms, and thus represent 'learning objects'. For example, social etiquette determines how users are expected to retweet a news article or mention a colleague on Facebook. Competence of this type is fundamental to language learning through social media, because such practices mediate how interaction unfolds; more importantly, such practices bind users together over time and space (Wenger, 1998). Using social media, in other words, is tantamount to being a community member.

The notion that social media is about participating in a community is based on the understanding that language learning is a situated activity. Learning a language through social media is inherently collaborative, requiring users to mutually engage in communicative actions for a common goal (e.g., commenting on a shared video, providing personal news updates to peers, and reviewing local restaurants). Although group norms help shape language behaviors (Postmes, Spears, and Lea, 2000), learning is not predetermined insofar as rules – that is, what is grammatically and communicatively right or wrong – are part of a dynamic system in a state of flux (Larsen-Freeman, 1997). The use of acronyms, abbreviations, and non-standard spelling in online text-based communication are only a few examples of how language 'rules' are socially-situated, malleable, and thus never fixed (cf. Crystal, 2004).

Being a member of a larger network of like-minded individuals brings to light the exceptional reach social media provides its users. This reach presents users with a number of learning opportunities and challenges; one of these pedagogical issues is discussed in the following section.

INTERCULTURAL LEARNING

Social media has partly made it possible, and necessary in some academic and professional contexts (e.g., language exchanges and international collaborations), to interact with geographically dispersed individuals. Communicating and collaborating across time zones, and between different regions, often entails interacting with peers from different linguistic and cultural backgrounds. It has been argued that the pervasiveness of these encounters has facilitated the global spread of English (Crystal, 2012). English as a lingua franca (ELF) is one of several global 'contact' languages that dominate online communication (e.g., Jenks, 2009). The online presence of ELF has forced researchers and practitioners to reconsider the dichotomies that have profoundly shaped the English language teaching literature. For example, individuals who speak English as an additional language far outnumber those who use it in largely monolingual contexts; as a result of the growing number of English speakers in contexts outside of so-called inner circle countries (e.g., the United States; see Kachru, 1985), notions of language competence and grammatical correctness have been transformed to reflect local and regional norms and expectations. Social media, in other words, complicates conceptualizations of, and approaches to, English language teaching. For instance, if English is being used as a lingua franca in a social media platform, then what is the target language (e.g., Standard American English), who is considered the learner, and what varieties are deemed more socially acceptable?

In addition to complicating fundamental categories used in understanding language teaching, social media creates opportunities to co-construct interculturality (see Chapter 28). The ongoing changes and demands of communicating and collaborating in a larger network of users represent learning opportunities (see previous section), but in addition to possessing the competence needed to adjust to group norms as they are presented, social media requires learners to fine-tune their language, in situ, to fit fellow interlocutors' linguistic and cultural norms and expectations.

Working on the premise that putting two interactants from different cultural backgrounds into a collaborative online space will *not* spontaneously generate intercultural awareness, O'Dowd (2003) investigated students from Spain and England communicating in a text-based environment in their respective target languages: English and Spanish. He found that students' ability to display empathy, provide linguistic accommodation to their peers, and engage in meaningful interactions were central to achieving intercultural communicative competence. In other words, online platforms provide the means to interact with individuals from different regions of the world, and language is central to achieving interculturality, but more crucial to the success of such encounters is the ability to form meaningful relationships.

IMPLICATIONS FOR TEACHING AND ASSESSMENT

Social media presents many intriguing opportunities for English language teaching and learning, as demonstrated above. However, care must be taken when incorporating social media in the language classroom. Social media platforms are intermeshed with much of what occurs in daily mundane activities, and thus students should be somewhat comfortable using such technologies, but teachers must be thoughtful of how online communicative and collaborative tools can enhance an existing curriculum of language instruction. That is to say, using social media for English language teaching and learning must be grounded in the understanding that such platforms exist because humans are inherently social beings.

How, then, can this primordial characteristic be exploited when incorporating technology in the language classroom? When using social media, users must be given long-term opportunities to establish relationships with peers, develop group norms and expectations; somewhat illogically, students should also be given opportunities to dictate, to some degree, how language should be used in such platforms. These requirements mirror what occurs naturally in, and through, social media. Indeed, scholarship has demonstrated that successful integration of such technologies is dependent on preserving the core functions of social media: communication and collaboration (e.g., Stevens, 2010). To this end, English language learning through social media requires giving students some autonomy in managing their learning experiences.

Although social media transforms traditional notions of language learning, teachers must grapple with the difficult task of assessing learnable 'objects' that are not clearly identifiable. For example, learnable (or learning) objects in traditional face-to-face classrooms may include the acquisition of vocabulary, the appropriate use of syntactic rules, or the pronunciation of consonant clusters. A long tradition of assessing such objects exists. How, on the other hand, can the development of group norms be evaluated? Are communicative empathy or linguistic accommodation assessable objects? What should a teacher analyze when grading the participation of students in synchronous chat? While the answers to these questions represent exciting areas of potential development in the technology-mediated learning literature, such gaps in knowledge do not immediately offer help to practitioners using social media.

CONCLUSION

Despite the aforementioned assessment challenges, social media provides learners with authentic opportunities to use the English language in spaces that are immediately relevant and socially applicable to their personal lives. As younger generations of students born into a world dominated by social media enter our classrooms, it becomes increasingly important to understand the strengths, affordances, limitations, and constraints of online communicative and collaborative tools. This chapter has provided a concise overview of some key issues in the use of social media for language teaching and learning. Although a wealth of knowledge exists in how technology mediates communication, much more work is needed in understanding how new social media platforms are being used for language learning. The discussion above has hopefully provided some inspiration and ideas for researchers and practitioners to continue working in this important area of language learning.

Discussion Questions

1. Social media is intertwined with much of what people do outside of classrooms. Do you think that the popularity of, and dependency on, social media presents teaching and learning opportunities? If so, what are some of these opportunities?

2. Social networking sites, like Facebook, represent a large part of how people communicate with family, friends, and colleagues. As younger generations are born into this technology-oriented world, what, if anything, must teachers do to adjust to the needs and experiences of students with greater knowledge of social media?

3. If social media presents users with unique, context-dependent ways of interacting that complicate notions of what is communicative and grammatically correct, how then can the language teacher promote, and assess, linguistic development?

Key Readings

Crystal, D. (2012). *English as a Global Language*. Cambridge: Cambridge University Press.

Herring, S. (1999). Interactional coherence in CMC. *Journal of Computer-Mediated Communication*, 4(4). https://doi.org/10.1111/j.1083-6101.1999.tb00106.x

Jenks, C. J. (2014). *Social Interaction in Second Language Chat Rooms*. Edinburgh, UK: Edinburgh University Press.

Stevens, V. (2010). Writing in a multiliterate flat world, part I: Multiliterate approaches to writing and collaboration through social networking. *Writing & Pedagogy*, 2(1), 117–131.

References

Abrams, Z. I. (2003). The effect of synchronous and asynchronous CMC on oral performance in German. *The Modern Language Journal*, 87(2), 157–167. https://doi.org/10.1111/1540-4781.00184

Augé, M. (2009). *Non-places: An Introduction to Supermodernity* (2nd ed.). London: Verso.

Crystal, D. (2004). *A Glossary of Netspeak and Textspeak*. Edinburgh: Edinburgh University Press.

Crystal, D. (2012). *English as a Global Language*. Cambridge: Cambridge University Press.

Herring, S. (1999). Interactional coherence in CMC. *Journal of Computer-Mediated Communication*, 4(4). https://doi.org/10.1111/j.1083-6101.1999.tb00106.x

Jenks, C. J. (2009). Getting acquainted in Skypecasts: Aspects of social organization in online chat rooms. *International Journal of Applied Linguistics*, 19(1), 26–46. https://doi.org/10.1111/j.1473-4192.2009.00211.x

Jenks, C. J. (2014). *Social Interaction in Second Language Chat Rooms*. Edinburgh: Edinburgh University Press.

Jepson, K. (2005). Conversation – and negotiated interaction – in text and voice chat rooms. *Language Learning & Technology*, 9(3), 79–98.

Kachru, B. B. (1985). Standards, codification, and sociolinguistic realism: The English language in the outer circle. In R. Quirk & H. G. Widdowson (Eds.), *English in the World: Teaching and Learning the Language and Literatures* (pp. 11–30). Cambridge: Cambridge University Press.

Kern, R. G. (1995). Restructuring classroom interaction with networked computers: Effects on quantity and characteristics of language production. *The Modern Language Journal*, 79(4), 457–476. https://doi.org/10.1111/j.1540-4781.1995.tb05445.x

Kress, G., & van Leeuwen, T. (2001). *Multimodal Discourse: The Modes and Media of Contemporary Communication*. London: Arnold.

Larsen-Freeman, D. (1997). Chaos/complexity science and second language acquisition. *Applied Linguistics*, 18(2), 141–165. https://doi.org/10.1093/applin/18.2.141

Mitchell, K. (2012) A social tool: Why and how ESOL students use Facebook. *CALICO Journal*, 29(3), 471–493. https://doi.org/10.11139/cj.29.3.471–493

Negretti, R. (1999). Web-based activities and SLA: A conversation analysis research approach. *Language Learning & Technology*, 3(1), 75–87.

O'Dowd, R. (2003). Understanding the "other side": Intercultural learning in a Spanish-English e-mail exchange. *Language Learning & Technology*, 7(2), 118–144.

Postmes, T., Spears, R., & Lea, M. (2000). The formation of group norms in computer-mediated communication'. *Human Communication Research*, 26(3), 341–371. https://doi.org/10.1111/j.1468-2958.2000.tb00761.x

Stevens, V. (2010). Writing in a multiliterate flat world, part I: Multiliterate approaches to writing and collaboration through social networking. *Writing & Pedagogy*, 2(1), 117–131. https://doi.org/10.1558/wap.v2i1.117

Wang, Y. (2006). Negotiation of meaning in desktop videoconferencing-supported distance language learning. *ReCALL*, 18(01), 122–146. https://doi.org/10.1017/s0958344006000814

Wenger, E. (1998). Communities of practice: Learning as a social system. *The Systems Thinker*, 9(5).

Yanguas, I. (2012). Task-based oral computer-mediated communication and L2 vocabulary acquisition. *CALICO Journal*, 29(3), 507–531. http://dx.doi.org/10.11139/cj.29.3.507–531

LIST OF CONTRIBUTORS

Oliver J. Ballance, Victoria University of Wellington, New Zealand

Helen Basturkmen, University of Auckland, New Zealand

Frank Boers, Victoria University of Wellington, New Zealand

Anne Burns, University of New South Wales, Sydney, Australia

Yuko Goto Butler, University of Pennsylvania, USA

Alice Chik, Macquarie University, Australia

Guy Cook, King's College London, UK

Tracey Costley, University of Essex, UK

Averil Coxhead, Victoria University of Wellington, New Zealand

Jean-Marc Dewaele, Birkbeck, University of London, UK

Gavin Dudeney, The Consultants-E, UK

Patricia A. Duff, University of British Columbia, Canada

Martin East, University of Auckland, New Zealand

Susan Feez, University of New England, Australia

Christine C. M. Goh, National Institute of Education, Nanyang Technological University, Singapore

Carol Griffiths, Auckland Institute of Studies, New Zealand

Gregory Hadley, Niigata University, Japan

Christoph A. Hafner, City University of Hong Kong, Hong Kong

David Hirsh, University of Sydney, Australia

Nicky Hockly, The Consultants-E, Spain

Elaine K. Horwitz, The University of Texas at Austin, USA

Christopher Jenks, Hong Kong Polytechnic University, Hong Kong

Rodney H. Jones, University of Reading, UK

Judit Kormos, Lancaster University, UK

Shaofeng Li, University of Auckland, New Zealand and Guangdong University of Foreign Studies, China

Ee Ling Low, National Institute of Education, Nanyang Technological University, Singapore

Jane Lockwood, Hong Kong Polytechnic University, Hong Kong

John Macalister, Victoria University of Wellington, New Zealand

Lama Nassif, Williams College, USA

Rebecca L. Oxford, University of Maryland, USA

Martha C. Pennington, Birkbeck and SOAS, University of London, UK

Jack C. Richards, University of Sydney, Australia and Victoria University of Wellington, New Zealand

Stephen Ryan, Waseda University, Japan

Farzad Sharifian, Monash University, Australia

Ali Shehadeh, United Arab Emirates University, United Arab Emirates

Joseph Siegel, Örebro University, Sweden

Adem Soruç, Sakarya University, Turkey

Marie Stevenson, University of Sydney, Australia

Neomy Storch, University of Melbourne, Australia

Victoria Surtees, University of British Columbia, Canada

Naoko Taguchi, Carnegie Mellon University, USA

Scott Thornbury, The New School, USA

John Witney, Birkbeck, University of London, UK

Lawrence Jun Zhang, University of Auckland, New Zealand

Zuocheng Zhang, University of New England, Australia

Index

CPSIA information can be obtained
at www.ICGtesting.com
Printed in the USA
LVOW09s0055260518
578592LV00001BA/1/P